A Publication Sponsored by
the Society for Industrial and Organizational Psychology, Inc.,
A Division of the American Psychological Association

Other books in the Professional Practice Series sponsored
by the Society and published by Jossey-Bass include:

Employees, Careers, and Job Creation
Manuel London, Editor

Organizational Surveys
Allen I. Kraut, Editor

Performance Appraisal
James W. Smither, Editor

Individual Psychological Assessment

Individual Psychological Assessment

Predicting Behavior in Organizational Settings

Richard Jeanneret

Rob Silzer

Editors

Foreword by Manuel London

Jossey-Bass Publishers • San Francisco

Jossey-Bass books and products are available through most bookstores. To contact Jossey-Bass directly, call (888) 378-2537, fax to (800) 605–2665, or visit our website at www.josseybass.com.

Substantial discounts on bulk quantities of Jossey-Bass books are available to corporations, professional associations, and other organizations. For details and discount information, contact the special sales department at Jossey-Bass.

For sales outside the United States, please contact your local Simon & Schuster International Office.

 Manufactured in the United States of America on Lyons Falls Turin Book. This paper is acid-free and 100 percent totally chlorine-free.

Library of Congress Cataloging-in-Publication Data

Individual psychological assessment : predicting behavior in organizational
  settings / Richard Jeanneret, Rob Silzer, editors; foreword by Manuel London.
      p.   cm. — (Jossey-Bass business & management series)   (Jossey-Bass
  social & behavioral science series)
    Includes bibliographical references and index.
    ISBN 0-7879-0861-4
    1. Employment tests.   2. Psychological tests.   3. Psychology, Industrial.
  I. Jeanneret, Richard.   II. Silzer, Robert Frank.   III. Series.   IV. Series:
  Jossey-Bass social and behavioral science series.
  HF5549.5.E5153   1998
  153.9—dc21   98-17395

FIRST EDITION
HB Printing   10 9 8 7 6 5 4 3 2 1

A joint publication in
The Jossey-Bass Business & Management Series
and
The Jossey-Bass Social & Behavioral Science Series

Society for Industrial and Organizational Psychology
Professional Practice Series

SERIES EDITOR

Manuel London
State University of New York, Stony Brook

EDITORIAL BOARD

Lawrence Fogli
Core Corporation

Nita R. French
French & Associates

A. Catherine Higgs
Allstate Insurance Company

Allen I. Kraut
Baruch College
City University of New York

Edward L. Levine
University of South Florida

Kenneth Pearlman
AT&T

Walter W. Tornow
Center for Creative Leadership

Contents

Foreword

This volume is part of the Professional Practice Series sponsored by the Society for Industrial and Organizational Psychology. The books in the series address contemporary ideas and problems, focus on how to get things done, and provide state-of-the-art technology based on theory and research from industrial and organizational psychology. They cover the needs of practitioners and those being trained for practice.

Four earlier volumes in this series, under the senior editorship of Douglas W. Bray, were published by Guilford Press and are now distributed by Jossey-Bass. Douglas W. Bray edited *Working with Organizations and Their People* (1991), which examines the role of industrial and organizational psychologists as practitioners involved in evaluation, training, and organization development.

The second book, *Diversity in the Workplace* (1992), edited by Susan E. Jackson, offers cases and methods for creating and assessing a diverse workplace and for managing workplace diversity through personal growth, team development, and strategic initiatives.

Abraham K. Korman's *Human Dilemmas in Work Organizations: Strategies for Resolution* (1994) considers the expanding world of the human resource practitioner. Readings describe programs for employee assistance, stress management, marginal performers, reorganizations, employee ethics, and elder care.

Ann Howard's book, *Diagnosis for Organizational Change* (1994), focuses on organizational diagnosis for design and development. The contributors examine the assessment of human talent for staffing and training. They also provide an overview of the high-involvement workplace with a consideration of organizational cultures, reward systems, and work teams.

As the new senior editor of the Professional Practice Series under our new publisher, Jossey-Bass, I edited *Employees, Careers, and Job Creation* (1995). This book examines ways that human resource development programs contribute to an organization's viability and growth in tough economic times. It describes programs that help employees maintain their value to their firm or find new employment after organizational downsizing. It shows how organizations, government, and universities can work together to help employees create new ventures and career opportunities.

The next book in the series, edited by Allen Kraut, is *Opinion Surveys in Organizations: Tools for Assessment and Change* (1996). It demonstrates the value of surveys for diagnosis of individual and organizational strengths and weaknesses, communication of organizational culture and expectations, and evaluation of human resource policies and programs. Cases describe best practices and methods by which organizations share items and compare results. The book shows how to link survey results to measures of organization effectiveness, such as customer satisfaction, financial performance, and employee turnover. Also it addresses tough issues such as holding managers accountable for survey results and avoiding treating survey results as necessarily reliable and valid data about individual capabilities.

James Smither's book, *Performance Appraisal: State of the Art in Practice* (1998), addresses the relationship between business strategy and appraisal systems, and covers evaluating both individuals and teams. It describes 360-degree feedback survey processes and shows how appraisal and feedback work in Total Quality Management cultures. It reviews legal issues in appraisal and examines cross-cultural issues of appraisal in multinational companies. The book contains many practical examples that have a solid research foundation.

This current volume on individual assessment is a valuable addition to the Professional Practice Series. Personnel selection is often thought of as the use of job analysis and test development and validation to select large numbers of people for the same job. Individual assessment is the evaluation of a few highly qualified candidates for one top-level job. Organizations are learning, sometimes the hard way, that seat-of-the-pants selection methods, such as search committees and do-it-yourself interviews, are insufficient for executive selection. Individual assessment is especially difficult because of the increasing complexity of organizational leadership.

Economic, global, and marketplace changes have led to flatter organizational structures, reengineered jobs, team processes, and methods for continuous, customer-driven quality improvement. Leaders serve as coaches, developers, negotiators, change agents, communicators, educators, and visionaries, as well as strategic planners and organizers. These organizational trends and their implications for the changing roles of executive managers make leadership selection a challenge.

Individual Psychological Assessment is a state-of-the-art reference for the design and implementation of individual assessment by qualified professionals. The editors, Richard Jeanneret and Rob Silzer, bring many years of experience to this growing area of practice in industrial and organizational psychology. They invited highly experienced practitioners to write about the science and art of individual assessment. The initial chapters present a theoretical framework for assessment, describe methods, and give examples of ways that assessment has been used. Other chapters debate whether assessment should focus on behavioral dimensions or the whole person and show how feedback of assessment results affects the individuals assessed and the organization. The contributors argue that assessment methods need to be adapted to the strategies and context of each organization. As such, assessment methods must fit new leadership models and deal with cross-cultural issues. Ethical and professional responsibilities are also addressed.

The editorial board contributed to this effort by setting the direction for the series and ensuring the high-quality results represented here. I thank the board members: Lawrence Fogli, Nita French, Catherine Higgs, Allen Kraut, Edward Levine, Kenneth Pearlman, and Walter Tornow. Also, I am grateful to the Society for Industrial and Organizational Psychology for sponsoring the series and supporting this volume.

April 1998   MANUEL LONDON
                                                State University of New York
                                                Series Editor

Preface

In August 1987, we conducted a workshop, "Psychological Assessment: Getting at Job-Related Skills and Abilities," which was sponsored by the Society for Industrial and Organizational Psychology during the annual convention of the American Psychological Association in New York City. Since that time, we have wanted to communicate further about individual assessment as it is specifically carried out in the context of industrial and organizational psychology. The opportunity to edit this book and write some of its chapters is a fulfillment of that goal.

This book explores the field of individual assessment as applied to the business world. It provides guidance to assessors and, more important, raises issues and discusses topics that are important to assessment practice. The book is relevant primarily for assessments that occur for work-related purposes, such as selection, promotion, or development. It does not address assessments that are conducted for clinical diagnosis or psychological evaluation in therapeutic settings, although some of our topics may have tangential relevance for clinical practice.

Audience

First and foremost, our target readers are assessors who conduct individual psychological assessments for some business-related purpose. They are typically licensed psychologists with doctoral degrees who practice as consultants either internal or external to the organizations they serve. A second audience is those in academia: faculty and advanced graduate students who are in psychology programs with interests in research and applications related to the assessment of individuals in the workplace. Readers will find references to important research in many of the chapters and also will benefit from the personal knowledge of authors whose careers are rich with assessment experience. Others who will find at least segments of this book to be of value are human resource professionals who are associated with individual assessments, most likely as clients, or who are using or considering the use of assessment in their organizations.

We fully recognize that the topic of individual assessment is closely allied to that of assessment centers and, more recently, the emphasis on multirater feedback processes. Although some chapter authors have included commentary and references to these two areas, they are not the primary focus of this book. Nevertheless, some chapters contain both conceptual and practical ideas that will be of real value to those interested in these topics.

Overview of the Contents

We have organized the book and selected chapter topics according to the following scheme. The first four chapters, in Part One, set the stage for the balance of the book and provide the framework for a sound assessment practice. The chapters in Part Two address assessment processes from several perspectives, including how assessments are designed and conducted and how results are interpreted and communicated to assessees and end users. The theme underlying the chapters in Part Three is that of context: How does assessment fit strategically to a business plan? How does it respond to the requirements of new leadership models? What are the relevant issues with respect to cultural differences? What are the possible influences that assessments can have on organizational effectiveness? The final chapter of the book (Part Four) provides our perspectives about individual assessment and insights about the future direction of assessment research and practice.

The majority of the chapter authors have extensive experience in the conduct of individual assessments, and they were selected foremost for that reason.

Chapter One begins with our overview, based on our more than fifty years of combined experience in assessment practice. It discusses the history, purposes, techniques, and strategies of individual assessment. Our introductory comments set the stage for the balance of the book by identifying issues that the chapter authors subsequently address.

Chapter Two is written by Joyce Hogan and Robert Hogan, who have both research and practical experience in the field of assessment. They provide a comprehensive understanding of the theoretical framework for assessment and present a strong rationale for psychologist assessors to conduct individual assessments with a clear theoretical view of human performance.

In Chapter Three, Ann Marie Ryan and Paul R. Sackett, whose pioneering survey research has resulted in a clear perspective on the scope of assessment practice within organizational settings, present a summary of the psychometric research regarding psychological instruments and assessor decisions as they occur in individual assessment practice. These findings point to the realities that assessment is still more art than science and that the outcomes from an assessment are often influenced as much by external variables as by the assessee. The authors also identify research opportunities and needs that should spark interest within the profession.

Chapter Four addresses ethical, professional, and legal responsibilities of both assessors and organizations using assessment results. Written by coeditor Richard Jeanneret, who has had a strong personal interest in this topic since the time he conducted his first individual assessment, this chapter identifies many ethical dilemmas and responsibilities faced by assessors and organizations using assessment results. It includes as well a framework for resolving ethical issues and a number of principles to follow in developing a sound assessment program. Many of the guidelines presented could apply equally to other forms of assessment, such as assessment centers or multirater feedback processes, and also to general human resource consulting assignments.

Chapter Five, by Michael H. Frisch, has a nuts-and-bolts flavor in that the emphasis is on the various factors that influence the design of an individual assessment process. Frisch makes the point that individual assessment typically represents some form of organizational intervention and that organizational influences have an impact on the assessment process from start to finish. The chapter addresses the basics: purposes, assessment components, understanding the assessee pool, and communicating results.

In Chapter Six, Robert E. Kaplan writes about how data collection and data reduction strategies can achieve interpretative simplicity and clarity. Based on his extensive experience using comprehensive assessment of an individual's development, he demonstrates how to use both an inductive approach, generating inferences from the data, and a deductive approach, based on existing theory, to arrive at conclusions. His interactive process relies on significant participation by the individual and reflects an insightful and thought-provoking approach to individual change and development.

Harry Levinson demonstrates in Chapter Seven how a comprehensive theory of personality, such as psychoanalysis, can be used as an integrating framework to assess executive candidates. He provides many clinical insights into important leadership traits and potentially limiting characteristics such as narcissism.

Pierre Meyer, in Chapter Eight, reviews oral and written assessment feedback approaches. He particularly explores our equal obligation to both the individual and the organization as dual clients and how feedback can be effectively used to leverage participant development. This chapter provides useful guidance on how to introduce and discuss psychological assessment in an organization.

Larry Fogli and Kristina Whitney, in Chapter Nine, describe how psychological assessment can be leveraged to assess individuals for new management roles in organizations. The authors not only define these newly emerging roles but demonstrate how both job analysis and assessment techniques can be adapted to accommodate them. This process should have broad applicability as organizations experience ongoing change. This chapter gives encouragement that with some adjustment, traditional tools can be useful in addressing emerging organizational issues.

John R. Fulkerson concentrates in Chapter Ten on the assessment of individuals who have different cultural backgrounds from those born and raised in the United States. Fulkerson has many years of firsthand experience in assessing managers who operate in the global marketplace, and his perspective blends well with the information that has been uncovered regarding cultural influences on assessment. There is considerable food for thought in this chapter as businesses become more global in operation and use individual assessment to support selection, placement, and growth decisions.

In Chapter Eleven, Sandra L. Davis provides a strategic view of individual assessment. She discusses how cultural factors, human resource plans, and business strategies provide the context for designing and implementing psychological assessment. Her organizational readiness model provides a guide for evaluating the potential effectiveness of assessment as an organizational intervention.

In Chapter Twelve, coeditor Rob Silzer discusses the application of psychological assessment for organizational development purposes, including succession planning, organizational change, and leadership development. He notes that organizations increasingly require that assessments have a tangible and meaningful benefit as an organizational intervention and reviews how assessment can be leveraged to influence organizational direction or effectiveness.

In Chapter Thirteen we summarize the issues and theories delineated in this book and extrapolate them into the future. Our focus shifts to anticipating future assessment applications and techniques, emerging issues, and research needs.

We hope all readers will find this book a valuable resource to confirm or change some of their current thinking about individual assessment, to stimulate their ideas for future research or practice, or to educate them if they will be conducting the assessments of tomorrow.

Ackowledgments

Writing this book has been both a challenging and rewarding experience for us, and we are most appreciative of the excellent efforts that have been made by all who have contributed to the completion of this book: the chapter authors, who were collaborative, professional, and committed to making a quality contribution; the Professional Practice Series board of the Society for Industrial and Organizational Psychology, particularly Manuel London and Walter Tornow; and Jossey-Bass editors Byron Schneider, Julianna Gustafson, and Mary Garrett.

We particularly want to thank the SIOP leadership for seeing the importance of recognizing and publishing advances in the practice of industrial and organizational psychology and particularly of individual psychological assessment.

And finally, we thank our families, friends, and colleagues, who supported our effort, stimulated our thinking, and helped advance our practice.

April 1998

RICHARD JEANNERET
Houston, Texas

ROB SILZER
New York, New York

The Authors

RICHARD JEANNERET is the founder and managing principal of Jeanneret & Associates, a management consulting firm headquartered in Houston. His consulting experience encompasses all aspects of human resource management, with emphasis on psychological assessment, job analysis, employee selection systems, performance measurement, and compensation programs. Jeanneret is a cofounder and current president of PAQ Services and an adjunct professor in the industrial-organizational psychology program at the University of Houston. He has served in an appointed chair and elected officer capacity in the Society for Industrial and Organizational Psychology (SIOP) and is a fellow of the American Psychological Association and SIOP. His substantial and long-term contributions to psychological practice were recognized by SIOP in 1990 when he was honored with the Distinguished Professional Contributions Award. Jeanneret received his B.A. degree from the University of Virginia, his M.A. degree from the University of Florida, and his Ph.D. degree in industrial and organizational psychology from Purdue University.

ROB SILZER is the founder and president of HR Assessment and Development, a human resource consulting firm based in New York City. He has broad experience consulting to U.S. and international corporations and provides a range of professional services, with an emphasis on executive and management development, staffing and selection, performance measurement, psychological assessment, and training and development. In collaboration with Richard Jeanneret, he has conducted numerous workshops, symposiums, tutorials, and presentations on individual psychological assessment and related topics. In addition, Silzer has served as director of personnel research for a Fortune 500 corporation and as president of the New York office for a major U.S. management consulting firm. He was cofounder of the Minnesota Society for Industrial/Organizational Psychology and recently served as president of the Metropolitan New York Applied Psychology Association. He is an adjunct professor in the Graduate School of Psychology at New York University. Silzer received his B.S. degree from Southern Illinois University, his M.S. degree in social psychology from Florida State University, and his Ph.D. degree in both industrial and organizational psychology and counseling psychology from the University of Minnesota.

Sandra L. Davis is cofounder and president of MDA Consulting Group, where she focuses on the identification and growth of leadership talent and the development of organizational systems that support peak performance. Her client work includes individual assessment and development, coaching, applied research, team building, training, cultural change, and organizational development. She is a nationally known expert in the use of the California Psychological Inventory (CPI) in organizations and has coauthored (with Pierre Meyer) an applications guide for using the CPI in organizations. Davis received her Ph.D. degree from the University of Minnesota.

Larry Fogli is president of CORE Corporation, a leading consulting firm providing business solutions in the design and implementation of management and human resource systems. As a corporate executive of human resource activities and external consultant, Fogli has had substantial experience in the financial, retail, manufacturing, professional sports, entertainment, and insurance industries. He has expertise in both strategic and specific functional human resource areas. He received his Ph.D. degree from the University of California, Berkeley.

Michael H. Frisch is a senior consultant in the New York City office of Personnel Decisions International (PDI), where he helps clients apply psychology to their organizations. In particular, he delivers selection and development assessments and directs the executive coaching practice for that office. Prior to joining PDI, Frisch led his own consulting practice, providing assessment and coaching services. He is a member of the Metropolitan New York Association for Applied Psychology, the Society for Industrial and Organizational Psychology, and the American Psychological Association. He received his B.A. degree from the State University of New York at Binghamton, his M.S. degree from Georgia Institute of Technology, and his Ph.D. degree from Rice University.

John R. Fulkerson is vice president of organization capability and training for K-Mart. For the majority of his career, he has worked and traveled internationally and has been vice president of organization and management development for PepsiCo Foods and Beverages International. Fulkerson received his B.S. degree from Texas A&M University and his Ph.D. degree from Baylor University.

Joyce Hogan is cofounder and vice president of Hogan Assessment Systems. She received her Ph.D. degree from the University of Maryland. Along with Robert Hogan, she has coauthored several individual differences inventories and test manuals. She is editor of *Human Performance* and a fellow of the American Psychological Association.

Robert Hogan is McFarlin Professor of Psychology at the University of Tulsa and cofounder of Hogan Assessment Systems. He is the former editor of *Journal of Personality and Social Psychology* and is a fellow of the American Psychological Association. He received his Ph.D. degree from the University of California, Berkeley, where he studied at the Institute for Personality Assessment Research.

Robert E. Kaplan is copresident of Kaplan DeVries, a consulting firm specializing in leadership consulting to executives. Before founding this firm in 1992, he spent twelve years doing research and management development at the Center for Creative Leadership. He is a coauthor of *Beyond Ambition: How Driven Managers Can Lead Better and Live Better* (1991, with Wilfred Drath and Joan Kofodimos). Kaplan received his Ph.D. degree from Yale University.

Harry Levinson is chairman of the Levinson Institute and clinical professor of psychology emeritus in the Department of Psychiatry, Harvard Medical School. In 1954 he created, and for the next fourteen years directed, the Division of Industrial Mental Health of the

Menninger Foundation. From 1968 to 1972 Levinson was Thomas Henry Carrol–Ford Foundation distinguished visiting professor in the Harvard Graduate School of Business Administration. In addition to numerous articles, he is the senior author or editor of fourteen books.

Pierre Meyer is president of MDA Consultants in San Francisco and an adjunct assistant professor at the University of Minnesota. His practice includes managerial and executive individual assessment, design and implementation of assessment centers, and coaching for development. His professional interests include leadership behavior, executive problem solving, team-based structure, and organizational change. He is coauthor of *The CPI Applications Guide* (1992, with Sandra Davis). He received his B.S., M.A., and Ph.D. degrees from the University of Minnesota.

Ann Marie Ryan is associate professor of psychology at Michigan State University. She received her Ph.D. degree from the University of Illinois, Chicago, and has served on the faculty at Bowling Green State University. Her primary research interest is in nonability influences on employee selection decisions. She serves on the editorial boards of *Journal of Applied Psychology, Journal of Management,* and *Personnel Psychology.*

Paul R. Sackett holds the Carlson Professorship in Industrial Relations at the University of Minnesota. He received his Ph.D. degree from the Ohio State University and has served on the faculties of the University of Kansas and the University of Illinois at Chicago. His research interests include the assessment of managerial potential, honesty in the workplace, psychological testing in workplace settings, and methodological issues in employee selection. He served as editor of *Personnel Psychology* from 1984 to 1990, and he is the coauthor of *Perspectives on Employee Staffing and Selection* (1993). From 1993 to 1994 he served as president of the Society for Industrial and Organizational Psychology. He is cochair of the American Psychological Association's Joint Committee on the Standards for Educational and Psychological Tests and a member of the National Research Council's Board on Testing and Assessment.

Kristina Whitney is manager of assessment and development services at CORE Corporation, a strategic human resource consulting firm, where she works with organizations to design and implement assessment and development programs that directly support strategic business objectives. She specializes in assessing and developing managers for new and changing organizational roles. This work includes individual assessment and coaching as well as the design and implementation of performance management systems. Her Ph.D. degree is from the University of California, Berkeley.

Individual Psychological Assessment

PART 1

Frameworks

CHAPTER 1

An Overview of Individual Psychological Assessment

Richard Jeanneret
Rob Silzer

Individual psychological assessment is particularly challenging because every assessee is unique and presents a combination of behaviors and characteristics that must be understood in the context of a particular setting, typically a specific organization with its own internal chemistry. Individual psychological assessment is also professionally rewarding because it allows practitioners to use the full range of their psychological knowledge and professional skills.

Defining Individual Psychological Assessment

In our first workshop on psychological assessment presented on behalf of the Society for Industrial and Organizational Psychology (SIOP) (Silzer & Jeanneret, 1987), we defined *individual psychological assessment* as a process of measuring a person's knowledge, skills, abilities, and personal style to evaluate characteristics and behavior that are relevant to (predictive of) successful job performance. Our definition is consistent with that of Sundberg (1977), who described assessment as "the set of processes used by a person or persons for developing impressions and images, making decisions and checking hypotheses about another person's pattern of characteristics which determine his or her behavior in interaction with the environment" (pp. 21–22). Typically, the focus is on normal psychological and behavioral factors, rather than on abnormal or latent psychological traits, although there is no question that some individual assessments (of nuclear power plant operators, for example) are designed to detect characteristics that might be outside a normal or acceptable range.

Both an organizational and an assessment psychologist can *evaluate* or *assess* people, but they do so from different perspectives, with different techniques, and often for different purposes. The organization's human resource and management representatives often are able to evaluate the specific knowledge and experience a candidate has relevant to the requirements of a particular job. Typically, they review applications or resumés, complete interviews, and perhaps make inquiries of past employers and references when appropriate. However, most organizations are less well equipped to assess an individual's aptitudes, general abilities, motivational needs, and temperament or personal style (often termed personality characteristics). This information is more reliably and effectively obtained by a psychological assessment process and used by assessors to describe individuals and make judgments about their performance or development potential. Typically, assessors collect the information they need using psychological instruments, simulations, and interviews, which are interpreted in terms of the job requirements and organizational context for the position of interest.

The purpose of an organization's evaluation or appraisal of an individual is often different from the purpose of psychological assessment. Relying on the measurement of psychological constructs and behavioral indicators, assessment usually is conducted to identify an individual's potential to perform successfully in the future (frequently in jobs that are different from past work experiences). An organization's evaluation is typically focused on determining an individual's effectiveness in his or her current job, focusing on very observable concrete behavior. When the purposes are switched, the evaluation and assessment techniques may have different results. When psychological assessment is used to evaluate current performance, the conclusions typically explore the underlying reasons why an individual is succeeding or failing, often extrapolating to future situations. When organizational evaluations attempt to predict future effectiveness, they tend to overrely on credentials (in external selection situations) or often fail to see the limits or abilities of the individual to adapt or to learn the complex factors in the future job (in internal promotion situations).

It is also important to distinguish individual psychological assessment from other types of evaluation that are carried out within an organizational setting. Two prominent evaluation techniques are performance appraisals and multirater feedback surveys. They may focus on evaluating an individual relative to a specific set of job expectations or competencies that might also be used to guide an individual psychological assessment. However, the perspective of the *evaluator* in such instances is very different. Those who complete performance appraisals or multirater surveys focus on observed behavior of the individual in the job. Conversely, the *assessor* conducting an individual psychological assessment is measuring more personal characteristics that underlie past and future expected behavior. Current on-the-job behavior is also considered but from a behavioral incident perspective, without the accompanying influences of having a personal, day-to-day working relationship with the individual. Thus our point is that individual assessment brings a type of reliable psychological measurement, a degree of objectivity, and an understanding of underlying psychological constructs to the process that cannot be achieved by organizational evaluations.

Table 1.1 compares performance evaluation and psychological assessment and outlines some of the clear advantages that individual assessment has relative to performance evaluations, but we do not intend to imply that individual assessments should replace or be used in the same manner as performance appraisals.

Although we recognize that certain assessment techniques measuring psychological constructs can be used with small to large groups, as well as with individuals, our focus is on individual assessment and not on what occurs when screening larger applicant pools (that is, group selection testing). Similarly, although many of the assessment tools and techniques for individual assessment are also commonly used in group assessment centers and in some cases, such as simulations, were first developed as part of an assessment center, we are concentrating on the assessment of a single individual. Sometimes, of course, what appears to be a group assessment process, such as a leaderless group discussion or a task force exercise, can be used to assess a single individual, with the

Table 1.1. Comparison of Psychological Assessment and Performance Evaluation.

Performance Evaluation	Psychological Assessment
Is typically focused on summarizing current behavior and results.	Is typically focused on predicting future behavior and performance potential.
Depends almost exclusively on evaluator's observation skills.	Depends on both reliable psychological tools and assessor's observation skills.
Uses techniques that are rarely researched or validated.	Uses tools and techniques that have been researched and validated.
Rarely includes systematic process for observing behavior or collecting data, which makes it difficult to compare individuals.	Includes systematic process for observing behavior, collecting data, and comparing individuals.
Involves an evaluator who is poorly trained, often subjective and influenced by organization hearsay.	Involves an assessor who is highly trained, objective, and removed from organizational influence.
Is guided by personal opinion.	Is guided by psychological constructs and theory.
Is usually seen as ineffective, and process is frequently revised.	Is usually viewed as useful, and process is often stable over time.
Evaluates only a small subset of skills and behaviors or fashionable performance areas.	Assesses a standard and comprehensive set of skills, abilities, and characteristics.
Becomes contaminated by other organizational systems like compensation.	Maintains independence from organizational systems.
Summarizes conclusions inconsistently or poorly.	Documents conclusions in consistent and professional manner.

other group members serving as confederates and having assigned roles. It is also not unusual for organizations to weigh the choice carefully between using individual psychological assessment and assessment centers. Often they are seen as equally effective approaches for some organizational objectives, with the choice depending on implementation logistics, costs, and available assessor staff. Furthermore, although the individual psychological assessment process is typically different from the assessment of a larger group, they often have the same objectives of selection or development.

Joseph Matarazzo (1990), in his American Psychological Association presidential address, provides a helpful summative definition that characterizes individual assessment: "It is the activity of a licensed professional, an artisan familiar with the accumulated findings of his or her young science, who in each instance uses tests, techniques, and a strategy that, whereas also identifying possible deficits, maximizes the chances of discovering each client's full ability and true potential" (p. 1000).

Finding the Origins

Matarazzo's definition implies that psychological assessment is part of a young science, but psychological assessment has roots that can be traced to the writings of Plato, which indicated that selection for state service in ancient Greece was made on the basis of assessed differences in the physical and cognitive abilities of candidates. In medieval China (A.D. 1368–1644), individual assessments, primarily competitive oral and written exams emphasizing communication skills and cognitive ability, were used in selecting among candidates for various civil service jobs throughout the governmental hierarchy (DuBois, 1970). The Chinese assessment approach later spread to India (1832), Europe (1855), and North America (1883) (Wiggins, 1973). In the late 1800s, Sir Francis Galton (1883) pioneered the development of nonverbal measures of individual differences such as sensory discrimination. Other researchers designed performance measures of intellectual functioning (Cattell, 1890; Seguin, 1907) and problem-solving ability (Binet & Simon, 1905).

Although individual assessment may have its historical beginnings more than twenty-two hundred years ago, the modern practices for industrial and organizational psychologists stem from the efforts of Hugo Munsterberg, who advocated vocational assessment to guide industrial employment; Louis Thurstone, who used auditory tests to select telegraphers; Robert Link, who used card sorting to select skilled inspectors; and Walter Bingham, who used personality measures to select sales representatives. Other early events included the development of Woodworth's Personal Data Sheet (PDS) in 1918 to screen U.S. Army recruits for maladjustments. The PDS was apparently used in conjunction with Thurstone's Personality Scale and Allport's Ascendance-Submission Test. Sundberg (1977) provides a historical background, citing fifty major events in psychological assessment beginning in 1869 with Galton's publication regarding individual differences and concluding with 1976 as the year that the "first major books on assessment with behavioral techniques are published" (p. 18).

Following defeat in World War I, Germany involved psychologists in military personnel affairs in order to evaluate the overall leadership skills of officer candidates and to put less reliance on single skills or credentials (Ansbacher, 1941, 1944; Farago, 1942; Fitts, 1946). The emphasis now switched from atomistic to holistic personnel assessments: "The unique emphases of German military psychology was on the assessment of the total person within the context in which he was expected to perform. . . . Within the holistic framework, 'atomistic' distinctions between abilities and character traits disappeared" (Simoneit, 1932, p. 357).

German psychologists established multiple assessment procedures for selecting military officers and specialists. The two-day assessment program collected performance, biographical, and psychological data using realistic situational performance tests as well as traditional intelligence measures, interviews, biographical questionnaires, and interest surveys (Farago, 1942; Wolfahrt, 1938).

Simultaneously in the United States, Murray (1938) and later the Office of Strategic Services (Office of Strategic Services Staff, 1948) pioneered the use of multiple assessment techniques and multiple assessors (MacKinnon, 1977). The OSS effort was the forerunner of assessment centers, which became popular in some business organizations in the 1960s. More than anyone else, Douglas Bray (1961, 1964, 1982) adapted multiple assessment procedures, later known as assessment centers, to business organizations and through the Management Progress Study (Bray, 1964) documented the validity of psychological assessment to predict management career advancement.

Psychological assessment was becoming so popular, said Miner (1970), that "conducting psychological evaluations may well be the largest single area of activity for industrial psychologists at the present time" (p. 393). Although the terminology may well have changed from *psychological evaluation* to *psychological assessment* some time ago, the activity itself was clearly a major component of the practice of industrial and organizational psychology. For example, in the 1960s the use of assessment centers in the business community was growing quickly; the pioneering efforts of Douglas Bray and Donald Grant (1966) at AT&T were being aggressively copied by other companies. Also, one of us, Richard Jeanneret, entered professional practice in 1969 and clearly recalls that many of the applied job openings, including the position he accepted, called for a significant portion of professional time to be spent in conducting individual assessments and providing developmental feedback to assessees. This continued to be true when Rob Silzer entered professional practice in 1975.

Finally, it should be noted that the one capability that sets apart psychologists from all other professionals is the capability to assess individual differences. Therefore, it is not unusual to find that a significant part of professional psychological practice has been and will continue to be devoted to individual psychological assessment within an organizational context.

Extent of Assessment Practice

It is impossible to determine how many assessments are conducted for U.S. organizations during the course of any time period, but we can make some estimates about the extent of the practice among SIOP members. Results from the SIOP membership survey (Howard, 1990) provide information about various practice areas performed by members. Membership survey data analyses were obtained that calculated the percentage of time certain SIOP members spent conducting individual psychological assessments for selection or promotion or performing vocational or career counseling (A. Howard, personal communication with requested data analysis of SIOP survey, July 17, 1990). The two categories of SIOP members selected were those whose primary job was reported as either external consultant or psychologist in a private-sector organization.

Table 1.2 presents these results, which indicate that external consultants (compared to industrial and organizational psychologists within organizations) devote more of their time to assessment and counseling functions and that assessment consumes considerably more time than vocational counseling. The median amount of time spent by assessing consultants (48 percent of consultant respondents) in the assessment process is approximately 18 percent (the equivalent percentage of time for psychologists within private-sector organizations is only about 4 percent). Given a 40-hour week, a consultant would devote, on average, 7.2 hours to assessment activities. If we assume a range of 2.3 to 3.6 hours spent per assessment, the typical consultant is completing two or three assessments per week. Of course, we recognize that these data are estimates at best, and personal experience tells us that some consultants complete two assessments per day, every day, for weeks at a time.

As part of his presidential address, Borman presented the results of a practice survey of 647 SIOP members (Borman & Cox, 1996). He reported that a significant area of practice (based on a factor analysis of time spent responses) was individual development, which consisted of individual coaching, executive development, individual assessment, succession planning, and outplacement. He also calculated that external consultants do approximately 69 percent of the work in individual development areas, whereas internal consultants perform 26 percent of the work and academics do about 5 percent of the work. (Howard estimated that 35 percent of academics do some consulting, whereas Borman estimated that 77 percent of academics consult.) Upon further analysis, we find the percentage of the individual development practice conducted by specific SIOP groups is as follows:

Consulting firms: 46 percent

Corporate consultants (internal): 21 percent

Table 1.2. Percentage of Time Spent in Assessment and Counseling Activities.

	Full-Time Employment	
	External Consultant	Psychologist in a Business Organization
Percentage of time conducting individual assessment		
0	52	74
Up to 25	30	23
26 to 50	10	2
51	8	1
Percentage of time doing vocational counseling		
0	65	75
Up to 10	23	22
11 and more	12	3

Source: A. Howard, personal communication (analysis of 1990 SIOP survey, July 17, 1990).

Self-employed: 21 percent

Government: 6 percent

Academia: 5 percent

Research firms: 1 percent

Clearly, individual development is a sizable area of practice and is primarily accomplished by external consultants (those who are working in consulting firms or who are self-employed).

Understanding What Assessors Are Doing

It is valuable for all assessors to step back from their day-to-day assessment activities and review what it is they are doing and the wide range of individual techniques that assessment practice comprises. Because of the variety that occurs in assessment process and technology, some have argued for standardization. For example, Lanyon and Goodstein (1982) believe that "there ought to be a relatively standard approach to the evaluation of executive potential . . . or leadership in particular situations. [However,] there tend to be rather substantial differences among actual practitioners as to which instruments are the most useful in a given instance, and as to what should be done with the responses once they are obtained. In general the behavior of psychologists in selecting assessment strategies seems to be governed more by tradition and superstition than by relevance or evidence" (p. 171).

Additionally, we are concerned that many assessors may simply function as data interpreters, without understanding the in-depth capabilities of the assessment process or recognizing the broad responsibilities that accompany it. For our purposes, data interpreters are those who administer one or more of their favorite psychological tests, obtain the scores for some set of dimensions purported to be measured by these tests, interpret the dimension scores in terms of the test manual descriptions and norms, and believe the assessment is complete. If this is an assessor's individual assessment practice, then that assessor's understanding of the individual is at best superficial and is likely to be wrong.

Making Inferences

The process of individual assessment involves making a series of judgments based on inferences and then integrating these judgments into descriptions of the individual and predictions regarding the fit between the person and the job and the person's future performance. These inferences are extremely important to the process. First, inferences are usually causal: that is, because the assessor has identified a specific characteristic in the individual, it will influence behavior in a certain way. Second, inferences typically imply positive or negative outcomes. Given that a characteristic will affect behavior in a specific way, it will enhance or detract from fit to a particular job or performance in that job. Finally, inferences establish expectations in terms of how pronounced a predicted behavior will be exhibited. In simplistic terms, if assessors observe the strength of a characteristic to be strong, then they might expect a clear impact on behavior (setting aside moderating effects of other characteristics for the moment).

The inferences that assessors make are derived from the information gathered by using the various tools and techniques available to psychologists. Of course, these tools and techniques are not perfect suppliers of information, and their psychometric characteristics must be understood and evaluated as part of the judgmental and integrative processes. Furthermore, assessors should be cognizant of the warning issued by Tryon (1979), who advised that the scale scores of psychological tests are not themselves measures of traits. Nor it is likely that responses to interview questions clearly measure specific traits. Consequently, descriptions of the traits of an individual occur as part of assessors' inferential thinking; the traits cannot be lifted directly from their instrumentation.

Identifying Self-Presentation Biases

Another consideration that assessors may overlook or take for granted in the assessment process is that the underlying source of all of their information is based on the self-presentations of the individual. This has both positive and potentially problematic implications. On the positive side the individual usually is a constant, single source of input. Thus responses to psychological tests or interview questions originate from the same source, which, in all likelihood, does not change during the course of the assessment process, thus providing cues for a relatively stable snapshot of the individual. On the problematic side the assessee is providing a single static snapshot of characteristics and behavior while participating in the assessment. To the extent there is a temporary distortion (intentional or unintentional) in responses, the assessor could make incorrect inferences and judgments when trying to describe the dynamic individual.

Information obtained by either instruments or interviews may be inaccurate for several reasons. Perhaps the reason that has been studied the most is that people do not like to admit to behavior or characteristics they consider to be socially undesirable; consequently, they may not be forthcoming about certain behaviors or feelings. A second reason is that people may forget relevant information or have a distorted memory. Third, questions are often stated in terms of time periods in people's lives, and most people lose track of time, especially for events that occurred years earlier. Fourth, and true especially in employment situations, assessees may respond in ways they believe fit their stereotype for the job or think will leave a good impression on the assessor, whom they perceive as having significant influence on the hiring decision. Sometimes individuals consciously decide not to tell the truth in response to test or interview questions. In addition, many of the assessment instruments can be influenced by particular response styles (for example, selecting or avoiding extreme ends of rating scales or always selecting a positive response) or by response unreliability (for example, selecting highly unusual responses or responding randomly). Unfortunately, research has not clearly determined the influence that response distortion has on the final assessment results or on predictions of performance. Consequently, assessors must rely on their experience and use their professional judgment when interpreting information that is potentially inaccurate or distorted.

There is some limited research in the personality testing domain that has implications for these concerns. Mount, Barrick, and

Strauss (1994) found that self-ratings by sales representatives of their personality characteristics were less predictive of job performance when compared to supervisor and coworker ratings of the same personality variables. In fact, for the variables of extroversion and agreeableness, the correlations between self-ratings and supervisor ratings of job performance were not even statistically significant. We could easily hypothesize that for these two personality constructs, there is considerable self-awareness, and we would expect significant predictability. The research of Nilsen (1995) also raises concern about the validity of self-report ratings of personality characteristics. Her results indicate that concurrent validities for executives were lower than validities for other individuals who completed either personality inventories or descriptions about the executive population being studied. In other words, executives responding to personality measures were less predictive of their work behaviors (self-descriptions) than were other individuals who observed and described the executives' characteristics using equivalent personality measures.

Although these studies are disconcerting, they are not conclusive. They suffer to some degree from method bias (that is, using the same instrumentation for different respondents) and from other potentially uncontrolled respondent sets. For example, the "observers" described the personalities of individuals only as they appeared at work; the participants' self-descriptions may have taken a whole life perspective, integrating their work life with their personal life. Even so, we wonder about the perspective of individuals when completing personality inventories and other behavioral questionnaires as part of a psychological assessment.

In general, however, many persons may not be fully aware of or understand their own functioning, especially when dealing with others. Consequently, what may seem to be honest self-reports may not be completely accurate in terms of describing actual behavior. Thus a failure of memory or a lack of insight can lead to distorted responses. We raise these concerns because assessors may place too much faith in instrumentation, the responses to interview questions, and their inferential powers, believing that the assessment information is fully reliable and highly valid. Of course, reality is that few, if any, assessment data are without some error.

Interpreting Assessment Information

One primary responsibility of the assessor is to understand the assessment information in order to make sound inferences and judgments. There are several considerations that may influence how the assessor goes about this interpretation process. One consideration relates to the assessor's understanding of the assessment purpose. Simplistically, on a bipolar continuum, one way to state the purpose is as either positive or negative. If, for example, the explicit purpose is to make a selection decision, the assessor could be focused on finding positive characteristics that match the job requirements, or conversely, looking for reasons that the individual should not be selected for the job. Similarly, one or the other of these perspectives might also be taken for a developmental assessment. Our concern is that although assessors might perceive themselves as neutral and as looking for both positive and negative characteristics, actual practice may be different.

For example, Richard Jeanneret, early in his career while he was learning about assessment, practiced with a psychologist who always seemed to view the assessment results in the most positive light and rarely considered negative information. However, another assessor was just the opposite. He seemed to focus on negative characteristics, and his recommendations were more likely to reflect reasons that an individual should not be selected. Despite candid discussion about these differing perspectives, there was little change in the actual practice of either assessor over a period of several years.

Independent of how assessors may interpret assessment data, they should also recognize that the purpose for the assessment may be expressed on a continuum of positive to negative selection. On the positive side for developmental assessments, assessors might assist already solid performers in becoming even more effective or better prepared to expand into new job roles. On the negative side during a selection assessment, they might consider screening out candidates for highly sensitive jobs (police officer or nuclear power plant operator, for instance) based on disqualifying information in order to prevent a "bad" hire rather than looking for information to find the "best" hire.

When assessment responds to an organizational need, its objective is not usually one of classification. Assessors are not attempting to assign individuals to categories of mental health disorders or treatment groups. Their interpretative strategies are usually focused on the prediction of performance in either a known work setting or one that they can describe with some degree of clarity in terms of performance requirements and expectations.

Choosing Normative or Ipsative Interpretations

One way to improve the relevance of assessment interpretations is to develop client-specific and job-specific norms. This is especially useful when evaluating the results of cognitive tests for which there may be only very generic normative data available from the publishers. The development of more specific norms applicable to the purpose and situational context of the assessment can be informative to both the assessor and the individual (during the feedback session).

A normative perspective also can be very useful when interpreting assessment instruments (such as personality tests). For example, assessing a number of incumbents in an organization can provide an assessor with valuable insights regarding success factors, personal chemistry, and organizational climate in advance of assessing candidates for the same position. Although the publisher may score the instrument using more traditional normative data, the baseline information is often very broad and may have limited relevance for the specific assessment purpose or may not be relevant for the assessee population of interest. For example, Scott and Sedlacek (1975), using cross-validated discriminant analyses, found significant differences in the California Psychological Inventory (CPI) and Vocational Preferences Inventory (VPI) profiles of men who were pursuing a career in physical science in comparison to the category "male engineer." In many normative data sets the two groups would be compiled together. Similarly, Braen, Grant, and Patton (1981) found significant differences for engineers and managers on four primary CPI scales. Hence, client-specific or occupation-specific normative data can be useful to assessment interpretations and can help build interpretative consistency across different assessors who are both assessing applicants for the same position.

Sackett and Wilk (1994) also make a valuable observation regarding the value of normative data when interpreting individual assessment results. Specifically, they point out that when a clinical interpretation of personality inventory test scores is being made by a psychologist, it might be reasonable for that interpretation to take into account gender differences (as expressed normatively by a publisher) on certain personality dimensions. They note that psychologists who believe the gender differences are meaningful and incorporate this knowledge as part of their data integration may be in violation of the 1991 Civil Rights Act's prohibition on score adjustments.

Ipsative interpretation of assessment results also can be a valuable technique for assessors. Although the psychometric deficiencies of ipsative scores have been well documented (Anastasi, 1976; Guilford, 1954; Johnson, Wood, & Blinkhorn, 1988), the value of comparing an individual's scores across scales on the same instrument or even across different tests (for example, the assessee is higher on one trait relative to a second trait) has not been the subject of rigorous research. However, as Harris (1980) argues, "It is at least as important to know how that trait relates to another trait in the same person as it is to know how that trait relates to the same trait in 1,000 other persons" (p. 742). Further, using an ipsative approach allows the assessor the opportunity to "correct" a profile for excessive faking or being overly "open" in responding to a particular test (such as obtaining very low fake scores on the Guilford Zimmerman Temperament Survey [GZT]). In the latter instance, one typically expects applicants' defense mechanisms to operate in such a way that their results for the emotional stability and objectivity scales will not fall below the lowest quartile. However, applicants who approach the assessment process with the intent of seeking counseling lower their defense mechanisms and "open" themselves by responding with a greater number of admissions to behaviors typically considered less desirable. In turn the assessor should be cautious about drawing conclusions from such data, especially if comparisons are being made with other applicants who have maintained their normal defense mechanisms.

Integrating Assessment Information

The process of integrating assessment information has long been a controversial and confused topic among psychologists. Over the years, some psychologists have advocated using clinical integration and prediction methods, relying on the assessor's judgment to weigh and integrate the data into assessment inclusions and predictions (Holt, 1958, 1975; Holtzman, 1960; Hunt, 1959; Korman, 1968); others have strongly argued for an actuarial approach, using statistical methods to combine data into final assessment conclusions and predictions (Dawes, 1979; Dawes, Faust, & Meehl, 1989; Goldberg, 1976; Meehl, 1954; P. E. Meehl, personal communication to R. Silzer, January 30, 1981; Sawyer, 1966). Part of the confusion has been in failing to distinguish between data collection methods and data combination methods, even though this distinction was pointed out several decades ago (Sawyer, 1966). Clinicians and assessors have long felt that even this distinction was a personal attack on their judgment and expertise.

There has been an emerging consensus in the literature that assessors' judgment is best used in collecting assessment data, not in making behavioral predictions. One author writes, "I have a great deal more confidence in the intrinsic validity of those trait ratings than I do in the clinical predictions because clinical psychologists are trained specifically in assessing personality not in making predictions of behavioral outcomes" (Holt, 1970, p. 341). Statistical methods of combining data, however, have proved more accurate than clinical methods of data combination (Dawes, 1979; Dawes, Faust, & Meehl 1989; Sawyer, 1966; Silzer, 1984).

Over the past twenty years, there has been a focus on blending the two approaches into some optimal method (DeGroot, 1961; Einhorn, 1972; Kleinmuntz, 1990; Silzer, 1984). Using both clinical and mechanical data collection methods is quite common. Most assessment psychologists clinically obtain data through interviews and mechanically collect data through tests and instruments. However, there is much less agreement on how to combine the data. The research literature (Dawes, Faust, & Meehl, 1989; Silzer, 1984; Wiggins, 1973) seems to advocate for either a "mechanical composite process," which mechanically combines both clinically and mechanically collected data, or a "mechanical synthesis," which is similar to a mechanical composite except that the clinical prediction is added in as an extra variable when mechanically combining the data. We know of no one who actually uses either of these methods to integrate individual psychological assessment data, although several attempts have been made when integrating assessment center data (Silzer, 1984).

Assessors are still primarily using a clinical data integration method. Some use what Holt (1958) calls "naive clinical prediction" (Sawyer, 1966, called this a "pure clinical approach"), which involves intuitive judgment of unknown validity. Assessors who use very lengthy interviews and few instruments (many clinical psychologists) are close to this model. Other assessors are closer to what Holt (1958) advocates as "sophisticated clinical prediction" (Sawyer, 1966, calls this a "clinical composite"), which uses a clinical combination of clinically and mechanically collected data. This approach also requires that the assessor have a good understanding of predictor-criterion relationships. This is a common approach among many psychologists who value the statistical underpinnings and validity support of assessment tools and instruments (Holt, 1975; Newton, 1965).

What may be emerging is a "clinical synthesis" approach (Kleinmuntz, 1990; Sawyer, 1966), which is similar to a clinical composite prediction except that a mechanically derived prediction is considered in the assessor's final judgment. Initially, this mechanically generated prediction can be based on predictor data norms, but as sample sizes grow and criterion data become available, it can be based on predictor-criterion correlations. Although some research supports the clinical synthesis approach (Silzer, 1984) over other clinical prediction approaches, there still is no single research study that convincingly demonstrates greater criterion validity for any clinical prediction process over mechanical predictions (Dawes, Faust, & Meehl, 1989). Some studies have shown equal validity between these two approaches, particularly when predicting a specific performance area, such as interpersonal skills (Silzer, 1984).

So why do assessors continue to use a clinical integration and prediction process that research routinely demonstrates is less accurate than a mechanical prediction process? There are several reasons. First, they might argue that individual psychological assessments may be unique situations. Meehl (personal communication to R. Silzer, January 30, 1981) believes that mechanical prediction strategies will always surpass clinical prediction strategies except in two instances: (1) when the predictor and criterion variables are very similar and (2) when faced with unique idiographic circumstances. Some assessors would argue that well-designed work simulations may often fall into the first exception, whereas many individual psychological assessments fall into the second category.

Second, some psychologists might believe that they themselves are more accurate judges than other assessors. There is some research support for accuracy differences based on the individual differences of assessors (Borman, 1977; Garner & Smith, 1976; Levenberg, 1975).

Third, some psychologists, particularly those with an industrial-organizational psychology background, might claim that they have a greater understanding of the work performance criterion and therefore can accurately predict successful matches of individuals to it. Although there is no research evidence to support this for psychological assessment, it is generally accepted that knowledge of the criterion improves prediction accuracy. A small unpublished study at an assessment provider did find that whereas counseling psychologists are more thorough in providing a rich description of assessed individuals, industrial-organizational psychologists make predictions that are more highly correlated with performance criterion measures (presumably based on their knowledge of work behaviors and job requirements). Of course, one could argue that both skills are needed in psychological assessment. Rich descriptions are useful for understanding and developing the individual, and more accurate predictions can provide a selection benefit to the organization.

If assessors continue to use clinical integration and prediction processes, they might consider ways in which they can strengthen their accuracy. Certainly, understanding the performance criterion will help them to choose assessment tools and techniques wisely, effectively integrate data, and accurately predict the potential success of individuals. Knowing the validity of the assessment tools and carefully weighing and incorporating assessment data from a variety of sources can also add to assessment utility. Further, using a standard assessment approach can help build useful norms, reliable integration procedures, interpretative expertise, and confidence in the assessor's judgment.

Other Issues Affecting the Interpretation of Assessment Data

Although industrial-organizational psychology has given extensive attention to both intervening and moderating variables that influence the effectiveness (and fairness) of selection systems, the focus of such research has been on preemployment test batteries, not individual assessment. However, research regarding influential variables on clinical assessment has addressed these issues for some time, and the findings are likely to have relevance or implications for individual assessment in organizations.

Topics worthy of exploration include cultural, racial, gender, age, and other demographic characteristics, as well as less obvious concerns, such as time of day that an assessment takes place (Westman & Canter, 1988, report diurnal changes to CPI responses). We are especially concerned about the research reported in Chapter Three by Ryan and Sackett, which indicates there may be considerable inconsistency in how assessment outcomes are derived based on differences in assessors and even how a single assessor interprets the same data from time one to time two.

Art or Science?

In this chapter, we have touched on topics that reflect both the scientific and artistic nature of individual psychological assessments. The scientific qualities of assessment are at the forefront when all of us, as assessors, examine the psychometric characteristics of many of our instruments and the objectivity we attempt to bring to the process. The artistic side is more evident when we examine how we interpret and integrate assessment data to make predictions regarding the fit of persons to specific jobs and organizational situations. The scientist may overlook unique idiographic information and situations, and the artisan may overweigh the uniqueness of each situation and miss reliable, predictable patterns. In the end the assessor must be both a scientist and an artisan. Certainly, this is a complex job. What if you had to assess candidates for the position of manager of assessors? What predictor data would you collect in the assessment? What performance criterion measures would you use to measure your prediction accuracy? This is roughly the spot that most organizations are in when trying to select an assessment provider. Because they frequently make the choice based on superficial qualities, we cannot count on the users of psychological assessment to make valid choices. Therefore the responsibility for maintaining professional psychological assessment services rests primarily on the assessors themselves. Individual assessors must look for ways to improve their validity and utility to the organization.

The challenge for the reader, in the course of reading the chapters that follow, is to ask how can we continue to improve our understanding of assessment processes through scientific inquiries and at the same time retain the value of the artistic contributions of assessors in examining assessment data in support of organizational decision making.

References

Anastasi, A. (1976). *Psychological testing* (4th ed.). New York: Macmillan.

Ansbacher, H. L. (1941). German military psychology. *Psychological Bulletin, 38,* 370–379.

Ansbacher, H. L. (1944). German industrial psychology in the fifth year of the war. *Psychology Bulletin, 41,* 605–614.

Binet, A., & Simon, T. (1905). Methodes nouvelles pour le diagnostic du niveau intellectuel des anormaux. *Année Psychologique, 11,* 191–244.

Borman, W. C. (1977). *Some raters are simply better than others in evaluating performance: Individual differences correlates of rating accuracy using behavior scales.* Paper presented at the annual conference of the American Psychological Association, San Francisco.

Borman, W. C., & Cox, G. L. (1996). Who's doing what: Patterns in the practice of I/O psychology. *Industrial Organizational Psychology, 33*(4), 21–29.

Braen, J. S., Grant, C. W., & Patton, M. J. (1981). A CPI comparison of engineers and managers. *Journal of Vocational Behavior, 18,* 255–264.

Bray, D. W. (1961). The Management Progress Study. In Educational Testing Service, *Identifying management talent.* Princeton, NJ: Conference on the Executive Study.

Bray, D. W. (1964). The Management Progress Study. *American Psychologist, 19,* 419–420.

Bray, D. W. (1982). The assessment center and the study of lives. *American Psychologist, 37*(2), 180–189.

Bray, D. W., & Grant, D. L. (1966). The assessment center in the measurement of potential for business management. *Psychological Monographs, 80.*

Cattell, J. M. (1890). Mental tests and measurements. *Mind, 15,* 373–380.

Dawes, R. M. (1979). The robust beauty of improper linear models in decision making. *American Psychologist, 34*(7), 571–582.

Dawes, R. M., Faust, D., & Meehl, P. E. (1989). Clinical versus actuarial judgment. *Science, 243,* 1668–1674.

DeGroot, A. D. (1961). Via clinical to statistical prediction. *Acta Psychologica, 18,* 274–284.

DuBois, P. H. (1970). *A history of psychological testing.* Needham Heights, MA: Allyn & Bacon.

Einhorn, H. J. (1972). Expert measurement and mechanical combination. *Organizational Behavior and Human Performance, 7,* 86–106

Farago, L. (Ed.). (1942). *German psychological warfare.* New York: Putnam.

Fitts, P. M. (1946). German applied psychology during World War II. *American Psychologist, 1,* 141–161.

Galton, F. (1883). *Inquiries into human faculty and its development.* London: Macmillan.

Garner, A. M., & Smith, G. M. (1976). An experimental videotape technique for evaluating trainer approaches to clinical judging. *Journal of Consulting and Clinical Psychology, 44,* 945–950.

Goldberg, L. R. (1976). Man versus model of man: Just how conflicting is the evidence? *Organizational Behavior and Human Performance, 16,* 13–22.

Guilford, J. P. (1954). *Psychometric methods* (2nd ed.). New York: McGraw-Hill.

Harris, J. G., Jr. (1980). Normvalidation and idiovalidation. A quest for the true personality profile. *American Psychologist, 35,* 729–744.

Holt, R. R. (1958). Clinical and statistical prediction: A reformulation and some new data. *Journal of Abnormal and Social Psychology, 56,* 1–12.

Holt, R. R. (1970). Yet another look at clinical and statistical prediction: Or is clinical psychology worthwhile? *American Psychologist, 25,* 337–349.

Holt, R. R. (1975). Clinical and statistical measurement and prediction: How not to survey its literature (Manuscript No. 837). *JSAS Catalog of Selected Documents in Psychology, 5,* 178.

Holtzman, W. H. (1960). Can the computer supplant the clinician? *Journal of Clinical Psychology, 16,* 119–122.

Howard, A. (1990). *The multiple facets of industrial-organizational psychology.* Bowling Green, OH: Society for Industrial and Organizational Psychology.

Hunt, W. A. (1959). An actuarial approach to clinical judgment. In B. M. Bass & I. A. Berg (Eds.), *Objective approaches to personality study* (pp. 169–191). New York: Van Nostrand Rinehold.

Johnson, C. E., Wood, R., & Blinkhorn, S. F. (1988). Spuriouser and spuriouser: The use of ipsative personality tests. *Journal of Occupational Psychology, 61,* 153–162.

Kleinmuntz, B. (1990). Why we still use our heads instead of the formulas: Toward an integrative approach. *Psychological Bulletin, 107,* 296–310.

Korman, A. K. (1968). The prediction of managerial performance: A review. *Personal Psychology, 21,* 295–322.

Lanyon, R. I., & Goodstein, L. D. (1982). *Personality assessment* (2nd ed.). New York: Wiley.

Levenberg, S. B. (1975). Professional training, psychodiagnostic skills and kinetic family drawings. *Journal of Personality Assessment, 39,* 389–393.

MacKinnon, D. W. (1977). From selecting spies to selecting managers: The OSS assessment program. In J. L. Moses and W. C. Byham (Eds.), *Applying the assessment center method* (pp. 13–30). New York: Pergammon Press.

Matarazzo, J. D. (1990). Psychological assessment versus psychological testing. *American Psychologist, 45,* 999–1017.

Meehl, P. E. (1954). *Clinical vs. statistical prediction.* Minneapolis: University of Minnesota Press.

Miner, J. B. (1970). Psychology evaluations as predictors of consulting success. *Personnel Psychology, 23,* 393–405.

Mount, M. K., Barrick, M. R., & Strauss, J. P. (1994). Validity of observer ratings of the Big Five personality factors. *Journal of Applied Psychology, 79,* 272–280.

Murray, H. A. (1938). *Exploration in personality.* New York: Oxford University Press.

Newton, J. (1965). Judgment and feedback in a quasi-clinical situation. *Journal of Personality and Social Psychology, 1,* 336–342.

Nilsen, D. (1995). *Investigation of the relationship between personality and leadership performance.* Unpublished doctoral dissertation, University of Minnesota.

Office of Strategic Services Staff. (1948). *The assessment of men.* Austin, TX: Holt, Rinehart and Winston.

Sackett, P. R., & Wilk, S. L. (1994). Within group norming and other forms of score adjustment in pre-employment testing. *American Psychologist, 49,* 929–954.

Sawyer, J. (1966). Measurement and prediction, clinical and statistical. *Psychological Bulletin, 66,* 178–200.

Scott, N. A., & Sedlacek, W. E. (1975). Personality differentiation and prediction of persistence in physical science and engineering. *Journal of Vocational Behavior, 6,* 205–216.

Seguin, E. (1907). *Idiocy: Its treatment by the psychological method.* New York: Columbia University Press. (Original work published 1886)

Silzer, R. F. (1984). *Statistical prediction in a management assessment center.* Unpublished doctoral dissertation, University of Minnesota.

Silzer, R. F., & Jeanneret, P. R. (1987). *Psychological assessment: Getting at job-related skills and abilities.* Society for Industrial and Organizational Psychology Workshop presented at the 35th convention of the American Psychological Association, New York.

Simoneit, M. (1932). Zur charakterologischen aus wetung von Reaktionspruefungen. *Archiv Fuer die Gesamte Psychologie, 83,* 357–384.

Sundberg, N. D. (1977). Assessment of persons. Upper Saddle River, NJ: Prentice Hall.

Tryon, W. W. (1979). The test-trait fallacy. *American Psychologist, 34,* 402–406.

Westman, W. H., & Canter, F. M. (1988). Diurnal changes on the California Personality Inventory on work and leisure days. *Psychological Reports, 62,* 863–866.

Wiggins, J. S. (1973). *Personality and prediction: Principles of personality assessment.* Reading, MA: Addison-Wesley.

Wolfahrt, E. (1938). Die Interessenforschung als Hilfsmittel der Persoenlichkeitsdiagnose. *Angew Psychologie, 79 (Beih. Z),* 118–131.

CHAPTER 2

Theoretical Frameworks for Assessment

Joyce Hogan
Robert Hogan

Assessment is one of the few contributions of psychological research that has materially influenced business and society. Even the most severe critics of psychology must acknowledge that carefully developed assessments work: scores from well-designed assessment procedures agree closely with observer-based descriptions of assessees, and they predict performance in virtually any job or activity for which there are reliable criterion data—in part because the criterion data are often observer descriptions.

Despite the pragmatic successes of assessment, it remains essentially a technology with few pretensions to being anything more than rude empiricism increasingly dressed up in the bells and whistles of computer-based video technology. This, we believe, is due in part to an indifference regarding the conceptual foundations of assessment and to an intense concern with its appeal or acceptability to clients. Our sense is that assessment vendors will increasingly feature gadgetry and gimmicks in order to sell tests and show how sophisticated the hardware and software have become. We also

Note: We thank the following colleagues who provided feedback and advice on an earlier draft of this chapter: Walter Borman, Judy Collins, Gordy Curphy, Marv Dunnette, Richard Jeanneret, John Johnson, Rob Silzer, and Ray Wolfe. We thank B. Dings, M. Gooch, and S. Gracie for their assistance in preparing the manuscript.

suspect that little attention will be given to the conceptual foundations of the process.

It would be a mistake to blame the relative mindlessness of assessment on technology. As it is now, so it seems always to have been. During the development of the first American assessment center, Henry Murray (1938) suppressed discussion of theoretical assumptions because he feared that if the staff at the Harvard Psychological Clinic began debating conceptual issues, civil war would break out. Consequently, the assessment procedures used at Harvard in the 1930s primarily reflected the charismatic Murray's idiosyncratic interests. So the trend was set at the outset: assessment center procedures are usually chosen and implemented based on the conceptual biases of the organizer.

This chapter surveys the options available at the various choice points in the assessment process; each section concerns a particular choice. The first section reviews theories of the origins of individual differences in social behavior; these theories tell where the important differences among people lie and are important guides to assessment. The second section reviews theories regarding the meaning of responses to assessment devices; this tells how to interpret scores on assessment procedures and evaluate the validity of inferences based on test scores. The third section reviews strategies for choosing assessment procedures. The final section reviews theories about how assessment data should be organized.

Theories of Individual Differences

This section reviews seven perspectives on the origins of individual differences. Each perspective has distinctly different implications for assessment.

Social Learning Theory

Social learning theory as developed by Bandura (1977) and others is a behaviorist model; behaviorism is arguably the prototypical American perspective in psychology and certainly a dominant viewpoint in industrial and organizational psychology. The seeming objectivity and simplicity of behaviorist models (among them, the One Minute Manager, situational leadership, and behavioral modeling) make them highly attractive. They argue that what people do at any time depends on the rewards and punishments operating in a particular environment. According to social learning theory, people differ from one another primarily in terms of what it is they have been rewarded for doing. Because there is no accepted taxonomy of reward systems, the model provides no systematic account of individual differences, which means that the assessment implications are not clear.

Despite the popularity of behaviorist models, they have four shortcomings as a conceptual basis for assessments. First, they are intended as *main effect* models; they focus on group effects, and individual differences are considered largely as error variance. Second, behaviorism largely ignores evolutionary theory; evolutionary theory allows informed speculation about the key dimensions of human ability and interpersonal behavior, a necessary starting point for any theory of human performance. Third, behaviorist theories concern how behaviors are acquired or maintained, not what they mean, despite the fact that social behavior carries meaning. People normally care more about how something is done than about what is done. Finally, behaviorism assumes that any behavior can be rewarded, which means that people will differ from one another in an infinite number of ways; this implies that assessment is a hopelessly complex task. In reality people reward only a limited number of behaviors in everyday life; thus social behavior is inevitably channeled into a limited number of dimensions.

Trait Theory

Although many people think of personality in terms of trait theory, trait theory is about variables, not people. Trait theory can be summarized in terms of two points. First, it states that behavior is controlled in significant ways by traits: hypothetical neurological, genetic, or biochemical structures (McCrae & Costa, 1996). Second, it offers alternative lists of trait terms as taxonomies of personality variables; discussions in trait theory largely concern the merits of the trait lists proposed by different theorists rather than the properties of people.

Trait theory begins with Allport's (Allport & Odbert, 1936) trait list; it extends through Cattell's research with the 16 PF, and culminates with the modern Five Factor Model (Goldberg, 1993) and its variants (Hough, 1989; Tellegen, 1993); the variants propose that there are more than five but usually fewer than twelve basic traits (Block, 1995). The original trait lists contained adjectives that observers used to describe others; today the trait lists are also used for *self-description*. Allport, whose prissiness was well known, chose only nonevaluative terms for his original list, a custom maintained until recently. Tellegen (1993) challenged this practice by arguing that trait attribution is inherently evaluative and that Allport's antiseptic list necessarily excluded valid information about others. We suspect that negative evaluative terms actually are more informative than positive terms—for example, "liar" versus "person who seems to tell the truth."

According to trait theory, people differ from one another primarily in terms of their profiles on the list of traits a theorist has identified. The goal of assessment from this perspective is to create a trait profile for each person assessed, which can be useful if the trait list has been properly validated by establishing correlations between trait scores and nontest performance.

Trait theory is a useful taxonomic exercise, but as a theory of performance, it has three drawbacks. First, it centers around variables, not people; it tells which behaviors covary but not why they do so. Second, trait theorists largely ignore evolutionary theory, and as a result the traits themselves have an existential quality; they just are, without any explicit reason or justification for their existence. This in turn means that some of the traits—for example, Costa and McCrae's Openness, Tellegen's Absorption—have few real-world performance implications. And third, trait theory is a version of *internalist metaphysics;* it explains individual differences in social behavior in terms of hypothesized neuropsychic or other biological mechanisms whose existence has never been and may never be verified.

Psychoanalysis

As originally proposed by Freud, psychoanalysis makes three interesting claims. The first is that by virtue of our evolutionary history, we all need—in a deep, unconscious way—love (sex, affiliation, closeness) and opportunities to bend others to our will (dominance, power, destruction). Second, the most important event in each person's development concerns learning to deal with authority—specifically, learning to deal with parental rules for suppressing, repressing, or expressing sexual and aggressive impulses. This process of accommodating to authority results in three kinds of adults: those who never repressed their instincts (criminals), those who successfully repressed them and now suffer the consequences (neurotics, who are by far the largest group), and those who have been psychoanalyzed. The third major claim of psychoanalysis is that people differ from one another primarily in terms of how they deal with the guilt that arises from the impossible task of repressing their sexual and aggressive impulses. Thus individual differences concern how people defend themselves against feelings of guilt and anxiety. Some attribute their impulses to others, some control anxiety by ritualistic behavior, and so forth. The goals of assessment from this perspective are to identify how guilty and anxious people feel, and how they protect themselves from these feelings of guilt and anxiety.

Although we are generally sympathetic with the implications of psychoanalysis, the theory itself has two major shortcomings. First, there is obviously more to human motivation than sex and aggression; for example, Baumeister and Leary (1995) make an excellent case for the importance of a broad human need for social attention. Second, psychoanalysis is a theory of incompetence and by definition can tell little about the factors associated with high-level performance. Human progress and accomplishment depend on effectiveness, not just the absence of incompetence.

Interpersonal Theory

Interpersonal theory as developed by Adler (1964) and Horney (1950) makes two valuable contributions. First, in a field dominated by men but where over half the participants are women, Adler and Horney contribute a sensible feminist emphasis to theories of social performance. Second, they shift the theoretical focus from private events inside people's heads to the public behaviors that disrupt social interaction. Their basic argument can be summarized quickly. During childhood, everyone has experiences that cause deep-seated feelings of inadequacy or inferiority about something—for example, grammar, hair color, eyesight, weight, coordination, academic ability—and these feelings persist into adulthood. People believe others will criticize them if they notice these inadequacies; to avoid criticism, people develop ways of compensating for their perceived shortcomings. These efforts to compensate for their insecurities drain energy from more productive activities. The bottom line here is that people differ from one another primarily in terms of what they feel insecure about and how they deal with their insecurities.

Horney developed an interesting taxonomy of strategies for dealing with insecurity. She argued that these strategies fall into three categories: subordinating oneself to the wishes of others, avoiding becoming involved with others, and competing with and dominating others. The *Diagnostic and Statistical Manual of Mental Disorders,* fourth edition (*DSM-IV*), Axis 2 personality disorders (American Psychiatric Association, 1994) can be organized in terms of these three strategies (Hogan & Hogan, 1996). The goals of assessment from this perspective are to identify the methods that people use to compensate for their feelings of inadequacy.

Although we generally agree with Adler and Horney's orientation, it has two major shortcomings. First, like psychoanalysis, it is a theory of incompetence, not effectiveness. Second, like the social learning theorists, Adler and Horney believe social circumstances determine individuals' lives, and they ignore biology and evolutionary theory.

Jungian and Humanistic Psychology

Carl Jung argued that people have an innate biological tendency toward growth and wholeness and become whole by committing themselves to a grand and powerful myth. Religion used to provide such a myth, but no longer; thus, for most people, the process of personal growth is blocked, and the solution is to develop a compelling personal vision and system of beliefs. Maslow (1943) adopted two of Jung's major themes: people have an innate tendency toward growth and development (self-actualization), and for most people this process is blocked by events in the environment. Jung defined growth in terms of increasing levels of self-understanding; Maslow defined growth in terms of the ability to live in accordance with one's personal and freely chosen values, which becomes possible after one satisfies more mundane needs for food, acceptance, security, and achievement. The bottom line here is that people differ from one another primarily in terms of their levels of self-actualization. Few people in the normal population become self-actualized; Maslow's list primarily contained cultural and artistic celebrities: Einstein, Eleanor Roosevelt, and himself. Today's list might include Mother Teresa and Timothy Leary. The goals of assessment therefore are to establish where each person is in his or her quest for self-actualization.

The self-actualization perspective of Jung and Maslow has the merit of being a theory about competence. Moreover, Maslow's ideas about self-actualization enjoy widespread acceptance in modern theories of management and organizational behavior (Hackman & Oldham, 1980). Nonetheless there are three problems with the theory. First, the concept of self-actualization is unintelligible from the perspective of evolutionary theory; there is no discernible adaptive advantage to being self-actualized. Moreover, some of Maslow's self-actualized heroes were loners with few friends or family. Second, efforts to measure individual differences in self-actualization have been largely unsuccessful, which suggests the concept is ineffable (Wahba & Bridwell, 1983). And third, the pursuit of self-actualization is a self-centered, even narcissistic, activity. Society would collapse if everyone followed Maslow's model.

Personal Construct Theory

George Kelly's *Psychology of Personal Constructs* (1955) brought the "cognitive revolution" to personality psychology. Kelly argued that people develop theories about what others expect of them during social interaction and use these theories to guide and interpret their dealings with others. Competent people have relatively valid theories that they are willing to test and revise; incompetent people have wrong-headed theories that they will not evaluate or modify. For example, good managers periodically ask their subordinates to evaluate their management practices and then act on this information. Conversely, Theodore Kaczynsky, the Harvard-trained mathematician accused of being the Unabomber, lived in an isolated cabin in Montana and spun out elaborate theories about how conspiratorial forces were ruining the environment, apparently with no desire to evaluate his ideas. In this view, people differ from one another primarily in terms of the validity of their theories and their willingness to verify them.

Kelly's theory concerns competence and seems sensible as far as it goes, but it suffers from two shortcomings. First, Kelly ignored evolutionary theory, which suggests that certain themes will appear more frequently in our theories than others; examples are desires for power and love. In Kelly's model, however, the content of people's theories is free to vary almost infinitely. And this leads to the second problem: the theory presents serious obstacles to assessment. How can we compare people on the basis of their theories of social interaction when each theory is, by definition, idiosyncratic and unique? Kelly's own role repertory (rep test) is cumbersome to the point of being impractical. In this rep test, a person lists a small number of significant others, then lists each of their salient characteristics. The assessor uses these materials along with Kelly's guidelines to identify the key elements of the person's interpersonal theory. We believe that people's theories of the world are also reflected in their values and interests. Thus measures of occupational goals may allow us to take advantage of Kelly's insight. In particular we regard Holland's (1985) occupational typology (RIASEC) as a major contribution to the assessment of individual worldviews, although Holland's types are rarely used to make such inferences.

Socioanalytic Theory

Our own perspective (Hogan, 1983, 1996) is a synthesis of the theories we have already set out. With Darwin, we believe that an adequate theory of social performance depends on some understanding of what people evolved to do. Along with Freud, Jung, and Maslow, we believe that behavior is significantly determined by a small number of unconscious biological drives or needs. Along with Adler and Horney, we believe that people are primarily concerned about social interaction; individuals' ability to build relations with others is a key element in the evolutionary survival kit. Along with social learning theory, we believe that experience, especially early experience, shapes behavior into characteristic channels. And finally, we agree with Kelly that what people do depends to a large degree on their theory about the person with whom they are interacting. Our viewpoint can be summarized as follows.

Evidence from many sources indicates that humans have always lived in groups, that every group has a status hierarchy, and that interaction within the group is regulated by local culture—but local cultures have some universal features (compare de Waal, 1996; Wright, 1994). This suggests that people are social animals, primarily motivated by needs for (1) status and the control of resources; (2) acceptance and positive regard; and (3) predictability, structure, and order. Social life consists of efforts to acquire more status or to avoid losing status, to acquire more respect and affection or to avoid losing respect and affection, and to gain some understanding of, and the ability to predict, social reality. In this view, people differ from one another in terms of their relative success in achieving power and status, respect and affection, and accurate understanding of their social worlds. From the perspective of socioanalytic theory, the goals of assessment are to measure factors associated with individual differences in status and power, in acceptance and respect, and in a valid understanding of social reality. Our approach relies heavily on observer ratings to avoid the metaphysical problems of trait theory; that is, we regard test scores as proxies for how a person would be described by others.

The major problem with this model is that, by relying on observers' ratings, it tends to ignore internal affective states, such as emotions, which many psychologists (Tompkins, 1962, 1963) consider to be crucial aspects of personality.

What Do Responses to Assessment Procedures Really Mean?

The meaning of responses to assessment procedures is an issue that rarely seems to come up, probably because people tend to think the answer is obvious. In fact, there are four distinct theories about these meanings, and the responsible practitioner should be clear about which model he or she is using because ideas have consequences.

Empirical Tradition

The first model of the meaning of responses to assessment procedures is associated with the so-called dust-bowl school of empirical test development. The perspective, nicely articulated by Meehl (1945) and Gough (1965), is the viewpoint behind the development of three of the most successful noncognitive assessment procedures in modern times: the Strong Interest Inventory (Strong, 1943), the Minnesota Multiphasic Personality Inventory (MMPI) (Hathaway & McKinley, 1943); and the California Psychological Inventory (CPI) (Gough, 1987).

The argument is based on a pragmatist theory of meaning in which a concept is defined by what it does or how it is used rather than by what it refers to (Wittgenstein, 1958). Thus, in this model, the meaning of a response to an assessment procedure is defined in terms of what a response predicts, and that must be determined empirically. The test author's or the assessor's theory of what a response means, in the absence of data, is irrelevant; the meaning of a response cannot be adequately determined a priori. This theory of meaning puts a heavy burden on test developers to demonstrate what their scale scores predict, which may partially explain why the view is so widely disparaged. The empirical view of meaning is largely out of favor today; although its limitations seem obvious, they are not profound, and we believe it still has much to recommend it.

Projective Tradition

The second theory of meaning, which comes from traditional depth psychology (advocated by Freud, Jung, and others), assumes that all test stimuli are ambiguous and that people's responses reflect the meanings that they assign to the ambiguous stimuli. The process of assigning meanings is unconscious or outside awareness. As a result a person's responses reveal aspects of personality of which he or she may not be aware. This viewpoint is used to interpret responses to the Rorschach, the Thematic Apperception Test (TAT) (McClelland, 1985), and sentence completion tests (Loevinger & Wessler, 1970; Miner, 1978). But in principle this theory explains responses to any open-ended assessment procedure, including leaderless group discussions and unstructured interviews.

This is an interesting viewpoint and undoubtedly true at some level. The problem is that it is hard for an observer to know whether an actor's response to open-ended materials reflects unconscious processes or conscious intentions. Moreover, projective tests present formidable problems in terms of developing standardized scoring systems, and scores from even the best scoring systems may be unreliable. Relative to the empirical theory, this model may seem extravagant and farfetched, but we believe it is no more so than the next viewpoint.

Trait Theory Tradition

Trait theory is probably the most popular item response theory in modern psychology. It depends on three assumptions (McCrae & Costa, 1996). First, it assumes that traits are real "neuropsychic structures" that exist inside people. Although these structures are still undefined, trait researchers believe that they will be discovered by neuroscientists some day. These neuropsychic structures cause or explain the regularities in overt behavior that are described with trait words. Thus extroverted people have extroverted *traits*—neuropsychic structures that cause them to be gregarious—inside them. This is the traditional reductionist view that characterizes the physical sciences: public events are explained in terms of underlying physical entities.

The second assumption of trait theory is that when people respond to items on questionnaires or questions in an interview, their responses are more or less veridical *self-reports*. People read or listen to a question, compare the question with information stored in their memory, and then respond accordingly. This assumption seems odd at best because it ignores the modern view that memory is largely constructed and that its correspondence to actual events in a person's past changes over time (Rubin, 1986; Schwarz & Sudman, 1994).

The third assumption is that, through the mechanism of self-report, people's neuropsychic structures or in-dwelling traits are projected, on a point-for-point basis, into their responses to items on questionnaires or questions in an interview. Thus a high score on a measure of extroversion signals the existence of a large or very active trait or neuropsychic structure that creates both high scores on the measure and extroverted behavior. In this model, psychological measurement is formally identical to physical measurement; scale scores correspond directly to the size or activity level of as-yet-undiscovered physical (neuropsychic) entities.

In our view, there is a vast conceptual distance between neuronal activity in the brain stem and responses to items on a test. The trait theory view of item responses is not impossible, just unlikely, and in any case is probably most relevant for measures of psychopathology (DePue, 1995). Moreover, the empirical approach seems logically more rigorous than the trait theory model. The next section describes a less metaphysical account of the same phenomena.

Socioanalytic View

In our view, people are motivated in a deep way to seek status, social acceptance, and predictability or meaning, essentially from birth. They acquire these *commodities* during social interaction. The motives are universal; the key differences among people concern the methods they use to pursue status, popularity, and understanding and how successful they are in their efforts.

Social and occupational life takes place primarily during social interaction, and every interaction has two major components: a pretext or agenda for the interaction, and roles for the participants to play. In many interactions the roles are well defined: examples are the bride in a wedding ceremony and the umpire in a baseball game. In less structured interactions, people bring their roles with them; these roles are their identities—their goals, aspirations, values, fears, idealized self-concepts, and images of themselves that they hope are or are not true. Identities guide behavior during interaction; there are things a person will or will not do or say because it is or is not him or her—that is, such actions make the person feel uncomfortable—or because it will give others the right or wrong impression of him or her. This process, called impression management, is not necessarily or even regularly conscious.

In our view the processes involved in responding to items on a questionnaire or to questions in an interview are formally identical to those that guide social interaction more generally. People use their answers to tell another person (the anonymous person behind the questionnaire items, the interviewer) how he or she wants to be regarded—as smart, loyal, ambitious, dangerous, sexy, pathetic, or world weary. Thus responses are *self-presentations*, not self-reports, although people typically respond in a more or less sincere manner. The persons who score an assessment procedure take the participant's self-presentations, code them, and use them for their own purposes. Thus there may be major differences between what a respondent intends when answering an item and the uses to which those responses are put (Johnson, 1997). For example, the Prudence scale of the Hogan Personality Inventory (HPI) (Hogan & Hogan, 1995) is a measure of the Big Five Conscientiousness dimension; the Prudence scale contains seven subscales, three of which are called Moralistic, Mastery, and Virtuous. Although persons who endorse the items on these three subscales may be attempting to appear incorruptible and utterly reliable, such responses are interpreted as evidence that they may be deceitful and trying to outwit the test by claiming to have virtues that are unlikely.

Conceptually, this view of item responding puts to rest the notion of faking. There is no faking; there is only impression management during an interaction, followed by an interpretation of that effort by the other participants in the interaction. Job applicants respond to a test or interview question in the role of a job applicant—that is what they are. They are not asked to fake being an applicant; they respond in a way designed to tell others how they want to be regarded: self-critical, a team player, flexible, autonomous, and realistic—or maybe self-confident, willing to take charge, dutiful, sensitive, and cultured. Observers interpret applicants' responses in terms of Big Five personality categories: as signs of their emotional stability, surgency, conscientiousness, agreeableness, and intellect/openness. It is the observer's interpretative scheme—the scoring keys or coding algorithms—whose accuracy is evaluated as a basis for decisions. Some interpretative schemes are obviously more valid than others.

The claim that personality measures can be "faked" by job applicants has recently resurfaced. Researchers debating the effects of intentional distortion seem more concerned with how faking affects validity than with a conceptual analysis of the faking process. The empirical findings from this research are summarized by Hough (in press). She points out that, when instructed, people can alter their responses to personality measures in both directions of desirability (Hough, Eaton, Dunnette, Kamp, & McCloy, 1990). In our view, this is evidence for self-presentation skill. In addition, she cites research indicating that whatever distortion takes place in real applicant settings is not as great as when experimental subjects in simulations are told to "fake good" for the purpose of obtaining a job (Hough, Eaton, Dunnette, Kamp, & McCloy, 1990). Hough (in press) reviews the effects of socially desirable responding on predictive and criterion-related validity and concludes that test validity is unaffected by social desirability. Moreover, Ones, Viswesvaran, and Reiss (1996) conclude that social desirability neither predicts, suppresses, nor mediates the personality and job performance relationship. Although Hough cites an impressive amount of evidence indicating that the consequences of response distortion are benign, she recommends that employers instruct applicants not to fake, for there will be "serious consequences" for "describing oneself in an overly virtuous way" (p. 16). We wonder why such warnings are needed when faking poses no problems. More important, would such instruction distort the self-presentation that the employer actually wants to evaluate? Again, in our view, there is no faking, only relatively sincere self-presentation in responding to test or interview items.

What Procedures Should Be Used?

There seem to be five conceptually distinct ways to approach the question of what procedures should be used; these approaches are discussed in the follow sections. This topic has not been analyzed in detail, and our comments should be taken as provisional.

Behaviorist Model

In behaviorist theory, there are few stable psychological structures underlying social behavior; as a result, people's actions are controlled by the reward contingencies found in each situation, and these vary. It seems to us that behaviorist theory requires face validity, so assessment procedures should model as closely as possible the situation in which performance will take place. Pilots should be tested in high-fidelity flight simulators, firefighters should be tested in fire scene simulations, managers should be assessed using incidents of actual performance problems, and so forth. Although not everyone who chooses face-valid simulations is a behaviorist, every behaviorist should choose face-valid simulations.

There are two problems with this approach. The first concerns how much verisimilitude is enough: How faithfully must a simulator replicate a target job? There is no formal answer to this question, and assessors may never develop a rule of thumb or general principle for figuring it out. But Motowidlo, Dunnette, and Carter (1990) found that even low-fidelity simulations can be effective (although they did not reliably measure the dimensions that were supposed to be built in). The second problem is that this approach makes generalization difficult because every situation is different; if generalization is the heart of science, then this approach may be inherently unscientific.

Empirical Model

The empirical approach to choosing assessment procedures begins with no assumptions about the performance requirements of particular tasks or undertakings. Rather, the content of an assessment process will depend on a job analysis. A competent job analysis will reveal the skills and abilities required to do a job, and the procedures used in an assessment process should measure individual differences in those skills and abilities. Dunnette (1971) provides one of the best descriptions of this approach to organizing assessments. In our judgment this popular and widely respected model has one major shortcoming: how to translate the skills and abilities revealed by a job analysis into measures of those skills. There are many important human abilities for which no adequate measures exist, among them good judgment, a sense of humor, and common sense. Interestingly, if a job analysis identifies an ability for which no measures exist, that ability will somehow get eliminated from the job analysis results. This is an unacknowledged reversal of the typical process; that is, available measures can dictate job requirements rather than vice versa.

Trait Theory Model

Trait theory leads to a clear and unambiguous specification of the measures to be included in an assessment process. As noted earlier, trait theories are taxonomies, and these taxonomies are by definition inclusive. Thus trait theory recommends that an assessment process include measures of each dimension of the taxonomy developed by a particular trait theorist.

Raymond Cattell, one of the original trait theorists, made an interesting addition to this recommendation. He argued that his taxonomy of traits should be assessed in three ways (Cattell, 1957). First, it should be assessed by having the individual complete measures of the traits. Second, observers should rate the individual for those traits. And third, the individual should complete a series of performance tests designed to measure the traits. Whatever one might think of Cattell's taxonomy, his methodological recommendation still seems valid, and he combines the trait model with the empirical model. If one follows Cattell's recommendation, then validity is built in.

Psychodynamic Models

Freud, Jung, Adler, and Horney disagreed about many things. They would all agree, however, that an assessment process should focus on the unconscious methods that a person uses to protect himself or herself from wishes and impulses that if recognized would cause embarrassment, anxiety, or worse. Whatever the merits of these ideas, they have not lent themselves readily to standardized assessment. Conversely, the best measures of flawed social behavior (for example, the MMPI) owe little allegiance to the ideas of these psychodynamic writers. Moreover, the history of assessment research in the United States indicates that standard measures of psychopathology, such as the MMPI, the Rorschach, and the TAT, are largely unrelated to positive occupational outcomes. We believe we have discovered an exception to this long-standing generalization. The *DSM-IV* Axis 2 personality disorders include such tendencies as narcissism, passive aggression, and psychopathy. These tendencies can coexist with good social skills and tend to predict managerial derailment (Bentz, 1985). Using a nonclinical inventory of these tendencies (Hogan & Hogan, 1996), we have assembled a good deal of data showing that these dispositions are highly undesirable in supervisors and managers; for example, narcissistic and histrionic managers, although colorful and dynamic, are unable to build a team, and subordinates will not willingly work for them. Conversely, some of these dispositions (for example, narcissistic, histrionic, and schizotypal tendencies) seem to facilitate high-level sales performance.

Competency-based Models

H. G. Gough, the author of the CPI, chose many of the measurement procedures used at the Institute of Personality Assessment and Research (IPAR), the University of California, Berkeley-based assessment center, between 1948 and 1985. IPAR was established to identify factors mediating effectiveness and high-level achievement, and in an unpublished memo to the Educational Testing Service, Gough (1954) suggested that any group should be assessed in terms of the following five areas:

1. *Intellectual competence.* Under this heading Gough emphasized two issues: knowledge of practical, routine, day-to-day matters, of which at least some "intellectuals" seem oblivious, and latent, functional knowledge, which a person must acquire indirectly by alert and attentive social observation. This second concept resembles Sternberg's (Sternberg, Wagner, Williams, & Horvath, 1995) concept of tacit knowledge.
2. *Personal stability.* Gough meant by this concept "balance, self-understanding, capacity for self-direction, self-acceptance, and freedom from crippling and inhibiting doubts and anxieties," and he suggested that personal stability could be assessed by the composite judgment of two or three observers based, at least in part, on MMPI profiles.
3. *Social acuity.* By this Gough meant perceptiveness and accuracy at reading subtle, often nonverbal, interpersonal cues. On this topic we would make four observations. First, we believe Gough

was right concerning the importance of this construct. Second, research on this topic was brought to a halt by Cronbach's review (1955), which concluded that the concept was extremely complex and almost impossible to measure. Third, Funder (1983) demonstrated that the concept is indeed meaningful and can be studied in a relatively straightforward manner. And finally, there are no well-constructed and well-validated measures of this crucial human capacity available today.

4. *Originality.* Gough defined this concept in terms of the ability to combine elements into new patterns, detect meaningful parts within larger wholes, think outside the lines, and be open to innovation and change. Several well-developed measures of originality are available today.

5. *Maturity and responsibility.* Gough defined this concept in terms of tolerance, integrity, and self-understanding with an emphasis on "ethical and human values." He noted that this concept can be reliably assessed with combinations of scales from the CPI.

Gough's sensible memo made no impact on the research agenda of the Educational Testing Service.

Socioanalytic theory focuses on factors leading to individual differences in status, power, and the control of resources; in respect, affection, and popularity; and in an accurate understanding of the social world. Predicting individual differences in these three broad areas drives the socioanalytic assessment agenda. We believe that the five constructs Gough (1954) identified are important in the pursuit of status and social acceptance. We would add to his list two additional concepts that we believe are essential components of any assessment process:

1. *Interpersonal skill.* By interpersonal skill we mean the ability to establish and maintain relationships with a wide range of people; to diffuse interpersonal tensions and solve social dilemmas; to charm, amuse, and disarm other people young and old, strange and familiar. Interpersonal skill is important for success in virtually any endeavor (Hogan & Lock, 1995). Mead (1934), Gough (1948), and Sarbin (1954) referred to this as

"role-taking ability" and saw it as the "g" factor in social performance.

2. *Ambition.* By ambition we mean competitiveness, a desire to get ahead, persistence in the face of obstacles, a sense of purpose—even destiny—and a feeling that one's ultimate success is a forgone conclusion. Ambition is a dirty word for many psychologists: Freud thought it reflected an unresolved Oedipus complex; Adler thought it indicated unresolved insecurities; Maslow thought it reflected derailed self-actualization; it does not appear in the Five Factor Model of personality (Hogan, 1996); and Type A researchers (Friedman & Rosenman, 1974) believe ambition will make you sick. In our opinion, ambition was engineered out of the Five Factor Model when the evaluative adjectives were excluded from the trait lists developed by Norman and Goldberg. Descriptors for persons with high scores on ambition include *competitive, persistent, assertive, bold, willful, willing to challenge superiors,* and *test the limits.* Despite the antipathy of many psychologists, ambition is the engine that drives significant careers, and it is an essential part of any assessment process designed to measure factors associated with individual differences in the ability to get ahead.

How Should the Data Be Organized?

There are four answers to this question, and they relate back to the question about what responses to questionnaires mean.

Empirical Tradition

In the data-oriented empirical tradition, a person's results on each assessment procedure is expressed in terms of a percentile score, followed perhaps by a ranking or standard score on a regression equation designed to predict performance in a job or other significant endeavor. Assessees are sometimes given interpretative material explaining what high and low scores on each procedure might mean; for example, persons with high scores on scale A are described by others who know them well as able, brave, capable, daring, easygoing, and so forth. The data will be organized to predict a performance outcome, not to instruct an individual client.

Trait Theory

In the empirical tradition the assessment process will contain any procedure that might be useful in predicting performance. In the trait theoretical tradition, however, the measures to be included are essentially prescribed in advance. The assessment process will include alternate measures of the traits defined by a particular trait theorist: scale scores, observer ratings, and perhaps some performance-based tests. The results themselves will be presented in terms of a profile—either normatively or ipsatively based—across the trait categories. Most practitioners find this model unduly restrictive.

Psychodynamic Tradition

The psychodynamic model for organizing assessment results in the United States probably starts with Henry Murray and his work at the Harvard Psychological Clinic. Murray (1938) believed the goal of assessment was to develop an in-depth psychological portrait of the person assessed. His procedure was to give the assessment data to an "assessment council," which assigned each person a summary rating on a set of dimensions deemed important and then composed a portrait of the person. For the purposes of predicting a person's subsequent job performance, the summary ratings on the assessment dimensions were sufficient, and the portrait was essentially useless. For the purposes of giving a person feedback on the assessment, the portrait was important, and the summary ratings were much less so.

In the psychodynamic tradition the core elements of the psychological portrait are a person's unconscious wishes, goals, desires, and defenses. In essence the portrait should educate a person regarding his or her unconscious processes and provide suggestions on how to deal with them.

Interpersonal Tradition

This model for organizing assessment results resembles the psychodynamic version but with a different emphasis. The assessor provides a portrait of the client, stressing factors associated with getting along and getting ahead in his or her career. Using test scores and observer descriptions, the assessor talks about the person's strengths and shortcomings as others perceive them, where strengths and shortcomings are defined relative to being liked and being successful at work. The scale scores are interpreted on the basis of their correlations with observer descriptions, and the interpretations can be constantly refined with new observer data. The assessor describes a person's perceived inadequacies and whether others notice them. In addition, it is possible to talk about a person's goals and aspirations, noting also what goals do not inspire him or her, and how these goals and values line up with this person's career choice and current work environment. Finally, the person is given suggestions regarding things he or she can do more efficiently to maximize personal strengths and minimize shortcomings in the pursuit of life goals.

In the psychodynamic tradition, assessment results are used to teach people about their hidden or neglected selves. In the interpersonal tradition, assessment results are used to coach people on their performance in the game of life; but like those in the psychodynamic tradition, we believe that without the aid of assessment people will often be unaware of their goals and strategies and oblivious to how others perceive and evaluate them.

Conclusions

Some themes from our discussion seem important for anyone who does assessment.

Examine Your Assumptions

Ideas have consequences. George Kelly (1955) tells of the disastrous consequences of bad ideas for individual lives; what is true for the average person is equally true for the assessment psychologist. What is *your* theory about the important dimensions of individual differences, and do you still believe it?

One of the most influential viewpoints in organizational psychology is humanistic psychology (Argyris, 1957; Hackman & Oldham, 1980; Herzberg, 1966). Humanistic psychology assumes that people need opportunities for growth and self-expansion. One then implements procedures in organizations designed to foster such growth—with predictably negligible results because one is trying to manipulate a nonexistent motive, but this seems not to be widely understood.

Nonetheless we believe a sense of identity is a crucial organizing point for social interaction, and we find that people with low scores on measures of sense of identity underperform in their careers. Our point is that assessors should be clear about what they see as the important dimensions of human performance, be clear about why they think these dimensions are important, and be willing to revisit their own views as data become available.

Trait Theory Is Wrong

We suggested that trait theory is wrong; it is a form of internalist metaphysics with a research agenda that can never be completed and a self-report theory of item responses that is contradicted by most modern students of memory (Rubin, 1986). Beyond intellectual honesty, there are three practical reasons that assessment psychologists should be wary of trait theory. First, to the degree that they buy into trait theory, the dimensions assessed will be prescribed by the taxonomy of the theorist whose model they have adopted; they will be the prisoner of another person's delusional system. Second, most existing trait theorists developed measurement models based on adjectival descriptors from which the more potent evaluative terms have been removed. This puts constraints on the validity of the models and on the dimensions that get used. And finally, trait theorists from Guilford to Costa and McCrae have been more interested in the degree to which their factor structures replicate across samples than they are in validity, defined in terms of predicting nontest outcomes. Although trait theories are not inherently hostile to the concept of validity, they have historically ignored it or minimized its importance. Academics can ignore validity at their discretion; practitioners can ignore validity at their peril.

Pay Attention to Validity

In our experience practitioners often act as if their job is done when they have conducted a job analysis and identified or developed some test procedures based on that information. They tend not to focus on the next step, which is determining the degree to which the test procedures actually predict performance.

On the issue of validity, we make four points. First, the standard methods of job analysis are designed to serve the purposes of content validity. Once those purposes have been served the research task is assumed to be over. This is a common disciplinary assumption that needs to be reevaluated because it serves to advance the interests of neither science nor the client.

Second, although the concept of validity is part of every well-trained psychologist's tool kit, our sense is that the concept is still poorly understood. It is normally defined in practice in terms of correlations between one measure and a few other measures and inventories, often chosen on the basis of sheer convenience. We define validity in terms of the number of empirically supported inferences about real-world performance that we can make about a particular score. The more inferences made, the more useful the measure is; the fewer the inferences made, the less useful the measure is. By far the most useful inferences are those concerning how others will describe people with high and low scores on a particular measure. Thus we consider correlations between scale scores and observer descriptions to be essential validity information.

Third, in addition to the question about the validity of an assessment procedure is one about the validity of the assessor's interpretation. To the degree that an assessor's interpretations are based on his or her experience, validity may be in trouble. To the degree that an assessor's interpretations are based on his or her knowledge of correlations between scale scores and observer descriptions, validity is on firm ground.

Finally, and in the strongest possible contrast with trait theory, we do not believe that scores on noncognitive measures tell us about qualities or features inside people. We believe that scores on noncognitive measures tell us how that person is likely to be described by others; again, we think this information is crucial.

Feedback Is a Moral Obligation

When assessment is used for hiring purposes, it may not be possible to give the applicants feedback. But people complete assessment procedures for a variety of reasons, including taking part in validation research. Although it may be inconvenient to give these people feedback, we believe assessors have an obligation to do so.

The feedback should also be valid. In our experience the validity of feedback is often compromised in two ways. The first is exemplified by a conversation we had recently with a successful psychologist who specializes in management development. In her view the crucial part of the feedback process consists of weaving together the various pieces of assessment information into a coherent story that she can tell her client. A coherent story is nice, but it is more important that it be true. In our view she had confused entertainment with education.

A desire to please and entertain the client is the source of the second way in which the validity of an interpretation can be compromised. People's performance can improve only if they are given feedback regarding what they are doing wrong—and doing right. In our experience, many assessors are reluctant to give their clients much negative feedback, a tendency that is understandable but not very helpful.

Everyone has a view of human nature. Practitioners need to spell out their views, ask what the implications are for human performance, and decide whether their views are consistent with the goals of their assessment practice. If not, it may be time for some conceptual renewal.

References

Adler, A. (1964). On the origin of the striving for superiority and of social interest. In H. L. Ansbacher & R. R. Ansbacher (Eds.), *Alfred Adler: Superiority and social interest* (pp. 29–40). New York: Viking Press. (Original work published 1933)

Allport, G. W., & Odbert, H. D. (1936). Trait names: A psycho-lexical study. *Psychological Monographs, 47*(1, Whole No. 211).

American Psychiatric Association. (1994). *Diagnostic and statistical manual of mental disorders* (4th ed.). Washington, DC: Author.

Argyris, C. (1957). *Personality and organizations.* New York: HarperCollins.

Bandura, A. (1977). *Social learning theory.* Upper Saddle River, NJ: Prentice Hall.

Baumeister, R. F., & Leary, M. R. (1995). The need to belong: Desire for interpersonal attachments as a fundamental human motivation. *Psychological Bulletin, 117,* 497–529.

Bentz, V. J. (1985, August). *A view from the top: A thirty year perspective of research devoted to discovery, description, and prediction of executive behavior.* Paper presented at the 93rd annual convention of the American Psychological Association, Los Angeles.

Block, J. (1995). A contrarian view of the five-factor approach to personality description. *Psychological Bulletin, 117,* 187–215.

Cattell, R. B. (1957). *Personality and motivational structure and measurement.* Chicago: World Book.

Cronbach, L. J. (1955). Processes affecting scores on "understanding of others" and "assumed similarity." *Psychological Bulletin, 52,* 177–193.

de Waal, F. (1996). *Good natured: The origins of right and wrong in humans and other animals.* Cambridge, MA: Harvard University Press.

DePue, R. A. (1995). Neurobiological factors in personality and depression. *European Journal of Personality, 9,* 413–439.

Dunnette, M. D. (1971). Assessment of managerial talent. In P. McReynolds (Ed.), *Advances in psychological assessment* (Vol. 2, pp. 79–108). Palo Alto, CA: Science and Behavior Books.

Friedman, M., & Rosenman, R. H. (1974). *Type A behavior and your heart.* New York: Knopf.

Funder, D. C. (1983). The "consistency" controversy and the accuracy of personality judgments. *Journal of Personality, 51,* 346–359.

Goldberg, L. R. (1993). The structure of phenotypic personality traits. *American Psychologist, 48,* 26–34.

Gough, H. G. (1948). A sociological theory of psychopathy. *American Journal of Sociology, 53,* 359–366.

Gough, H. G. (1954). *Some general areas of assessment which should be considered in the study of any group.* Consultant's memorandum submitted to the Educational Testing Service, Princeton, NJ.

Gough, H. G. (1965). Conceptual analysis of psychological test scores and other diagnostic variables. *Journal of Abnormal Psychology, 70,* 294–302.

Gough, H. G. (1987). *Manual: The California Psychological Inventory.* Palo Alto, CA: Consulting Psychologists Press.

Hackman, J. R., & Oldham, G. R. (1980). *Work redesign.* Reading, MA: Addison-Wesley.

Hathaway, S. R., & McKinley, J. C. (1943). *Manual for the Minnesota Multiphasic Personality Inventory.* New York: Psychological Corporation.

Herzberg, F. (1966). *Working and the nature of man.* New York: Crowell.

Hogan, J., & Lock, J. (1995, May). *A taxonomy of interpersonal skills for business interactions.* Paper presented at the tenth annual conference of the Society for Industrial and Organizational Psychology, Orlando, FL.

Hogan, R. (1983). A socioanalytic theory of personality. In M. M. Page & R. Dienstbier (Eds.), *1982 Nebraska Symposium on Motivation* (pp. 55–89). Lincoln: University of Nebraska Press.

Hogan, R. (1996). A socioanalytic perspective on the five-factor model. In J. S. Wiggins (Ed.), *The five-factor model of personality* (pp. 163–179). New York: Guilford Press.

Hogan, R., & Hogan, J. (1995). *Hogan Personality Inventory manual* (2nd ed.). Tulsa, OK: Hogan Assessment Systems.

Hogan, R., & Hogan, J. (1996). *Hogan Development Survey manual.* Tulsa, OK: Hogan Assessment Systems.

Holland, J. L. (1985). *Making vocational choices: A theory of careers.* Upper Saddle River, NJ: Prentice Hall.

Horney, K. (1950). *Neurosis and human growth.* New York: Norton.

Hough, L. M. (1989). Development of personality measures to supplement selection decisions. In B. J. Fallon, H. P. Pfister, & J. Brebner (Eds.), *Advances in industrial organizational psychology* (pp. 365–375). Amsterdam: Elsevier Science.

Hough, L. M. (in press). The millennium for personality psychology: New horizons or good old daze. *Applied Psychology: An International Review.*

Hough, L. M., Eaton, N. L., Dunnette, M. D., Kamp, J. D., & McCloy, R. A. (1990). Criterion-related validities of personality constructs and the effect of response distortion on those validities [Monograph]. *Journal of Applied Psychology, 75,* 581–595.

Johnson, J. A. (1997). Seven social performance scales on the California Psychological Inventory. *Human Performance, 10,* 1–31.

Kelly, G. A. (1955). *The psychology of personal constructs.* New York: Anchor Books.

Loevinger, J., & Wessler, R. (1970). *Measuring ego development I: Construction and use of a sentence completion test.* San Francisco: Jossey-Bass.

Maslow, A. H. (1943). A theory of human motivation. *Psychological Review, 50,* 370–396.

McClelland, D. C. (1985). *Human motivation.* Glenview, IL: Scott, Foresman.

McCrae, R. R., & Costa, P. T., Jr. (1996). Toward a new generation of personality theories: Theoretical contexts for the five factor model. In J. S. Wiggins (Ed.), *The five-factor model of personality* (pp. 51–87). New York: Guilford Press.

Mead, G. H. (1934). *Mind, self, and society.* Chicago: University of Chicago Press.

Meehl, P. H. (1945). The "dynamics" of structured personality tests. *Journal of Clinical Psychology, 1,* 296–303.

Miner, J. B. (1978). Twenty years of research on role motivation theory of managerial effectiveness. *Personnel Psychology, 31,* 739–760.

Mischel, W. (1968). *Personality and assessment.* New York: Wiley.

Motowidlo, S. J., Dunnette, M. D., & Carter, G. W. (1990). An alternative selection procedure: The low-fidelity simulation. *Journal of Applied Psychology, 75,* 640–647.

Murray, H. A. (1938). *Explorations in personality.* New York: Oxford University Press.

Ones, D. S., Viswesvaran, C., & Reiss, A. D. (1996). Role of social desirability in personality testing for personnel selection: The red herring. *Journal of Applied Psychology, 81,* 660–679.

Rubin, D. C. (Ed.). (1986). *Autobiographical memory.* Cambridge, England: Cambridge University Press.

Sarbin, T. R. (1954). Role theory. In G. Lindzey (Ed.), *Handbook of social psychology* (pp. 223–258). Reading, MA: Addison-Wesley.

Schwarz, N., & Sudman, S. (Eds.). (1994). *Autobiographical memory and the validity of retrospective reports.* New York: Springer.

Sternberg, R. J., Wagner, R. K., Williams, W. M., & Horvath, J. A. (1995). Testing common sense. *American Psychologist, 50,* 912–927.

Strong, E. K. (1943). *Vocational interests of men and women.* Stanford, CA: Stanford University Press.

Tellegen, A. (1993). Folk concepts and psychological concepts of personality and personality disorder. *Psychological Inquiry, 4,* 122–130.

Tompkins, S. S. (1962). *Affect, imagery, and consciousness* (Vol. 1). New York: Springer.

Tompkins, S. S. (1963). *Affect, imagery, and consciousness* (Vol. 2). New York: Springer.

Wahba, M. A., & Bridwell, L. G. (1983). Maslow reconsidered: A review of research on the need hierarchy theory. In R. M. Steers & L. W. Porter (Eds.), *Motivation and work behavior* (pp. 51–58). New York: McGraw-Hill.

Wittgenstein, L. (1958). *Philosophical investigations.* Oxford, England: Blackwell.

Wright, R. (1994). *The moral animal.* New York: Pantheon.

CHAPTER 3

Individual Assessment
The Research Base
Ann Marie Ryan
Paul R. Sackett

About a decade ago we found ourselves somewhat puzzled by the fact that although we knew of many psychologists who derived the bread and butter of their consulting work from individual assessment, there was very little research or even description of the practice in the literature. Thus we embarked on a series of studies to inform the field more fully about the scope of the practice. In this chapter we review our own research findings and summarize the existing research literature on the individual assessment process and its effectiveness, and we suggest directions for research and practice that will enable individual assessment to be a more effective tool in the work environment. The research on this topic falls into two broad categories: descriptive, which presents the commonalities and sources of variance in assessment practice, and evaluative, which addresses issues of the reliability and validity of both components of the assessment process and the assessor's overall evaluation.

Empirical research dealing directly with the individual psychological assessment process in personnel decision making is relatively limited. However, the research relevant to individual psychological assessments is voluminous, encompassing such topics as specific assessment tools (for example, cognitive ability tests and interviews), specific aspects of the assessment process (data integration, decision making, and feedback), and selection and development generally. We focus primarily on studies directly related to individual assessment for employment decision-making purposes, first presenting descriptive research, followed by evaluative research. (Readers are referred to the primary journal articles for in-depth presentation of research results; we present only summaries here.) We have noted elsewhere that individual assessment may be used for many purposes (Ryan & Sackett, 1987, 1992); we restrict our focus here to selection and promotion contexts, the most common purpose. We end with a presentation of what we see as practice themes and suggestions for future directions.

Descriptive Research on Assessment Practices

In 1986, we surveyed members of the Society for Industrial and Organizational Psychology (SIOP) to gain a better understanding of what the practice of individual assessment entailed (Ryan & Sackett, 1987). Our own working acquaintances with various assessment practitioners suggested wide variability in approaches to practice, and the survey provided a chance to validate that perception. Responses from 163 SIOP members who conducted individual assessment and also from 153 individuals with assessment-related interests who were not themselves involved in the practice provided us with some data regarding the scope of the practice and how individual assessment practice was perceived by those in the field of industrial and organizational psychology.

A number of respondents commented that although our survey might provide an accurate picture of how SIOP members conducted individual assessments, many of those conducting individual assessments for personnel decision-making purposes were psychologists with other affiliations, and so our survey would not truly capture the scope of the practice. In 1988, we conducted another highly similar survey to address this issue (Ryan & Sackett, 1992). The second survey, which had 158 respondents, was sent to random samples of members of two other American Psychological Association (APA) divisions, Division 12 (Clinical Psychology) and Division 13 (Consulting Psychology), as well as to a list of names of some non-SIOP members obtained from respondents to the first survey and of some individuals and firms listed in the Yellow Pages for major U.S. cities and advertising themselves as assessors or otherwise indicating that they were psychologists involved in personnel decision-making services. Rather than review the results of these surveys separately, we briefly review the integrated findings (see Ryan & Sackett, 1987, 1992, for more detailed descriptions).

It is important to note that although survey respondents were engaged in conducting individual assessments, most spent less than half their time conducting assessments, with over 40 percent spending less than 10 percent of their time engaged in individual assessments. Thus individual assessment is a component of the practice of many individuals rather than the primary focus.

Assessment Content and Methods

The most common type of assessment conducted was for selection purposes, and this has also been the focus of virtually all of the research in the individual assessment area. An important concern, then, is how assessors choose methods and techniques for selection assessments and whether those coincide with what is considered "good selection practice." We found that most of those conducting individual assessments used a personal history form, ability tests, personality inventories, and an interview. Table 3.1 provides more detail on the use of different types of assessment methods and on the frequency of use of specific ability and personality measures.

Most assessors based their selection of tests on published or in-house research data, or both, and most conducted an unstructured or only moderately structured interview. Descriptive information was also gathered on specific tests used and on views on the effectiveness of various methods (see Ryan & Sackett, 1992, for a complete reporting). Although there were some differences in tests employed based on background (that is, degree and affiliation), assessors tended to use commonly known tests. Respondents indicated that the typical assessment content included interpersonal skills, judgment and analytical skills, organization and planning skills, intelligence, supervisory skills, emotional maturity, leadership, and energy/drive (Ryan & Sackett, 1987). Most assessors did not employ a formal job analysis method, with SIOP members and SIOP members with industrial and organizational (I/O) psychology degrees more likely to use standardized methods and more formal means of gathering information.

Table 3.1. Percentage of Assessors Using Assessment Methods and Specific Tests.

	I/O SIOP	Non-I/O SIOP	Non-I/O Non-SIOP	Total
Assessment methods[a]				
Personal history form	81.5	83.0	81.1	81.9
Ability tests	77.8	78.8	66.4	74.3
Personality inventories	79.6	79.0	77.9	78.9
Projective tests	32.4	45.0	48.1	41.7
Simulation exercises	41.9	26.5	17.5	28.8***
Interview	96.3	94.0	96.2	95.5[b]
Specific tests[c]				
WAIS-R	8.3	19.8	26.2	18.0**
Wonderlic	1.9	8.9	8.4	6.3
Watson Glaser-CTA	30.6	20.8	7.5	19.6***
EAS	15.7	8.9	4.7	9.8*
Wesman PCT	15.7	9.9	1.9	9.2**
GZTS	31.5	13.9	9.4	18.4***
MMPI	10.2	22.8	40.2	24.4***
MBTI	13.0	16.8	15.0	14.9
16PF	23.2	31.7	26.2	26.9
EPPS	13.9	8.9	1.9	8.2**
CPI	22.2	16.8	18.7	19.3
TAT	13.0	21.8	28.0	20.9*
Rorschach	4.6	14.9	23.4	14.2***
Sentence completion	4.6	5.0	16.8	8.9**

[a]Percentages are of those using a particular test type (ability, personality, or projective tests).
[b]Valid chi-square test could not be conducted.
[c]WAIS-R = Wechsler Adult Intelligence Scale, Revised; CTA = Critical Thinking Appraisal; EAS = Employee Aptitude Series; PCT = Personnel Classification Test; GZTS = Guilford Zimmerman Temperament Survey; MMPI = Minnesota Multiphasic Inventory; MBTI = Myers-Briggs Type Indicator; 16PF = Sixteen Personality Factor; EPPS = Edwards Personal Preference Schedule; CPI = California Psychological Inventory; TAT = Thematic Apperception Test.
$*p < .025; **p < .01; ***p < .001$.

Source: Ryan & Sackett (1992). Used with permission.

One area where practitioners did vary tremendously was in the percentage of individuals recommended for a given decision-making purpose, with survey responses varying from 7 percent to 100 percent, with a mean of 59.7 percent. It appears that most assessors believe they approach assessment with a screen-in (they are looking for desirable characteristics) rather than a screen-out (looking for disqualifiers) approach; only 21.6 percent reported they screened out. Additionally, assessors typically combine information using a judgmental or both a judgmental and statistical approach.

Differences Between Individual Assessment and Textbook Selection

It is useful to contrast individual assessment practices with what might be considered a more typical or traditional approach to selection. There are several areas in which differences between assessment practice and "textbook" selection suggest potential lines of future research.

Use of Personality Measures

The prevalence of personality inventories in individual assessment is in striking contrast to data about the extent of use of personality measures in selection in general. Gatewood and Feild (1994) reported survey data showing that although the use of personality testing for selection is increasing, only 17 percent of companies used these measures in 1988. The heavy reliance in individual assessment on personality measures (over 75 percent) has long differed from I/O psychology's generally negative stance toward the use of such measures. The recent revival of interest in the I/O literature in personality as a predictor of job performance bridges what had been a major gap between individual assessment practice and received wisdom within I/O psychology.

It is interesting to compare findings from recent research on personality as a predictor of job performance and findings from our survey of individual assessment practices. Recent personality research has focused on the generalizability of conscientiousness (Barrick & Mount, 1991), and specifically on integrity tests (Ones, Viswesvaran, & Schmidt, 1993). Our earlier survey indicated that on average, assessors saw integrity as one of the less predictive dimensions they assessed. A wide range of possibilities exists: assessors are mistaken in their beliefs about the limited value of assessing integrity, assessors use tests that do not measure integrity per se but tap related constructs, the validity of integrity measures is not generalizable to the high-level positions for which individual assessment is commonly used, and other market mechanisms produce a candidate pool that is heavily prescreened on the integrity dimension, thus severely restricting the value of further attention to that dimension. Research aimed at reconciling these research findings with typical assessment practice would be useful.

We also note that none of the most commonly used personality inventories mentioned by survey respondents and listed in Table 3.1 was a Big Five–based instrument, since our data collection predated the widespread interest in the Big Five framework. We do not know whether Big Five–influenced instruments are being incorporated in individual assessment practice; an investigation of the usefulness of this framework in the context of individual assessment would be valuable.

One common criticism regarding the use of personality testing for employment decision-making purposes is faking on the part of the test taker. Hough and Schneider (1996) noted that the pervasiveness of distortion in applicant settings is lower than that in research settings where individuals are instructed to fake, and distortion does not appear to affect criterion-related validities of personality instruments. Hogan, Hogan, and Roberts (1996) believe that corrections for faking may reduce scale validities. We do not know the extent of this practice among assessors; however, we do know that many of the personality measures typically employed by assessors have social desirability or faking scales. The typical assessor, in clinically interpreting the data rather than using test scores directly as predictors, may make "corrections" mentally for high-impression management scores. If Hogan and colleagues are correct, mentally adjusting scores for social desirability or impression management may reduce validity. We would like to see more research on the impact of score corrections before viewing this as a closed issue.

Structured Versus Unstructured Interviews

A second difference from textbook selection practice is the use of an unstructured or only moderately structured interview. Given the substantial research support for the superior validity of the structured interview (Campion, Pursell, & Brown, 1988; Wiesner & Cronshaw, 1988), one might question why individual assessors tend not to use this format. Unstructured formats may be preferred because of the perception of greater interviewer control and greater flexibility. The capacity to make changes during the process allows an assessor to be flexible and perhaps to be more diagnostic than he or she could be with a more structured selection system. Stratton (1991) noted that through data collection, assessors may form hypotheses that can then be tested, which would otherwise (that is, in a more mechanical approach) not be considered.

Some interviewers may achieve high validities with unstructured formats, as research suggests the possibility of individual differences in interviewer validity with such formats (Dreher, Ash, & Hancock, 1988; Dougherty, Ebert, & Callender, 1986). Further, Dipboye (1992) noted that the social competence of the interviewer (including both personality traits and social intelligence) is likely to affect the conduct of the interview. Assessors are likely to make choices during the assessment process influenced by their personal characteristics (for example, flexibility versus rigidity). Situational factors such as time pressure, selection ratios, and affirmative action pressures are also likely to affect the assessor, just as they would any other interviewer (see Dipboye, 1992, for a review).

Thus the issue of interview structure is another area worthy of investigation. An immediate reaction may be that assessors are erroneously ignoring persuasive literature on the value of the structured interview; it should be noted, however, that the research on interview structure has focused on the situation in which large numbers of candidates are being screened for a single position. In contrast, individual assessment is often used to render an opinion about a single job candidate or about two or three finalists for a position. Also, assessments are often performed for unique or high-level jobs (such as chief executive officer) where assessees have varied backgrounds that perhaps necessitate greater flexibility in questioning to allow an adequate evaluation of candidate capability. Arguments can be made for the value of flexibility on the part of a skilled assessor in conducting an in-depth evaluation of a candidate.

Data Integration

That relatively few individual assessors use statistical approaches to data integration seems at odds with the literature on data combination. Dawes, Faust, and Meehl (1989) found that nearly one hundred studies have replicated the superiority of actuarial or statistical methods of data combination over judgmental or clinical methods in terms of predictive ability. Stratton (1991) noted there are many practical reasons why assessors choose not to use statistical methods: small sample sizes, the required speed of decision making, facing one-of-a-kind personnel decisions, and the need for understanding (such as for career or personal development) rather than just accurate prediction.

Stratton (1991) used a lens model approach to examine the manner of data combination of seven individual assessors who used test and interview data to rate candidates on a series of dimensions and to make an overall recommendation for hire. She found that these assessors' models differed in the predictors they used and contained substantially fewer predictors than were available for the assessors to use. Regressing assessor overall ratings on various predictors (tests and assessor ratings, for example) resulted in coefficients in the .50 to .60 range. She noted that these moderate relations may be attributable to inconsistent use of data by the assessors, but also to the fact that assessors may use variables (such as clinical judgments on certain areas) that are not explicitly portions of the model (that is, are not test scores or rated dimensions).

Although there is little research on data integration and judgment that directly examines individual assessors, there is much relevant psychological research on decision making that can help us understand how individual assessors combine information in a nonstatistical manner. For example, Shanteau and Stewart (1992), in a review of research on expert decision making, noted that experts use only a small number of factors in making judgments and that they are subject to the same biases from using heuristics as novices.

Some may suggest that individual assessors use judgmental approaches because they tend to employ configural policies in integrating assessment data. However, Shanteau (1992) noted that decision-making research indicates that judgments of experts in a variety of domains can be described by linear models. Schneider

(1996) noted that "people are whole people," but we conceptualize them in terms of constructs that we view one dimension at a time in relation to a criterion. Individual assessors discuss profiles of attributes and *profess* to use configural ways of thinking about job-related skills and traits. Although individual assessors may have the right view on how to think about the evaluation of people (as whole people), there are scant data to support how people are viewed as wholes in the typical individual assessment process.

Assessment Reports and Feedback to Candidates

Some descriptive data also exist on the typical feedback process conducted by individual assessors. We found that feedback to clients typically consisted of a narrative description, a stated recommendation, a list of the individual's strengths and developmental needs, developmental suggestions, and a follow-up telephone or face-to-face discussion (Ryan & Sackett, 1987, 1992). Most of those in the second survey responded that their reports were used by clients as an equally weighted component in decision making; few noted that reports indicated if and when they should be destroyed. Most assessors give feedback to those assessed. Such feedback paralleled that given to the client organization, with a number choosing not to disclose the specific recommendation to the organization. Interestingly, we found that 42.1 percent allowed assessees to read the narrative report (Ryan & Sackett, 1992). Those surveyed felt that negative reactions to being assessed were rare.

A review of sample individual assessment feedback reports by a variety of organizations (Ryan, 1988) led us to some general observations about the client feedback given by many assessors. First, the relationship of the report content to the job analysis is often unclear. Stating in a narrative report that a candidate "harbors underlying uneasiness," "is ethically and morally sound," or "reacted defensively to our questions" is not acceptable unless the report reader has a clear understanding of how the statements connect to ability to do the job. Some firms do organize their reports around knowledge, skills, and abilities (KSAs) identified through job and organizational analyses, but it appears many others assume that the reader is correctly inferring the job relatedness of the narrative.

Second, reports typically do not say what areas of importance were not assessed. Although individual assessors often state that the evaluation is only one component of the organization's decision making, the reports generated provide no indication of what the other components could or should be. For example, many assessors focus on interpersonal and motivational requirements of the job and assume the organization will evaluate job knowledge and experience. It should be clear that the recommendation made by an assessor is not based on the total set of job requirements. We found that few assessors think their clients use their reports as a primary basis for making a personnel decision (7.4 percent); instead they think that clients use these reports only with other information (Ryan & Sackett, 1992). Holliman (1985) also found that 64 percent of the ministry boards using individual assessment she surveyed reported using reports as one piece of datum in their decision process about clergy.

Third, reports often seem to include information that might be better assessed or at least easily gathered by the client—for example, the individual's employment history. Although assessors may be quite correct in seeing work history as one of the most predictive aspects of the assessment process (Ryan & Sackett, 1987), we can question whether an external psychologist is better suited to evaluate that history than those in the organization.

Fourth, the developmental suggestions in reports often lack specificity, so much so that it is doubtful change could be implemented. For example, pointing out that a candidate "would benefit from developing some additional insights into some of the important underlying factors which are a part of her" is hardly a concrete suggestion.

Fifth, the labeling of reports regarding confidentiality, use of information, and disposal is often insufficient. Managers have told us about reading reports left in the personnel files of others long after they have outlived their usefulness. Most of those in our second survey did not have such labeling on their reports. Although an assessor cannot control a client's behavior, providing thorough statements on written reports regarding use seems a necessary step.

Finally, reports are often generic and not individual. One should be able to tell more about the differences between two assessees after reading two reports than about the style of the assessor.

We know very little about the practice of giving feedback to assessees in the individual assessment context. Considerable research in the performance appraisal arena has supported Ilgen, Fisher, and Taylor's proposition (1979) that an individual's willingness to accept feedback is influenced by the perceived credibility of the source of feedback and the favorableness of the feedback (Halperin, Snyder, Shenkel, & Houston, 1976; Stone, Gueutel, & McIntosh, 1984; Stone & Stone, 1984, 1985). An examination of the credibility of individual assessors in the eyes of candidates might be informative.

For example, Davey (1982) stated that the most common reaction of a manager about to undergo an assessment is one of apprehension. Despite recent attention to applicant reactions to selection procedures (Kluger & Rothstein, 1993; Macan, Avedon, Paese, & Smith, 1994; Smither, Reilly, Millsap, Pearlman, & Stoffey, 1993), we could locate only one unpublished study on reactions to individual assessment. Ryan and Laser (1989) examined pre- and postassessment (prefeedback) data from 161 job candidates (58 percent private sector, 42 percent public safety) and found generally positive reactions, with most reporting an understanding of the process and finding nothing objectionable about it. Public safety position candidates were more likely to know someone who had been through an assessment, expect the assessment as part of the selection or promotion process, and be aware of why the assessment was part of the process. The recommendations of the psychologist were unrelated to self-evaluations or perceptions of candidates. Other research on reactions to individual assessment, employing paradigms such as organizational justice (Gilliland, 1993), might be beneficial.

In sum, this descriptive research provides a picture of typical assessment practice. The second area individual assessment research has focused on is the question, Does it work? One caveat to keep in mind in reviewing the evaluation research is that because of the wide variability in practice, any single evaluative study may be viewing an assessment process that is not representative of any one assessor's practice.

Evaluative Research on Assessment Practices

Our survey work found that most individual assessment practitioners, regardless of graduate training or professional affiliation, did not regularly attempt to validate their assessment process empirically. Only 41.4 percent did so always or often. Additionally, many (32.3 percent) did not always or often attempt to follow up with client organizations to monitor the performance of the individual assessed. These findings suggest that most assessors do not follow a criterion-related validity strategy. We might then infer that these assessors use other forms of validity evidence to support their practices. However, there is little in the literature to provide guidance to the individual assessor in pursuing other lines of evidence. We provide an overview of the literature on the reliability and validity of individual assessments and highlight why evaluation practices may be so lax.

Validation of Individual Assessment

Figure 3.1 highlights some of the complexities of validating the individual assessment process. This model identifies a variety of issues of interest. First, it indicates that criterion-related validity research can be conducted on at least the three linkages shown in the model: (1) Are the methods used (for example, test scores) directly predictive of the criterion of interest? (2) Are dimensional judgments predictive of the criterion? and (3) Is the overall recommendation predictive of the criterion? Second, it suggests questions about how information is integrated to form dimensional judgments and overall recommendations, and about the incremental contribution added by the judgment process. The SIOP Principles (Society for Industrial and Organizational Psychology, 1987) state that "decision makers who interpret and act upon predictor data interject something of themselves into the interpretative or decision making process. The judgments or decisions thus become at least an additional predictor, or, at the most, the only predictor. For example, if the decision strategy is to combine test and non-test data . . . into a subjective judgment, the actual predictor is the judgment reached by the person who weights and summarizes all the information. It is this decision that should be validated in addition to the information which was available to the decision maker" (p. 12). Thus there is a need for evidence that the individual components of the process are appropriate and that the psychologist's integration of the information represents a valid inference.

Figure 3.1. Model of Individual Assessment Validation Process.

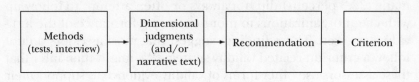

We envision four potential scenarios in which criterion-related validity evidence for individual assessment could be obtained. They represent the cells of a two-by-two table:

1. *Validation of a single assessor's inferences for a single job or job family.* Such empirical validation is feasible in only two situations: the relatively uncommon situation in which individual assessment is done for a job with a large number of incumbents and the instance in which a single assessor has a long-term relationship with an organization and a large number of assessments can be aggregated over time. For example, an assessor evaluates police officer candidates for promotion for an agency over a period of years.
2. *Validation of a single assessor's inferences aggregated across jobs and organizations.* A meaningful criterion across the job or the organization is a major obstacle.
3. *Validation aggregated across assessors for a single job or job family in a single organization.* Here the focus shifts from validating an assessor to validating a process common to a group of assessors (say, a consulting firm that trains all assessors in a particular approach to assessment). This approach is dependent on comparability of assessors; evidence to that effect, such as inter-assessor agreement when evaluating the same candidate, is called for.
4. Validation aggregated across assessors and across jobs and organizations.

As one moves from Scenario One to Scenario Four, the sample size component of technical feasibility is eliminated as a problem.

However, other significant problems remain, the most critical of which is criterion contamination. If organizational level is used as a criterion, a positive correlation can be viewed simply as evidence that the psychologist's recommendations are being followed. If performance in the target job is used as a criterion, a correlation between a go/no-go recommendation by a psychologist and a criterion can be computed only if some no-go candidates are selected or promoted despite the negative recommendation of the psychologist. It seems likely that promoted no-go and nonpromoted no-go candidates may differ in any number of important ways, making the interpretation of a validity coefficient difficult.

As a result of factors such as these, we would expect it to be the exception rather than the rule for a psychologist practicing individual assessment to be able to produce criterion-related validity evidence for his or her assessment practices. We review here the relatively limited number of validation studies that have been published and also describe two more recent unpublished studies.

Hilton, Bolin, Parker, Taylor, and Walker (1955) conducted a study of the validity of assessments made by psychologists in the Personnel Audit Program of the Personnel Research Institute. Assessments were made for a variety of positions (sales, engineering, accounting, supervisory) in eighteen different companies and usually consisted of paper-and-pencil testing, an interview by two psychologists, and projective techniques. This information was integrated into a final report by one psychologist. Ratings on five areas (sociability, organizational ability, drive, overall performance, and potential) based on the final report were used as predictors. These ratings were made by two psychologists who read the test results, interview notes, and final report, not by the assessor who wrote the final report. Criteria were ratings on the same five scales made by one or more supervisors. Interrater reliabilities on the predictors (corrected by the Spearman-Brown formula) ranged from .29 to .75; validities ranged from .21 to .38.

In 1962, seven reports on this same assessment program at Western Reserve University were published in *Personnel Psychology*. Campbell (1962) noted that the procedures used in the assessments varied but generally included interviewing and objective and projective tests, gathered by different sources and then integrated into a report by one individual.

Campbell, Otis, Liske, and Prien (1962) examined the validity of ratings (on social skills, persuasiveness, leadership, intellectual capacity, creativeness, planning, motivation and energy, and overall effectiveness) made by the individual who wrote the final report. The criteria were ratings of first- and second-level supervisors on the same scales, as well as an "action rating" of whether the individual would be promoted, retained, or let go. They concluded that there was general agreement between the supervisors' and psychologists' ratings, although there was low discriminant validity. Correlations between psychologists' and supervisors' ratings on identical scales ranged from −.05 to .39 for sales applicants and from .04 to .50 for nonsales applicants. Correlations of psychologists' scale ratings with the action rating ranged from −.05 to .49 for sales and from −.18 to .29 for nonsales individuals.

In the final article in the series, Otis, Campbell, and Prien (1962) noted that ratings based on the final report showed a consistent drop in validity when compared to ratings made by the individual who actually prepared the final report. They concluded that poor communication of information in the narrative report decreases the value of the appraisal.

Trankell (1959) examined validity in predictions of airplane pilot success. Correlations of −.21 to .55 with a median of .34 were reported across fourteen assessment dimensions, with all but three being statistically significant. Trankell also reported a 96 percent hit rate in judging individuals as suitable who then performed well and a 46 percent hit rate in judging individuals as unsuitable who were hired and subsequently dismissed.

Albrecht, Glaser, and Marks (1964) reported a validation study of assessments conducted by three psychologists from the same consulting firm on individuals who had already been hired. Candidates were ranked on four areas: forecasting and budgeting effectiveness, sales performance, effectiveness in interpersonal relationships, and overall performance. Rankings on these same scales were made by regional supervisors and peers, and ratings on these same scales were made by the immediate supervisor. Nine of the twelve validity coefficients involving ranking criteria were significant; none involving the rating criteria was significant.

Dicken and Black (1965) reported a validation study with reports written by one psychologist and ratings made by four other psychologists who reviewed the reports. The reliabilities of the report readers on the eight areas rated ranged from .85 to .98. The authors concluded that satisfactory validity was found in the sample from one organization but not in the sample from a second organization.

DeNelsky and McKee (1969) had seven psychologists review reports of Central Intelligence Agency employees made by one of eight psychologists twelve to fifty-seven months earlier. These psychologists rated thirty-two assessees on twenty-five performance and personality areas, and sorted reports into five overall categories in a modified Q-sort distribution. Criterion data were ratings of fitness by supervisors and a sort of current fitness reports by the same group of psychologists (with assessee names deleted). A significant relationship was found between a composite rating of effectiveness based on the assessment reports and the sorted judgment of effectiveness from the fitness reports.

Miner (1970) described a series of studies on assessments of individuals hired by management consulting firms. He classified report recommendations into a five-point scale to serve as the predictor and used tenure, mean increase in compensation rate per year, and a rating by the office manager as criteria. Predictive validity was not found in any of the five samples for any of the criteria.

Note that the most recent study was published in 1970. We now turn to two more recent large-scale unpublished studies. Silzer (1986) reported a study of 1,749 individuals assessed by a psychological consulting firm. A "management success" criterion, which was a composite of management level, number of subordinates, and salary, was created. Silzer reported that psychologist ratings on the dimensions of motivation ($r = .21$), administrative ($r = .15$), communication ($r = .17$), interpersonal ($r = .16$), leadership ($r = .28$), and adjustment ($r = .18$) correlated significantly with the composite criterion. Silzer also reported correlations between test scores and the same criterion, and found that several test scores correlated with the criterion at essentially the same level as the psychologist's dimensional rating ($r = .26$ for management interests and $r = .24$ for leadership potential). Thus, although the study provides evidence of the validity of assessors' dimensional judgments, there is not strong support for incremental validity of the assessor's judgment over test scores.

A second recent unpublished study also focuses on a single consulting firm. DeMann (1988) followed up on 3,298 individuals assessed by psychologists in the firm. In contrast to the Silzer study, in which psychologists made dimensional ratings, DeMann's study focuses on the overall recommendation made by the psychologists. We show the relationship between psychologists' recommendations and hiring decisions in Table 3.2. These data show a relatively strong relationship between the psychologists' recommendation and the hiring decision. Note that the "not hired" condition includes both situations in which the firm decided not to extend a job offer and situations in which the candidate declined a job offer.

For purposes of the validation study, only those hired were available. Thus the 1,217 individuals recommended and hired were contrasted with the 270 individuals hired despite the psychologists' recommendation against hiring. Criterion measures were obtained from the employer at least two years after the assessment. Performance ratings of above-average or superior were obtained for 56 percent of those recommended and 34 percent of those not recommended, and those not recommended were more likely to have been let go by the company (26.4 percent) than those recommended (13.7 percent).

Thus both large-scale recent studies show evidence of criterion-related validity, one for dimensional judgments and the other for overall recommendations. Both are studies of operational assessment programs, and thus issues of criterion contamination and sample representativeness (such as the degree to which individuals hired despite a negative recommendation from the psycholo-

Table 3.2. Relationship Between Recommendations and Hiring Decisions in DeMann's Study.

	Recommended		Not Recommended		Total	
	(N)	(percent)	(N)	(percent)	(N)	(percent)
Hired	1,217	67.0	270	18.0	1,487	45.1
Not hired	600	33.0	1,211	81.8	1,811	54.9
Total	1,817	55.1	1,481	44.9	3,298	

gist are representative of individuals receiving a negative recommendation from the psychologist) cannot be ruled out. We see it as unlikely, though, that these obstacles can be overcome, unless sponsorship for a large-scale "for research only" assessment program were to be obtained.

A number of issues emerge from this review. First, one must ask what the predictor and the purpose are for which we are establishing validity evidence. Of the studies reviewed, a number used ratings on dimensions as predictors, with some using ratings made by someone other than the individual assessor. Only 15.1 percent of those we surveyed combined their assessment results to yield an overall rating, and only 28.8 percent included ratings on specific dimensions in their assessment reports. Because many assessors (60.7 percent in Ryan and Sackett's 1992 survey) make specific recommendations, the more appropriate predictor to examine in many cases might be this recommendation.

Second, range restriction may play an important role in considerations of individual assessment validity. Candidates may have been through several screening hurdles prior to the psychological assessment, so psychologists seldom see the entire applicant pool.

A third issue in providing validity evidence for the individual assessment process is how the information from the assessment is integrated into the organization's personnel decision making. In some cases the assessment information may be the deciding factor; in others it may be ignored or differentially weighted from candidate to candidate or selectively included (for example, only report information on certain characteristics is considered). Care must be taken in separating the discussion of the validity of the assessor's inferences from the validity of the organization's decision.

Fourth, some may argue that because many methods used by individual assessors (cognitive ability tests, in-basket tasks, personality measures, and others) have been established as valid predictors of job performance, then individual assessment as a process is valid. The issue is much more complex, because the assessor's judgment is often a clinical combination of the information gathered from these methods, which may enhance or detract from the validity of the overall process. As we noted in the model presented in Figure 3.1, validation research can be conducted on methods, dimensional judgments, and overall recommendations.

A fifth issue is the validity of predictions as a question separate from the validity of descriptions. Differences between description and prediction purposes and how one approaches them is not without precedent in I/O psychology. Two central areas of individual differences—cognitive ability and personality—have been the focus of debates between those who have looked exclusively at prediction maximization and those who demand greater description and understanding. For example, Murphy (1996) noted that research on cognitive ability in I/O psychology has focused on the prediction of performance without focusing on describing the structure of specific abilities that underlie "g."

What should be done in individual assessment validation? The difficulties of conducting criterion-related studies should lead to the use of different validation strategies rather than abandonment of validation attempts. Sackett and Arvey (1993) have argued that an assessor claiming he or she makes valid inferences must explicate the constructs assessed, the linkage between the methods of assessment and these constructs, and a causal model relating the constructs to the overall decision. However, research on decision making indicates that individuals often do not have insight into the policies they use to integrate information (Shanteau & Stewart, 1992). Even if an assessor can articulate the model of performance and information integration used, we might question whether he or she is actually following it in practice.

Clearly, much more research is needed on the validity of individual assessment processes. Such research should include a detailed description of the individual assessment process used, to enable the accumulation of information about how variations in practice relate to effectiveness.

Reliability Issues in Individual Assessment

Interrater agreement has received some attention from individual assessment researchers. Several studies have looked at agreement in ratings made by those reading assessment reports (DeNelsky & McKee, 1969; Dicken & Black, 1965; Walker, 1955). Others have examined agreement among raters who had access to test scores and interview notes (Hilton, Bolin, Parker, Taylor, & Walker, 1955). We looked at agreement both among those reviewing test scores and interview tapes and among three individuals who conducted their own assessments of the same three job candidates (Ryan & Sackett, 1989). We also looked at reliability in terms of the semantics of assessments, to examine whether those examining reports written by the same individual for the same purpose would identify them as such (Ryan, Barbera, & Sackett, 1990).

As we have noted elsewhere (Ryan & Sackett, 1989), each of these methodologies provides information on only part of the interrater reliability question. One can examine assessor agreement across assessees, across methods or data sources, or across both. In doing so, one must also consider candidate reliability in terms of individuals' not presenting themselves consistently. One question that must be addressed in this line of research concerns the purpose of assessing agreement. The question is, Agreement on what? On ratings (which are not always used or provided by individual assessors), on recommendations with respect to specific personnel decisions, or on the descriptions of individuals given?

Research on individual assessment reliability has not consistently reached positive conclusions. We (Ryan & Sackett, 1989) found that three assessors who each evaluated the same three candidates for a position had much disagreement over specific candidate attributes as well as overall job suitability. One of the candidates was described by the first assessor as "counterdependent," the second as "lacks independence," and the third as "independent." Another candidate was described by one assessor as having limited self-confidence and by a second as having high self-confidence. Although the three assessors did rank-order the three candidates consistently, they did not agree on whether they would recommend a given job candidate. We also examined reliability indirectly by having fifty I/O psychologists review the materials from the assessments and rate candidates using a Latin squares design. Ratings were made based on reviewing the assessment materials (such as test scores and tapes of interviews) but not the assessor's report. Only one-third of the raters agreed with the conclusions of the assessor whose materials they were reviewing.

Ryan, Barbera, and Sackett (1990) took a different approach to examining reliability, providing subjects with nine narrative reports: three reports about each of three individuals. Reports were edited for identifiability, and subjects were asked to group the nine reports according to the individual they had written about, with specific directions to create three groups of three reports. None of the subjects correctly grouped the reports by candidate, and a sizable percentage did no better than random in grouping.

One key difference between these and early studies on individual assessment reliability is that these focused on agreement in conclusions (on ratings, recommendations, and rankings) *and* in candidate descriptions. Why is reliability with regard to description important above and beyond reliability for purposes of prediction? As Ryan, Barbera, and Sackett (1990) noted, assessors may agree in describing an individual as outgoing but might differ in the predictive inferences they make based on that description. They might also agree in recommending a candidate but have different descriptions of how that individual will act on the job. The reliability of descriptions becomes more important as information is used for more than one purpose or for describing performance in a dynamic and evolving environment. As the field of I/O psychology attempts to address predicting a moving target (rapidly changing work), so too must its methods of evaluating practices.

An examination of the literature on expert judgment provides some useful reasons why there might there be disagreement among individual assessors. One reason is incompetence of one or more individual assessors (Hammond, 1996); that is, an individual assessor may not be truly an expert in terms of qualifications. This begs the question, however, of what the criteria are for considering someone an expert in the individual assessment area. A second explanation is differences in ideology. Research has shown some differences in assessor approaches based on training and professional affiliation (Ryan & Sackett, 1992), although these differences appear to play only a minimal role in explaining practice variation.

Differences in judgment may be due to differences in how assessors organize and use the same information. Mumpower and Stewart (in press) noted that because experts often do not get adequate feedback on the outcomes of their judgments or receive ambiguous feedback, differences in expert judgment occur. They also noted that often expert judgments are made with proxy variables because relevant data are unavailable (the assessor does not have a prior supervisor's view, for example). As Mumpower and

Stewart remind us, people (including experts) overestimate the quality of their own judgments based on biased recall of positive outcomes and a lack of consideration of base rates and selection ratios. Experts having the same information in front of them can also organize that information in different ways, employing different mental models and different cognitive processes to aggregate the information into a judgment.

Thus individual assessor disagreements are not unexpected by those who research human judgment; nonetheless, this disagreement has important implications for practice. Without established reliability of assessor judgments, it is impossible to make claims regarding the typical effectiveness of individual assessment.

One other reliability concern relates to the internal consistency of an assessor. Assessor consistency can be evaluated in overall dimensional judgments and recommendations about the same individual and also in how inferences are formed across individuals. For example, does the assessor consistently make the same inferences based on the same data (say, test scores, interview answers, and simulation performance)? Are these inferences presented in a consistent manner to clients? Note that there may be cases where inconsistency in the interpretation of test data might be viewed as appropriate by an assessor. For example, an assessor might believe that ipsative evaluation of test results is necessary because one should consider a pattern of scores across tests rather than interpretation of a single scale in isolation or that a particular individual's score should be "corrected" for obvious impression management attempts. The concern is whether inconsistency on the part of the assessor is truly warranted.

Other Evaluation Criteria

Criteria other than psychometric ones for evaluating the effectiveness of individual assessment may merit some attention. One consideration is whether the goals of the user of individual assessment results (the organization) have been met. A related criterion is whether the individual assessment results in a greater achievement of client goals (or greater validity or reliability) than alternative processes do. Organizations may use a psychologist rather than relying on in-house or other resources to evaluate an individual because of a perception of the capability of the psychologist to assess areas different from ones the organization can assess or to assess those areas more effectively. The veracity of these beliefs should be established. Utility analyses might provide further information on individual assessment effectiveness. An effective individual assessment process is one that is worthwhile from a cost-benefit perspective; that is, considering the cost of poor performance and the accuracy of individual assessment recommendations, is the assessment worth the cost?

Fairness and Adverse Impact

There is no published research on fairness and individual assessment, although there is much research on test bias and the adverse impact of the types of selection procedures used in individual assessment. Our survey research indicated that although few assessors have been subject to legal action, most (particularly non-SIOP members) were unaware of whether their assessment process conformed to professional and legal guidelines.

Given the subjective nature of individual assessment decision making, bias on the part of the assessor is clearly a concern. A less obvious concern is the use of idiosyncratic score adjustments. Assessors often consider applicant gender or age when interpreting personality or interest test results. Sackett and Wilk (1994) presented standardized male-female difference scores for personality measures most often used in individual assessments and noted sizable differences for some dimensions. They noted that the lack of studies on the predictive bias of personality measures by gender or race precludes a determination of whether systematic underprediction exists and therefore whether score adjustment is warranted. However, they pointed out that psychologists making clinical judgments, as in the individual assessment context, may mentally adjust scores based on their knowledge of differences. Several concerns with such mental adjustments when forming interpretations exist: (1) Is the within-group norming justified due to actual bias in measurement? (2) Is the adjustment made consistently by the assessor across candidates? and (3) Is the adjustment based on empirical evidence or the assessor's idiosyncratic beliefs?

Recent research on perceptions of the fairness of selection procedures has adopted an organizational justice framework (Gilliland, 1993, 1994); as we noted earlier, examination of assessee perceptions of the fairness of individual assessment is needed. For example, considerable empirical support exists for the influence of consistency on perceptions of fairness (Gilliland & Beckstein, 1996; Greenberg, 1986; Sheppard & Lewicki, 1987). The use of unstructured interviews and score interpretations practices by assessors suggests that individual assessment procedures are not consistent across candidates; whether this inconsistency is perceived by assessees and influences their evaluations of process fairness remains to be addressed.

Variations in Practice

Our review of the research on the practice of individual assessment has led us to identify several specific variations that seem to distinguish approaches to practice (Ryan & Sackett, 1992). We recognize that there may be other themes unidentified by our research, and those may also be important indicators of how the practice of individual assessment is approached. Nonetheless, these variations serve as a useful starting heuristic for understanding the scope of individual assessment practice.

Job Versus Whole Life Focus

One variation that emerges from descriptive research on individual assessment is whether assessors take a job-relevant versus a whole life approach to assessment. We noted in 1992 that some assessors take a whole life approach to assessment, questioning candidates on family life, hobbies, and other areas not explicitly job relevant. Although we can admonish those who ask invasive or illegal questions, the whole life approach may have greater relevance for selection in certain situations than is traditionally acknowledged. There is a growing body of research on the effects of family and other nonwork issues on work effectiveness (Crouter, 1984; Gutek, Nakamura, & Nieva, 1981; Near, Rice, & Hunt, 1980; Zedeck, 1992). For example, research suggests the influence of family in success in expatriate assignments (Black & Gregerson, 1991; Black, Mendenhall, & Oddou, 1991; Black & Stephens, 1989) and willingness to relocate (Brett, Stroh, & Reilly, 1992). Family social support is important for those in highly stressful positions (Cohen & Wills, 1985; Fletcher & Jones, 1993; Granrose, Greenhaus, & Parasuraman, 1992; Parasuraman, Greenhaus, & Granrose, 1992). The key issue is whether the assessor's whole life focus is nondiscriminatory and considers only factors documented through job analysis to be relevant to job success.

A second research area that supports a whole life focus concerns the validity of biodata for predicting success on the job (Rothstein, Schmidt, Erwin, Owens, & Sparks, 1990). Again, as biodata developers have noted (Mael, 1991), assessors should ask for biographical information that is nondiscriminatory, noninvasive, and job relevant. Mael, Connerley, and Morath (1996) found that biodata items that dealt with traumatic events, stigmatizing issues, religion and politics, and intimate behavior were considered invasive. In our second survey sample (Ryan & Sackett, 1992), the majority of individual assessors asked questions that are likely to be problematic (about parents, spouse, children, medical status, and criminal history). Such a focus may be reflective of inappropriate views of the relation between developmental experiences and job performance. For example, Hansen (1991) stated that asking about family history in individual assessments can be revealing as "it is unlikely that a bricklayer's child will have the necessary developmental experiences while growing up to become an advertising executive" (p. 12).

A third area that may indirectly support a whole life focus is research on employee fit (see Kristof, 1996, for a review). Consideration is given by both applicant and organization as to whether there is a good fit of the individual's values, beliefs, characteristics, and skills to the organizational climate and job requirements. The individual assessor may garner much of this information from standardized assessment devices; however, adequately assessing fit may require extending beyond a sole focus on an individual's behavior at work. For example, judging the value congruence between an individual and an organization may involve a whole life focus.

Research is needed on the effects of this practice variation. Are assessments based on a whole life focus likely to produce less or more valid inferences? Do assessees react negatively to a whole life focus? Do clients seek assessors who can provide them with valid inferences based on non-job-specific information?

Examining Test Results Before or After the Interview

A second theme that emerges from our review of practice is that assessors differ in how they view the interview and noninterview components of the assessment process as relating. Specifically, many assessors (40 percent) formulate the interview questions after reviewing personal history and test score information (Ryan & Sackett, 1987, 1992).

Much has been written in the interviewing literature regarding the influence of prior impressions on the interviewer's behavior. In a review of the evidence for whether interviewers tend to be confirmatory, disconfirmatory, or diagnostic due to prior opinions, Dipboye (1992) concluded that research supports the possibility that each of these processes affects information gathering. He also noted that the interviewer's questioning strategy might be different—say, diagnostic—from his or her nonverbal behaviors—say, confirmatory. Dipboye concluded that the evidence is mixed regarding the effect of prior impressions on information processing, but he noted that the research seems to support disconfirmatory effects, with interviewers more likely to notice and remember information that violates prior expectancies. Research on information integration and judgment appears to support the view that interviewers' behavior and judgments are affected by their preinterview impressions.

Examining test or other data during the assessment process provides the assessor with an impression that will more heavily influence the final conclusions than the interview. Some might argue that given the unstructured nature of most individual assessment interviews, this is not a bad thing. However, research on how this variation in individual assessment practice relates to effectiveness is warranted.

Proportions of Recommended Candidates

A third variation theme across assessment practices is variability in recommendation rates. Miner (1970) pointed out that assessors may differ in the percentages of candidates they recommend for hiring or promoting. This was supported by our survey, which found a range of 7 percent to 100 percent of candidates (mean 59.7 percent) recommended, with significantly more being recommended for nonmanagement positions. Stratton (1991) found hiring recommendation rates ranging from 21 percent to 54 percent among the assessors in her study.

What drives the rate of recommendation? If it is the nature of the position and the purpose of assessment or the characteristics of the candidate pool, we might find such differences in rates acceptable. For example, if there are primarily internal candidates under consideration for a position, we might expect a higher recommendation rate than if there are primarily external candidates. However, if assessors differ in their "leniency," we must be concerned how this error affects the accuracy of organizational decisions that use individual assessment information.

Harvey (1992) noted that expert decision makers might have a variety of goals when approaching a judgment process: "to maximize the percentage correct; to maximize the hit rate for a constant false alarm rate; to achieve a specific number of misses for each false alarm; to maximize the expected value, given that the benefit of each type of correct judgement and the cost of each type of incorrect judgment is known" (p. 235). These goal differences are likely to translate into different recommendation rates. Further, Harvey pointed out, the consumers of expert opinion may have very different goals from those of the expert decision maker and may have difficulty using the expert information without knowledge of the expert's goals. Thus we need to link assessment goals and applicant pool characteristics with expected rates of recommendation in order to evaluate whether a particular assessor's rate is too high or too low.

Inclusion or Exclusion Focus

A fourth issue in individual assessment information integration is the use of an inclusion or exclusion focus. Butcher (1985) stated that assessment for sensitive positions operates primarily by using exclusion criteria—that is, by detecting characteristics of the individual that might hinder success on the job—not by using inclusion criteria (that is, not by looking for desirable characteristics that might contribute to success). Whether exclusion or inclusion criteria are used in individual assessments of other purposes is unknown. Our survey (Ryan & Sackett, 1992) found that 21.6 percent of assessors reported using a screen-out approach.

Holliman (1985), in her review of psychological assessment for selection into the ministry, found that a survey of ministry boards indicated the emphasis was on remediation of weaknesses rather than nonacceptance; however, her survey of clergy applicants indicated that 33 percent felt the purpose of assessment was to select out. Thus we might conclude that beyond the psychologist, the client organization might also drive the emphasis on inclusion or exclusion and that the candidates may perceive the emphasis quite differently than intended.

Conclusions: Trends and Directions

Our data on the state of the practice of individual assessment are already several years old. What may have changed since our more recent survey, or what is likely to have changed? The use of certain assessment methods, in both generic form and specific measures, may be changing. We would anticipate that even more assessors are now using simulations, because many off-the-shelf individual exercises (such as in-basket exercises) are available that are easily scored. Situational judgment tests (both paper-and-pencil and video) have become increasingly popular, and we expect their incorporation into individual assessment practice. Additionally, the validity evidence regarding measures of integrity and conscientiousness supports their greater use. A number of personality instruments designed specifically for selection contexts are now marketed heavily. One method that has gained increasing popularity for assessing others (although perhaps not in the selection context) is 360-degree feedback instruments. We anticipate that individual assessors are incorporating these types of data into both developmental and promotion assessments.

In terms of assessment content, we hope that assessors are responsive to the changing nature of work. The evaluation of interpersonal skills has always been a focus of individual assessment and often a primary reason for its use. We suspect that current individual assessment practice has an increased focus on particular types of interpersonal skills, such as ability to work well on a team and with diverse populations and to exhibit service-oriented behaviors, as trends in the workplace necessitate these emphases. We also note that assessors surveyed often mentioned flexibility or adaptability as an area evaluated; the increased pace of change in the workplace appears to make evaluation of this area critical.

One thing that we suspect has not been revolutionized in the past few years is the attention to individual assessment in graduate training. Although our evidence is only anecdotal, we see few I/O programs providing practica in testing and interviewing or even courses on specific assessment methods. We see few clinical or counseling programs that incorporate discussions of equal employment opportunity requirements and job analysis methods. We also suspect that our conclusions regarding the state of the practice have not changed (Ryan & Sackett, 1992). Many assessors are not up to standard in terms of licensing requirements, conducting job analyses, conducting interviews, and evaluating the validity of their practices.

In the clinical arena, recent research has indicated that psychological assessment as practiced now is remarkably similar to psychological assessment as it was practiced thirty years ago (Watkins, Campbell, Nieberding, & Hallmark, 1995). A review of our survey results and the Western Reserve validity studies of the early 1960s does not indicate that individual assessment practice is evolving at a more rapid rate. We hope that greater attention to individual assessment by researchers and greater communication of knowledge to practitioners will enable the state of the practice to coincide more closely with the state of the knowledge.

References

Albrecht, P. A., Glaser, E. M., & Marks, J. (1964). Validation of a multiple-assessment procedure for managerial personnel. *Journal of Applied Psychology, 48,* 351–360.

Barrick, M. R., & Mount, M. K. (1991). The Big Five personality dimensions and job performance: A meta-analysis. *Personnel Psychology, 44,* 1–26.

Black, J. S., & Gregerson, H. (1991). The other half of the picture: Antecedents of spouse cross-cultural adjustment. *Journal of International Business Studies, 22,* 461–477.

Black, J. S., Mendenhall, M., & Oddou, G. (1991). Toward a comprehensive model of intercultural adjustment: An integration of multiple theoretical perspectives. *Academy of Management Review, 16,* 291–317.

Black, J. S., & Stephens, G. K. (1989). The influence of the spouse on American expatriate adjustment and intent to stay in Pacific Rim overseas assignments. *Journal of Management, 15,* 529–544.

Brett, J. M., Stroh, L. K., & Reilly, A. H. (1992). What is it like being a dual-career manager in the 1990s? In S. Zedeck (Ed.), *Work, families, and organizations* (pp. 138–167). San Francisco: Jossey-Bass.

Butcher, J. N. (1985). Personality assessment in industry: Theoretical issues and illustrations. In H. J. Bernardin & D. Bownas (Eds.), *Personality assessment in organizations* (pp. 277–309). New York: Praeger.

Campbell, J. T. (1962). Assessment of higher-level personnel: I. Background and scope of research. *Personnel Psychology, 15,* 57–62.

Campbell, J. T., Otis, J. L., Liske, R. E., & Prien, E. P. (1962). Assessments of higher-level personnel: II. Validity of the over-all assessment process. *Personnel Psychology, 15,* 63–74.

Campion, M. A., Pursell, E. D., & Brown, B. K. (1988). Structured interviewing: Raising the psychometric properties of the employment interview. *Personnel Psychology, 41,* 25–42.

Cohen, S., & Wills, T. A. (1985). Stress, social support, and the buffering hypothesis. *Psychological Bulletin, 98,* 310–357.

Crouter, A. C. (1984). Spillover from family to work: The neglected side of the work-family interface. *Human Relations, 37,* 425–442.

Davey, D. M. (1982). Conventional techniques: An industrial psychologist's approach to the assessment of managers. In D. M. Davey & M. Harris (Eds.), *Judging people: A guide to orthodox and unorthodox methods of assessment* (pp. 27–41). London: McGraw-Hill.

Dawes, R. M., Faust, D., & Meehl, P. E. (1989). Clinical versus actuarial judgment. *Science, 243,* 1668–1674.

DeMann Ltd. (1988). *A follow-up study of psychological assessment in selection.* Minneapolis: Author.

DeNelsky, G. Y., & McKee, M. G. (1969). Prediction of job performance from assessment reports: Use of a modified Q-sort technique to expand predictor and criterion variance. *Journal of Applied Psychology, 53,* 439–445.

Dicken, C. F., & Black, J. D. (1965). Predictive validity of psychometric evaluations of supervisors. *Journal of Applied Psychology, 49,* 34–47.

Dipboye, R. L. (1992). *Selection interviews: Process perspectives.* Cincinnati, OH: South-Western Publishing.

Dougherty, T. W., Ebert, R. J., & Callender, J. C. (1986). Policy capturing in the employment interview. *Journal of Applied Psychology, 71,* 9–15.

Dreher, G. F., Ash, R. A., & Hancock, P. (1988). The role of traditional research designs in underestimating the validity of the employment interview. *Personnel Psychology, 41,* 315–327.

Fletcher, B. C., & Jones, F. (1993). An empirical study of occupational stress transmission in working couples. *Human Relations, 46,* 881–903.

Gatewood, R. D., & Feild, H. S. (1994). *Human resource selection.* Fort Worth, TX: Dryden Press.

Gilliland, S. W. (1993). The perceived fairness of selection systems: An organizational justice perspective. *Academy of Management Review, 18,* 694–734.

Gilliland, S. W. (1994). Effects of procedural and distributive justice on reactions to a selection system. *Journal of Applied Psychology, 79,* 691–701.

Gilliland, S. W., & Beckstein, B. A. (1996). Procedural and distributive justice in the editorial review process. *Personnel Psychology, 49,* 669–691.

Granrose, C. S., Greenhaus, J. H., & Parasuraman, S. (1992). A proposed model of support provided by two-earner couples. *Human Relations, 45,* 1367–1393.

Greenberg, J. (1986). Determinants of perceived fairness of performance evaluations. *Journal of Applied Psychology, 71,* 340–342.

Gutek, B. A., Nakamura, C. Y., & Nieva, V. (1981). The interdependence of work and family roles. *Journal of Occupational Behavior, 2,* 1–16.

Halperin, K., Snyder, C. R., Shenkel, R. J., & Houston, B. K. (1976). Effects of source status and message favorability on acceptance of personality feedback. *Journal of Applied Psychology, 61,* 85–88.

Hammond, K. R. (1996). *When judgments fail: Irreducible uncertainty, inevitable error, unavoidable injustice.* New York: Oxford University Press.

Hansen, C. P. (1991). What is psychological assessment? In C. P. Hansen & K. A. Conrad (Eds.), *A handbook of psychological assessment in business* (pp. 1–22). Westport, CT: Quorum Books.

Harvey, L. O. (1992). The critical operating characteristic and the evaluation of expert judgment. *Organizational Behavior and Human Decision Processes, 53,* 229–251.

Hilton, A. C., Bolin, S. F., Parker, J. W., Jr., Taylor, E. K., & Walker, W. B. (1955). The validity of personnel assessment by professional psychologists. *Journal of Applied Psychology, 39,* 287–293.

Hogan, R., Hogan, J., & Roberts, B. W. (1996). Personality measurement and employment decisions: Questions and answers. *American Psychologist, 51,* 469–477.

Holliman, P. J. (1985). *A study of psychological assessment procedures as adjunctive to personnel selection processes in a religious organization.* Unpublished doctoral dissertation, Northwestern University.

Hough, L. M., & Schneider, R. J. (1996). Personality traits, taxonomies, and applications in organizations. In K. R. Murphy (Ed.), *Individual differences and behavior in organizations* (pp. 31–88). San Francisco: Jossey-Bass.

Ilgen, D. R., Fisher, C. D., & Taylor, M. S. (1979). Consequences of individual feedback on behavior in organizations. *Journal of Applied Psychology, 64,* 349–371.

Kluger, A. N., & Rothstein, H. R. (1993). The influence of selection test type on applicant reactions to employment testing. *Journal of Business and Psychology, 8,* 3–25.

Kristof, A. L. (1996). Person-organization fit: An integrative review of its conceptualizations, measurement, and implications. *Personnel Psychology, 49,* 1–50.

Macan, T. H., Avedon, M. J., Paese, M., & Smith, D. E. (1994). The effects of applicant reactions to cognitive ability tests and an assessment center. *Personnel Psychology, 47,* 715–738.

Mael, F. A. (1991). A conceptual rationale for the domain and attributes of biodata items. *Personnel Psychology, 44,* 763–792.

Mael, F. A., Connerley, M., & Morath, R. A. (1996). None of your business: Parameters of biodata invasiveness. *Personnel Psychology, 49,* 613–650.

Miner, J. B. (1970). Psychological evaluations as predictors of consulting success. *Personnel Psychology, 23,* 393–405.

Mumpower, J. L., & Stewart, T. R. (in press). Expert judgment and expert disagreement. *Thinking and Reasoning.*

Murphy, K. R. (1996). Individual differences and behavior in organizations: Much more than g. In K. R. Murphy (Ed.), *Individual differences and behavior in organizations* (pp. 3–30). San Francisco: Jossey-Bass.

Near, J. P., Rice, R. W., & Hunt, R. G. (1980). The relationship between work and nonwork domains: A review of empirical research. *Academy of Management Review, 5,* 415–429.

Ones, D. S., Viswesvaran, C., & Schmidt, F. L. (1993). Comprehensive meta-analysis of integrity test validities: Findings and implications for personnel selection and theories of job performance. *Journal of Applied Psychology, 78,* 679–703.

Otis, J. L., Campbell, J. T., & Prien, E. P. (1962). Assessment of higher level personnel: VII. The nature of assessments. *Personnel Psychology, 15,* 441–446.

Parasuraman, S., Greenhaus, J. H., & Granrose, C. S. (1992). Role stressors, social support and well-being among two-career couples. *Journal of Organizational Behavior, 13,* 339–356.

Rothstein, H. R., Schmidt, F. L., Erwin, F. W., Owens, W. A., & Sparks, C. P. (1990). Biographical data in employment selection: Can validities be made generalizable? *Journal of Applied Psychology, 75,* 175–184.

Ryan, A. M. (1988, April). *Individual assessment reports and reactions to assessment.* Paper presented at the third annual conference of the Society for Industrial and Organizational Psychology, Dallas, TX.

Ryan, A. M., Barbera, K. M., & Sackett, P. R. (1990). Strategic individual assessment: Issues in providing reliable descriptions. *Human Resource Management, 29,* 271–284.

Ryan, A. M., & Laser, S. A. (1989, June). *Assessee reactions to individual assessments for personnel selection decisions.* Paper presented at the first annual American Psychological Society conference, Alexandria, VA.

Ryan, A. M., & Sackett, P. R. (1987). A survey of individual assessment practices by I/O psychologists. *Personnel Psychology, 40,* 455–488.

Ryan, A. M., & Sackett, P. R. (1989). Exploratory study of individual assessment practices: Interrater reliability and judgments of assessor effectiveness. *Journal of Applied Psychology, 74,* 568–579.

Ryan, A. M., & Sackett, P. R. (1992). Relationships between graduate training, professional affiliation, and individual psychological assessment practices for personnel decisions. *Personnel Psychology, 45,* 363–385.

Sackett, P. R., & Arvey, R. D. (1993). Selection in small N settings. In N. Schmitt, W. C. Borman, & Associates, *Personnel selection in organizations* (pp. 418–447). San Francisco: Jossey-Bass.

Sackett, P. R., & Wilk, S. L. (1994). Within-group norming and other forms of score adjustment in preemployment testing. *American Psychologist, 49,* 929–954.

Sawyer, J. (1966). Measurement and prediction: Clinical and statistical. *Psychological Bulletin, 66,* 178–200.

Schneider, B. (1996). When individual differences aren't. In K. R. Murphy (Ed.), *Individual differences and behavior in organizations* (pp. 548–572). San Francisco: Jossey-Bass.

Shanteau, J. (1992). Competence in experts: The role of task characteristics. *Organizational Behavior and Human Decision Processes, 53,* 252–266.

Shanteau, J., & Stewart, T. R. (1992). Why study expert decision making? Some historical perspectives and comments. *Organizational Behavior and Human Decision Processes, 53,* 95–106.

Sheppard, B. H., & Lewicki, R. J. (1987). Toward general principles of managerial fairness. *Social Justice Research, 1,* 161–176.

Silzer, R. F. (1986, April). *Predictions of prophecies: By data or by divinity?* Paper presented at the annual conference of the Society for Industrial and Organizational Psychology, Chicago.

Smither, J. W., Reilly, R. R., Millsap, R., Pearlman, K., & Stoffey, R. W. (1993). Applicant reactions to selection procedures. *Personnel Psychology, 46,* 58–60.

Society for Industrial and Organizational Psychology. (1987). *Principles for the validation and use of personnel selection procedures* (3rd ed.). College Park, MD: Author.

Stone, D. L., Gueutel, H. G., & McIntosh, B. (1984). The effect of feedback sequence and expertise of the rater on perceived feedback accuracy. *Personnel Psychology, 37,* 487–506.

Stone, D. L., & Stone, E. F. (1985). Effects of feedback consistency and feedback favorability on self-perceived task competence and perceived feedback accuracy. *Organizational Behavior and Human Decision Processes, 36,* 167–185.

Stone, E. F., & Stone, D. L. (1984). Effects of multiple sources of performance feedback and feedback favorability on self-perceived task competence and perceived feedback accuracy. *Journal of Management, 10,* 371–378.

Stratton, S. A. (1991). *Judgment theory applied to data combination in individual psychological assessment.* Unpublished doctoral dissertation, University of Houston.

Trankell, A. (1959). The psychologist as an instrument of prediction. *Journal of Applied Psychology, 43,* 170–175.

Walker, W. B. (1955). *An investigation of the effectiveness of communication between psychologists and sales executives through personnel audit reports.* Unpublished doctoral dissertation, Western Reserve University.

Watkins, C. E., Jr., Campbell, V. L., Nieberding, R., & Hallmark, R. (1995). Contemporary practice of psychological assessment by clinical psychologists. *Professional Psychology: Research and Practice, 26,* 54–60.

Wiesner, W. H., & Cronshaw, S. F. (1988). The moderating impact of interview format and degree of structure on the validity of the employment interview. *Journal of Occupational Psychology, 61,* 275–290.

Zedeck, S. (1992). Introduction: Exploring the domain of work and family concerns. In S. Zedeck (Ed.), *Work, families, and organizations* (pp. 1–32). San Francisco: Jossey-Bass.

CHAPTER 4

Ethical, Legal, and Professional Issues for Individual Assessment

Richard Jeanneret

Very early in my consulting career, when I was providing assessment services for a Fortune 100 company with regional facilities throughout the United States, I encountered my first ethical dilemma. It was easy for me to solve but had some unfortunate personal repercussions. The ethical concern arose when I was scheduled to review the test results and provide feedback to a client's employee, whom I immediately discovered was my cousin.

The purposes of the assessment were twofold: client management considered the results in making career decisions (on promotions, assignments, and transfers), and the employee was expected to use the results for personal development and career planning. Schedules were prepared and sent to employees about two weeks in advance, and one of these schedules indicated that I was assigned to complete the feedback assessment for my cousin. After receiving the schedule, I notified the client of the ethical conflict, and the schedule was revised so that another psychologist could complete my cousin's assessment. However, the assessment did not occur until some months later, and a promotional opportunity for which my cousin was qualified went to another employee in the interim. My cousin always believed that if I had completed the assessment as scheduled, he would have received the promotion. From his perspective, I was at fault for raising the ethical issue in the first place, and thus preventing him from being considered for a promotion he believed he deserved. Although there have been some unfortunate family consequences, there is no question in my mind as to the correctness of my ethical decision.

An assessing psychologist working in the context of providing consultation to an organizational client must be cognizant of and responsive to a wide range of ethical, legal, and professional issues that underlie the conduct of an individual psychological assessment. This chapter identifies many of these issues and provides a framework for assessing psychologists to use. In discussions about how several of these issues should be addressed, I have taken a strong stance. By no means, however, are my responses without alternatives that may be equally appropriate in terms of ethical, legal, and professional responsibilities. That is what makes ethical issues important to the delivery of assessment services. Alternatives must be identified and judgments made, but there can be more than one ethically sound approach or solution.

I begin with a brief discussion of the relevance of ethics to individual assessment and follow with a review of the primary resources that assessors should understand in order to develop a sound ethical code. I refer to the legal issues that have evolved regarding assessment and point out that little, if any, case law has directly addressed the fairness or legality of individual assessment in the industrial and organizational (I/O) psychology or business context. The chapter next focuses on the professional practice matters that assessors encounter. Note that separating the discussions of ethical principles and professional practice in this chapter is for purposes of conveniently organizing my commentary; it is not intended to mean that ethical principles and professional practice are in any way separable. They are not. The concluding section develops a set of recommendations for meeting the ethical, legal, and professional responsibilities associated with individual psychological assessment, and it is my intention that these suggestions integrate ethical, legal, and professional practices.

I have written this chapter from the perspective of an I/O psychologist who provides individual assessment services to organizations. However, I realize there are many other psychologists with training in other specialty areas (including clinical and counseling) who also complete individual assessments, often using processes that are similar and sometimes identical to those found in the domain of I/O psychology. Consequently, this chapter has relevance for psychologists with somewhat different backgrounds from those labeled as I/O, but who have similar purposes and client relationships when providing assessment services.

Ethical Issues

The matter of professional ethics is of greatest importance to psychologists providing consultation to organizations in the context of individual assessment. This is particularly true because the assessing psychologist typically has a dual client relationship; the assessee and the organization sponsoring the assessment are both clients of the assessor. (An exception occurs in vocational assessment, where the assessee is the only client.) Accordingly, it is especially important that assessing psychologists and the organizations they serve have a strong appreciation of the ethical parameters that define the context in which an individual assessment takes place. Further, it should be understood that ethics are part of the everyday practice of assessment rather than unique issues that arise only in extraordinary situations. Perhaps this is why many define ethics as a matter of moral behavior on the part of the assessing psychologist. In effect, one who acts unethically has behaved in a manner deemed inappropriate in terms of a recognized moral code or value system.

Understanding What Constitutes an Ethical Dilemma

The term *ethics* is derived from the Greek word *ethos*, which is translated as "custom" or "character." Thus the expectation is that ethical behavior is behavior consistent with societal customs or in accord with moral human character.

Rushworth Kidder (1995) has recently described an ethical paradigm as a dilemma that arises when one has to make a "tough choice" between two alternatives. From Kidder's perspective, which

I find especially compelling, ethical issues are not matters of right versus wrong; one of the alternatives is not immoral or illegal. Rather, either alternative is potentially the right one. Here is a hypothetical example:

> A client organization you have served for many years has a chief executive officer (CEO) whose attitudes are very well known to you. One of these attitudes is a strong opposition to marital divorce, and you are quite certain that the CEO gives little respect to a divorced individual (especially one employed by the company), regardless of the circumstances leading to the divorce and of the individual's job performance.
>
> You are conducting an assessment of a candidate seeking a position that will report directly to the CEO. It is your understanding that the candidate is well regarded so far, and the individual assessment is the last step before a final decision is made. The assessment results are outstanding from your perspective, and you have not seen an equally or better-qualified candidate for this position. However, during the course of the interview, and with no inquiry from you, the assessee confides in you that a marital separation has occurred and a divorce is imminent. You realize that had that information been known to the client, this candidate would not have made it to the assessment stage of the selection process.
>
> What, if anything, do you reveal to the candidate about the attitude of the CEO regarding divorce? What feedback and recommendation do you provide to the CEO about the candidate's fit to the job and the potential chemistry of their working relationship?

The responses to my questions and many others that could be asked about this hypothetical example must be developed in the context of the specific assessment situation. However, in developing such responses the psychologist could cast the issue into one or more of the four types of Kidder's (1995) ethical dilemmas: truth versus loyalty, individual versus community, short term versus long term, or justice versus mercy. Here are some examples of the choices these dilemmas might present within the context of an individual assessment:

- Completely honest feedback to a candidate versus loyalty to a long-term client
- Privacy rights of an assessee versus client avoidance of turmoil
- Potential for immediate impact versus likelihood of longer-term distrust

- Consideration of all the assessment results (positive and negative) versus the overlooking of certain negative results given unfortunate life history circumstances

All of Kidder's dilemmas can be found in the context of individual assessment, and each can provide alternatives that will be "right." Given the hypothetical example, one characterization within the Kidder model, truth versus loyalty, might be as follows:

Truth	*Loyalty*
Inform assessee that the organization is not tolerant of divorce and that you (the assessor) would either (1) like the assessee's permission to tell the CEO about the marital situation or (2) encourage the assessee to make the pending divorce known to the CEO as soon as possible and potentially prior to any other feedback to the client from you. The psychologist's feedback to the CEO could be completely candid about all information, including the pending divorce, if permission is granted to reveal this confidential information.	Tell the assessee that the chemistry with the CEO (including value judgment compatibility) is critical to success. Inform the CEO that you have assessed a very strong candidate, but you are concerned about "their chemistry." Do not reveal the specific issue of the pending divorce, but emphasize that based on your understanding of the CEO's expectations and value system, the working relationship could be jeopardized.

These brief characterizations are offered as a framework of potential strategies for the psychologist to consider. Certainly there are many alternative approaches, even trying to change the CEO's viewpoint regarding divorce.

Interestingly, in a study that asked ten consulting psychologists to describe how they would respond given two ethical dilemmas, George (1994) found a wide divergence in how these psychologists would resolve the issues. This divergence occurred with respect to some fundamental matters, such as who the client is, what the principles are for the client engagement, and what degree of confidentiality should be recognized. I would not be surprised if many readers have very different viewpoints from mine on how to resolve the issue in the example and other ethical and professional issues discussed in this chapter.

Participant Roles and Ethics

Understanding the ethics of assessment within an organizational setting is akin to recognizing the relevance of the issues raised by Mirvis and Seashore (1979) in their discussion of ethical consultation to organizations. The authors clearly point out that when conducting research or providing consultation to a business, the consultant must have an appreciation for the varied roles performed by all the participants: being an employee, a manager, or a member of one or more organizational units and also participating in a larger society.

Mirvis and Seashore (1979) hold that ethical consultation begins with identifying role ambiguities or conflicts and ends by resolving them through open communications. In the context of assessment the assessor's role should be clarified for each assessee, and depending on the role of any specific assessee, potential conflicts or ambiguities should be resolved at the outset. This is particularly compelling when assessees are current employees, each with unique roles and perceptions of the assessor-assessee relationship and the purpose of the assessment process. Similarly, the psychologist's role and responsibilities must be equally clear to individuals within the client organization who authorize, receive, and use assessment results. In particular it is important to define the boundaries of the assessing psychologist's role in terms of what information she or he can (or will) provide to the client organization. If we accept the traditional meaning of assessment in the broadest context, the psychologist's role is one of description, explanation, and prediction. Matters of evaluation and decision making then rest with client representatives. However, often the assessing psychologist is asked to go beyond the traditional model in terms of what conclusions can be drawn about the assessee—for example, what the likelihood of success is, what risks are associated with the assessee's selection or promotion, or what misgivings there are regarding certain undesirable behaviors. If the role is not clarified from the outset, conflict and possible ethical dilemmas are sure to arise.

Ethical Principles and Standards

Ethics evolve as the theory and practice of assessment merge. Because individual assessment has always been within the domain of psychology, a significant body of information and a number of principles exist to guide assessing psychologists. Many of these principles stem from the clinical and counseling fields of psychology, but their origin does not in any way limit their applicability to psychologists providing assessment services to organizations. These ethics are continually evolving and have become a body of knowledge concentrated in understanding the relevant issues and providing guidance for decision making. How a psychologist completes an assessment is in itself the ethics of the practice of assessment. In other words, how we treat assessees, communicate with clients, relate to professional colleagues, and use assessment results defines our ethics. Consequently, ethical principles are often not the answer to a particular problem but rather provide the perspective and prescribe the analytical process the assessor should follow to reach an appropriate answer or solution. In essence, assessors must develop and abide by a sound ethical code that guides their assessment practices. By doing so they will be able to fulfill their responsibility to both assessees and client organizations.

The foundation for an ethical assessment practice is set forth in the Ethical Principles of Psychologists and Code of Conduct published by the American Psychological Association (1992). These principles supersede those published by the APA in 1990, and they in turn will be superseded in a continuing process. The next major revision was authorized by the APA board of directors at its December 1994 meeting and is expected to take several years.

Six general principles were set forth in the 1992 ethical principles, and all apply to individual assessment. They address the areas of

1. Competence
2. Integrity

3. Professional and scientific responsibility
4. Respect for people's rights and dignity
5. Concern for others' welfare
6. Social responsibility

The areas addressed by these principles alone convey considerable information in terms of what is expected in an ethical assessment practice. The following is a brief interpretation of each principle, from my own perspective, that aligns the principle with assessment practice:

1. *Competence.* Psychologists have appropriate education, training, and experience to conduct assessments; they update their knowledge in assessment practices and properly use assessment techniques and information for their intended purposes.
2. *Integrity.* Psychologists provide truthful information and deal fairly with others; they clarify their roles and relationships; and they avoid conflicts of interest related to assessment practices.
3. *Professional and scientific responsibility.* Psychologists accept responsibility for the influences of assessment results; they confer, refer, or cooperate with other psychologists when appropriate; they do not promote the practice of assessment by unqualified individuals; and they do not use instruments that scientific research has found not to meet professionally accepted standards.
4. *Respect for people's rights and dignity.* Psychologists recognize the rights of assessees to privacy, confidentiality, self-determination, and autonomy; they are respectful of individual differences and the diversity of others; they realize that individuals' participation in assessment is voluntary; and they understand that assessees have a right to receive feedback about their assessment results.
5. *Concern for others' welfare.* Psychologists are sensitive to the welfare and needs of assessees; they attempt to avoid or minimize any harm that might result because of the assessment process; and they are cognizant of the individual's well-being when interpreting assessment results.
6. *Social responsibility.* Psychologists comply with the law and maintain awareness of social conditions that might influence how they conduct assessments.

Within the 1992 ethical principles, two major sets of standards directly apply to assessment. Standard 2 addresses evaluation, assessment, or intervention and contains ten specific guidelines related to the conduct, interpretation, feedback, and security of assessments. Standard 5 addresses privacy and confidentiality and has eleven specific guidelines applicable to the treatment and maintenance of assessment information.

Many other standards given throughout different sections of the ethical principles have either direct or tangential relevance for individual assessment matters. Examples include understanding one's boundaries of competence, nondiscrimination, maintenance of records and data, supervision of subordinates, and referral fees. George (1994) reports in her limited study the unfortunate finding that few psychologists refer to the APA ethical principles for guidance. (Canter, Bennett, Jones, & Nagy, 1994, provide an evolutionary discussion of the ethics code and describe each section of the principles in detail. Their commentary and explanations are extremely helpful for practitioners looking for further interpretation of particular principles.)

Relevant Guidelines for Ethical Practice

The APA ethical principles are augmented by the General Guidelines for Providers of Psychological Services (American Psychological Association, 1987a) and the Specialty Guidelines for the Delivery of Service (American Psychological Association, 1981b); a subset of the specialty guidelines is relevant to I/O psychology, and three of these guidelines are important for assessors. They define who providers are (setting out assessor qualifications), set forth professional considerations related to the rights of those receiving services, and establish expectations of accountability so that the effectiveness of services can be evaluated with respect to service objectives and the promotion of human welfare. In addition, a working group of the Joint Committee on Testing Practices is developing a set of test taker rights and responsibilities; its draft of these rights and responsibilities encompasses all of the concepts discussed in this chapter. Furthermore the APA has established the Task Force on Test User Qualifications, which is expected to develop a set of guidelines relevant to the knowledge and skills necessary for the responsible and competent administration, scoring, and interpretation of assessment instruments.

The *Casebook on Ethical Standards of Psychologists* (American Psychological Association, 1963) was initiated to describe matters of ethics that occurred within psychology from 1959 to 1962. The cases were descriptive of the Ethical Standards of Psychologists first published in 1953, revised in 1959, and reprinted in 1967. Additions to the casebook were published by the APA Committee on Professional Standards in the summer of every year from 1981 through 1988 and in 1994 and 1995 (American Psychological Association 1981a, 1982a, 1983, 1984, 1985, 1986, 1987a, 1988, 1994, 1995). Further the 1981 to 1986 cases have been summarized in a revised casebook (American Psychological Association, 1987b).

The Society for Industrial and Organizational Psychology (SIOP) sponsored the *Casebook on Ethics and Standards for the Practice of Psychology in Organizations* (Lowman, 1985) and its revision (Lowman, 1998). At least five of the cases in the I/O casebook have direct implications for the conduct of individual assessments. Throughout all of the available casebook materials, the underlying emphasis is on maintaining the dignity of the assessee and protecting his or her human rights. The cases are descriptive of the proper use of assessment results; the assessee's right to knowledge about the assessment techniques and the derived results, conclusions, and recommendations; confidentiality and security; and adherence to appropriate psychometric procedures. These topics and related ethical matters also have been thoroughly discussed by London and Bray (1980) and Keith-Spiegel and Koocher (1985).

Additional Resources

There are several other resources regarding ethical practice that have some relevance for those conducting psychological assessments, including some of the articles in the special issue of the *American Psychologist* devoted to testing policy, concepts, practice, and research (Glaser & Bond, 1981). Also, the Ethical Principles in the Conduct of Research with Human Participants (American Psychological Association, 1982b), now undergoing revision, are important to psychologists who may use assessment data for research purposes. These principles provide guidance with respect to matters of informed confidentiality, consent, and feedback of results. Another resource is the evolving position recently developed by the APA's Committee on Psychological Tests and Assessments with regard to the disclosure of test items, scores, and protocols (American Psychological Association, 1996). In a similar vein the APA's Joint Committee on Testing Practices has been working on the development of a code of fair testing practices, and part of its effort has been published as a code to apply to testing in education (Fremer, Diamond, & Camara, 1989).

For those using an assessment center methodology the Standards and Ethical Considerations for Assessment Center Operations (Guidelines and Ethical Considerations for Assessment Center Operations, 1989) is a valuable resource. Also, information has been published that is particularly relevant to assessments that have an underlying computer-based scoring and interpretative system. (See Eyde & Korval, 1987; Fowler, 1985; and Ryabik, Olson, & Klein, 1984.)

One final resource is the ethical statements set forth by state boards governing the certification and licensing of psychologists. Often these statements not only reinforce the APA principles but also establish guidelines for the revocation, cancellation, or suspension of certification or license due to unethical practice.

Culture and Ethics

What is considered to be ethical varies from one culture to the next. (Chapter Ten of this book discusses assessment in the context of different cultures.) As psychologists, we believe that privacy and confidentiality are universally recognized and establish the necessary trust between psychologist and assessee, but these beliefs may not always be accepted in practice. For example, some cultures outside the Judeo-Christian traditions view the basic rights of individuals and what constitutes respect for others in a very different way. These cultural differences could influence the respect given by an organization to the confidentiality of assessment reports, or organizational concern for providing feedback to assessees regarding their assessment results. Hence a psychologist whose training and experience have been confined to the United States should carefully evaluate what constitutes ethical expectations and practice if assessments are to be accomplished in other cultures. In some instances this could mean changing the assessment process to conform to cultural norms while still maintaining standards consistent with those set forth in this chapter.

Ethical Theory and Decision Making

Ethical decisions are derived from one or more ethical theories. Carroll, Schneider, and Wesley (1985) have defined three common ethical theories and point out that sometimes these theories are in conflict. One theory is ethical relativism: right and wrong actions are determined by what is approved by society, the situational context, or some other source. A second common ethical theory is utilitarianism: do that which creates the least amount of discomfort and the greatest happiness for the most number of individuals. The third theory emanates from Kant's moral philosophy: treat each person with dignity and respect, and never manipulate a person as an object. The ethical principles of psychology seem to reflect these theories, and there is every reason to make a decision regarding one matter on the basis of one ethical theory and rely on another theory for some other ethical decision.

Ethical decision making is required when the behavior of one individual affects or will affect the welfare of another. The decision maker has several sources that might be available to help her or him determine a course of action or response. Certainly, reviewing the relevant written materials referred to in this chapter is one source. A second valuable resource is to consult with colleagues and peers, and a third related strategy is to obtain some other professional advice (from a psychiatrist or lawyer, for example). Additionally, one should be certain that there is a rational reason for the decision and that it is consistent with previous decisions. Thus, one might test a solution (or alternative solutions) before a final decision is made, and as part of that test be sure that the decision promotes the welfare of the affected individual.

Ethics in Summary

Ethics attempt to make sense of issues by drawing on experience and past practices to derive guidelines and standards of professional practice and behavior that are consistent with the purpose of psychology and the application of a relevant body of associated knowledge and techniques labeled individual psychological assessment. There are times when the ethics of business and those of assessment professionals are incompatible. The business manager may well expect from the assessor personal information about an assessee that is clearly confidential within the context of the assessment. Because assessing psychologists are in a position of trust and directly influence the welfare of assessees, these psychologists must have an ethical perspective to guide their actions and decisions to the benefit of those involved in the assessment process. Unfortunately, according to Carroll, Schneider, and Wesley (1985), after examining complaints against consulting psychologists, it was evident that these psychologists identified more with their clients' interests than with those of the individuals who complained. A subsequent section of this chapter provides a framework for addressing potential conflicts that might arise for psychologists when working with both assessees and clients. Further, at the conclusion of the chapter I suggest a set of ethical principles specifically intended to guide individual assessments in organizations.

Legal Issues Underlying Individual Assessment

Individual assessment, like other forms of testing and evaluation associated with employment, is within the purview of the Civil Rights Acts of 1866, 1964 (Title VII), and 1991; the Uniform Guidelines on Employee Selection Procedures (43 Fed. Reg. 38 [1978], 290–38, 315); and associated case law (Bersoff, 1981; Jeanneret, 1988; Novick, 1981). Assessment procedures and outcomes are also covered by the Age Discrimination in Employment Act (1967), section 504 of the Rehabilitation Act of 1973, and the Americans with Disabilities Act of 1990.

I am not aware of any legal suit based on civil rights and equal employment opportunity law that specifically complains about a traditional individual psychological assessment conducted by an assessing psychologist for an employment or organizational purpose. This does not mean we should ignore the warning of Carroll, Schneider, and Wesley (1985), who believe that organizational psychologists are especially vulnerable to litigation. Furthermore there are several tangential cases that may be establishing some relevant precedents in the event of an individual assessment lawsuit.

Lawsuits that involve assessment centers clearly have identified relevant issues underlying the potential for illegal discrimination, although to date the decisions regarding such suits have generally supported the assessment center process (*Progressive Officer's Club* v. *Metropolitan Dade County* [U.S., Southern District of Florida, 1989]; *Wilson* v. *Michigan Bell Telephone Co.* 550 F. Supp. 1296. [D.C. Michigan 1978]), although not in every case (for example, *Firefighters Institute for Racial Equality* v. *City of St. Louis, Missouri*, 616 F.2d 350 [8th Cir. 1980]). The reasonableness of filing a suit alleging discrimination by an assessment has been given credence by the U.S. Supreme Court's ruling in *Watson* v. *Fort Worth Bank and Trust* (108 S.Ct. 2791 [1988]) that a subjective employment-related decision (such as the outcome of an individual assessment) could be examined by a court of law under a disparate impact model (see Bersoff, 1988). Another tangential legal issue has evolved from *Tarasoff* v. *Regents of the University of California* (Cal. Rptr. 14, No. S.F. 23042 [1976]), which held that an assessor must protect potential victims from an assessee's violence. *Tarasoff* is the model for all psychologists, even though the case involved a psychotherapeutic relationship. Other matters of law that may influence the conduct of assessments are privacy rights, open records laws, and defamation issues (Kress, 1989). Finally, legal disputes primarily evolving within the education arena that may have relevance for assessment procedures include the use of standardized tests to place individuals (*Larry P. by Lucille P.* v. *Riles*, 793 F.2d 969 [9th Cir. 1984]; *PASE* v. *Hannon*, 506 F. Supp. 831 [N.D. Ill. 1980]), truth-in-testing matters (see Elliott, 1987), and security of test materials (*Detroit Edison Co.* v. *National Labor Relations Board*, 440 U.S. 301 [1979]).

State laws governing the certification and licensing of psychologists also establish a legal framework for psychological assessments. Although the matter of licensing also may be considered an ethical-professional issue, it is clear that any psychologist conducting an assessment in a state with laws governing the practice of psychology must be licensed. Licensure is designed to offer the public some assurance that an individual practitioner is qualified to provide the professional service offered to a client. When psychologists offer an individual assessment service, they have immediate and direct influence on the personal lives and careers of assessees; these assessees therefore are entitled to some assurance that the psychologists are competent to render their services.

Although the licensing process cannot make guarantees of competence, particularly with respect to one type of service (in this case, individual assessment), it does provide a mechanism for complaint and review, and it reinforces for psychologists their obligations and ethical responsibilities regarding the assessments they complete. Consequently, a psychologist offering individual assessment services would be operating outside the scope of any state law that includes assessment practice as a part of the psychological services covered by the statute.

Although there has been opposition to licensure within the field of I/O psychology (Howard & Lowman, 1985), the majority (73 percent) of assessing psychologists responding to a survey of SIOP members report they are licensed (Ryan & Sackett, 1987). Some I/O psychologists are not licensed because the state where they practice does not offer them a licensing opportunity. This is regrettable, but occurs in only a few states. Ryan and Sackett (1987) also have reported that research and testing represented areas of work activity for 55 percent of individual assessors and that an academic institution was the primary employment setting for 23 percent of the assessors. (This latter finding also might account in part for why some assessors are not licensed, because some states provide exemption from licensure to psychologists employed in academia.) However, the Ryan and Sackett findings are still rather surprising given the type and intensity of experience appropriate for assessing psychologists, the legal parameters that encompass assessment techniques and decisions, and the ethical considerations that should guide an assessment practice.

Professional Practice Issues

Closely allied to the topic of ethics is the matter of professional practice. In fact many would equate unprofessional practice and unethical practice. I am specifically referring to the technical standards and resources that are relevant for assessing psychologists. These resources are well known to I/O psychologists, because the standards apply to a major segment of the profession, not just to the conduct of individual assessments. The most relevant references are the Standards for Education and Psychological Testing (American Educational Research Association, American Psychological Association, & National Council on Measurement in Education, 1985), which are undergoing revision, and the Principles for the Validation and Use of Personnel Selection Procedures (Society for Industrial and Organizational Psychology, 1987). These two primary references set forth the fundamental psychometric parameters that must be met by any assessment technique or procedure. In addition to the overriding message that any assessment measure should be reliable and valid, both documents address matters related to interpreting results, selection decision making, administration of assessment instruments, and periodic auditing of procedures.

Also included within the realm of professional practice are topics associated with the proper administration of assessment materials. The qualifications of test users and administrators have long been a concern of the APA, as well as many commercial test publishers. The qualifications issue was recently studied by Moreland, Eyde, Robertson, Primoff, and Most (1995), who identified eighty-six competencies for test users and seven factors that accounted for potential test misuse. The authors contend that emphasizing competencies in test use and administration is more valuable than relying solely on some credentialing process. Thus the intent is to educate users in proper testing practices rather than restrict the availability or use of tests. In this scenario good professional practice also will be good ethical practice.

The Interface of Ethics and Practice

The essence of assessment ethics is that the application of the assessment process should be evaluated in terms of its potential consequences: Is the assessment appropriate for the intended purpose, and will it be conducted in an appropriate manner? Messick (1965) was the first to raise this issue, pointing out that whether a test is appropriate for the intended purpose is a psychometric question; how a test is implemented is an ethical matter. In a similar way, Haney (1981) reasoned that social concerns and political philosophies affect issues of a psychometric nature such as validity, utility, and evaluations of fairness. Burton (1978) suggested that the underlying linkage was accomplished through validation: that the validity of a test in effect is an "ethical guarantee" (requirement) that a test can be used for the intended purpose. If the validity evidence is sufficient, then the ethical issue can be answered in terms of social values.

Messick (1975) has argued that all validity evidence should be "construct referenced," and his argument is strongly supported by Guion (1976) when considered in the context of selection and placement. Following from that position, Messick (1980) has developed a model linking construct validity, test interpretations, and ethical considerations. The lesson to be learned from the Messick model is that we base our interpretations of assessment results on a construct validity argument and then verify the ethical implications of our interpretations. Let us say that a psychologist assesses a specific job-related construct, perhaps conscientiousness, and interprets the assessment measure for a particular individual as presenting very low conscientiousness. The psychologist will make several ethical decisions in how the assessee's result for conscientiousness is treated. These decisions include whether it is appropriate to assess conscientiousness as part of the assessment in the first place, whether it is consistent with the proposed use and utility of the assessment, whether there are any social implications, and what other consequences might be associated with the conscientiousness measurement and interpretation. For example, would the low score mean that the assessee might mishandle monies if he or she were in a position of financial responsibility? And should that interpretation be communicated to the client or the assessee? As Messick (1980) has stated, the purpose of the model is to "emphasize the point that tests are rarely used in isolation but rather in combination with other information in broader decision systems" (p. 1025). Clearly, one of these decision systems is the ethical implications of the assessment process, and the implications that arise for determining assessment use, interpreting results, and making employment-related decisions with these assessment results.

Ethical and Practice Issues for Assessors

The following ethical and practice issues that every assessor should consider address relationships, procedures, and individual rights. Although the coverage is not exhaustive, I consider it representative. (Some of these topics are also discussed in the *Statement on the*

Disclosure of Test Data, a report of the APA Committee on Psychological Tests and Assessment (American Psychological Association, 1996).

To begin with, two topics are often of immediate concern to an individual (assessee) entering an assessment process: confidentiality and consent. Both emerge from the individual's right of privacy.

Confidentiality

Confidentiality is a broad topic that encompasses many subtopics and issues that interact with other ethical and professional practice matters. It has important and somewhat different meanings from the perspective of the assessor, the assessee, and the client organization. The assessor has a responsibility to manage confidentiality issues for all three of these entities.

In its most straightforward form, confidentiality means that there is a high degree of trust between two parties (the assessor and the assessee or the assessor and the client organization) and that the assessor will protect the well-being of the assessee. For the assessor this responsibility begins with the intent to keep privileged communications confidential. From the assessee's perspective there is clearly potential concern regarding the power the assessor might hold because of information revealed by test responses, by interpretations of test responses, or by admissions that come forth during an interview. By the same token, this level of trust implies that the assessee will be honest and truthful in responding to the assessment methodology.

Robinson and Gross (1985) extend the degree of trust even further with the proposition that all information obtained about an assessee should be confidential. If we examine this assertion more closely, there is reason to argue that confidentiality issues fall along a continuum. At one end are assessor-assessee understandings that all assessment findings are confidential in the sense that they are not to be shared with other individuals. This might be a reasonable expectation for assessments of a purely developmental or career counseling nature. At the other end of the continuum is the assessment conducted with the explicit purpose of uncovering any behavior that may be associated with instability or some asocial characteristic, and all information obtained about the assessee will be available to those with a need to know. In most instances that assessors working in organizational settings would encounter, this latter end of the continuum will be a rare event, if it occurs at all. Accordingly, when information is obtained that would be unfavorable to the assessee, the psychologist usually is not in a position of having to reveal it to others. One side of the confidentiality equation involves the relationship between the assessor and client organization. In this instance the psychologist is advised to establish the level of confidentiality to be expected at the time of engagement so there are no misunderstandings later.

One of the most effective means for addressing the psychologist-assessee confidentiality issue is for the assessor to describe the ground rules to the assessee up front. Included in this explanation is information about the purpose of the assessment, the nature of the assessment process, who will receive the assessment results and in what form, and what the assessee can expect once the assessment is concluded. Also, I inform the assessee at the outset of an interview that if he or she intends to confide in me information that may be especially sensitive or confidential, to let me know when the information is forthcoming. In that way I can more readily judge whether it is information I even want to learn about, and I can be careful not to ask questions that may merely serve my own curiosity and otherwise would be invasive of the assessee's privacy.

I also inform assessees that confidentiality includes the protection of their results from third parties. No one without a clear need to know should have access to the results of an assessment. I do not divulge assessment results to anyone else without the written permission of the assessee and the client organization. If written permission is granted, I will release results to a qualified psychologist or psychiatrist as directed by the assessee. I have been able to follow this practice throughout my entire career with two exceptions, and then the releases were made only after court orders and protective custody covenants were granted for the assessment records. Anyone who has a need for guidance in responding to legal notices requesting confidential information can refer to "Strategies for Private Practitioners Coping with Subpoenas or Compelled Testimony for Client Records or Test Data," prepared by the APA's Committee on Legal Issues (obtainable from the Office of the APA

General Counsel, 750 First Street, NE, Washington, DC 20002). This document offers suggestions for managing the conflicting demands of litigation, privacy rights, and ethical principles.

Confidentiality has a few other meanings for the assessing psychologist. One is that the psychologist will protect assessment instruments (uncompleted and completed) and related information (scoring keys, norms, manuals, and so forth) and also interview notes and other documents developed during the course of an assessment. In this context the protection includes not releasing assessment instruments or associated documents to unauthorized individuals or organizations. It also means maintaining adequate records of the assessment. Although the guidelines are not completely clear for assessments conducted for work-related purposes, I believe assessment records should be maintained for a minimum of seven years. Subsequently, the records can be destroyed in a manner that befits any confidential document (such as shredding). Note that record-keeping duration does not certify that the assessment information is in fact valid for that length of time. Rather, it may be that certain types of assessment information are relevant for only a specific situation and for a short period of time. The reason for the longer record-keeping period will be to conform to other record retention practices, make assessment comparisons over time, and be responsive to legitimate assessee inquiries.

Still another aspect of confidentiality involves how the client organization retains assessment reports. Clearly such reports are not part of the standard personnel file, and the assessing psychologist needs to educate the client on how to store reports so that they are retained in a highly secure manner with very limited access to only those who have a need to know. In a discussion of the issue of confidentiality within the context of organizational consulting, Newman and Robinson (1991) point out that confidentiality depends not only on the behavior of the psychologist, but also on the actions of those in an organization, depending on who has access to confidential information. They imply that the parameters of confidentiality are not inherent to the assessing psychologist-organization relationship but must be negotiated up front and that such negotiations should define who has access to what information.

Consent

Although the matter of consent seems to be relatively straight-forward on the surface, it has extensive implications for ethical practice. In the most obvious sense the assessee gives consent by participating in the assessment process. In this case, there are several immediate implications:

- The assessee is participating voluntarily and is not being coerced.
- The assessee is informed as to the nature of the process, the purpose of the assessment, and the use of the results.
- The assessment results can be shared with the designated individual(s) representing the client organization.
- The assessee has a right to know the results of the assessment.

Most psychologists expect that assessees appear for assessments voluntarily, but I have seen exceptions. Sometimes I have been made aware of assessees' concerns about being "required" to participate in an assessment the moment they arrived at my office, other times I have learned this information during the course of test administration, and still other concerns about coercion have not arisen until the assessment interview was underway. My position has always been that the assessee has the right to discontinue participation in the assessment at any time, and my responsibility is to be sure the individual has enough accurate and adequate information about the assessment to make a rational decision. The connection between consent and individual rights to privacy is clear, as is the fact that the assessor must respect the assessee's freedom to choose whether to participate in an assessment process. In essence, consent is always required before an assessment can begin.

I noted in the section on confidentiality the need to provide information to an assessee about the assessment process, its purpose, and the use of its results. Such information is also relevant to the concept of consent. In essence a person cannot rationally consent to participate in a process unless he or she has an adequate understanding of its contents, purposes, and outcomes. Also, it is important that the assessment be conducted under conditions that create minimal anxiety for the assessee—for example, quiet testing and interview settings, adequate lighting, and professional administration of all assessment measures. The issue of the assessee's consent to share information with either a client representative or a third party is best addressed before the assessment begins by having the assessee read and sign a specific form explaining the assessment process. (Exhibit 4.1 provides an example of such a form.) In essence the assessee knows who will receive the assessment results and that no information will be released to a third-party professional without explicit permission from the assessee

Exhibit 4.1. Informed Consent Form for Individual Assessment.

Informed Consent for Assessment

Name _____   SSN _____

Address _____

Occupation _____

Home Phone _____   Work Phone _____

I consent to participate in an assessment by the firm of _____ _____. I understand that this assessment is being performed at the request of _____ as part of an overall process to determine my suitability for employment as _____. I understand that I will take a battery of written tests and will be interviewed by a psychologist. I understand that a report will be provided to the requesting organization and will become property of _____ _____ and that such files will be kept confidential and will be released: (a) only to another qualified professional and only with prior written consent from both myself and the original client organization; or (b) for personal therapeutic treatment and/or services, only to another qualified professional and only with my prior written consent.

Signed _____

Date   _____

and the client. The consent form also specifically identifies the job title of the position to which the assessment applies, if it is known, so there is no misunderstanding as to the position for which the individual is being considered by the client organization. Another component of consent is related to the ownership of the assessment data. When completing responses to tests and giving answers to interview questions, the assessee creates a data file for the psychologist. Under the parameters of consent the psychologist has ownership of that data and assumes all the attendant responsibilities for it.

The final aspect of consent in my opinion is the most important issue of all. An individual's consent to participate in an assessment establishes his or her right to receive feedback about the results, as long as that feedback does not adversely affect the assessee's welfare. Stated in another way, because assessment is a form of invasion of privacy, the assessee has a right to know what aspects of his or her public and private life have been revealed and what interpretations are being made about those revelations.

One caution that the psychologist must exercise is how to communicate information that might have severe negative implications from the assessee's viewpoint. Two major issues emerge here: what to tell the client representative and what to tell the assessee. With respect to the former the psychologist could be faced with determining when the welfare of the client takes precedence over the assessee's right to confidentiality. For example, say that an assessing psychologist learns that an assessee has a substance abuse problem. If the assessment is being conducted for selection into a safety-sensitive job (security officer or nuclear plant operations manager, for instance), then the psychologist would seem obliged to inform the client. Further the assessee should be told that the problem was going to be revealed to the client, and the assessee should be encouraged to seek treatment. The problem perhaps becomes more difficult if the job is, say, that of chief financial officer or perhaps regional sales manager. Because it is not possible to develop all of the circumstances that might be encountered, no general rule or standard can be defined. However, the existing ethical principles should be followed as closely as possible, and the psychologist should use those principles as a foundation for all decision making associated with what to tell a client.

The second issue concerns the feedback of negative information to the assessee. Under some circumstances the assessor's judgment could be to withhold information if it was believed to be harmful to the assessee's welfare—for example, if a psychologist determined the presence of severe depression or concluded that the assessee had an asocial personality disorder. Rather than communicate that information directly, the psychologist might find avenues to guide the assessee to consider counseling with a professional with clinical training, with referral services if so requested by the assessee. (For further discussion of the feedback issue, see Petzelt & Craddick, 1978, and Chapter Eight.)

Assessment feedback can be oral or written; my preference is for oral feedback at the conclusion of the assessment interview, especially if the purpose is for selection rather than development or career planning. If written reports are prepared, there are the questions of who has access to the reports and whether the assessees should receive copies. This is a matter of choice and not a matter of ethics in my view, and either or both forms of feedback may be appropriate. (Chapters Five and Eight provide more detail regarding the purpose and content of oral and written reports.)

In the eyes of the APA ethical principles not all assessments require feedback; exceptions include organizational consulting and preemployment screening. Unfortunately, the APA language is subject to varying interpretation and provides a loophole that may not be justified. On the one hand, for example, if preemployment screening refers to the administration of a battery of tests (typically comprising ability and job-specific measures and frequently administered to groups of candidates), then specific feedback may not be justified or practical. Often there are large numbers of test takers, tests with established cutoff scores, and no opportunities for assessees to have individual interviews with a psychologist. Many such testing programs are focused on skills and abilities rather than personal characteristics, and there may not be much diagnostic information available other than that the candidate passed or failed. On the other hand, if preemployment screening refers to an individual assessment of an external candidate for an executive, managerial, sales, or other type of organizational position, then I believe assessee feedback is required. Similarly, because most individual assessments are used for succession planning, management development, and similar activities, I find no justification for not providing assessees with feedback.

The APA ethical principles are not fully explicit in terms of who may provide the feedback. They state, "Regardless of whether the screening and interpretation are done by the psychologist, by assistants, or by automated or other outside services, psychologists take reasonable steps to ensure that appropriate explanations of results are given." One interpretation of this statement might be that a psychologist could delegate feedback to an assistant or perhaps a computer. I believe, however, that the assessing psychologist, or an equally competent colleague if necessary, should always provide the feedback. Thus, with respect to both "exceptions" and the feedback "source," I find the ethical principles to be less than definitive and perhaps misleading as to what should be required of I/O psychologists providing individual assessment services. At least the ethical principles do require the assessing psychologist to explain and reach agreement in advance of the assessment process if feedback to the assessee will not be provided. Presumably at this point if there is not to be feedback, the individual would have full justification for not participating in the assessment.

Finally, consideration should be given to the content of the feedback. Although this is not entirely a matter of ethics, there is, in part, an ethical rationale for determining what to include in the assessment feedback. Specifically, the assessee must receive explanations that are understandable and not couched in psychological jargon; the assessee must receive interpretations rather than specific raw test scores and these interpretations must be described in normative, ipsative, or comparative ways; the assessee must understand the limitations as well as the capabilities of assessment to provide relevant information about him or her; and the assessment results should have meaningful relationships to other indicators, including an assessee's life history, job performance, feedback from others, and self-appraisals of behavior. This last point can be especially valuable, allowing the assessee to understand the assessment outcome in terms of actual life experiences—for example, that the assessment tells him that he is not very detail oriented and has received feedback from others at work and at home that he is sometimes careless or otherwise prone to make unnecessary mistakes.

Procedures

Many topics that define the boundaries of ethical practice can be considered procedural. In this section, I discuss those few that have come to my attention with some degree of regularity.

Marketing Assessment Services Ethically

Ethical marketing of individual assessment services is no different from ethical delivery of those services. However, certain marketing strategies may be judged unethical in themselves—for example, advertising that "guarantees" specific increases in workforce productivity, or that provides a comprehensive written analysis of a person's effectiveness as an executive through "mail-order testing," or that offers a referral fee to the person who sends an assessment user prospect to your business doorstep. (As a matter of ethical practice, any payments tendered should be for professional services and not referrals; see the APA's 1992 Ethical Code of Conduct, 1.27.) Still another example would be to assert that a specific assessment technique has established psychometric capabilities and is in conformance with professional and legal standards when in fact no scientific research has been conducted to verify such assertions. (Any form of misrepresentation would be in violation of the 1992 Ethical Code of Conduct; see 3.03.)

Using Assessment Instruments Without Established Validity

The reality is that few, if any, of the most frequently used assessment instruments, including the individual assessment interview, have reported validity in the form of specific research studies within the context of an individual assessment, let alone for an assessment conducted for a specific purpose within a particular organization. Yet most, if not all, of the well-constructed instruments do have established construct validity. Furthermore there is growing evidence in the research literature that predictors used in assessment settings, as well as assessment outcomes (predictions) and interviews, have some predictive validity. (See Chapters Three and Nine for discussions of this validity evidence.) Consequently, I believe most psychologist-assessors generalize from what validity data do exist to their specific applications and are satisfied that they are not practicing in an unethical manner.

This does not relieve psychologists of all responsibility for testing hypotheses about the validity of instruments and evaluative processes when used within the context of individual assessment. Follow-up research is recommended whenever possible so that we can more fully understand the validity and effectiveness of individual assessment practices.

Location of Test Completion

Should assessees be allowed to complete tests in another environment (say, at home)? There is no clear-cut answer to this question, and the most recent information from the APA's Ethics Panel, dating back to July 1973, gives some guidance but no single conclusion. In effect the decision is that of the assessor, who must consider the nature and purpose of the assessment, standardization of procedures across assessees, publisher restrictions, and related topics. I would argue that instruments that have a level C restriction (use only by a qualified psychologist) should not be given as take-home materials under any circumstance, and obviously tests of cognitive ability should be administered only under the conditions specified by the test developers.

Responsibilities of Organizations Using Psychological Assessment

The information on ethical and professional issues in the conduct of individual assessments is all directed toward the assessing psychologist. What is usually missing is guidance to the organization sponsoring the assessment with regard to relevant ethical matters (Jeanneret, 1989). Yet the organization has responsibilities to the assessee and the assessor that can influence the professional and ethical environment in which the assessment takes place.

An organization is responsible for providing the assessee with appropriate preparatory information regarding the assessment itself and maintaining the confidentiality of assessment results. The organization also should have a well-defined procedure for integrating the assessment information into its decision making and for communicating (internally and to assessees) decisions based on assessment results and opportunities for future reassessment. Finally, the organization must respect the dignity and rights of the assessee, and not try to gain from the assessor information that is privileged or otherwise is not relevant to the expressed purpose of the assessment.

Because organizations typically do not have a comprehensive understanding of their assessment responsibilities, the most likely source of such information is the assessment psychologist. However, there are indications, based on a relatively limited number of psychologist and client interviews by George (1994), that consulting psychologists are not as diligent as clinical psychologists in defining the client relationship. Further, she found the client representatives (chief executive officers) did not give much thought to the ethics of how a consulting psychologist was practicing in the organization. These officers seemed to conclude that the psychologist would do what was ethically correct.

There are several ways in which the psychologist can promote effective organizational practices with respect to assessment matters. One strategy is to prepare an assessment policy template covering the organization's responsibilities, which each organization can then modify and adopt. Additionally, the psychologist can assist the organization in preparing a written description of the assessment process that can be given to an individual in advance. (Exhibit 4.2 contains an example of such a description.) Finally, to help maintain confidentiality and enhance the understanding of the strengths and limitations of assessment results, the written reports submitted to an organization should provide proper notification. (An example of one type of statement that appears as an introduction to an assessment report is presented in Exhibit 4.3).

Responsibilities of the organization to the assessing psychologist include providing access to relevant job analysis and organizational and performance data that bear on the assessment process and interpretation of results. This is important because often the assessment is providing as much information about the fit of an individual to an organization and its culture as it is about the match between the assessee's characteristics and the requirements of a specific job. Ideally, organizations also will be supportive of research to evaluate assessment techniques and outcomes.

Table 4.1 presents a summary of the responsibilities of both the psychologist and the client organization with respect to the delivery of individual assessment services. Typically the psychologist will

Exhibit 4.2. Descriptive Information About the Assessment Process Provided to Assessees.

Individual Assessment

You will be participating in an individual assessment process that will give you the opportunity to provide information about yourself, your interests, and your abilities. The assessment includes:

- Some paper-and-pencil tests that are designed to evaluate cognitive abilities, interests, and individual characteristics
- An interview with one of our licensed psychologists, during which you can provide more details about yourself, and any questions you may have about the process can be addressed
- A summary review of the assessment results that will let you know the kind of information that will be reported about you and can help you determine how closely the job you are considering matches the way you work

Our goal is to provide an environment in which you can do your best. We recognize that a variety of factors can influence your willingness and ability to respond to the test items. We will attempt to reduce the influence of any hindering factors.

Understanding Instructions

You need to have a clear understanding of the test instructions. If you are unsure about what you are to do or have questions about any test, please ask. The Test Administrator will answer your questions or arrange for a psychologist to do so.

Noise or Distractions

If background noise is bothering you during the testing process, please let the Test Administrator know about it. While we make every attempt to provide a quiet testing environment, there are a variety of activities taking place in our offices. The Test Administrator will take steps to reduce any noise or other distractions.

Physical Conditions

If you have problems with lighting, temperature, or other conditions in the testing area, let the Test Administrator know. Although our ability to control some aspects of the environment (such as building temperature) is limited, we will make every effort to correct the problem.

Breaks and Refreshments

During the testing, if you need to stretch your legs, get some fresh air or a bite to eat, make a phone call, or take a break for any other reason, please feel free to tell the Test Administrator. The Test Administrator also will direct you to the rest room facilities. Water, coffee, juices, and soft drinks will be available to you.

**Exhibit 4.2. Descriptive Information About the
Assessment Process Provided to Assessees** (continued).

Accommodating Disabilities

If you have a disability that would make it difficult for you to complete the assessment tests in their usual formats, in the allowable time limits, or in the testing location, we will make every attempt to accommodate you. If you need a particular accommodation, please notify the Test Administrator of your request. The Test Administrator will work with you and the assessing psychologist, if necessary, to identify possible accommodations that will enable you to complete the assessment while maintaining the integrity of the process.

Taking Tests

The tests you will be taking cover a broad range of subjects, some of which you may be more comfortable with than others. If you think that you will not perform well on one test or another, do not worry about it. Everyone has different areas of strength and weakness. How all the parts of your assessment fit together is more important than how you perform on any single test.

We encourage you to be accurate and forthright in responding to the test items and to attempt to respond to all of them. Eliminating items can reduce the accuracy of the assessment. Please keep in mind that your responses to items will be grouped for analysis, resulting in an overall profile. However, if you find an item particularly upsetting or offensive and would be uncomfortable answering it, you may choose to skip that item.

Feedback and Report

At the conclusion of the interview, the psychologist will review the assessment results with you. If you have questions about the results, please discuss them with the assessing psychologist.

The written and oral information you provide will be used to prepare a report that describes your particular abilities, interests, and work style. This report will be used as one part of the overall process. The report will focus on the extent to which your individual strengths match those needed in the job for which you are being assessed.

It is important to us that the assessment process be as productive as possible and that, regardless of the purpose and outcome, you are given an opportunity to perform as well as possible.

Complaints

Our assessment practice is under the purview of the _____ Board of Examiners of Psychologists. If you have a complaint that is not satisfactorily handled by our psychological staff, a representative of the Board can be reached at _____ or by writing to

_____ .

Exhibit 4.3. Statement About Confidentiality and Use of Assessment Reports.

Value and Use of Assessment Reports

The enclosed assessment report contains information about this individual that can aid you in making selection, placement, or promotional decisions. The report provides insight into the individual's occupational interests, work habits, motivational characteristics, and likely reactions to various work environments and supervisory styles.

Since everyone has strengths and weaknesses, special caution must be exercised to consider this assessment as a whole. Be careful not to overemphasize specific statements, but rather take into account the person's overall suitability for the specific position in your particular organizational environment.

The primary purpose of the assessment is to describe the individual's characteristics as accurately as possible. To minimize chances of erroneous decisions, you should integrate this report with information from other sources (for example, interview impressions, employment references, work experience, job competence, work habits, and personal background). Occasionally you may encounter a statement that surprises you. Evaluation of the other information sources should indicate whether the statement is more reflective of overt behavior or of rarely surfaced tendencies. Further, the assessment may provide indications of areas on which to focus during reference checks or interviews with the individual.

Of course, people may change over the years, sometimes in unpredictable ways. If more than a few years have elapsed since the date of this report, its findings must be carefully weighed and modified by new evidence and information. Organizations change too, and these changes could well affect the recommendations of this report. Assessments that are clearly out of date or affect individuals who are not employed by your organization should be destroyed.

Amplifications

During an assessment we collect many more data than are possible to communicate in this report. These data are available should you want clarification of points or have other questions. We will be happy to answer your questions and otherwise to assist you in understanding this assessment through personal contact. All of our data will remain in our files and will be released only to a qualified psychologist at the specific request of our client and the individual assessed.

Confidentiality

Because of the nature of appraisal information and the dangers of its misuse, the report is a confidential document, and its contents should be restricted to as few people as possible. During personal interviews with the psychologist, individuals are normally given feedback on their test results. Whether they received feedback or not, assessment reports should not be shown to them or specific contents discussed with them. Unless a qualified psychologist or counselor is present during the feedback session, there is a strong possibility of erroneous interpretation, misunderstandings, dissension, or disclosure of information that the individual may be unable to handle psychologically.

Table 4.1. Summary of Responsibilities
for Assessors and Organizations.

Assessor Responsibilities	Organization Responsibilities
Confidentiality	*Confidentiality*
Keep privileged communications with assessee confidential in accord with assessment purpose.	Maintain strict confidentiality of all assessment communications, including reports.
Inform organization of parameters associated with the confidentiality of assessment information aligned with the purpose of the assessment.	Keep assessment reports separate from the standard personnel file.
	Define who can have access to assessment information.
Safeguard confidentiality of assessment instruments and related materials, interview notes, and reports.	Provide relevant information to the assessee about the assessment purpose and use of the results.
Consent	Respect the dignity and privacy rights of the assessee.
Only expect voluntary participation on part of assessee.	Inform the assessee regarding how assessment results are communicated internally.
Explain assessment ground rules to assessee up front (purpose; who receives results; what assessee can expect in terms of feedback; how results are used; and so forth).	*Other*
	Guide the assessor in terms of providing information that describes the organizational context, job requirements (competencies), and explicit purpose for assessment.
Obtain assessee consent in writing.	
Provide assessee with feedback regarding assessment results that is understandable.	Give assessee adequate information in advance of assessment.
Properly select, use, and interpret assessment instruments, consistent with the organizational context, job requirements, and assessment purpose.	Make commitment that all assessees will receive feedback.
	Make appropriate use of assessment results in decision making.
Other	Ensure that the assessor is competent.
Encourage research regarding assessment processes.	Do not extend life of assessment data.
Market assessment capabilities accurately and without guarantees.	Support assessment research.

take the initiative on these matters and provide assistance to the organization in meeting its responsibilities. Although having the organization create a written policy covering its responsibilities clearly represents the ideal, there is no reason that these obligations cannot be carried out in practice without a written policy.

Meeting Legal, Ethical, and Professional Requirements

Individual psychological assessment cannot be separated from the professional training, competence, and ethical values of those psychologists rendering assessment services. How closely psychologists adhere to the legal, ethical, and professional requirements has been addressed to some degree by Ryan and Sackett (1987). They report that among a sample of individual assessors who responded to their survey, 73 percent are licensed, 80 percent offer feedback to the assessee, 73 percent make at least some attempt to validate the assessment process, and only 7 percent and 4 percent do not believe that their procedures conform to the Uniform Guidelines or the APA Test Standards, respectively. These, of course, are self-report data and in some instances may be presented from the most favorable perspective. I believe that ethical and professional obligations in the context of individual assessment require the following:

- All assessors should be licensed. To the degree that licensure adds to the likelihood that the assessee will be treated in accord with the ethical code of psychology and provides penalties if that is not the case, then the licensure requirement is appropriate and accomplishes its intended objective.
- All assessees should receive feedback. No doubt there are exceptions to this premise, but as long as the individual assessment process includes interaction between the psychologist and assessee, there is ample opportunity for feedback at the time of an assessment or shortly after.
- Every attempt should be made to ensure that the assessment procedures are valid and in compliance with relevant standards, principles, and legislation. This is an admittedly difficult requirement because of the lack of knowledge about the psychometrics of most instruments when used in the individ-

ual assessment setting. Consequently, the assessing psychologist should select instruments and procedures that have established reliability and validity and some relevance to the assessment setting (for instance, used in selection studies or with demonstrated applicability for measuring requirements of jobs to which the assessment will apply).

There are four fundamental precepts that can guide the conduct of individual psychological assessments and also meet the relevant legal, ethical, and professional requirements (Jeanneret, 1989, 1990). The first requires the development and implementation of formal written assessment policies on the part of both the assessor and the organization sponsoring the assessment. These policies should set forth the purpose of an assessment and dictate the use of the results. The policies should directly address the feedback of assessment results and otherwise ensure the protection of all assessee rights. Finally, the policies should document the administrative issues associated with assessment, and especially matters related to assessment report storage and access by those with a reason to know.

Second, the development and conduct of assessment procedures should be guided by appropriate job analysis, job requirements, and organizational environment information. Essential activities include defining job requirements, demands, and competencies and establishing assessment dimensions on the basis of both job-relevant and organizational data; determining how assessment dimensions are going to be measured using the best available psychometric techniques; and, when feasible, developing organization-specific normative data as quickly as possible.

Third, assessors should be qualified professionally and legally and fit well with the sponsoring organization. This includes having an assessment style and practice consistent with the organization's assessment policy. Assessors must recognize their own limits and capabilities in terms of both services offered and requests that may be made of them. Under no circumstances should they misrepresent those capabilities.

Fourth, it should be recognized that assessment results are usually not meant to stand alone; rather, these results should be integrated with other relevant information obtained from various components of an organization's human resource information and management system.

Resolving Ethical Dilemmas

From the writings of Carroll, Schneider, and Wesley (1985), Kidder (1995), Messick (1965, 1975, 1980), and all those who have participated in the preparation of ethical principles and cases, we have learned that making decisions regarding an ethical issue or resolving an ethical dilemma is no different from any other cognitive problem solving. However, the decision making or resolution cannot begin unless one realizes that an ethical dilemma exists. If you know you are facing an ethical issue, and it is one for which you are a responsible party, then you should initiate a fact-finding effort. Once the facts are in hand, there are three principles that can be queried to guide the resolution of the dilemma:

1. *Follow-the-rule principle.* Select the alternative that you expect anyone else to follow. In effect you follow the rule regardless of how you might envision the outcome.
2. *Utilitarian principle.* Select the alternative that provides the greatest benefit to the largest number of people. In this instance the outcome is most important and justifies the decision.
3. *Golden Rule principle.* Select the alternative that would treat others the way you would want to be treated. This principle is focused on an empathic concern for people rather than on rules or outcomes.

It is possible that two or even three of the principles could apply to a specific ethical dilemma, and certainly no one principle is superior to another. However, within the context of ethical issues that arise regarding individual assessment, it is very likely that the Golden Rule principle is the one many assessors would use to resolve their dilemmas. Furthermore, to the extent that rules are developed that take the form of assessment policies for both the assessor and sponsoring organization, then such rules can frequently guide the resolution of ethical dilemmas.

Staying Ethically Fit

Kidder titled Chapter Three of his 1995 book "Ethical Fitness," a term that I find especially relevant for assessing psychologists. Ethical fitness means being both intellectually involved and emotionally committed to resolving ethical dilemmas. Kidder writes: "Ethics is not blind impartiality, doling out right and wrong according to some stone-cold canon of ancient and immutable law. It's a warm and supremely human activity that cares enough for others to want right to prevail. And it's not mere analysis. It doesn't come from woollying around with apparently insolvable dilemmas or arguing endlessly and inconclusively over case studies" (pp. 59–60).

Kidder informs us that you do not become ethically fit by being a passive bystander or by treating ethics as an intellectual game. Rather, you already have an understanding of what is ethical, where your values lie, and what impulses you may need to control. Thus, you are prepared to address the dilemma forthright and reach a decision so that your world and that of others you touch is a better place.

Staying ethically fit means that you confront ethical issues head on and express your values and intentions. You do so with colleagues and representatives of the client organizations you serve. By *confrontation* I mean not only identifying the issue and reaching some resolution but also trying to prevent its reoccurrence. Ethical fitness to the assessing psychologist is no different from physical fitness for the athlete. It is one way that we can prepare to do our very best.

Training of I/O Psychologists

A fundamental matter concerns how competency is developed among psychologists who provide assessment services to business organizations. The Guidelines on Education and Training at the Doctoral Level in Industrial/Organizational Psychology (Society for Industrial and Organizational Psychology, 1985) indicate that psychological assessment is an important competency, yet Ryan and Sackett (1987) have reported from their survey that 52 percent of assessors were self-taught, and only 76 percent were given any training under qualified supervision. They concluded that few graduate programs offer appropriate curricula. Although courses on individual differences, tests and measures, and psychometrics are typically available, particular needs that appear to be unmet within most I/O graduate training programs are specific courses in assessment interviewing and psychological test and construct interpretation, supervised practice, and a foundation in ethical and professional assessment practices (Jeanneret, 1986). Apart from such academic training, it is important to note Wiggins's (1973) conclusion that professional experience in assessment rather than educational background in psychology is a "more relevant variable on several counts" (p. 132).

Accepting Wiggins's position argues that most assessment knowledge and skill will develop as part of on-the-job training. This clearly is how the majority of assessors learned, according to Ryan and Sackett (1987). Considerations for carrying out an on-the-job training program include the following:

1. Learning in some detail about the developmental and psychometric characteristics of assessment instruments and procedures, especially the relevant theory underlying each instrument and also its reliability, validity (both construct and criterion related), and fairness.
2. Understanding how the instruments are scored, the characteristics of normative sources, corrections for faking when appropriate, and other mechanisms associated with the derivation of test results and profiles.
3. Learning how to interpret the test results and profiles, including interpretations within and across test constructs being measured. Generally this knowledge is gained as an experienced assessor and learning psychologist work together. First the psychologist in training observes the experienced psychologist. Subsequently, he or she learns how to interpret assessment information and then tries this work alone, with the experienced partner providing feedback. Both normative and ipsative interpretations should be considered.
4. Learning how to conduct an assessment interview. This can be a two-stage process, with the trainee observing an experienced assessor, followed by the trainee's conducting the interview with

guidance and feedback from the experienced psychologist. Part of this process would include learning how to provide feedback, although that would not be accomplished by the trainee until after the last stage of the learning process.

5. Learning how to integrate all the assessment information and make job-related predictions about assessee behavior. This is clearly the most challenging part of the training process, and it requires a skilled assessor to convey all of the relevant knowledge to a trainee about the final conclusions obtained from both assessment instruments and the inferences drawn from them.

6. Learning how to communicate (orally and in writing) the assessment results to the client organization and the assessee. Again trainee observation of the experienced psychologist followed by opportunities to perform independently with subsequent review is the process most likely to develop effective assessment communication skills.

Conclusions

Although we often believe that ethical concerns exist only when certain types of problems arise, a fundamental thesis of this chapter is that the entire scope of assessment services in an organizational context offered by a psychologist is a continuing matter of ethical practice. The ethical responsibilities emanate from the psychologist's relationship with two sources: the organization and the assessee. These responsibilities begin when a relationship develops with an organization to provide assessment services and continues until that relationship is formally severed. Similarly, as soon as there is contact between the psychologist and assessee, ethical responsibility is initiated, and it continues even if an assessee does not maintain affiliation with the sponsoring organization. These relationships are equally true of the legal and the professional issues that have been discussed in this chapter. Nevertheless, satisfying legal or professional standards is not sufficient; the moral treatment of assessees goes well beyond any legal acceptability requirements.

Table 4.2 outlines many of the primary ethical issues. For each issue there are several representative responsibilities that establish a framework for how the issue might be addressed. These

Table 4.2. Ethical Issues and Responsibilities of Assessment Psychologists.

Ethical Issues	Representative Ethical Responsibilities
Identification and understanding of the roles of all parties involved in the conduct and use of individual psychological assessments	Identify conflicts of interest. Clarify assessor role to assessee. Clarify assessor role and responsibilities to client organization.
Competence in conducting individual psychological assessments	Update knowledge of assessment practices and developments. Properly use all assessment techniques.
Integrity in dealing with all parties receiving information about individual psychological assessment	Provide truthful information to assessees and clients. Deal fairly with all parties.
Professional and scientific responsibility for use of individual psychological assessment instruments and their results	Confer, refer, or cooperate with the psychologists when appropriate. Promote and provide assessment services only by qualified professionals. Do not use instruments that do not meet professionally accepted standards.
Respect for people's rights and their dignity, including the rights to privacy, confidentiality, self-determination, autonomy, and feedback about their assessment results	Learn about and respect individual differences and the diversity of others. Minimize assessee anxiety. Recognize that assessee participation is voluntary. Provide feedback to assessees in terms they can understand.
Concern for others' welfare, especially when providing feedback and making recommendations about assessment results	Attempt to avoid or minimize any harm that might result from the assessment process. Place assessment results in the proper context for the assessee.
Social responsibility, including compliance with the statutes that govern the delivery of individual psychological assessment services in one's practice domain (and including meeting licensure requirements)	Respect and abide by licensing and all other requirements set forth by state regulatory bodies. Recognize social or cultural conditions that might influence assessment practices.

**Table 4.2. Ethical Issues and Responsibilities
of Assessment Psychologists** *(continued).*

Ethical Issues	Representative Ethical Responsibilities
Maintaining confidentiality of all assessment information	Protect information provided by the assessee to the assessor in confidence at all cost.
	Describe ground rules to assessee at the outset regarding who will receive assessment results and who has access to assessment information.
	Maintain the security of all assessment instruments and related documents, including test questions, answer keys, and manuals.
	Retain assessment records for a reasonable period of time (seven years is recommended).
	Destroy assessment documents in a manner used with other confidential documents.
	Advise client organizations regarding the storage of assessment reports.
Obtaining consent of assessee for his or her participation in the assessment	Advise assessee as to the purpose, content, and associated outcomes that apply to the assessment process.
	Provide feedback to assessees about the results and implications.

responsibilities are offered as examples and to stimulate the reader's thoughts, not as ready-made answers.

Ethical behavior is not simply a matter of "doing it right." In fact, if the choice is between "right" and "wrong," there is no ethical dilemma. Ethical choices occur when there are two potentially appropriate alternatives with no clear or ready answer. Sometimes we must choose between competing alternatives, and at other times there may be a compromise alternative that becomes the best solution. The ethical guidelines that are available do not remove the ambiguities we are going to encounter in the delivery of assessment services. Thus, although we can review the APA ethical principles, read commentaries and interpretations related to ethical matters, and discuss ethical problems with colleagues, the final determination of our ethical decision making is reflected in every aspect of how we conduct our individual assessment practices. Assessing psychologists must be ethically fit at all times.

References

American Educational Research Association (AERA), American Psychological Association (APA), and National Council on Measurement in Education (NCME). (1985). *Standards for educational and psychological testing.* Washington, DC: American Psychological Association.

American Psychological Association. (1963). *Casebook on ethical standards of psychologists.* Washington DC: Author.

American Psychological Association. (1981a). Casebook for providers of psychological services. *American Psychologist, 36,* 682–685.

American Psychological Association. (1981b). *Specialty guidelines for the delivery of service.* Washington, DC: Author.

American Psychological Association. (1982a). Casebook for providers of psychological services. *American Psychologist, 37,* 698–701.

American Psychological Association. (1982b). *Ethical principles in the conduct of research with human participants.* Washington, DC: Author.

American Psychological Association. (1983). Casebook for providers of psychological services. *American Psychologist, 38,* 708–729.

American Psychological Association. (1984). Casebook for providers of psychological services. *American Psychologist, 39,* 663–668.

American Psychological Association. (1985). Casebook for providers of psychological services. *American Psychologist, 40,* 678–684.

American Psychological Association. (1986). Casebook for providers of psychological services. *American Psychologist, 41,* 688–693.

American Psychological Association. (1987a). Casebook for providers of psychological services. *American Psychologist, 42,* 704–711.

American Psychological Association. (1987b). *Casebook on ethical principles of psychologists.* Washington, DC: Author.

American Psychological Association. (1987c). General guidelines for providers of psychological services. *American Psychologist, 47,* 1597–1611.

American Psychological Association. (1988). Casebook for providers of psychological services. *American Psychologist, 43,* 557–563.

American Psychological Association. (1992). Ethical principles of psychologists and code of conduct. *American Psychologist, 47,* 1597–1611.

American Psychological Association. (1994). Report of the Ethics Committee, 1993. *American Psychologist, 49,* 659–666.

American Psychological Association. (1995). Report of the Ethics Committee, 1994. *American Psychologist, 50,* 706–713.

American Psychological Association. Committee on Psychological Tests and Assessment. (1996). Statement on disclosure of test data. *American Psychologist, 51,* 644–648.

Bersoff, D. N. (1981). Testing and the law. *American Psychologist, 36,* 1047–1056.

Bersoff, D. N. (1988). Should subjective employment devices be scrutinized? *American Psychologist, 43,* 1016–1018.

Burton, N. W. (1978). Societal standards. *Journal of Educational Measurement, 15,* 263–271.

Canter, M. B., Bennett, B. E., Jones, S. E., & Nagy, T. F. (1994). *Ethics for psychologists, APA.* Washington, DC: American Psychological Association.

Carroll, M. A., Schneider, H. G., & Wesley, G. R. (1985). *Ethics in the practice of psychology.* Upper Saddle River, NJ: Prentice Hall.

Elliott, R. (1987). *Litigating intelligence: IQ tests, special education, and social science in the courtroom.* Dover, MA: Auburn House.

Eyde, L. D., & Korval, D. M. (1987). Computerized test interpretation services: Ethical and professional concerns regarding U.S. producers and users. *Applied Psychology, 36,* 401–417.

Fowler, R. D. (1985). Landmarks in computer-assisted psychological assessment. *Journal of Consulting and Clinical Psychology, 53,* 748–759.

Fremer, J., Diamond, E. E., & Camara, W. J. (1989). Developing a code of fair testing practices in education. *American Psychologist, 44,* 1062–1067.

George, P. P. (1994). *In service to two masters: The ethical predicament of consulting psychologists.* Unpublished doctoral project, University of St. Thomas, St. Paul, MN.

Glaser, R., & Bond, L. (Eds.). (1981). Testing: Concepts, policy, practice and research. *American Psychologist, 36,* 1–215.

Guidelines and ethical considerations for assessment center operations. (1989, Winter). *Public Personnel Management, 18*(4), 457–470.

Guion, R. M. (1976). Recruiting, selection and job placement. In M. D. Dunnette (Ed.), *Handbook of industrial and organizational psychology.* Skokie, IL: Rand McNally.

Haney, W. (1981). Validity, vaudeville, and values: A short history of social concerns over standardized testing. *American Psychologist, 36,* 1021–1034.

Howard, A., & Lowman, R. L. (1985). Should industrial/organizational psychologists be licensed? *American Psychologist, 40,* 40–47.

Jeanneret, P. R. (1986). Discussant. *The design and conduct of individual psychological assessments in industry.* Symposium conducted at the first annual conference of the Society for Industrial and Organizational Psychology, Chicago.

Jeanneret, P. R. (1988, April). Marketing and planning psychological assessments. In *Individual assessment for personnel selection,* symposium conducted at the third annual conference of the Society for Industrial and Organizational Psychology, Dallas.

Jeanneret, P. R. (1989). Are psychological assessments legal and ethical in the selection and hiring process? In *Proceedings of the 1988 National Assessment Conference.* Minneapolis: Personnel Decisions.

Jeanneret, P. R. (1990). *Ethical/legal issues: Individual psychological assessment for personnel decisions.* Master tutorial presented at the fifth annual conference of the Society for Industrial and Organizational Psychology, Miami Beach.

Keith-Spiegel, P., & Koocher, G. P. (1985). *Ethics in psychology: Professional standards and cases.* New York: Random House.

Kidder, R. M. (1995). *How good people make tough choices.* New York: Morrow.

Kress, M. M. (1989, Spring). Psychological assessment programs: Their use in employment decisions. *Employment Relations Today,* pp. 1–8.

London, M., & Bray, D. W. (1980). Ethical issues in testing and evaluation for personnel decisions. *American Psychologist, 35,* 890–901.

Lowman, R. L. (Ed.). (1985). *Casebook on ethics and standards for the practice of psychology in organizations.* College Park, MD: Society for Industrial and Organizational Psychology.

Lowman, R. L. (Ed.). (1998). *The ethical practice of psychology in organizations.* Washington, DC: APA Books.

Messick, S. (1965). Personality measurement and the ethics of assessment. *American Psychologist, 20,* 136–142.

Messick, S. (1975). The standard problem: Meaning and values in measurement evaluation. *American Psychologist, 30,* 955–966.

Messick, S. (1980). Test validity and the ethics of assessment. *American Psychologist, 35,* 1012–1027.

Mirvis, P. H., & Seashore, S. E. (1979). Being ethical in organizational research. *American Psychologist, 34,* 766–780.

Moreland, K. L., Eyde, L. D., Robertson, G. J., Primoff, E. S., & Most, R. B. (1995). Assessment of test user qualifications. *American Psychologist, 50,* 14–23.

Newman, J. L., & Robinson, S. E. (1991). In the best interests of the consultee: Ethical issues in consultation. *Consulting Psychology Bulletin, 43,* 23–29.

Novick, M. R. (1981). Federal guidelines and professional standards. *American Psychologist, 36,* 1035–1046.

Petzelt, J. T., & Craddick, R. (1978). Present meaning of assessment in psychology. *Professional Psychology*, pp. 587–591.

Robinson, S. E., & Gross, D. R. (1985). Ethics of consultation: The Centerville ghost. *Counseling Psychologist, 13*, 444–465.

Ryabik, J. E., Olson, K. R., & Klein, D. M. (1984). Ethical issues in computerized psychological assessment. *Professional Practice of Psychology, 5*, 31–39.

Ryan, A. M., & Sackett, P. R. (1987). A survey of individual assessment practices by I/O psychologists. *Personnel Psychology, 40*, 455–488.

Society for Industrial and Organizational Psychology. (1985). *Guidelines for education and training at the doctoral level in industrial/organizational psychology.* College Park, MD: Author.

Society for Industrial and Organizational Psychology. (1987). *Principles for the validation and use of personnel selection procedures* (3rd ed.). College Park, MD: Author.

Wiggins, J. S. (1973). *Personality and prediction: Principles of personality assessment.* Reading, MA: Addison-Wesley.

Processes

Processes

CHAPTER 5

Designing the Individual Assessment Process

Michael H. Frisch

Designing an assessment process is akin to menu planning for a formal dinner. Practical, logistical, and technical requirements must be considered. Critics and contributors to the process, as well as consumers of it, must feel satisfied with its integrity, internal structure, and outcome. Whether intended to be a unique meal for a particular diner or to be repeated many times for many people, the menu designer draws from a palette of options, each representing a category that must be included if the meal is to feel complete.

Just as in the culinary arts the choice and assembly of assessment elements allow assessors to express their professional judgment and sensibilities toward maximizing the results, always constrained by time, cost, and context. Reading this chapter cannot, of course, replace actual design experience and the learning that provides. Using the guidance it offers, however, assessors can be assured that an assessment will not flop. Furthermore, it provides a foundation

Note: I thank all of my colleagues at Personnel Decisions International, whether they contributed directly to this chapter or not. Our collective consciousness about assessment is inseparable from the tangible lessons I have learned since joining the firm. My New York office colleagues have been especially supportive. I particularly thank Dixie Harper and Gwen Stucker for their assistance in readying the chapter for publication.

on which new assessors can add less familiar elements, thereby expanding their competence into more complex designs.

This chapter outlines the many specific elements that can be assembled into an assessment process. It provides a template with which those interested in the design process can check their thinking and ensure comprehensive coverage. The rationale for each element is provided, with occasional specific examples and suggestions. An overall example at the end of the chapter highlights key decision points in the design process. References to published tests and measures are excluded, owing to the impossibility of comprehensive coverage. Experienced assessors may find some new design ideas that they can try; novices, I hope, will feel encouraged to seek out opportunities to contribute to assessment design decisions.

I give attention to describing how key organizational context variables influence design considerations. To a greater or a lesser degree, an assessment process is an organizational intervention; it is sponsored by an organization for specific purposes and with broad organizational implications. As a result, several aspects of the organization directly influence design decisions: the organization's culture and climate, the organizational goals for the assessment process, the jobs or managerial levels for which assessments are performed, and the characteristics of the assessee pool, such as normative years of experience, education, and primary language. The organizational context variables must be understood before assessment design begins so that the design can be aligned with important aspects of the organization.

Consider an organization facing a future shortage of executive talent for succession planning that is seeking to implement an assessment process to enrich and accelerate the development of managers. If development has not previously been a high priority for that organization, neither assessees nor organizational processes may be ready to implement the more specific developmental plans that will be produced using developmental assessments. Assessment designers will need to consider organizational context issues as they seek ways of linking assessment results with performance management and succession planning systems. They will need to modify specific assessment elements, such as report formats and follow-up meetings, toward providing maximum support for development action plans. Without such clear links between organizational considerations and assessment elements, an assessment process is unlikely to deliver on expectations set for it.

Reflecting both organizational variables and assessment design options, this chapter is divided into two broad topics. It examines organizational contextual variables with an eye toward their implications for assessment design and presents the options and elements available for assembling individual assessments. It ends with a detailed case study example describing a realistic organizational context and the resulting assessment design. Figure 5.1 illustrates the general relationship between key contextual variables and core assessment design considerations. Because aspects of the organizational context potentially influence all elements of the assessment design, they are shown surrounding the assessment alternatives, in equal contact with all design issues.

Figure 5.1. Organizational Variables and Assessment Design.

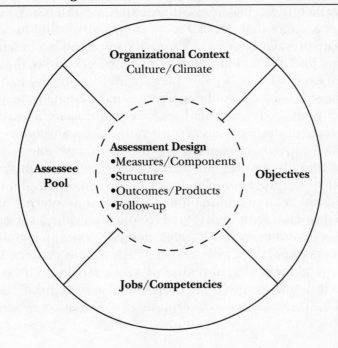

Definitions and Assumptions

Individual assessment has a broad objective: to produce comprehensive insights about an individual's skills, motivation, and interpersonal style. Technical and functional skills are usually deemphasized in individual assessment, while general dimensions of effectiveness, such as problem solving, communications, and adjustment, are the focus. Because it is aimed at broad characteristics, individual assessment is most frequently applied to managers and supervisors but also has found wide use in other job families, such as sales, public safety, and staff roles. In addition, insights from an assessment should be interpretable with respect to specific job demands and organizational contexts.

The tools used to accomplish these ambitious goals are varied and gather job-relevant information from a current employee or candidate during a day or two at most. Even if an assessor could follow an employee for several weeks and shadow all interactions, the observations might not include the breadth of situations that the assessment is intended to predict, especially when that employee is being considered for a job that he or she has yet to perform.

Typically individual assessors are external consultants, but this chapter assumes that internal staff psychologists could be used as well. The prevalence of using external consultants is a function of the time intensity and intermittence of the work and of the objectivity of external staff, because they are unlikely to have had prior contact with assessees. Additionally, external consultants may be in a better position to benchmark assessee performance against what is expected at similar levels across a range of organizations. If appropriate expertise in applied organizational psychology is available internally, assessments can certainly be accomplished by specialists employed by the organization. For example, I have worked with a large multinational bank that has internal organizational psychologists available to conduct individual assessments and assessment centers. Although many organizations train line managers to perform as assessors in assessment centers, I have never found them to perform individual assessments. This is probably as it should be, given the professional and technical requirements for conducting and interpreting individual assessments.

Another assumption concerns the professional standards that apply to assessments. Assessment aimed at selection must conform to practices that are consistent with legal and professional guidelines for selection procedures (see the Uniform Guidelines on Employee Selection Procedures, 43 Fed. Reg. 166 [1978]). Although these Equal Employment Opportunity Commission (EEOC) guidelines are not articulated in terms of an individual assessment process, their spirit and intent should be followed. Even when it is impossible to validate a selection assessment process that may be used only once or for single-incumbency positions, the tools employed should be job related and reliable and have demonstrated generalizable validity. Even if there is no immediate selection decision pending and an assessment is developmental, the approach should not be less rigorous than selection assessments. The broad conclusions from developmental assessments can have important implications for job assignments and placement. Therefore developmental assessments should be held to the same standards as selection assessments. For assessors and organizational sponsors to feel comfortable with their assessment practices, those practices need to conform to the professional standards for selection, regardless of the intended application.

A more recent major piece of legislation that affects selection assessment is the Americans with Disability Act (ADA) (56 Fed. Reg. 144 [1991]). Although less targeted than the EEOC guidelines toward assessment issues, the ADA does have important implications for the design of assessment. These include formally offering accommodation to assessees who request it; being able to provide such accommodation if requested; and using assessment measures that are not restricted under the ADA, such as tests or interview questions classified as *medical*. Assessment firms usually provide a legally accurate *accommodation* statement to all assessees, requesting a signature to acknowledge its receipt. Accommodation itself, when requested, can range from the simple, such as adjusting the assessment schedule for an assessee whose hand functioning limits speed of writing, to the complex, such as having instructions and testing materials available, and validated, in braille. (For more information on ADA and assessment, see U.S. Department of Justice, 1991; U.S. Department of Labor, 1992.)

This chapter also assumes that assessments are designed to measure and predict behavior in a job context. In keeping with behavioral job descriptions and competency models that categorize success factors for on-the-job performance, the results of individual assessments should align with that vocabulary to make interpretation more directly applicable to job performance. Using behaviorally defined competencies such as "managing execution," "building organizational relationships," and "fostering teamwork" allows assessment designers to select measures and make interpretations with greater relevance to a job than does evaluating personal traits, such as "social effectiveness" or "affiliation." Competency models also ensure comprehensive coverage of important on-the-job behaviors, because they typically have been developed consensually and apply to large segments of an organization through performance appraisal or management development processes.

In addition, the content of this chapter is meant to apply to any type of individual assessment used in organizational settings. That could range from screening large numbers of customer service applicants, to qualifying craft union members for advancement to broader responsibility, to evaluating candidates for positions with responsibility for public safety, or to selecting managers from a pool of internal candidates. In practice, individual assessment aimed at managerial and executive positions uses the most comprehensive complement of assessment components. Also, my most challenging assessment experiences have involved predicting managerial behavior. For these reasons this chapter's examples tend to use managerial- or executive-level individual assessment. The points made are nevertheless intended to be universally useful, regardless of the assessment application.

Finally, it is assumed that assessors must balance the needs of two masters: the organization paying for assessment and the individual experiencing it. The organization must be provided with findings that enrich its understanding of the person and, where appropriate, aid in evaluating the fit between that person's skills and available job opportunities. The organization does not need, nor should unqualified staff be allowed access to, all information collected during an assessment process. Conversely, every individual undergoing assessment should be offered meaningful and comprehensive feedback about performance in the process. Experiencing assessment as a black box, where the only feedback assessees get is the job offer or not, is unacceptable. Every assessee should have the opportunity to discuss with skilled and knowledgeable staff the results of the assessment and consider its implications for professional growth (American Psychological Association, 1996). Provision for such discussions needs to be considered along with all other assessment design issues.

Organizational Context

Four aspects of the organizational context are essential to consider in designing an individual assessment process: (1) the organization's culture and climate, especially as it relates to assessment in particular and evaluation in general; (2) the organization's objectives in conducting assessments; (3) the job, organizational level, and competencies to be targeted by the assessment; and (4) characteristics of the likely assessee pool.

Organizational Culture and Climate

Organizational characteristics that influence how people are treated and evaluated—organizational values, human resource initiatives, the general norms of behavior, and criteria for individual success—require consideration in the design process.

Even mundane historical information about an organization's prior use of assessment can be important to understand; positive outcomes or frustrations from such use are particularly important. For example, a client planning to use assessment for executive development had negative experiences with how cognitive test results had been handled in the past. It was essential to understand that prior experience so that concerns could be addressed through the assessment design. Similarly, it is very useful to understand the organization's pace, pressures, and time typically devoted to developmental or hiring processes. If managers in the organization will reject anything longer than a one-day process, it is best to know that before designing something more elaborate.

Other organizational culture factors that are especially important for assessment design focus on the centralization of decisions and the interplay between staff and line units. In practice these variables can be understood in terms of process sponsorship: who in the organization experiences a need for assessment and who will establish and monitor the process. Usually, the process owners reside in the human resource function, typically in staffing or management development, whereas the process sponsor often is a senior line executive. For managerial and executive assessment, senior-level sponsorship is important due to the sensitivity of the information and the likely concerns about its use. For example, a client organization had expanded its sales force, yielding additional sales management positions. An individual assessment process was proposed and designed to bring greater objectivity to the selection process for those openings. The process owner was the human resource executive in charge of succession planning, who happened to be an organizational psychologist. The sponsor was the senior vice president of sales and marketing, who had a large stake in launching a restructured sales function and a budget dedicated to achieving that goal.

Framing a written organizational policy governing the use of assessment is an excellent means to align assessment design with the organizational context. Such a policy should clearly state why assessment is being conducted, what benefits the organization expects to derive from it, when and for what purposes it is to be administered, and how the results will be used for individuals and the organization. It may even be as detailed as to define the job levels where assessment will be used, the steps in the process, the assessment components, and how reports will be distributed. Such a policy may be difficult to craft and implement, but it has great value in facilitating the consistent application of assessment, especially in large or decentralized organizations. Equally important, it assures each assessee that he or she is not somehow being targeted for unusual scrutiny; assessees accept that they are part of a process with organizational backing. In such situations, assessments are used consistently as determined by the criteria described in the policy, with the assurance of professionalism and value for both the organization and assessees.

Organizational Objectives for Assessment

Understanding an organization's objectives in initiating an assessment program is essential to all design decisions. These objectives can be differentiated according to two primary goals: selection or development. In a selection assessment, on the one hand, the focus is on helping organizational decision makers optimize the likelihood that those they select for, or place in, particular jobs will perform well. In other words a selection assessment is aimed at making a prediction about a candidate's future job performance. In addition, the prediction may involve comparisons among a slate of candidates, resulting in hiring recommendations, or even a rank ordering.

Developmental assessments, on the other hand, focus on helping assessees gain insight into their portfolio of skills to guide their efforts in strengthening their performance and potential for advancement. With purely developmental assessments, no immediate job placement question is being considered. Organizations provide developmental assessment with the expectation that assessees will create and implement plans for professional growth that are comprehensive, concrete, and achievable. Organizational sponsors of developmental assessments believe, or have done evaluation research to prove, that such an investment in employee development supports organizational success. The payoffs include improving managerial bench strength, hiring from the outside less frequently, building better leadership to support business objectives, and spending training dollars more wisely by having more accurate, focused plans for development.

In practice, selection and developmental goals are not mutually exclusive and usually reflect a greater emphasis on one without totally excluding the other. For example, even when assessment is clearly used for selection purposes, feedback in some form should be available to aid in each candidate's development. Especially where candidates are internal to an organization, time and attention should be devoted to extracting developmental value from a selection assessment, whether an assessee is selected at that point or not. From a professional standpoint, assessment psychologists should feel a strong commitment to ensuring a positive experience for assessees, even where the client is the selection committee or hiring manager. Discussing the assessment and providing useful feedback are critical elements of that positive experience.

Conversely, when the primary goal of an assessment is developmental and no immediate job change is being considered, developmental recommendations and plans are likely to augment employee information available to organizational decision makers. During the normal course of organizational life, that information is often accessed to identify internal candidates for openings. Along with performance history, jobs held, education, and other information, developmental assessment results can provide valuable insights about the overlap between an employee's skills and the demands of an available position. In some cases assessment-revealed gaps may be actively matched with job assignments likely to provide a platform for development. These developmental placements, informed by assessment results, may accelerate the "lessons of experience" that most executives cite as being key to their success (McCall, Lombardo, & Morrison, 1988).

Individual assessments sometimes address both goals. In these hybrid situations the primary focus is often developmental, which has implications for designing feedback and developmental planning steps, but the assessee understands that results also are to be used for pending placement or promotion decisions. In such situations, assessment reports and developmental plans are retained not only by assessees and their managers but also by the organizational unit responsible for staffing or human resource planning. If this dual purpose is to be credible, it is critical that sponsoring organizations follow through on supporting development. A process must exist to aid in translating assessment results into developmental plans, resources for development must be available, and the organization must value such efforts. Wherever possible the resulting job placements should reference developmental plans and provide opportunities for implementing them.

An organization's goal in sponsoring individual assessments influences the style and emphasis of the assessment design more than its substance. There will always be developmental value from a selection assessment; similarly, the plans and actions coming from developmental assessments are likely to be considered, along with other information, for succession and placement decisions. Understanding which goal is prominent for the organization, however, remains useful because that emphasis does affect elements of the design, especially steps before and after the assessment. For example, if developmental assessments for managers are being planned, comprehensive feedback on all assessment components needs to be designed into the schedule of activities during the assessment. Prework and follow-up discussions should reflect that developmental focus as well. If selection is the goal, feedback to the organization becomes a prominent step in the design. Given these differences, assessment designers often provide separate advice for selection versus developmental applications.

Depending on which organizational goal is prominent, assessment designers need to make provision for linkages with various human resource systems and processes. Guided by the organization's assessment policy, assessors may need to translate assessment results into systems that aid in placement, succession planning, individual development, and broad-scale training needs analysis. These systems vary a great deal across organizations, but all serve to centralize employee information organization-wide, especially for managerial ranks. Career paths can be constructed across divisional and departmental boundaries to maximize the internal candidate pool and provide more varied career path options. Assessment results provide a rich source of information, made more valuable if standardized and consolidated in a sophisticated database. Of course, access to that information must be carefully controlled and monitored, like other sensitive human resource data.

Linking the Assessment with the Job: Defining the Relevant Competencies

A short digression may help to clarify the importance of this organizational context variable. Early in my graduate training I took an interesting course on responding to a request for proposal (RFP). Using a realistic RFP document, I diligently constructed a proposal to implement a selection assessment system—and got a disappointing grade. The professor felt that I had neglected the job analysis step. Although I had implied it in the steps of the proposal, it had not been made a cornerstone of the project. This one-trial learning proved to be a valuable lesson for me. Regardless of our theoretical orientation, specialties, or approaches, all services that industrial and organizational (I/O) psychologists offer need to be grounded in an understanding of actual job duties and responsibilities within an organizational context.

Job analysis is the foundation of selection. It determines which measures will be investigated and later validated. I have used rigorous job analyses in designing selection processes for police officers, chemical plant operators, banking relationship managers, and audit staff. There are many methods and processes available for job analysis aimed at particular applications. If a formal job analysis exists for positions where individual assessment is to be used, it will provide valuable input to design decisions.

More likely, formal, structured job analysis approaches are not feasible for individual assessments. The number of incumbents is often very small, openings occur one at a time, and there may be only one or two candidates for an opening. Other methods of gathering and categorizing job-related information for individual assessment have evolved—for example, asking human resource staff, hiring managers, or other subject matter experts about the key accountabilities of a job or managerial level, the knowledge, skills, and abilities required, and situational factors relevant to performance. To help this process, most assessors have favorite questions they ask to gather revealing information about the job, often similar to the critical incident technique (for example, "Describe examples of particularly good or poor performance") (Flanagan, 1954). Job descriptions can be a useful reference where they are up-to-date. When more formal documentation is needed or several sponsors want to have input, short questionnaires that ask for job highlights and success factors are helpful.

A useful approach to categorizing and describing the elements of jobs, especially for managerial and executive positions, is the application of competency models. Competency models contain dimensions that are broader than skills and attempt to organize behavior into categories applicable across many jobs. Development of comprehensive lists of competency dimensions has become standard operating procedure in large organizations. The models provide a consistent job analysis vocabulary for many applications, including selection, development, performance management, and training (Boam & Sparrow, 1992; Bognanno, 1992; Boyatzis, 1982; Spencer & Spencer, 1993).

Because these models aim to go beyond technical requirements, dimensions required for leading others and working collaboratively are more explicitly recognized than in the typical job description. Another appeal of competency models is that the language used describes skills and behaviors that successful incumbents need, thereby avoiding a logical leap from descriptions of accountabilities to the managerial or leadership characteristics that are often evaluated in an assessment process. Exhibit 5.1 provides an example of a standardized senior management competency model.

Given their prevalence and utility, competency models, usually differentiated by organizational level, are often used to structure managerial assessment processes. Even in an organization that has not devoted much effort to this, executive and middle manager competency models can be created in fairly direct ways or tailored

---

Exhibit 5.1. Senior Management Competency Model.

Competency Factors and Dimensions

Thinking factor
1. Seasoned judgment
2. Visionary thinking
3. Global perspective

Strategic management factor
4. Strategic business planning
5. Managing execution

Leadership factor
6. Attracting and developing talent
7. Empowering others
8. Leadership versatility

Interpersonal factor
9. Influencing and negotiating
10. Building and sustaining relationships

Communication factor
11. Fostering open dialogue
12. High-impact delivery

Motivation factor
13. Drive for stakeholder success
14. Entrepreneurial risk taking

Adjustment factor
15. Mature confidence
16. Adaptability
17. Career and self-direction

Source: Executive Success Profile, Personnel Decisions International. Copyright © 1991, Personnel Decisions International Corporation. Used by permission.

from those in the literature. Other models can be adapted for first-line supervisors, individual contributors, sales representatives, and other job families. With a competency model shaped and accepted, assessments can be designed to provide multiple measures of each competency dimension.

An early step in any assessment engagement is to review the competency models used in the organization. Employees often feel commitment to these particular models and their phrasing; these models reflect committed efforts by human resource departments and executives to reach consensus on what is critical for success at particular levels. Assessment firms often have their own general models that can be used to structure comprehensive assessment processes. A comparison of an organization's competency model with the model used by an assessor to design a standard assessment process—an activity called mapping—evaluates how well the organization's performance criteria overlap with those measured in an assessment process. Adjustments then can be made in that process, usually by adding elements, to be sure it measures essential aspects of the organization's competency model.

Especially for selection assessments, competency models can provide useful information about which job dimensions are most critical to success. Frequently a hiring manager will highlight those dimensions for assessors. This information can be used to strengthen the measurement of those dimensions and to focus the interpretation of results and feedback to the organization. Written reports may be tailored to highlight those success factors as well.

A large U.S. consumer goods company decided to use an assessment process to staff the managerial jobs in a newly restructured information technology department. Internal human resource staff, in conjunction with line managers, created a managerial competency model for the new department. The assessment process was needed to measure the nontechnical competencies in that model. The consulting firm contracted to do the assessments had a well-developed middle manager assessment process based on its own standardized competency model. That model was mapped to the organization's model to check for gaps and translate dimensional language into behavioral definitions. Assessment measures were selected and adjusted to focus on the organization's competencies. Customization of the report and feedback handouts to be consistent with the organization's model was also agreed on. In these ways the links were clear between assessment elements and job requirements.

General Characteristics of the Assessee Pool

The likely participants in an individual assessment process need to be considered when studying the organizational context. For example, assessees' typical education and work experience are factors in the selection of the measures to be used. If all are at least college educated but have little if any managerial experience, paper-and-pencil testing may provide more options than management-oriented job samples or simulations. Conversely, if all are experienced executives who are participating in the assessment process for their own development, then devoting most time to face-valid simulations, with relatively less time, if any, allocated for testing, may be a trade-off to consider.

Conducting assessments across cultures has become an important topic. Multinational corporations with global business operations pose the challenge of using a consistent assessment process on a worldwide basis. Language and culture affect many aspects of the design and use of assessments. However, cultures influence the design of assessment processes in ways well beyond choosing the language on tests. Cultural implications need to be considered, starting with the assessment's foundation: the job analysis or competency model that describes the job. If no internal competency model exists, a general or literature-supplied model can be adjusted to capture which dimensions are important in a particular cultural setting and how those dimensions should be described behaviorally. For example, effectively managing task execution may require indirect but persistent requests in some cultures but more demanding or directive behavior in others. Such adjustments are necessary in U.S.-built competency models for accurately predicting effective managerial behavior in each of several European and Asian countries (Hazucha, Hezlett, Bontems-Wackens, & Ronnqvist, 1995; Bognanno, 1992). Although these adjustments may not be radical, they are important for evaluating assessment performance at the behavioral level. (For a complete review of cross-cultural assessment issues, see Chapter Ten.)

Language and cultural issues have an obvious impact on the choice of cognitive, personality, and interest tests. Verbally loaded abilities tests developed in the United States reflect aspects of the culture beyond the language in which they are written. These concerns lead to a preference for instruments that focus on abstract, numerical, or other nonverbal abilities when the assessment crosses cultural lines. Several cognitive tests exist that have equivalent forms in multiple languages or are completely nonverbal (numerical or pictorial) in depicting items. Unfortunately, in personality and interest testing, the impact of crossing cultural boundaries is less well understood. Whether tools developed in the United States are interpretable for candidates raised in other cultures is an unresolved question, although recent research has supported the universality of personality structure (McCrae & Costa, 1997). Such questions about traditional testing make including job samples and realistic simulations all the more important.

Assessment Design

Assembling elements into a complete assessment design requires the consideration of four categories of variables: (1) the components, such as tests and other measures of assessee performance; (2) the structure of the process and the sequence of the components; (3) the work product outcomes that emanate from the assessment process; and (4) the follow-up steps that should be considered.

Assessment Components

The components described emphasize the utility of using multiple measures with some overlap (at least two measures per competency), multiple methods (such as tests, simulations, and interview), and multiple assessor input for each assessee. This multimeasure, multimethod, multirater process is most often associated with assessment centers, where it is applied to small groups of assessees, but it is directly applicable to the design of individual assessments as well. Using multiple methods reassures assessees that conclusions are not based on the results of a single measure or how well they present in an interview. Especially for measuring assessees on complex or managerial competency models, individual assessments can capitalize on the wisdom of the assessment center methodology.

When warranted and feasible, multiple measures, including simulations, are used, several assessors are involved, and during the course of the assessment, each competency is rated more than once. This approach results in a matrix of competencies by measures (see Exhibit 5.2).

The primary assessor, usually the interviewer, needs to make two types of evaluations for each assessee. He or she needs to (1) integrate ratings across each competency, considering the relative contribution of each data source, to arrive at final competency ratings, and (2) interpret information from each method to arrive at behavioral themes that describe the assessee's strengths and developmental needs. These two broad conclusions—one quantitative, normative, and grounded in a competency model and the other ipsative and descriptive, relying on the assessor's interpretative insight into the measures being used—are different but complementary. There should be consistency between them; that is, relatively higher-scoring dimensions should be consistent with descriptions of the assessee's strengths and lower-scoring dimensions with developmental needs. The integration matrix of competencies by measures adds rigor to the individual assessment process by linking the assessor's qualitative and quantitative judgments.

This approach to individual assessment, combined with the premise that selection guidelines should set the standards for assessment, has important implications for the measures used. Measures not objectively scored, not clearly linked to job competencies, or frequently used in clinical settings are deemphasized here. This includes both projective and standardized clinical instruments. Although projective tests could be interpreted conceptually by competency, implementation of the ADA has relegated such measures to applications within clinical or medical assessment (Fischer, 1994). This act has also resulted in restrictions on the use of standardized tests aimed at clinical interpretations, except in employment assessments with significant public safety exposure, such as those for police officers or nuclear power plant operators. Experienced assessors continue to augment their batteries with simpler clinical measures, such as sentence completion forms, although legal rulings may yet constrain even that limited use.

Exhibit 5.2. Sample Assessment Integration Form.

Competencies	Interview	Tests	In-Basket Simulation	Dir. Report Simulation	Peer Meeting	Dimension Rating	Factor Rating	360 Profile
Assessor Initials								
Thinking Skills								
1. Seasoned Judgment								
2. Visionary Thinking								
3. Global Perspective								
Strategic Management								
4. Strategic Business Planning								
5. Managing Execution								
Leadership								
6. Attracting and Developing Talent								
7. Empowering Others								
8. Leadership Versatility								
Interpersonal Skills								
9. Influencing and Negotiating								
10. Building and Sustaining Relationships								
Communication								
11. Fostering Open Dialogue								
12. High-Impact Delivery								
Motivation								
13. Drive for Stakeholder Success								
14. Entrepreneurial Risk Taking								
Adjustment								
15. Mature Confidence								
16. Adaptability								
17. Career and Self-direction								
Person/Job Fit or Overall Rating								

Source: Executive Success Profile, Personnel Decisions International. Copyright © 1991, Personnel Decisions International Corporation. Used by permission.

Given these considerations the specific components selected for an assessment can be divided into three broad types, with an optional fourth category aimed at augmenting developmental assessments: (1) simulations and assessment center exercises; (2) paper-and-pencil measures of cognitive skills, personality dimensions, and vocational interests; and (3) interviews and self-descriptive background forms. The fourth category includes multirater tools for use in developmental assessments, such as 360-degree surveys, open-ended write-in comments, referent interviews, or focus groups about an assessee.

Simulations and Assessment Center Exercises

Individual assessment has often excluded assessment center–like simulations because of difficulties in their design, construction, and execution. Nevertheless they add such significant value to the validity and utility of an assessment, not to mention credibility in the eyes of assessees, that every effort should be made to include them (Gaugler, Rosenthal, Thornton, & Bentson, 1987). Especially applicable to assessments at managerial and executive levels, simulations are potentially useful for any job that requires complex interactions with others, including sales, customer service, project management, and internal consulting roles. Using simulations does require multiple assessors as independent raters of an assessee's performance, but a skilled staff of one lead assessor to interview and interpret results, aided by one to three experienced colleagues, depending on the number of simulations used, is sufficient. Ideally, each of these assessors should evaluate an assessee in only one simulation. As a result, leaderless group problem-solving exercises, often observed in assessment centers, are not included in individual assessments. (Many excellent references exist on assessment center philosophy and general methods, such as Bray & Grant, 1966; Howard, 1983; Thornton, 1992; Thornton & Byham, 1982.)

Typical simulations include situations reflective of the broad types of interactions that job incumbents are likely to face. Generally applicable simulations include administering the accumulated mail of an in-box, presenting to a decision-making committee, resolving a disagreement with a peer, and meeting with a customer. Managerial assessments use simulations more relevant to managerial jobs: meeting with a direct report, leading a meeting of one or two peers to address an organizational initiative, responding face-to-face to an immediate superior's request for a business recommendation, and even being interviewed by a journalist about an organizational issue. Two to four of these simulations can be chosen for a one- to two-day assessment, determined by the critical tasks likely to be faced on the job and the complexity of the underlying competency model being measured.

The assessment is much more compelling, and efficient, if these simulated meetings or behavioral demonstrations are embedded in a scenario that describes in detail a usually fictitious, but realistic, organization. Ideally, the scenario's stage is set with organizational charts, company history, memos and correspondence, summaries of issues, performance appraisals, letters from customers, plans and proposals, and even mock annual reports and mission statements. Every effort should be made to convey a sense of realism about the invented organization.

During the assessment, assessees can be "assigned" to a position within this realistic organization. The level of the position they are assigned to is an important decision for assessment designers. In a selection assessment, that position should overlap with the competencies required in the position for which candidates are being evaluated, usually a position at or above a candidate's current job. For developmental assessments, an assessee can be slotted into a more advanced position or one reflecting likely promotions. Those positions should not be too big a jump from an assessee's experience base but can be a stretch to provide insight into assessee preparedness for future challenges. Organizations going through significant change actually have sponsored the design of simulations tied to a future vision or virtual organization to obtain feedback about likely gaps so employees can determine future directions for their developmental needs.

In preparing for such assessment variations, it is useful to have several scenarios or several versions of the same scenario. For example, one variation might be based on an assessee's assuming a position as a middle manager in a sales function, another might assign an assessee to a corporate staff role, and another might place an assessee at the top of a business unit with multiple functions reporting to that position. Obviously, these variations require significant time and effort to create and refine. Accompanying elements must also be developed, including behaviorally anchored scoring guides for each simulation and instructions for both assessees and assessors. Training assessors is also a significant investment, so, depending on the scenario, assessors can be asked to evaluate any one of several simulations. There is both art and science in creating and applying simulations for individual assessment, but the resulting enrichment of the assessment data makes simulations well worth the effort.

Standardized Paper-and-Pencil Measures: Cognitive, Personality, and Interest Tests

Paper-and-pencil tests used in assessment fall into the traditional three categories: cognitive, personality, and interest measures. (Many resources are available, both publishers' catalogues and professional critiques, to aid in the selection of tests, such as Conoley & Kramer, 1989, and Hogan & Hogan, 1990.) Assessment batteries are built around these three broad classifications with a variety of considerations in mind, chief among them being job relatedness but also including the assessor's experience with the measures, availability of norms, difficulty level, overlap of scales across instruments, and, in the case of cognitive tests, speed versus power. In assessments using simulations, tests, and an interview, test-taking time must be balanced with what can be reasonably asked of an assessee. For example, in a typical one-day selection assessment using two or three simulations, there may be no more than one or two hours available for paper-and-pencil measures. To maximize the time available, assessors often allow completion of some instruments, usually personality or interest inventories, before the assessment. That arrangement leaves only cognitive ability testing during the assessment day.

Cognitive tests should be linked with the task demands likely to be experienced on the job. With those factors in mind, instruments can be assembled into a battery covering skills such as conceptual reasoning, problem solving, numerical reasoning, verbal reasoning, and vocabulary. Some of these may be time bound to evaluate the assessee's functioning under time pressure, whereas others could be untimed power tests. Specialized knowledge tests may also be helpful for particular applications, such as sales or supervisory comprehension tests.

Although cognitive ability testing is important and an expected part of an individual assessment, test scores alone do not determine conclusions about mental abilities. Rather, cognitive test results, interview findings, and performance in simulations are integrated across appropriate problem-solving competency dimensions to yield conclusions about intellectual functioning. Combining test "brightness" with practical problem solving applied to realistic situations provides a much broader sample of intellectual functioning than cognitive test scores alone. Integrating data from several methods of measuring cognitive skills adds interpretative richness to the assessor's job, as well as eases assessees' concerns about performance on standardized tests. By considering how thinking skills are applied in simulations as well as how cognitive test scores compare with appropriate norm groups, assessors can add more value to insights about intellectual functioning.

Personality testing is a standard part of most assessment batteries. Although ADA considerations have restricted the range of choices, concerns that all personality tests would be restricted have eased. Assessment psychologists usually have several instruments focused on dimensions of "normal" personality that they know well, allowing more insightful interpretation. The more time an assessor invests in learning to use a personality measure, the richer the possible interpretations are, especially for unusual response patterns and interactions between test scales. (The theoretical question of whether personality exists as a viable scientific construct is not considered here. In my experience, all assessment psychologists, regardless of their education and training, use measures of personality or temperament. The term *personality* will continue to be used, indicating behavioral tendencies and characteristics of individuals that endure across specific situations and especially those that involve interpersonal style.) (For reviews of personality tests, see Conoley & Kramer, 1989.)

In order for personality tests to be preferred for use in assessment, their subscales should have been validated and business norms should be provided, often by organizational level. Widely used tests measure all of the so-called Big Five personality dimensions: adjustment, sociability, conscientiousness, agreeableness, and intellectual curiosity (Digman, 1990; McCrae & Costa, 1997). Test batteries often contain some redundancies in scales measuring these or similar dimensions to provide greater assurance in making interpretations.

As with other tests, it is important to obtain and use norms with personality measures that reflect referent groups similar to the assessee or the organizational level of an available job. Test manuals often supply norms for supervisors or middle managers, and assessors usually accumulate norms based on their own, or their clients', use of particular tests. These may be used to confirm published norms or, if sufficient numbers can be captured, create specialized norms for a specific organization (usually divided by organizational level, such as executives or middle managers) or for functional departments (such as marketing or sales). Customized norms are especially helpful in making inferences between test scores and leadership competency dimensions being measured during an assessment.

Assessors can use personality tests to indicate the strength of behavioral characteristics observed through the interview or simulations and to suggest questions that could be asked of the other data in the assessment. For example, an assessee may describe during the interview his or her approach to managing tasks or leading groups. Scores on specific scales or scale combinations on personality measures can be compared with that self-descriptive information to strengthen its meaning. In addition, personality scores compared with simulation findings on such items as assertiveness or communication skills can stimulate new perspectives on a candidate. A particularly useful scale in this regard is a social desirability or so-called good impression measure. Knowing a candidate's drive to self-promote can be a useful filter on the interpretation of the other assessment data.

For developmental assessments, questionnaires are often included where the objective aims more for description and self-insight than for predicting behavior. Although not validated for use in selection, these questionnaires allow classification of assessees into *types,* or categories, and are popular with assessees. The *typologies* used often suggest descriptions of assessees' preferred approach to others and likely pitfalls. Normative information about predominant types in particular organizations can be interesting to assessees in understanding interpersonal experiences they have had, or are likely to have, in those organizations.

Because interest inventories are aimed primarily at self-insight, they are frequently used in developmental assessments. My own informal survey among assessors, however, found that some assessors always use a vocational interest test, whereas others reserve them for developmental assessments where assessees have raised career choice questions. Some assessment test batteries do include vocational interest measures as a matter of course, although in selection assessments they are interpreted along with other data to help indicate fit with a particular job or level. They can be a very useful addition to discussions with an assessee about likely satisfying avenues in which skills can be applied in the current job or in considering future career paths. The results of interest inventories can also contribute to discussions about motivation relative to the current job or to an open position.

Interview and Self-Description Forms

The most pervasive, and probably inconsistently applied, assessment tool is the interview. All interviews must conform to legal restrictions on the types of information elicited (see the Uniform Guidelines on Employee Selection Procedures, 43 Fed. Reg. 166 [1978]). Although clinically oriented, chronological interviews can produce insights about skills, motivation, and personality, research indicates that more structured interviews using behavioral prompts show better validity (Arvey & Campion, 1982; Janz, 1982; Orpen, 1985). These *behavior description* and *competency-based* approaches have similar principles, although they differ in the exact phrasing of questions and evaluation of answers. Both provide opportunities for assessees to give detailed descriptions of their work behavior so that their answers can be evaluated using scorable behavioral anchors based on job requirements.

Most professional assessors strongly recommend these types of structured interview approaches to their clients in line management and human resources. When internal interviewers use such methods, their evaluations of candidates are more likely to be comparable to assessment findings, making for more productive assessment feedback discussions. In their own interviewing, however, assessors amend their advice and appear to prefer a conversational, chronological flow along with behavioral prompts to probe work and educational history. There are several likely reasons for this "do as I say but not as I do" advice. First, the superiority of purely competency-based interview methods is based on research using the interview as a predictor of performance. It may be that assessors, who must integrate multiple assessment data, find that a more clinical interview style adds to their ability to interpret assessee themes. Second, professionals who interview frequently appreciate that rapport building during the interview is a good investment in eliciting information. Whatever the explanation, there remains art in achieving a symbiotic balance of Rogerian positive regard and targeted, competency-based questions (Smart, 1983; Swan, 1989). Assessors need to have a repertoire of interview techniques and find an overall approach that works best for them, tailoring it to specific assessment situations.

Also covered here are biographical information forms and questionnaires that ask assessees interviewlike questions. Scorable biodata forms, developed and validated for specific jobs, may be used, but more frequently, background questionnaires are simply job applications, covering an assessee's education and work history. Especially useful is the inclusion of open-ended questions about job likes and dislikes, work style self-descriptions, career aspirations, and self-insight questions about strengths and developmental plans. When used as prework, this type of form has several benefits, not the least of which is to stimulate the assessee's self-reflection prior to the assessment. Assessors find value in augmenting their interview data with the contents of the form, in effect extending the coverage of the interview. It is also useful to discuss answers with assessees during the interview. Especially in developmental assessments, written responses to such self-evaluation questions can provide a window into assessees' self-insight and readiness for feedback. Although simplistic compared with psychometric tools, open-ended self-report forms make a valuable contribution to gathering assessment data.

Multirater Feedback Tools and Developmental Profiles

The final category of assessment tools summarized here includes the increasingly popular multirater or 360-degree surveys and various forms of qualitative information gathering about an assessee, such as referent interviews and focus group discussions. Typically used only for development, these measures aim at softer information: perceptions by colleagues and coworkers of an assessee's work style, strengths, developmental needs, and potential. Such feedback can have a significant impact on assessees' insight into how they are viewed by others. Also, it provides a real-world perspective for assessment findings and helps to build buy-in to developmental needs, prioritize developmental objectives, and suggest specific behaviors to change. This information usually is consistent with other assessment findings, but surprises can stimulate fruitful discussion by shedding light on situational factors or unintended effects of an assessee's behavior.

Well-developed 360-degree tools, whether constructed in-house or purchased, should be based on a comprehensive competency model sanctioned by the organization and appropriate to the assessee's job, the same requirements that exist for other assessment components. Raters, usually the assessee, his or her immediate manager, direct reports, peers, or other colleagues, use a standardized questionnaire to evaluate the assessee's on-the-job behavior. Various question-and-response formats are available, but the more behavioral the questions are, the easier it is for assessees to understand and use the results. Output formats vary as well but usually show average ratings by competency dimension and item scores sorted by rater group. It is useful if norms are provided for each of these groups so that assessees can compare the ratings they receive from their own direct reports, for example, with how direct reports typically rate their managers. Anonymous open-ended comments from the raters are a useful addition, augmenting the quantitative printouts that 360-degree questionnaires produce.

Like the open-ended comments that an assessee might receive from a 360-degree profile, referent interviews or focus groups bring the assessor into direct contact with the assessee's coworkers. Questions to those individuals should be broadly drawn, covering such topics as interpersonal style, key strengths, developmental needs, contributions to the organization, critical incidents, and advice they would give. When assessors have knowledge of assessment results, they should not indicate agreement or disagreement with answers or inadvertently share anything about the assessee. Assessors typically do a content analysis of their notes from such interviews and present themes to the assessee, masking any information that could identify a particular source. This is an expensive and time-consuming process, but when it is handled objectively, very useful behavioral examples and specifics can be gathered, facilitating developmental action planning.

Structuring the Assessment

The flow of the events in an assessment needs to be considered as part of its design. Every effort should be made to construct a process that is sensitive to the needs of assessees and consistent with professional treatment. It should be efficient but not at the expense of reasonable breaks during the day. Setting the tone even before the assessment begins, a personalized letter to assessees is a detail they are likely to appreciate. It can be used to confirm the date, time, and place of the assessment; introduce the assessor and his or her firm; and outline the assessment process. When personality or background questionnaires are being sent in advance of the assessment, such a letter also can describe that prework and provide instructions. Other steps to help make assessees feel welcome should be considered to send a clear message of mutual respect and sensitivity to the time and effort that they will be devoting to the process.

For selection assessments of candidates for unique openings or those with managerial responsibilities, it is also valuable to schedule a telephone call between the assessor and the organizational sponsors, including the hiring manager and a representative from the human resource or staffing department. In keeping with the need to link assessment design with job requirements, this conversation between assessor and organization should be a recognized step in the process. The twenty to thirty minutes that an assessor takes to ask about the job, its organizational context, and *person-specifications* information are well worth the effort. Time can also be taken in such a call to answer questions about the assessment process and clarify expectations for feedback and reporting.

On the day of the assessment the sequence of events should be clearly organized in advance so that the assessee can be briefed on what to expect. Various trade-offs should be considered in arranging such a schedule. For example, typically the interview is first, to acclimate the assessee and answer any questions. Assessees often wonder how the results will be used, who receives reports, and when feedback to them will be available, and so it is useful to resolve those questions early in the process. An alternative strategy is to place the interview at the end, thereby allowing assessors to ask assessees about their experiences during the process. Interviewing at the end of the assessment also affords assessors the opportunity to use test or other results available at that point to inform their line of inquiry, although this practice is sometimes criticized as biasing the interview. Regardless of the sequence, the assessor or a knowledgeable colleague should orient the assessee and resolve any questions before the assessment begins.

Another general guideline is to place the cognitive testing as early as possible in the process, when assessees are likely to be most alert. Simulations, when used, are quite engaging and therefore can be arranged more flexibly, although they are often anchored by an in-basket simulation. Other simulations, such as direct report and peer meetings, follow the in-basket simulation, which establishes the organizational scenario, although they do not require a particular sequence. Logistical constraints, such as multiple assessments administered simultaneously and assessor availability, often determine the sequence of the interpersonal simulations.

An important factor in structuring assessment elements is whether selection or development is the focus. Selection assessments typically do not contain significant time for feedback. Abbreviated feedback using normed test results can be provided immediately after selection assessments, but this does not require much time on the schedule. Most sponsoring organizations are unwilling to invest in thorough feedback for candidates who may not be joining the organization. More important, having a fruitful feedback discussion is aided by a developmental focus, undistracted by selection pressures and grounded in a known job context. These circumstances will not exist until after the hiring decision has been made and all candidates have been informed of the decision.

With little or no immediate feedback, selection assessments can be completed in less overall time than developmental assessments. A typical schedule for a managerial selection assessment with interview, cognitive testing, and three simulations can be accomplished in one day, assuming personality testing is completed as prework. By contrast, a developmental assessment with the same components requires almost two days, which includes time for feedback after each simulation and comprehensive feedback from a lead assessor that integrates all results into strength and developmental need themes. In addition, developmental assessments may use more measures than those used for selection, such as 360-degree surveys, results from colleague interviews, or vocational preference inventories. These require additional discussion time to interpret and compare with other assessment findings.

Exhibits 5.3 and 5.4 illustrate typical assessment schedules and, respectively, point out differences between selection and developmental assessment time requirements. These samples depict a managerial or executive assessment with simulations in order to show how more numerous elements may be sequenced. Fewer assessment elements obviously result in shorter, simpler schedules.

Assessment Outcomes: Oral and Written Reports

After assessments are conducted the assembled data about assessees must be interpreted or integrated. Assessors evolve their own process for integrating the data, some choosing to focus on more free-form interpretations of strengths and developmental needs, others using a more structured or competency-based process. Because these integration methods do not influence assessment design, they are not covered here. How those interpretations are reported, however, does need to be factored into the design of the overall process.

Exhibit 5.3. Sample Selection Assessment Schedule.

9:00–10:45	Interview
10:45–11:00	Break
11:00–12:00	Cognitive testing
12:00–1:00	Lunch
1:00–3:00	In-basket simulation
3:00–3:15	Break
3:15–4:15	Direct report simulation: preparation and meeting
4:15–5:15	Peer meeting simulation: preparation and meeting
5:30	Departure

Exhibit 5.4. Sample Development Assessment Schedule.

Day One

9:00–10:45	Interview
10:45–11:00	Break
11:00–12:00	Cognitive testing
12:00–1:00	Lunch
1:00–3:00	In-basket simulation
3:00–3:15	Break
3:15–4:15	Direct report simulation: preparation and meeting
4:15–4:45	Direct report simulation: feedback discussion
5:00	Departure

Day Two

9:00–10:00	Peer meeting simulation: preparation and meeting
10:00–10:30	Peer meeting simulation: feedback discussion
10:30–10:45	Break
10:45–12:45	Comprehensive feedback
	In-basket simulation
	Test results: prework and cognitive
	360-degree profile
	Summary and developmental themes
1:00	Departure

Reports come in both oral and written forms, and the time when assessees and organizational sponsors will receive them should be understood from the beginning of an assessment process. As in other design issues, whether the goal of an assessment is selection or development has a major impact on how and when assessor interpretations are reported. For selection assessments, assessors typically provide an oral summary to human resources or a hiring manager, or both, within a day or two after the assessment. That oral summary usually covers the assessee's strengths and developmental needs, especially in terms of fit for the available position. Multiple candidates assessed for the same job can be discussed at that time as well. Written reports then follow within one or two weeks. For developmental assessments the assessee is the main recipient of oral feedback, usually consisting of a detailed discussion of the assessment elements provided immediately or soon after the assessment. Again, the written summary is generated later. My experience is that the written report should be the same for both organizational sponsors and assessees. Different versions of a report about the same assessee, regardless of the intention, can raise unsettling questions for assessees about full disclosure.

Oral feedback to candidates who are already employees of the sponsoring organization and to external applicants who are hired should be a routine follow-up step to selection assessments. Such feedback should clearly emphasize extracting the most developmental benefit from the assessment, especially in preparing selected candidates to move into a new job. That feedback should include the assessment report, discussion about the process, and an opportunity to deconstruct and understand components of the assessment, including tests and simulations.

Selection assessment feedback to external candidates who are not hired is often perfunctory or overlooked completely. This is unfortunate. Assessors have a professional obligation to make each assessment experience as useful as possible for those who participate. Also, sponsoring organizations have a significant stake in candidates' positive reactions to the hiring process. As a professional and public relations practice, it is worth the investment of time to review assessment findings with external candidates who are not hired and to discuss with them possible developmental implications of the results. Written reports, however, are often viewed as the property of the sponsoring organization, especially if they are customized to a specific competency model, and so are not usually provided. Nonetheless the feedback should help to balance the time and effort expended by an assessee against developmental value that enriches self-insight, even if the job was not offered or, if offered, not taken.

Design considerations also apply to the structure of written reports. For selection assessments the written report may contain subsections: a narrative summary covering the assessee's education, work experience, key strengths and gaps relative to the available job, career aspirations, and job-fit recommendation. These topics allow the assessor to paint a clear picture of each assessee. It is also useful to view the assessee through the lens of the competency model that the organization uses, potentially highlighting the competencies of critical importance to the job. Therefore, written reports often have sections that describe assessees using competency factors, such as leadership, communication skills, and interpersonal skills. Short paragraphs or bulleted statements can be used to describe assessees on each competency or factor. These provide another view of assessees and make for standardized comparisons across all candidates for a particular job.

Selection assessment reports may include charts or graphs showing the normed results of standardized cognitive ability testing. These results, however, tend to receive undue emphasis from organizational sponsors: any "below-average" score could taint a hiring manager's thinking about a candidate out of proportion with that particular instrument's predictive utility. In addition, reporting on the results of individual tests is inconsistent with competency language and the focus on job-related success factors. Furthermore the primary task of the assessor is to interpret assessment results relative to the demands of the available job. Listing how an assessee performed on various assessment components shifts part of that interpretative task to organizational sponsors, who are unlikely to be trained assessors. For these reasons the presentation of cognitive test results in assessment reports has frequently been replaced by ratings of performance on competency factors.

Discussion of normed cognitive test results fits well into the report sections about competencies tied to cognitive functioning, such as problem solving or judgment. More important, where simulations are used, cognitive test results should be interpreted in the context of how assessees actually apply cognitive abilities to realistic situations. Ratings of effectiveness on each competency, or factor (group of related competencies), can be reported with a chart or graph based on a five-point scale. Integrating all assessment measures, including tests, into ratings of job-specific competency dimensions is especially appealing when results are being reported to nonpsychologists who need to compare a number of candidates for the same position.

Such slates of candidates for specific positions represent a special challenge for assessors. After identical assessment processes have been applied to all candidates, organizational sponsors usually want to discuss how the candidates compare. Simply reviewing each candidate's unique lists of strengths and weaknesses will not yield clear conclusions on how they may be ranked. In those cases a structure is needed that can be applied uniformly to all candidates' assessment performances and that is linked with factors important to success on the job.

The organization's competency model fulfills these requirements, especially if it has been the basis of the job specification process and at least some of the written report has been dedicated to the dimensions of the model. Assessment performance on competency factors by each candidate can be shown easily in a matrix (see Exhibit 5.5) that allows for comprehensive comparisons. To make such a chart more accessible, assessment performance ratings are usually reduced to several broad categories, such as "clear strength," "competent," and "needs development." These categories lend themselves to graphic symbols or colors, making it possible to scan the chart visually to compare candidates on key competencies. Finally, an overall job-fit rating for each candidate can be added to the chart, thereby showing a complete summary of how each candidate stacks up against all others.

Developmental assessment reports can have a structure similar to selection assessment reports, including a narrative summary of assessee background, career, strengths, developmental needs, and evaluation by competency, but without comparisons to particular job requirements. In addition, developmental reports may have a more personal tone, aimed at the assessee by being written in the second person. Within a developmental assessment report, assessment evaluations by competency dimensions may or may not be included, depending on the organization's preference. Such evaluations do provide useful normative feedback to assessees, but some organizational sponsors feel that ratings or scores may be viewed by assessees as inconsistent with encouraging development.

Developmental reports also should contain concrete suggestions as to actions that assessees might take to further their growth. Suggestions should be linked to the developmental needs identified by the assessment and can be quite extensive. They can cover

Exhibit 5.5. Candidate Slate Comparison Chart.

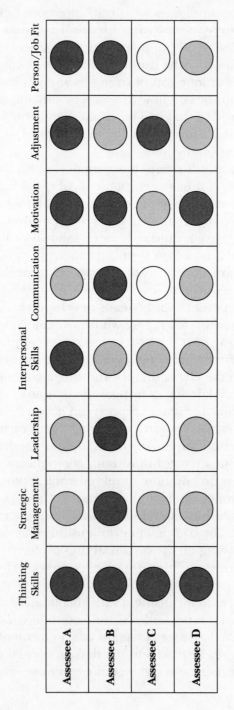

Source: Executive Success Profile, Personnel Decisions International. Copyright © 1991, Personnel Decisions International Corporation. Used by permission.

the typical course listings and readings but also should emphasize practical, on-the-job activities that assessees can use to improve a particular skill or competency. Providing these suggestions demonstrates the organization's commitment to applying assessment results to development. This commitment is emphasized by expecting that these suggestions will be used judiciously as the raw material for developmental plans created and implemented after assessment (Davis, Skube, Hellervik, Gebelein, & Sheard, 1996).

Assessment Follow-up Steps

Even after an assessment is complete, reports delivered, and feedback given, there are subsequent steps that should be built into the process from the start. Because the goal of a developmental assessment is to produce committed action on well-founded developmental objectives, a written developmental plan should be a key deliverable. Oral commitments are not robust enough to support developmental actions over the course of a year or more with multiple stakeholders, such as an assessee, a manager, and human resource representatives. In addition, unwritten plans are too vulnerable to lapses of memory and lead to inconsistent organizational encouragement. Among the various formats for constructing developmental plans are computerized tools with developmental suggestions built in. An effective developmental plan, however, may be no more complex than identifying a clear developmental need and action steps to help improve it. Underused or overused strengths are also often included in a developmental plan. This helps lessen the plan's focus on shortcomings and highlights the natural interdependence of strengths and developmental needs. For example, more effective use of a strength such as "task execution" could be used to aid in the development of related skills, such as "empowerment" or "providing feedback."

Similar follow-up efforts should be made to extract developmental value from selection assessments. Although full feedback and developmental planning steps may be delayed by the hiring process, the assessment results remain useful to assessees. For the selected candidate, assessment results can aid that individual's transition to the new job or organization by anticipating difficulties and pitfalls. For assessees who did not receive a job offer, turning the selection assessment results into developmental action plans allows them to focus efforts productively on areas that may be holding them back. In that way even disappointing outcomes can be translated into hopeful and motivating plans.

To ensure the creation of assessment-based developmental plans with commitment from both assessee and immediate manager, a planning meeting is invaluable, facilitated by the assessor and often attended by a human resource representative. The meeting objective is to review the assessment results to foster their on-the-job application. Even before a developmental assessment occurs, the meeting can be placed on calendars as an assessment follow-up step, signaling the organization's commitment to using the process for development. This meeting is also useful in encouraging discussion of the report to be sure that it is clear and has useful developmental suggestions and that those suggestions, or others, are actionable within the context of the assessee's job. Finally, it sets an expectation that assessees will produce developmental plans based on the discussion.

When approved by the organization, ongoing follow-up to an assessment can be useful. Assessees often benefit from assistance in completing the developmental plan and in brainstorming about how to apply it. Although enlightened managers and human resource sponsors can help with this support, the assessor may be more experienced with writing such plans and available by telephone, fax, or E-mail. Periodic follow-up conversations with the assessor, who at that point may become the assessee's coach, may also be useful to maintain commitment to development and strategize around obstacles. Similarly, assessor follow-up contact with the immediate manager can provide him or her with specific advice and suggestions about supporting the assessee's development.

From an organizational perspective, various additional analytical steps can be useful, although these are not strictly design elements of an individual assessment. For example, when multiple assessments are conducted for the same organization, results can be evaluated to reveal common developmental needs, which can be useful to an organization's training department in curriculum planning. Assessment reports and developmental plans can inform succession planning processes, both to ensure that candidates have requisite skills before promotion and to tie individual developmental needs into particular assignments that will provide opportunities for growth. Groupwide assessment results can also have implications for outside recruitment where current or future skill gaps are revealed on the management team.

More quantitative follow-up is possible when larger numbers of assessments from the same organization are available. Organization-specific personality and cognitive testing results can be used to create customized norms, a valuable aid in interpreting future assessments for that organization. Also, there may be opportunities for validation research. Although individual assessment typically relies on the metavalidity and job relatedness of the components, testing hypotheses about relationships among assessment results and subsequent job performance, promotions, and other criterion measures is highly desirable. It can serve to inform adjustments in the assessment process to increase the validity and improve the efficiency of that process, and if presented at professional meetings or published, it can add to the field.

Individual Assessment Design Case Study

As an aid to understanding the interplay between organizational and assessment design issues, the following descriptive case study is provided. Based on an actual application of selection assessment for executive-level positions, the case describes both organizational variables and assessment design decisions. The organization in question evaluates approximately four hundred internal and external candidates for executive openings over a four-year period. Although the assessment design is complex and costly, the organization views it as a good investment of time and resources. Because it enriches and standardizes the candidate information, the assessment process is viewed as a significant contributor to the organization's invigorated growth and to a share price that has more than doubled.

Organizational Context

A successful and well-known financial services organization, Financial Edge (FE), with a worldwide presence, faced increasing challenges to its future growth. Competitive pressures had become intense, surprising senior management, who had taken FE's industry prominence for granted. Innovative services and incentives that captured consumer attention were being launched by competitors, with only defensive, also-ran responses from FE. Market share was eroding, and the organization had little, if any, visionary leadership.

A board shake-up resulted in a new CEO. Having successfully run a sister organization in the same corporation, the new CEO was well versed in FE's strengths and challenges. He also knew most of the key executives and realized that the type of leadership that helped FE to its past successes would not be sufficient in the financial marketplace of the future. He initiated programs on several fronts, both to stem the market share slide and build revenues back up. He also began articulating essential changes in leadership behavior. He sought to change the definition of success, from emphasizing sales and operations to highlighting marketing and entrepreneurship. FE needed a senior management team that would face the heat of their "burning platform" and champion new initiatives to foster growth.

Seeing the gap between current managerial behavior and what the new CEO described, senior human resource managers sought to create communication, appraisal, and training processes to support that vision. The cornerstone of those efforts was a competency model for the entire managerial population. Using interviews, focus groups, and questionnaires, a model was drafted, tested, revised, and accepted by that population. It was rapidly installed in a new performance management system and also applied elsewhere.

Also, a committee of senior managers focused on ways to bring new talent to the organization. They were concerned that current managers would not be able to evaluate some of the newly defined competencies. Structured interview training and tools for evaluating those competencies were implemented. Staffing efforts were centralized and procedures established to expand the reach of recruiting efforts. Candidates were viewed more objectively, in light of the key competencies, than they had been in the past.

Assessment Design

The CEO, having had experience with individual assessment processes, requested that individual assessment be used with all candidates for executive positions. It was his view that such a process would level the playing field by providing a consistent evaluative tool for both internal and external candidates aimed at the competencies needed for FE's future.

Assessment firms were identified and interviewed, with several human resource managers actually experiencing the assessment processes of the finalist firms. The vendor selected had a long track record of simulation-based executive selection assessment. The human resource managers knew that the process had to be engaging and credible if it were to be taken seriously by their critical, smart, and vocal users. Simulations were an advantage in that regard.

The CEO crafted and distributed a policy memo that explained the rationale for implementing selection assessment and clearly defined when it would be used. The memo also introduced the vendor, described the general nature of the process, and discussed outcomes. It even specified how reports would be distributed and feedback provided to assessees.

This clarity aided the assessment vendor in structuring a process that would meet the objectives established by the CEO. In partnership with a committee of human resource managers, the vendor's existing one-day executive assessment process was tailored for FE. Mapping of FE's new competency model against the assessment vendor's executive model showed much overlap. In order to measure several of FE's competencies better, changes were made in the issues built into the fictitious organization that formed the basis of the simulations. Given the comprehensiveness of FE's model, three simulations were chosen: a meeting with a direct report, a meeting with two peers, and a meeting with the immediate manager. Customized simulation score forms were constructed using FE's competencies, with behavioral anchors, and the vendor's consultants were trained to use them.

Other elements of the assessment process were tailored as well. FE and the vendor decided to amend the vendor's standard cognitive test battery to achieve the goals of providing objective measures of problem-solving competencies and of keeping testing time at a minimum. Two measures of general reasoning, one timed and one untimed, were retained. Also, to maximize time available during the process for simulations, a standardized personality measure and background form would be sent to assessees prior to their assessment appointment.

Because the assessments were focused on finalist candidates for executive-level openings, scheduling responsiveness was essential. This required clear understanding of standard procedures by both client contacts and the assessment vendor's staff. FE's executive staffing function was made the coordinator between candidates and the vendor. Internal placements would not be approved without the staffing department's involvement in scheduling assessments. Candidate information was communicated to a central scheduler at the vendor, who then contacted the candidates, found agreeable dates, and shipped prework to them with an orientation letter. The scheduler also coordinated precall and feedback telephone calls between the hiring manager, human resource representative, and the consultant-assessor responsible for interviewing and producing the report. Any special scheduling needs were discussed with the vendor contact.

Other decisions focused on the assessee pool. Although the organization had offices around the world, English fluency was expected at the executive level. All executives worked with headquarters staff and made presentations to senior leaders in English. All aspects of the process, including testing, interviewing, and simulations, would therefore be conducted in English. If, over time, another assessment process were to be implemented at other levels of management, the English-language basis would be reevaluated.

Feedback expectations were established. Within forty-eight hours after an assessment was finished, the hiring manager and a human resource sponsor could request verbal feedback from the assessor. Written reports would follow within five working days, and two copies would be provided, one for the hiring manager and one to be stored in a central, secure area in human resources. The written report was divided into two main sections: an overall summary of background, assessment results, and fit with the job requirements, and bulleted highlights organized around FE's competency model. Feedback to assessees would be provided after the hiring decision was announced. Each candidate would be scheduled for a one-hour meeting with the assessor. At that meeting, a copy of the report would be provided, along with normed test scores, and a discussion of the process would ensue. Developmental suggestions would also be abstracted, based on the assessment results, and provided as a separate document. External candidates not hired would receive the same feedback, excluding their actual report, because it was customized for FE, and developmental suggestions. A follow-up developmental planning meeting between the hiring manager and the selected candidate was available as an option, facilitated by the assessor.

Where multiple candidates were assessed for the same job, which was expected to occur with some frequency, the vendor would designate a lead assessor who could deliver all, or most, of the assessments for that job. That assessor would be responsible for gathering job-related information, coordinating report consistency, and providing overall, comparative feedback on all the candidates.

Over the course of two years the CEO's initiatives have achieved positive results. FE's place in the market is growing and it is broader as well, with more products and services and a leaner structure. FE launched several innovative business lines and has built upon its worldwide network. The vendor created FE-specific norms and also used overall assessment results to highlight broader strengths and developmental needs in the executive population at FE. These were used to guide communications and in-house management training. A validity study was designed and planned so that the assessment process may be improved in the future.

Conclusions

As an experienced assessor, I continue to learn about the process by applying it within changing business contexts to find ways of enhancing its effectiveness. In this chapter, I have attempted to comprehensively review all the content and process factors that play a role in designing an individual assessment process, and I have also endeavored to supply rationales for my preferences in order to stimulate the thinking of others as they too continue to expand both the science and practice of individual assessment.

Five or six years ago, one of my mentors, the psychologist who twenty years ago taught me interviewing and edited my first assessment reports, was bemoaning the future of assessment. "No one seems interested in individual assessment anymore," he complained, resigned to the decline of one of industrial and organizational psychology's traditional practice areas. I am pleased to report, however, that rumors of the demise of individual assessment have been greatly exaggerated. My colleagues and I continue to conduct individual assessments for both new clients and long-standing ones at a healthy rate, shaping assessment designs to fulfill specific organizational needs. Although the emphasis has shifted to include more equal numbers of selection and developmental assessments, individual assessment still holds an important place in our tool kit. Changes and advances in assessment practices, processes, and measures help to keep individual assessment a vibrant practice area.

References

American Psychological Association. Science Directorate. Joint Committee on Testing Practice. (1996). *The rights and responsibilities of test takers.* Washington, DC: Author.

Arvey, R. D., & Campion, J. E. (1982). The employment interview: A summary and review of recent research. *Personnel Psychology, 35,* 281–322.

Boam, R., & Sparrow, P. (Eds.). (1992). *Designing and achieving competency: A competency-based approach to managing people and organizations.* London: McGraw-Hill.

Bognanno, M. (1992). Linking executive competencies to a cultural competency model. In *Conference on the latest developments in identifying, measuring, and applying competencies.* London: IIR.

Boyatzis, R. (1982). *The competent manager.* Wiley: New York.

Bray, D. W., & Grant, D. L. (Eds.). (1966). The assessment center in the measurement of potential for business management. *Psychological Monographs, 80*(17, Whole No. 625).

Conoley, J. C., & Kramer, J. J. (1989). *The tenth mental measurements yearbook.* Lincoln: University of Nebraska Press.

Davis, B. L., Skube, C. J., Hellervik, L. W., Gebelein, S. H., & Sheard, J. L. (1996). *Successful manager's handbook.* Minneapolis: Personnel Decisions International.

Digman, J. M. (1990). Personality structure: Emergence of the five-factor model. *Annual Review of Psychology, 41,* 417–440.

Fischer, R. J. (1994, Fall). The Americans with Disabilities Act: Implications for measurement. *Educational Measurement,* pp. 17–37.

Flanagan, J. C. (1954). The critical incident technique. *Psychological Bulletin, 51,* 327–355.

Gaugler, B. B., Rosenthal, D. B., Thornton, G. C., III, & Bentson, C. (1987). Meta-analysis and assessment center validity [Monograph]. *Journal of Applied Psychology, 72,* 493–511.

Hazucha, J. F., Hezlett, S. A., Bontems-Wackens, S., & Ronnqvist, A. (1995,

May). *In search of the Euro-manager: Management competencies in France, Germany, Italy, and the United States.* Paper presented at the tenth annual conference of the Society for Industrial and Organizational Psychology, Orlando.

Hogan, R., & Hogan, J. (Eds.). (1990). *Business and industry testing: Current practices and test reviews.* Austin, TX: Pro-Ed.

Howard, A. (1983). Work samples and simulations in competency evaluation. *Professional Psychology: Research and Practice, 14,* 780–796.

Janz, T. (1982). Initial comparisons of patterned behavior description interviews versus unstructured interviews. *Journal of Applied Psychology, 67,* 577–580.

McCall, M. W., Lombardo, M. M., & Morrison, A. M. (1988). *The lessons of experience: How successful executives develop on the job.* San Francisco: New Lexington Press.

McCrae, R. R., & Costa, P. T., Jr. (1997). Personality trait structure as a human universal. *American Psychologist, 52,* 509–516.

Orpen, C. (1985). Patterned behavior description interviews versus unstructured interviews: A comparative validity study. *Journal of Applied Psychology, 70,* 774–776.

Ryan, A. M., & Sackett, P. R. (1987). A survey of individual assessment practices by industrial organizational psychologists. *Personnel Psychology, 40,* 455–488.

Smart, B. D. (1983). *Selection interviewing: A management psychologist's recommended approach.* New York: Wiley.

Society for Industrial and Organizational Psychology. (1987). *Principles for the validation and use of personnel selection procedures* (3rd ed.). College Park, MD: Author.

Spencer, L. M., & Spencer, S. M. (1993). *Competence at work.* New York: Wiley.

Swan, W. S. (1989). *Swan's how to pick the right people program.* New York: Wiley.

Thornton, G. C. (1992). *Assessment centers in human resource management.* Reading, MA: Addison-Wesley.

Thornton, G. C., & Byham, W. C. (1982). *Assessment centers and managerial performance.* Orlando: Academic Press.

U.S. Department of Justice. (1991). *ADA handbook.* Washington, DC: U.S. Department of Justice and Equal Employment Opportunity Commission.

U.S. Department of Labor. Equal Employment Opportunity Commission. (1992). *A technical assistance manual on the employment provisions (Title I) of the Americans with Disabilities Act, resource directory.* Washington, DC: Author.

CHAPTER 6

Getting at Character
The Simplicity on the Other Side of Complexity
Robert E. Kaplan

There is no telling how long systematic assessment has been used to select people for jobs. As early as 200 B.C., for example, the Han dynasty used methods of assessment to determine a person's qualifications for a job in the civil service (Wiggins, 1973). The purpose of this kind of assessment was, and is, to educate decision makers about candidates for a position. Only recently, in the last twenty-five years, has assessment been widely used for another purpose: to educate individuals about themselves. If the first kind can be called assessment for selection, this more recent type is assessment for development.

The purpose of assessment for development is to stimulate individuals to see themselves differently and therefore to behave differently and more effectively. To do this the assessment must help individuals clearly understand the problems with their current ways of operating and, correspondingly, the opportunities to operate more effectively. What individuals understand about themselves must be clear and powerful enough to compel them to change

Note: I thank the following people for helping me take account of the first draft of this chapter and make the organization and content more powerful and clearer: David DeVries, Bill Drath, Rebecca Henson, Denise Lyons, Connie McArthur, Chuck Palus, and Amy Webb. And I extend special thanks to Bill Drath for his close editing of the final draft.

their minds about themselves and, as a result, change the way they behave.

This chapter describes one strategy for helping managers achieve this kind of compelling clarity about themselves. It is an approach that my colleagues and I have developed over a number of years in our work with senior managers, CEOs included, and that we continue to practice. Although this approach is not unique to us, it is a departure from standard practices such as 360-degree feedback and the assessment component of much executive coaching. In comparison with data obtained by standard methods, the data we collect are more comprehensive in both quantity and its diversity. Additionally, we probably do a more complete job of funneling all the data down to their essence. For assessment to lead to significant self-realization, what is needed is a great multiplicity of data points followed by a profound simplicity in the conclusions based on the data. Data collection therefore is an expansively, even explosively, divergent activity; data reduction is an intensely convergent activity.

Probably the chief benefit of going to all this trouble is the significance that the eventual output has for the individual. The quantity and diversity of the data set leave little question in the minds of most participants about the validity of the findings. And the definition of the individual's essential problem-and-opportunity that emerges from the systematic, iterative, and collaborative process of analyzing and interpreting the data has obvious relevance and importance for that person. Whereas the output from most assessments is a list of possibly unrelated characteristics, positive and negative, the output of this process is a coherent picture of the person's basic character, which encompasses and unifies the disparate characteristics. In systematically and yet creatively searching for a way to organize the mass of data, consultant and participant eventually hit upon an organizing principle, which turns out to be an approximation of the way the individual organizes himself or herself—in other words the person's character. The person's disparate characteristics, so often the only output of an assessment, are put in the context of the individual's character, and this increases the meaning of the various pieces.

Participants almost never question the relevance of the picture of themselves that develops out of the assessment process, largely because it is theory fashioned from their own data. The definition fits because it was tailor-made from empirical material that contained no preconceived idea of its eventual design. Different from standard assessment practice, which relies principally on generic data collection instruments constructed on the basis of a conceptual framework that in effect is imposed on the individual's data, this approach relies heavily on verbal descriptions elicited from people interviewed using open-ended questions. As a result, this becomes a process of discovery, of groping toward a formulation of a theory expressly designed to fit this case.

As inductive and faithful to the individual's data as this is, the assessment process also includes a deductive component whereby the consultants, always careful not to force-fit, draw on existing theory to help in the formulation of the individual-specific framework. This chapter includes a description of larger, unifying concepts that have proved helpful in accounting for the data about the executive population with whom we work.

Although I concentrate here on the uses of data to precipitate change, this is by no means the only lever for change in assessment. Another critical lever is the social process used to conduct the assessment. It includes the consultant's relationship with the manager in going about this work, for example, the close, highly personal cooperation that develops as the work of constructing a picture takes place. The social process also includes the involvement of significant others at work and possibly also outside work. The involvement of others in a process of self-discovery can be crucial. It can make all the difference when other individuals, whether certain coworkers, family members, friends, or professionals, get personally involved.

In addition, the approach we use is unusually powerful and must be handled with care. Not all managers are up to participating in it. Not all consultants or executive coaches are equipped to use it.

The Importance of Clarity

The outcome sought from assessment for development is clarity. Becoming clearer about oneself, gaining insight, can be a powerful impetus for development, especially if it reveals a basic problem with one's current way of operating and simultaneously points the way to improvement. The kind of clarity that leads to change is compelling when it arouses a mix of fear and inspiration—fear of the consequences of continuing on the same path and inspiration at the prospect of finding a better way.

The task of coming to know oneself is a lifelong one, a gradual and halting progression toward greater clarity about oneself. A character in one of John Updike's short stories makes this point vividly: "You land, it seemed to him, on the shore of your own being in total innocence, like an explorer who was looking for something else, and it takes decades to penetrate inland and map the mountain passes and trace the rivers to their sources. Even then there are large blanks, where monsters roam" (Updike, 1995, p. 243). The job of understanding oneself is never complete, if only because people change over time as their circumstances change.

If clarity about oneself is the desired outcome of assessment, then in what sense can a person be said to be lacking in clarity and therefore in need of increased clarity? Sometimes people are simply unaware of some aspect of themselves. They may never have turned their attention to it, or they may have been denying or avoiding certain painful truths about themselves. As a result of the assessment they dis-cover this thing about themselves; they remove the cover from it, as it were, and it is no longer hidden from them. They may be in for an unpleasant surprise, having had no idea, for example, that they intimidate people. Or the surprise may be pleasant; they hear for the first time that other people think they are appealing personally or exceptionally smart.

Typically, managers already know these things about themselves, and this knowledge is confirmed, made firmer, or underscored. Perhaps this is why, after reading the assessment report, participants say almost without fail that there were "no surprises." Of course the fact that they are aware of some characteristic does not mean that they have nothing more to learn about it, as they themselves later acknowledge. In particular they may not have appreciated the significance of a characteristic, the extent of its impact, or how pervasive it is. Its importance is underlined for them, and in that way they bring something already seen into sharper focus. When people go from having only a blurry awareness to a sharp clarity, they can be shocked by what they see and may be moved to act as a result.

Even when people are quite clear about most aspects of themselves, their understanding of other aspects can be absolutely muddled. Otherwise intelligent human beings are capable of being mixed up on certain points, particularly those near and dear to their hearts. In fact, an appreciable proportion of the executives we work with, bright as they are, are muddled on the subject of their own intelligence. Convinced that they are "not that smart," they dismiss comments to the contrary from their coworkers. Some may have been poor students who got poor grades in school and therefore have concluded that they are not bright. Never mind that in the work world they have learned hand over fist and developed their intellectual capability. They still make a false equation between poor grades and intelligence. Now emotions enter in. They are not able to define themselves as smart on the basis of how smart they actually are or on the basis of what they actually know, how quickly they catch on, or how well they think things through. Their negative associations with formal education left them with negative feelings about themselves intellectually, and these prove to be a difficult feelings to shed. Not only poor students make this mistake. Managers with stellar records in school are also capable of underestimating their intelligence.

On those sensitive points where managers persist in a perception that flies in the face of the evidence, we have observed that fear of inadequacy is often the culprit. They are afraid of not being smart or not smart enough, and that fear closes their minds to a contrary view, including a more favorable assessment. We tell the manager: "You're not that smart, but you're smart enough to know that these other people are wrong about how smart you are." Emotions cloud people's judgments, including their judgments about themselves. Their thinking is muddled. It is con-fused in the sense that they merge things that ought to be kept separate. One manager, I'll call him Richard, whom we will return to later, consistently underrated himself and was hampered by self-doubt that hurt his performance. When we suggested that he focus on the strengths that other people saw in him, he said he couldn't do that. Why not? "Because that would make me arrogant." His thinking was confused on this point: he equated feeling good about himself with arrogance.

Another manager was described by a coworker as "muddled" because the manager had trouble hearing about any of his weaknesses without its spilling over onto other aspects of himself. The coworker said, "He hears suggestions for improving his communications skills as being critical of his thinking, and that's not the case. It's *all muddled up* in there—the weaknesses and the strengths—all in this one big unit, so a sorting out would be useful so he could see clearly what he is doing." Given his confusion, what he needed was to sort out his experience of his strengths and weaknesses and make them distinct. This is not a simple matter.

To clear up confusions and make things more distinct from one another is one way to gain clarity. The main character in the novel *A Thousand Acres* describes how her experience of herself as well as her experience of the important people in her life have "swum around [her] in complicated patterns." Those things that she "had at best dimly perceived through murky water now all became clear" (Smiley, 1991, p. 305). Coming to this realization, where things were made real, left her feeling "drenched with insight, swollen with it like a wet sponge."

Clarity about oneself can come at a higher level of abstraction. This kind of clarity comes from seeing how various characteristics are synthesized into a larger pattern—one's character or identity. This organizing principle gives heightened order to a person's experience of self. This is a step beyond insight into one behavior or another or even insight into a set of behaviors that are not tied together. When the organizing principle is basic enough, it is one of those simple truths that enables a person to see himself or herself in a wholly new light. The organizing principle can make self-awareness coherent. The individual sees an underlying pattern that pulls together the previously scattered elements of his or her self-view. The protagonist in *A Thousand Acres* remarked on her sister's ability to find the "simple truth" of situations, "as if we'd found the basic atoms of things, hard as they were" (Smiley, 1991, p. 239).

An organizing principle introduces a hierarchy of ideas that clarifies what is fundamental and what is not. Assessments can offer not just a catalogue of characteristics about a manager but a unified view that crystallizes an individual's essential character as a leader—what is fundamental to that person's leadership.

One executive, having made his way through a one hundred–page report that itemized his various managerial characteristics, came to a realization that stuck with him and later helped him to make some adjustments. He spoke of "this revelation that they want me to lead more." (The root of the word *revelation* is "veil"; *to reveal* is to remove the veil.) He came up himself with the summary idea of "leading more" in response to several weaknesses that came out clearly in the data: not decisive, slow to state his own views, reluctant to confront performance problems, not aggressive enough in pushing the organization to change. The injunction to lead more became a hook on which he was able to hang several specific weaknesses.

At its most basic an increase in clarity about one's character represents a shift to a new stage of development. People alter the way they think about themselves as they make a shift from one stage to another. Kegan (1982) used the term *re-cognition* to describe a developmental shift in the way a person experiences himself or herself, a process by which, Kegan said, a worldview the individual was subject to, and captive to, becomes object. In general, to become clearer about oneself is to become more objective: one holds one's subjective experience out at arm's length and examines it, much as one would examine any object. In this way people gain a fresh perspective on themselves—in this case from the vantage point of the next stage of development.

This discussion of a re-cognition should not leave the impression that the learning available through assessment is only cognitive. There is also a sizable emotional component. Frequently a jump in self-awareness requires managers to poke through a haze of emotions. The experience of seeing oneself in a new light is always stimulating, often unsettling, and sometimes disturbing and painful, depending on what is revealed. Without an emotional impact, there would be no possibility of change. The desired outcome of assessment for development is, after all, not the information itself, however psychometrically sound the instruments or however expert the analysis. The goal is to generate enough spark so that the assessment changes the way an individual thinks and feels about himself or herself and thereby changes the way he or she acts. Intellectual awareness is not enough. Emotional impact is also required. Clarity is achieved when an intellectual insight is charged with emotional energy. When a gain in clarity has an emotional as well as intellectual impact, it has a good chance of being compelling enough to precipitate change.

Data Collection: Establishing Credibility

On top of their obvious purpose of serving as input to an assessment, the data are important in establishing the credibility of the assessment or evaluation itself. If the evaluation seems accurate to the individual but the data are skimpy, it will not have the same impact as it would if the data were extensive. (Especially because they are extensive, *all* data we collect, as well as the discussions fostered, are held in confidence. This is all the more important when data about a manager's personal life are collected.)

The output of an assessment process is only as credible and powerful as the input to that process. The quantity of the data is important. A great multiplicity of data points adds to the confidence that the participant and the consultant can have. Beyond sheer numbers, the types of data points matter. It is helpful to have multiple sources—not just the individual himself or herself, but other people who know this person: superiors, peers, and subordinates. It adds to the credibility of the data if these others are not limited to people at work but include, if feasible, family members and friends.

In addition to using multiple sources, using multiple methods for collecting the data strengthens data impact. Ratings are standard in gathering input from coworkers, but the message is more powerful when interviews are also used. In gathering information from the participant, interviews, managerial ratings, and personality tests are all possibilities. It is ideal to do all three. Also, in addition to these second-hand accounts of the manager's behavior and characteristics, the consultant can benefit from observing the individual directly, either in natural settings or in artificial situations like role plays.

The consultant should seek variety in the characteristics of the manager that are assessed, that is, the content. The assessment is more nearly complete when it is not confined to managerial behavior but also includes motivation, those forces operating in the person's inner life that affect his or her outward behavior. Further the assessment has more impact when it covers the manager's behavior outside work as well and not just the current behavior but also formative influences, beginning in childhood, on that behavior.

The chief benefit of a comprehensive assessment, with a large quantity of data and variety in the data, is convergence: convergence across sources, methods, and types of content (see Table 6.1). When participants see this convergence along with the weight of the evidence, they are likely to judge the results to be credible. Of course there is also a certain amount of divergence among the different subsets of data, but in case after case, there is much less divergence than convergence. Moreover, these inconsistencies turn out, after discussion, to be understandable in the context of a multifaceted picture of the individual.

Large Quantities of Data

On the premise that systematic data collection is leverage for creating clarity that leads to change, we first follow the principle that more is better and routinely collect great quantities of data. We want there to be no question about what the major messages are, and as a result it is almost always true that the headlines pop out of the data clearly. There is no hunting in search of further clues as to what the message is. One executive announced to us: "There is a lot of redundancy in this report; in the whole thing there really are only three or four major themes!" He meant redundancy in a positive, clarifying, sense.

The need for a substantial database is evident when one considers what it takes to change managers' minds about themselves. Their view of themselves is well established, with beliefs and values buttressing it and lines of defense they can instantly deploy when that view is disputed. The data, especially when there are points of difference, must be strong enough to counter their established concepts of themselves. So having a sheer mass of data, a kind of phalanx of data points lined up facing the manager, is useful.

Table 6.1. Diversity in the Database.

Multiple Sources	Multiple Methods	Multiple Settings and Levels
Not just the participant but others	Both ratings and verbal descriptions	The addition of private life
Not just a single group but multiple groups	Not just accounts of behavior but direct observation	Motivation as well as behavior
Not just coworkers but family and friends		The addition of a biographical perspective

In the full-scale version of our assessment process, we present the manager with a five-volume report, three or four inches thick. That sheer mass makes an implicit statement that there is a sound empirical basis for the picture to be developed of the manager, with nothing arbitrary or seat-of-the-pants about the process. Data in great quantity and systematically and impartially collected acquire a property critical for the purpose of changing managers' minds about themselves: credibility.

Multiple Sources

Diversity in the database is also a big factor in gaining the confidence of the participant. It builds in an opportunity for cross-validation, another credibility-bestowing feature. In their daily lives, managers typically hear about themselves from one person at a time, whether at appraisal time or informally from a coworker on a trip or after tennis or over a glass of wine. What that other person has to say is usually to some degree suspect, at the very least because of the inescapable fact that it is one person's view. Rarely do managers hear from as many as fifteen or twenty coworkers at once. When they do, and when certain observations are repeated by most or all of this collection of people, the validity of the observation is much harder to question. This might be called consensual validation in the sense that a virtual consensus on certain of the manager's characteristics exists among those surveyed.

Reflecting at the end of a day in which he had received a comprehensive feedback report, one executive said:

> I think that the most important thing is that the information to me is credible. I've never done anything like this before. The exercises like this that I have done, the problem is the information itself. It's too easy to question the credibility of it one way or another. Therefore it's relatively meaningless to you. You don't buy it or it's meaningless. This information is very different, so the decision about what to do doesn't involve the credibility of the information. I think that's the most important thing.
>
> I believe the information. I perceive it to be not only accurate, but it fits together so you can't deny it. It is so well linked that it is indisputable really. So it makes it easier to focus on what you are going to do about it. There are some things that might seem to

conflict with one another, but they're easily resolved. So I find this extremely helpful. It's something I can work with.

The "things that might seem to conflict with one another," that is, divergence in the data, usually turn out to be different facets of the same thing. For example, what might initially seem to be contradictory—that an executive reported to be good with people is shy—is cleared up by appreciating that in relating to other people, the executive is warm, friendly, open, and constructive but she is also nevertheless unsure of herself with people and therefore reluctant to be the one who initiates contact.

Three points are especially important with respect to using multiple sources. First, not just the participant is the source. Some assessments, perfectly respectable and evidently quite useful, rely exclusively on the subject of the assessment as the sole source of data (Tobias, 1990). Yet as rich a source as people can be on themselves, they are limited by what they have not yet discovered about themselves. Whatever lack of clarity about themselves they come to the assessment in need of transcending will limit the utility of the input they provide. Therefore, it seems self-defeating to limit an assessment to a self-report when it can be supplemented powerfully by the views of others, especially coworkers. And if the desired outcome is clarity compelling enough to move the individual to change, then the impact of what others have to say is indispensable. Knowing what potent sources of observation and insight other people can be, we would find it strange to conduct an assessment exclusively on the basis of what managers had to say about themselves.

The second factor is the use of multiple groups. When other people's experience of a manager is tapped, the cross-validation possible is greater when those individuals are drawn from multiple groups and not, for instance, just subordinates. Multiple groups are standard practice for 360-degree feedback, a term that implies a wraparound view of the individual, from the vantage points of people below, above, and beside him or her. If in addition to different individuals, different categories of individuals say the same thing, then the point is emphasized that much more. An individual whose relationships with peers are rivalrous might be inclined to discount reports from those peers that he is competitive and arrogant, but if superiors and subordinates, with whom he is on better terms, describe him in the same way, then he is more likely to view the characterization as valid. Of course, when a characteristic is reported by one category of coworkers and not by others, that too is revealing and provides important differentiation in the description of a manager's behavior.

Third, a comprehensive assessment gets truly comprehensive when it gathers data not just from coworkers but also from family members and friends. These people have less to say about the manager's leadership and more about his or her characteristics outside work. On the assumption that a manager's personal makeup affects how he or she performs, this reading on the manager outside work can have high relevance. As unusual and tricky as it can be to cross the line separating work and private life, it is useful to do so if it proves feasible and responsible. This type of information adds credibility to the results (Kaplan & Palus, 1994).

These family members and friends fall into two categories: those who know the manager in the present, as an adult, and those who knew him or her in the past, as a young person growing up. By making connections between the manager's current characteristics and youthful formative influences, the consultants build in another form of cross-validation. Talking to members of the original family or to childhood friends is not the only way of taking account of a person's childhood. The consultants can also take a history from the participant.

Multiple Methods

To continue building this cross-validation, we also use different methods of collecting data. A common strategy in behavioral science and assessment centers for a long time, a multimethod approach generally means some combination of verbal reports by people who know the person, ratings of the person, personality tests, direct observation of the person in natural settings, and observation in controlled environments like role plays or simulations. It is very useful to include, for example, both ratings and verbal descriptions of the manager's behavior.

When people today refer to 360-degree feedback, they usually mean ratings—quantitative data. This is standard practice: ratings are generated using a commercially available instrument, and they are sometimes supplemented by a page or so of write-in comments. The ratings are the main event or the only event. Yet we have found that the impact of the data is greatly amplified when the verbal part is as large as or larger than the quantitative part. The power of people's words, recorded verbatim, is considerable, especially because these other people are intelligent, perceptive, and articulate. Once managers have read what their coworkers have to say about their strengths and weaknesses, those observations are corroborated by the quantitative data and much more precisely calibrated. By the same token the ratings—typically, average scores on various scales and items, precise but disembodied—are nicely fleshed out by the prose descriptions. At its best, this combination is a happy marriage of the scientific and oral traditions of studying and representing people.

For example, an executive received a low rating on the item, "abrasive; tends to antagonize." (The instrument used, SKILLscope for Managers, presents results not as averages but as frequencies. Out of sixteen raters, fourteen endorsed this item.) There was no question that this individual was abrasive, and the point was driven home by statements made in the interviews:

> He doesn't have to be rude to make his point. His confrontational style is to—bang—be at the guy's throat.
>
> He tends to trash people. When he starts working people over, it's clearly mental and verbal abuse.
>
> He's a bully. He abuses people verbally. He will berate. He will call you an idiot in a meeting. He will humiliate you.

These comments gave texture to the quantitative result and conveyed something of the tone—indignant, in this case—that people took. They added detail and power to the words "abrasive" and "antagonizes" in the questionnaire item.

Personality tests are another kind of quantitative data cum self-report. Results on tests like the Myers-Briggs Type Indicator, the Firo-B, the Adjective Check List, the California Psychological Inventory, and the Minnesota Multiphasic Personality Inventory provide yet another source of cross-validation. One executive read through the leadership report, ratings, and verbatim descriptions, and the next morning still had his doubts, in part because he distrusted many of the people who provided the input. His jaundiced view of his fellow managers carried over to their evaluation of him. But when he discovered that the test results told a similar story, his skepticism dissipated. The thick report on his leadership that piled up evidence of both his leadership ability and his potentially tragic flaws could not by itself do what the addition of the relatively thin set of several test results accomplished. The contribution of the tests is heightened when a clinical psychologist, going only on the tests and knowing nothing else about the individual, writes up authoritative interpretations of each of the tests and also does an overall interpretation based on all the tests.

As informative as verbal descriptions and ratings of the manager are, they are not firsthand experience for the consultant. The consultant can gain this experience by sitting in on meetings or by spending a day or two following the manager. Offsetting the vividness of seeing the manager in action, however, is the inefficiency of this method of collecting data and the confounding effects of having an observer present. Primarily for this reason, we no longer use systematic observation ourselves. We do, of course, observe managers as they interact with us, which is a window into their defenses as they react to the report. We get a further chance to observe if we play an on-site consulting role during the application phase, as managers attempt to apply their newfound insights. Although usually not systematic, this opportunistic observation, the results of which we may very well pass on to the manager, helps us refine the picture of the manager as we go.

Observation can also be done in artificial settings. Simulations such as in-basket exercises and role plays in groups are a regular part of assessment centers. In our current practice we do not use simulations because we collect enough data, as well as enough variety in those data, by other methods. In addition, simulations take time, and we already take a day or more of each executive's time in interviewing and in filling out instruments.

Multiple Settings and Levels

Assessments are generally confined to the work setting, a perfectly reasonable approach when the purpose is to assess leadership. If it is practical to approach the assessment in a holistic fashion, the view of the individual as a manager is enriched. And when, as is usually the case, parallels to the individual's managerial behavior turn up elsewhere in his or her life, the leadership assessment gains additional credibility. Participants are regularly impressed with how consistent the data are across settings. After reading a report the spouse of an executive remarked, "It's amazing to me, the tie-ins between friends and family and colleagues."

A holistic approach can also include the manager's inner life—his or her motivation and inhibitions—as those correspond to the person's managerial behavior. When, as is usually the case, it becomes apparent that the manager's behavior is an outward expression of his or her emotional needs, this convergence bolsters the credibility of the assessment.

Private Life

Although retaining a focus on leadership, a biographically oriented assessment places the individual's leadership in the context of his or her life. This means moving beyond the work setting to, with explicit permission, the private lives of managers. We interview family and sometimes friends and therefore create an opportunity for an additional form of cross-validation. Almost always, the descriptions of managers in their home life parallel the descriptions at work. When managers see these parallels, they are more likely to regard the results as valid and not attribute them to, for example, the corporate culture. And where managers act differently in some respects outside of work, the differences are instructive.

The more extensive the assessment, especially when it is personal as well as professional, the more responsibility the consultants assume and the greater the commitment to the client must be. When we conduct a comprehensive assessment, we use two consultants and do everything we can to make sure that the client works through the data. The assessment process and our commitment to the client do not end with feedback. We remain available to the client and continue to meet. We talk on the telephone a few days after the feedback session. We talk with the spouse about the data and in fact quite often include that person in the consulting process. We finish what we start.

Motivation

We do not consider an assessment of a manager to be complete without a reading on what lies behind that individual's behavior as a manager: his motivation. Much of what accounts for managers' performance is their motivation—their drives and their fears. If the objective is to understand a manager's behavior, then we can always do a better job if we consider what needs the individual is meeting in acting the way he does. This answers the question of why: Why this effective behavior? Why that ineffective behavior?

In assessing motivation, psychological tests and direct questions asked of coworkers are both useful. We ask directly about needs and inhibitions, questions such as: "What motivates this person?" and, "What does this manager avoid or shy away from?" The answers run the gamut: from achievement to challenge, from getting ahead to advancing the company's interest, from recognition to doing the right thing. Of course, power, ego, status, and money are also included. We hear less about inhibitions. Two of the most common we do hear about are avoiding conflict and avoiding close relationships.

Personal History

Assessments are usually limited to the manager's current behavior. This produces a slice of life but suffers from being ahistorical. A person's history, whether career history or early history, adds some idea of how the past affects current behavior and provides clues to what might have shaped the person's behavior. For example, the types of job assignments a person has had help to account for what skills have or have not been developed. Childhood experiences contribute to the development of an individual's basic character, still evident decades later.

Managers who were severely and consistently criticized as children, for example, are likely as a result to possess a mix of sensitivities and predispositions, including a tendency to be hypersensitive to criticism, hypercritical of others, poor at giving praise and recognition, and almost desperate to dispel a painful sense of inadequacy. When managers' emotional needs can be seen to match up with their behavior, that inward view lends an extra dimension of understanding. And when what we are able to learn about early formative influences lines up with the manager's current behavior or motivation, then the apparent validity of the assessment is strengthened. These are two additional types of validation, two additional ways in which the puzzle pieces can fit together.

A comprehensive approach puts a manager's leadership, character, current life, and life history on the table, so to speak, making it possible to look at all of the elements at once. By revealing how characteristics of the person repeat themselves in different settings and at different levels, we confirm the characteristics' existence. This is what the executive speaking to the credibility of the data meant when he said, "The pieces fit together."

To gain managers' full trust and confidence in the data, a comprehensive assessment takes the form of an expansively, even explosively divergent exercise in data gathering, a casting of nets widely. Having hauled in the various piles of data, however, the client and the consultant have on their hands the daunting task of reducing this input to something manageable and useful.

Data Reduction: Achieving Simplicity

Once we have assembled a data set complete enough to be credible to the manager, the issue then becomes: What do we make of the data? How do we order the multiplicity of data points and the many different types of data points so that the major messages become clear? How do we arrive at a unifying idea or two that tie the data together? How do we analyze and interpret the mass of data in order to move from a loose, fragmented collection of observations and insights to a compact, higher-order interpretation?

The French writer Paul Valéry asserted: "Tout ce que est simple est faux; tout ce que ne l'est pas est inutilisable" (all that is simple is foolish and all that is not simple is useless). A comprehensive assessment avoids the simplistic attributions that people so often make about others, but it runs the risk of being so complicated that it is useless. Once all the data are in, the challenge is to reduce this material to a form that is neither superficial nor hopelessly complex. At the end of the feedback session, with the several reports sitting on the conference table, we sometimes quote Oliver Wendell Holmes and describe the goal of data reduction as finding the simplicity on the other side of complexity. This is the simplicity obtainable following an assessment informed and supported by careful study of a considerable body of data. The analysis and interpretation must result in conclusions that are simple yet profound.

We use two approaches to reducing the data. The first approach is highly structured and systematic, akin to the way scientists analyze data. Through an iterative process, we organize the various types of data and distill them to their essence. It is a thoroughly inductive approach, where the categories used to classify the data are largely derived from the data and not from a preconceived theory or categories imported from psychology or the management literature. This is not to say that the consultants or the participant are blank screens. But the picture that emerges respects the uniqueness of that client as it is reflected in that person's own data. The inductive process produces a "theory of the case" that is directly informed by the data. A fair amount of this analytical work is done as homework, with the consultant and participant working independently.

The second approach to reducing the data is unstructured, opportunistic, and interactive. The consultant and participant work together to boil down the material to its essential properties. This is an exploratory process done jointly and interactively for the most part. In the course of exploring one promising area or another, the participant provides additional information about that area, and so together the consultant and participant fill in the sketchy picture and add depth to it. The report, in its original or summarized form, serves as a jumping-off point for this process of defining the major problem or problems facing the manager. As consultant and manager delve into the problem, shaping and solidifying their understanding, additional data come out. The interactive nature of the process is an opportunity for the consultant to challenge the participant to see himself as others see him while providing emotional support as the manager does that difficult work.

Structured, Systematic Approach

Although this part of the work of data reduction is structured and systematic, it is not merely mechanical and without creativity. This part of the process, which proceeds step by step, is in fact an extended act of discovery. From the mass of data, a theory of the individual's leadership is defined, in the way a potter shapes a pot from clay or a sculptor finds a sculpture in a block of granite.

The process we use closely resembles a strategy for building theory in the social sciences formulated by Glaser and Strauss (1967) in their classic book, *The Discovery of Grounded Theory*. Arguing that theory development should not be limited to verifying or testing small pieces of grand theories through tight, restrictive studies, Glaser and Strauss introduce a complementary approach whereby social scientists, with no preconceived notions about the topic, "accumulate a vast number of diverse facts" from which they carefully discover a theory (p. 243). Because the theory is so thoroughly grounded in the data, it is highly likely to fit the facts and to be useful in informing practical application. The goal is to "develop a theory that accounts for much of the relevant behavior" (p. 23).

Theory is discovered from the data less often by great intuitive leaps than by exhaustive analysis. The first step in analyzing the data is to sort similar types of data points into groups, each of which becomes a conceptual category. Once all the data have been sorted and the categories created, the categories themselves are ordered into an integrated conceptual framework. "Lower level categories emerge rather quickly during the early phases of data collection," wrote Glaser and Stuart. "Higher level, overriding, and integrating, conceptualizations . . . tend to come later" (p. 36).

In our practice we proceed through a process of discovering grounded theory in roughly four steps (the "outputs" column in Table 6.2 corresponds to the four steps).

Step one: organize data by interview question. The first step is to order the data enough so that they are not in complete disarray but not so much that the participant is robbed of the chance to participate in the discovery of the theory. We organize the data by interview question, reproducing everyone's answer to each question. Thus the large part of what we present initially to the manager consists of verbatim descriptions: scores of pages of other people's actual words characterizing the individual at work and outside work. Each set of answers to a question is subdivided into the categories of people responding—for example, subordinates, nondirect reports, peers, superiors, board members, customers,

Table 6.2. Steps in Systematically Reducing the Data.

Steps in the Process	Activity	Outputs
Preparation for feedback session	Consultants and administrative staff assemble report.	Data organized by interview question (and, within each question, by category of respondent)
Feedback session	Consultants and participant discuss the data and come to a preliminary closure.	A preliminary list of themes: a rough, partial summary of the data
Preparation for summary session	Participants review the report and identify themes.	Data reorganized by conceptual category
	Consultants analyze the data systematically—content-analyze each major section.	
Summary session	Consultants and participant cooperate in ordering categories and weaknesses into an integrated conceptual framework.	Categories organized into a conceptual framework: lists of leadership strengths and weaknesses, each reduced to a one-page diagram

and the like. The report does not include an executive summary because we want the client to encounter the data in a more or less raw form.

Step two: put together a preliminary list of themes. This step, which takes place during the feedback session, amounts to an eyeball analysis, typical of what researchers do early in the process of making sense of results and what one would expect to do in taking initial account of a large body of assessment data, which is to spread out the material on the table and look for patterns. This step, which we choose to do with the manager rather than completing it before the feedback session, is necessarily broad-brush, preliminary, and incomplete given the quantity of data. In the course of this session, which lasts a day or two depending on how extensive the assessment was, we join the manager in making observations as we go through the material and in drawing initial conclusions at the end of the session. Typically, the consultants and the manager come up with a few buckets that contain portions of the data. By the time this session is over the manager has some closure on the messages in the data, but a closure that is quite partial and preliminary.

Step three: reorganize data by conceptual category. The third step consists of analyzing the data systematically. Participants are assigned the task of rereading the report and creating lists of themes for each major category of data: leadership, personal life, early history, tests. Participants vary considerably in how thoroughly they perform this task. The consultants, however, do an extremely careful job of combing through the material. The crux of this analytical step is to organize the data tightly.

The poet Shelley captured the spirit and intent and patience with which this work needs to be done (Holmes, 1994, p. 456):

> I imagined that if day by day
> I watched him, and seldom went away,
> And studied all the beatings of his heart
> With zeal, as men study some stubborn art
> For their own good, [I] could by patience find
> An entrance to the caverns of his mind.

Our method of studying the data is highly inductive. We create a set of categories from an initial reading of the data and then sort data, bit by bit, into those categories. This is what social scientists call content analysis, and it is a laborious process but one that strengthens our grasp of the material. This stage takes us beyond an impressionistic reading of the data, however insightful those impressions might have been, to a highly systematic analysis, which provides a basis on which the individual and the staff can make sound judgments. Whereas in the initial report the interview data were organized around the interview questions, this time the data are reordered under headings that are defined by the answers to the questions.

The content analysis of the interview data on leadership proceeds as follows. In the beginning of the section on leadership are the answers to two broad questions: "What are this individual's major strengths?" and, "What are this individual's major weaknesses or limitations?" All strengths or weaknesses mentioned at least once in these two sets of answers receive a tentative place on the list of conceptual categories. Then, using this list, the consultants go through the rest of the report, all 75 or 100 or 125 pages of it, sentence by sentence, and sometimes phrase by phrase, considering whether a particular mention of a strength or weakness belongs in one of the categories identified. If it does, that mention is coded accordingly. If it does not, a new category is added to the list, or an existing category is revised to include this particular characteristic. A characteristic that originally looked like a single entity may receive so many mentions over the course of the content analysis that it subdivides into two or more distinct subcharacteristics. Something that did not appear in the early part of the report may emerge in the later material and warrant a place on the list. A characteristic that makes the list because it was mentioned in the beginning of the report may wash out if it turns out that it receives only one or two mentions in the entire report. In a process requiring real creativity, the consultants continually test the viability of categories and revise them as necessary. And at the end of the process, when the new product, consisting of the list of categories and all the quotations appearing under their respective categories, is in front of the consultants, they take another close look at the categories in the light of the evidence marshaled for each one. The content analysis entails great interplay between theory and data. As Glaser and

Strauss (1967) described it, "In discovering theory one generates conceptual categories . . . from evidence; then the evidence from which the category emerged is used to illustrate the concept" (p. 23).

This highly analytical reading of the text picks up weak signals that might otherwise be missed but also distinguishes between the weak and the strong signals. The output of this consolidated version of the data consists of the lists of strengths and weaknesses plus the weights placed on each of those strengths or weaknesses in accordance with the number of comments that fall under each one. Those few strengths or weaknesses that are followed by long lists of comments are obviously the ones that stand out for other people. Of course, the enthusiasm people have for the strengths and the frustration or dismay they express about the weaknesses also come through and contribute to the emphasis placed on one or another. Also, grouping the quotations that pertain to a given characteristic, rather than having them scattered throughout the first set of reports, concentrates the message and heightens the impact, increasing the chance that the message gets through.

Step four: organize categories into a conceptual framework. This step of the inductive work takes the output from the previous stage and reduces it still further. In our practice, this step takes place during the session in which we cover the consolidated version of the data. After having discussed the consolidated leadership data in depth, we set ourselves the task of detecting the underlying structure of the individual's leadership. Working separately and then together, the two staff members and manager, with the list of strengths in front of them, try to identify the core strength—the basic quality that ties together most or all of the various positive characteristics. Then they do the same with the list of leadership weaknesses to tie together the negative characteristics.

It is almost always possible to distill the weaknesses down to a single basic quality: the manager's fundamental developmental need. This core weakness or developmental need then has several specific weaknesses branching off it. The core weakness encompasses the various characteristics, just as the characteristics themselves were a reduction from the many specific data points (see Figures 6.1 and 6.2). It is usually possible to reduce the list of strengths to a single basic capability.

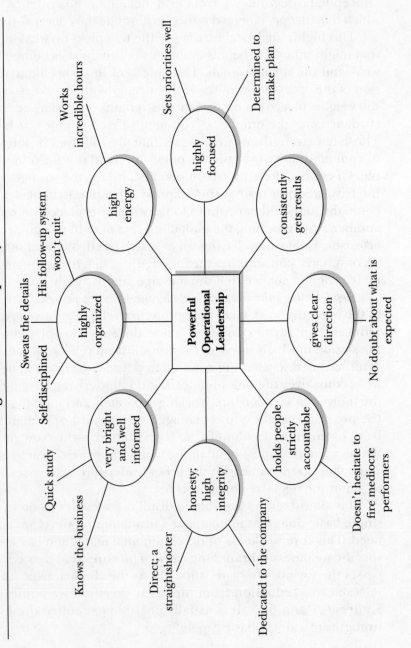

Figure 6.1. Core Capability.

- Works incredible hours
- Sets priorities well
- Determined to make plan
- highly focused
- high energy
- consistently gets results
- Sweats the details
- His follow-up system won't quit
- Self-disciplined
- highly organized
- **Powerful Operational Leadership**
- gives clear direction
- No doubt about what is expected
- Quick study
- Knows the business
- very bright and well informed
- honesty; high integrity
- holds people strictly accountable
- Doesn't hesitate to fire mediocre performers
- Direct; a straightshooter
- Dedicated to the company

Figure 6.2. Core Weakness or Limitation.

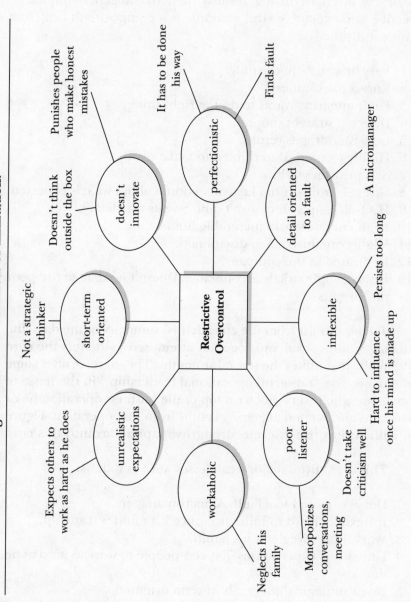

Following is the list of categories of major strengths prepared by the consultants during their content analysis of data from an assessment of a hard-driving, results-oriented, and generally quite effective line executive (this example is a composite drawn from three individuals):

1. Very bright. A quick study.
2. Knows the business.
3. High integrity. Wants to do the right thing.
4. Direct; a straight shooter.
5. Consistently gets results.
6. Highly focused. Determined to make plan.
7. Sets priorities well.
8. Gives clear direction. Leaves no doubt about what is expected.
9. His follow-up system won't quit. Sweats the details.
10. High energy. Works incredible hours.
11. Highly organized. Self-disciplined.
12. Dedicated to the company.
13. Holds people strictly accountable. Doesn't hesitate to fire poor performers.

Taking this list from the consultants' summary of the data, the manager and consultants together attempted to identify the core capability that unites the several strengths. They agreed, after some discussion, on "powerful operational leadership," in the sense of someone who is very much on top of the business operation he or she runs and is good at getting results from that operation. Figure 6.1 illustrates the discrete strengths mapped around this core capability.

This executive's major weaknesses were as follows:

1. Detail oriented to a fault. A micromanager.
2. Inflexible. Hard to influence once his mind is made up.
3. Workaholic. Neglects his family.
4. Unrealistic expectations. Expects people to work as hard as he does.
5. Not a strategic thinker. Short-term oriented.
6. Perfectionistic. Tends to find fault.
7. Overly controlling. Things have to be done his way.

8. Poor listener. Monopolizes conversations.
9. Not creative. Doesn't think outside the box.
10. Does not encourage innovation. Not receptive to new ideas.
11. Reacts badly when people make mistakes, even honest ones.
12. Persists too long when a course of action he has chosen isn't working.
13. Doesn't take criticism well.
14. Doesn't take good care of himself.

Figure 6.2 illustrates this set of weaknesses mapped around a single core issue: "restrictive overcontrol."

This manager's core strength and his core weakness actually amount to two sides of the same coin. His basic strength was that he focused his operation intently on getting good short-term results, and his basic weakness was that he went too far in doing this. As is so often the case, his weaknesses were his strengths taken to an extreme.

The two maps are the ultimate output of the structured, systematic approach to reducing the leadership data. We could create similar maps for the participant's personal life and childhood, but consistent with the focus of the assessment on leadership, we take the leadership data only that far. Even if not synthesized to the same degree, the rest of the data serve as extremely important input to the exploration of the individual's leadership.

Unstructured, Exploratory, Collaborative Approach

Much of the highly systematic, structured reduction of the data is done by the consultants, and the results could be taken as the final word on the client. After all, the database is unusually broad, the consultants have taken great care in sorting through the separate batches of data, and they have had years of experience with managers and this kind of analytical work. However, the purpose of this assessment is not ultimately for the consultants to understand the manager but for the manager to gain insight into himself or herself. Thus the process of analysis and interpretation needs to be conducted so that the managers do their share of the discovering. Rather than figure it out for managers, the staff's role is to help managers figure it out for themselves. As in ordinary managerial life, people are more likely to accept decisions that they participate in making, including decisions about their makeup, growth, and development. At the same time, we do not hesitate to tell participants how we read the data or to make clear recommendations at the appropriate times.

The results of the consultants' summary serve as the input to another equally important analytical and interpretative effort. This is the series of discussions that the consultants and participant have about the data, not once but at several stages. This second approach is indispensable because these discussions generate additional data, critical puzzle pieces without which the puzzle would not come together. Also, the purpose of helping the participants attain greater clarity about themselves would be less likely to be served if they were relegated to a passive role, a receptacle to be filled with knowledge gained by the professionals. It is critical that managers engage actively and fully in the process of discovering the truth about themselves.

This approach is as unstructured, emergent, dynamic, and interactive as the other is structured, systematic, and planned. Nevertheless, we do plan this approach, and we introduce structure, even as the process is largely spontaneous and opportunistic. Working together, the consultants and manager explore the data in their original form or in consolidated form, ranging widely across the subsets of data, the individual's characteristics, and the various spheres of his or her life.

The purpose of this series of joint explorations is to work out a full definition of the most significant developmental issues. The jumping-off point for this exploratory process often is the highly distilled output of the systematic analysis: the definition of a core capability and a core weakness. In particular, we delve into the weaknesses, the performance problems. Beyond the symptoms, what are the underlying causes? What are the emotional needs that seem to give rise to the behavior? How entrenched is the problem, and how long has the person had it? How serious is it? Is it confined to work, or does it also manifest itself in other areas of the manager's life?

In the course of exploring a major developmental issue, we keep our eye out for possible solutions to the problem. For one executive, let us call him Zachary, the presenting problem was poor interpersonal relationships. He was sometimes arrogant or abrasive. In truth the interpersonal problems were less by commission than omission; generally he failed to develop his relationships beyond a certain superficial point. He kept people at a distance. He failed to engage often or fully enough. People complained that he was not available to them, traveled too much, did not initiate contact enough, did not give them sufficient direction or sufficient coaching to carry out direction. In addition the little interaction he did have with people, at work and at home, tended to leave them with a bad feeling. He was extremely critical and conspicuously unsupportive.

He knew coming into the feedback session that he wanted to improve his relationships. The data only confirmed the need to do that. He put it this way: "What I'm seeking is a higher capacity for relationships. I'm confident in all areas of my life but this one." Later in the session, in searching for a better understanding of the problem, we discussed his interpersonal history. The precollected data had revealed the difficult family environment in which he had grown up, and as we discussed his childhood during this session, he added to what had come out in the interviews. His father was an alcoholic, who, though he did not beat Zach physically, showered abuse on him verbally. As Zach put it, "I couldn't please him when he was sober, and he was hell on wheels when he was drunk." Zach's father, at best unsupportive, was at his worst scathingly critical, sarcastic, and caustic, and Zach, the firstborn, bore the brunt of it. Zach's mother, though well intended, was ineffectual in countering or containing his father's bad habits. She harbored resentment, however, and the tension between his parents made for an aversive climate.

Very bright, Zach threw himself into his schoolwork, and except for a two-year rebellious period in high school when he slacked off, he was an excellent student. He also read voraciously, holed up in his room. From the time he was nine or ten, he had part-time jobs, all of them solitary: a paper route, selling magazines door to door, driving a delivery truck.

This excursion into his childhood, aided by the report and amplified by his further comments during the discussion, made the simple point that his interpersonal difficulties had powerful antecedents in his past and reinforced the significance of his current problem. It also led to a clear identification of the problem. At the end of the discussion of these early influences, he said, "I have never been close to people, even my children. The only exception has been my wife." And by Zach's own admission, even with his wife he kept his distance. She certainly felt the lack of closeness and expressiveness on his part.

As grim as the content of this discussion was, its tone was upbeat because Zach was actively and courageously exploring the problem. We gave him credit for being able to stand outside the patterns to which he had long been captive and see them for what they were.

The next morning, however, he came in sounding discouraged. He had lost much of the confidence of the previous day that he could overcome his interpersonal problems. "I'm such a solitary person, I'm not sure I will be able to correct this problem."

For a while the session stalled. Nothing that the consultants said, no discussion they initiated with Zach, was productive. Concerned, one of the consultants, a man, decided to reflect back Zach's present mood to him.

Consultant A: The wind seems to have gone out of your sails.
    Zachary: I know what you're talking about. Reading the report last night I was overwhelmed.

In reading the portion of the leadership report not covered during the day, Zach had been surprised by how dissatisfied some of his subordinates were and how turned off by the way he treated them. This left him feeling deflated and ready to give up.

    Zachary: I have to go back and regroup about where I am on this.
Consultant B [a woman]: You thought you were further ahead with your people.
    Zachary: Yes.

In the past few months, Zach, sensing that his subordinates had a problem with him, had called a meeting and gamely invited them to get their feelings off their chests. The discussion had gone well, and he thought this had cleared the air. His emotional reaction to the reemergence of this relationship problem, we established that morning, turned out to be extremely telling. He felt like avoiding the whole thing, just as in general he tended to "escape" (his word) when a relationship got uncomfortable.

The discussion of his reaction to this leadership issue turned into another discussion of formative influences.

Consultant B: There must have been a point in time in your life when you decided you would meet your own needs.

Zachary: I can't remember the first time I said that, but I've said it a lot in my lifetime.

Consultant A: You were in a hostile environment growing up. The only way to survive was to look after yourself. You had to find a way to survive in a hostile environment.

Consultant B: It may be that your mood changed today because you again felt, in this case with your subordinates, that you were in a hostile environment—because of those negative comments your subordinates made in the report.

The discussion of formative influences gave way to one of the pattern of his relationships. The staff raised the question of safety. As a result of his early experiences, he did not feel safe in relationships. The staff also suggested that just as his desire for relationships was nearly extinguished as a child, his interest in having strong relationships with his subordinates was nearly snuffed out when their critical comments made him feel unsafe. Zachary's response was, "I hide from relationships." Later in the session he made another striking, confessional statement: "I like to keep relationships distant. So I don't get hurt."

A little later in the discussion, appreciating in another way the effect of his early experience on his way of coping, Zachary asked an intriguing question: If aversive early relationships put him off relationships, would the opposite condition, a nurturing environment, have encouraged a capacity for relationships? In raising this question, he came up with the seed of his relationship development. We built on that idea. And in our own relationship with him we tried to offer him a model or prototype for a safe, nurturing, yet robust relationship.

We then moved to a more precise definition of the problem, with implications for how he might learn to solve the problem. The diagnosis rested on the distinction between his fear of relationships and his urge to flee. Zach confirmed this reading: "Yes, I'm afraid, and I immediately escape." What he experienced was the need to leave the scene; what he was coming to realize in this session was the fear that precipitated that urge. This was evidently fear of a repetition of the pain he had experienced in his early relationships. We suggested that he learn to interrupt the reflex reaction, to recognize the fear and pause before acting, to ask himself whether what he experienced was the old fear as opposed to a realistic threat in the current situation. If he could catch himself as he was about to have that knee-jerk reaction, and if he could determine that the current situation was in fact not threatening, then he could elect to stay engaged with the other party. An increase in his capacity to engage would be a big step toward improving his relationships.

This long sequence with Zachary took place off and on over two days, during which he was able to get to the bottom of his relationship problem. The definition we arrived at near the end of the session was not the whole story; no doubt Zach would deepen and refine his understanding as he went forward. But it was a solid working understanding that fit the facts available at the time, and it served as a solid platform for him to attempt to change.

As scripted and prescribed as the strict data analytic work is (and it is not without a creative component), this fluid, opportunistic process has an artistry to it (though it is not without its own emergent structure). Each exploratory sequence runs a different course depending on the client and his or her issues and also depending on the staff and how they think and work.

Though unique to him and the staff working with him, the particular sequence with Zach contains a number of the elements found in a successful exploratory process. It began with the client's complaint: that his relationships left a lot to be desired. This statement of the situation was, in this case, an effective statement of the problem; the work to be done was to add definition to his understanding of the problem. This we proceeded to do by delving into his early experience in relationships—not to dwell on childhood trauma but to appreciate the magnitude of the problem and identify the conditions that prompted him to adopt his pattern of relating. We wanted to help him see that the patterns that served him badly as an adult were necessary for his emotional survival as a child. As maladaptive as they might be now, they were adaptive for the conditions in which he found himself as a child.

The exploration of the problem took us into his inner life and the emotional needs that corresponded to his interpersonal inadequacies. He was able to develop a more differentiated view of his emotions in interpersonal situations. In particular, he was able to uncover emotions lying a level or two below the surface. He could recognize the reflex-like need to leave uncomfortable situations—change the subject, end the conversation—and a level beneath that he could see, and own up to, the fear that prompted the urge to escape. And in exposing the way he mismanaged interpersonal situations, he saw the potential for managing interactions more effectively.

In the search for the manager's most basic issue or issues, we use the data presented in the report and its summary as a point of departure, but the search itself becomes an occasion to gather additional data. Once Zach's early relationships became a focal point, he volunteered, as others tend to do at this point in the process, new, vivid facts about influential individuals in his family. Once the psychology of his interpersonal relationships became relevant, he offered fresh insights into his emotional life—really gaining those insights as we went. In this rolling, investigative process the parts of a person's performance, character, and life that become salient go from being sketchy to filled out. The picture of the critical features gains detail, texture, and depth. The problem is defined fully and complexly and at the same time simply and clearly. In this way the diagnosis penetrates to the core.

Deductive Approach: The Uses of Existing Theory

The structured, systematic approach to reducing the data is an essentially inductive process out of which comes a *theory of the case* that is heavily determined by the data. It is an inductive approach in that theory is inferred from concrete data. Yet it is not entirely that. Consultants, after all, are not blank screens; they cannot encounter the data completely free of preconceived ideas. Nor should they. In fact they are in a much stronger position to understand an individual if they are bolstered in that effort by what they have learned about other human beings. And the more applicable the consultants' repertoire of concepts, the better able the consultants are to guide managers to the approximate truth about themselves.

The one condition for effectiveness is that they do not force-fit their theories onto the data, that is, they do not impose their favorite conceptual framework. The data must slip snugly into the category or theory as if they were made for that person's data. As this proviso implies, existing theory is not introduced until the analytical and interpretative process has progressed to the point where a definition of the individual's leadership character has begun to take shape. The application of theory in a deductive sense must not be premature. And when the time is right to apply existing theory, it almost never fits perfectly in its generic form. It almost always must be altered to fit the contours of the emerging organization of the particular person's data. Glaser and Strauss (1967), advocates for an aggressively inductive approach to building theory, reached the same conclusion: "Categories can be borrowed from existing theory, provided the data are continually studied to make certain the categories fit" (p. 36).

It is useful to approach the interpretative task deductively—that is, to make inferences about the individual on the basis of existing theory. To do so does not contradict or undermine the inductive process, with its high reverence for the data. Dropping in existing theory at the right time in the process of organizing the data lends clarity to the emerging definition of the individual's leadership character. As that definition takes on still greater sharpness and clarity, the individual is struck by its relevance and fit and aroused by a realization of his or her historic governing patterns and by the possibility, and even the necessity, of future growth.

The consultant's grab bag of theory fragments, imported from the literature or derived from experience, comes in handy in seeing the significance of one or another characteristic. Even more useful is a broad unifying idea or framework that encompasses the bulk of the data and integrates the otherwise fragmented set of findings about the person.

A unifying idea helps to define the person's basic identity as a manager and as a person. Identity is the sameness that unites the many otherwise seemingly disparate characteristics of the person— in other words, it is the higher-order consistency in a person that cuts across many of the particularities, including those that are apparently unrelated or contradictory.

One unifying theory that I find has particular relevance for the executive population we work with is the distinction between orientation to self and orientation to others. This is a fundamental theory, one that potentially encompasses much or all of human personality. Although this theory has not dominated the personality literature in psychology, it has surfaced quite a bit in one form or another. David Bakan (1966), writing philosophy and theology as much as social science, proposed two basic sides of human nature: agency (the individual as agent) and communion. Wiggins (1973), in his textbook on assessment, adopted agency and communion as a framework for accounting for much of the literature on personality. Kegan (1982) formulated a stage theory of human development on the basis of two sides of personality: autonomy and inclusion. Beck (1983), a specialist in cognitive therapy, identified two modes of personality, individuality and sociality. McAdams (1988), developing a narrative theory of personality, found that people typically tell the story of themselves and their lives in terms of power and intimacy. Bowlby (1988), a psychiatrist who has studied the effects of relationship deprivation since World War II, identified two components of human nature: the tendency to form strong emotional bonds and the urge to explore the environment. Blatt (1995) wrote a review of the literature on depression that was organized around the distinction between self-definition and interpersonal relatedness.

Each of these orientations—toward self and toward others— while coupled in a dialectical relationship, is so basic as to be a way of life. It is not just a motivation to be that way, not just the value placed on being that way, not just the skill to behave that way, but all of these things. Kegan (1982) talked about the yearning for autonomy or inclusion and the capacity to meet each of these needs.

The literature on orientation to self and orientation to others (Blatt, 1995; Beck, 1983; Wiggins, 1982) divides the distinction into two parts. The first is the difference between being a separate individual and being in relationship to others—that is, separateness versus inclusion.

Separateness Versus Inclusion

To be separate is to be autonomous and independent: to rely on oneself, take care of oneself, have freedom of movement, keep one's own counsel, keep others at a distance. All of these are healthy and useful capabilities. To be inclusive is to be in relationship: to form attachments with others, join with others (including in groups), achieve closeness and a sense of belonging, trust others, rely on others, allow others to take care of you, open up to others. This is an equally healthy and functional set of capabilities. At a higher level of abstraction, this is a distinction between differentiation (as in self-differentiation) and integration.

Both of these orientations are valuable. Because human beings tend to develop unevenly, however, many people do not possess both orientations in roughly equal measure. In a sense, this is how human development goes wrong. The individual develops a strong preference for one side, relies heavily on it, believes in it, and develops it to a high degree, sometimes to the point where it becomes exaggerated and dysfunctional.

The separateness or autonomy orientation in the extreme case takes the form of being withdrawn or isolated and avoiding relationships (Blatt, 1995). In the extreme case, individuals become completely alienated, cut themselves off from other people, and take a paranoid stance in which they live in fear of losing their autonomy or having their boundaries invaded. They may also become compulsively self-reliant, as a result of a history of being rejected and rebuffed when they needed care as children (Bowlby, 1988). In other words, too much self-orientation amounts to too little other-orientation.

An exaggeration of the inclusion orientation, conversely, takes the form of an unhealthy attachment: a clinging to dominant individuals, a need for continual reassurance (that one is lovable), a fear of being abandoned (Blatt, 1995). It is characterized by a difficulty asserting oneself for fear of alienating the other party (Beck, 1983). In the extreme case, it becomes an excessive preoccupation with relationships, a state of being anxiously attached; this pattern results from a history of not being able to count on the parent when needed (Bowlby, 1988). It is also associated with a submission to others and to relationships with others that leads to a loss of a sense of self. In other words, too much other-orientation amounts to the too little self-orientation. It is often the case that when individuals place a heavy emphasis on one side, they place a correspondingly lighter emphasis on the other side. They become lopsided.

To return to the case of Zachary, we offered him this distinction during the summary session. Having heard a brief explanation of the idea, he remarked after a break, "The idea of self-orientation got to me. It brought extra clarity." Being exposed to the theory helped him see how one-sided he had become and stimulated him to reflect further on his childhood and the roots of his relationship orientation. Looking back to the objective he had tentatively set at the end of the feedback session, he declared it to be "directionally correct but too nebulous."

> *Zachary:* I'm just like my parents. It's the way I was raised. They're divorced, and neither one of them has any friends, and they don't want any. I was raised to be self-reliant, self-sufficient. There was no hugging in my family. That's what my upbringing was like. It pushed me to that extreme. In my heart of hearts, I am personally closed. It's a defense.
>
> *Consultant B:* Were you always that way?
>
> *Zachary:* I was worse in high school. I've always been self-reliant. I have never relied on a support structure.
>
> *Consultant A:* Do you have close friends?
>
> *Zachary:* No, I don't have any. If I had to name one, it is my wife, and I'm reserved with her. I've become an island and not let anyone into my circle and not let anyone close enough to see a weakness. I see that's exactly what I've been doing. So I've got to let people into my circle.

Self-orientation and other-orientation, the pair, represent a polarity—an opposition of equally virtuous qualities that potentially, in the best case, complement each other. Frequently, however, they do not operate as complements in individuals because one side is much better developed than the other, and one side of the polarity is cultivated at the expense of the other. Zach had learned to rely on himself, to function as an autonomous human being, but his ability to rely on others to meet his needs had been stunted. In his case, rather than acting as complements to each other, the two orientations become almost mutually exclusive. This lopsided condition represented Zach's core problem and his core developmental opportunity rolled into one.

Entering the assessment process, Zach had some awareness of his interpersonal problems at work, and the data and analysis and also the interpretation of the data heightened that awareness. If in constructing a theory about him, we had never uttered a word about personality theory, he would still have left the process much clearer about himself. Yet the brief explanation of the self-and-other polarity helped to clinch his discovery of his basic pattern. Once he saw the application of the polarity to himself, he again recognized not only how the pattern manifested itself at work but how it extended its reach throughout his life. By coming to an encompassing understanding about himself, the clarity became that much more compelling, and his interest in changing to become more effective at work was amplified by a desire to be more effective in his life. Zach declared: "I don't want to be like my parents. And I don't want to be that way with my children." He had found a personal motivation as well as a work motivation to change. In deciding what developmental objectives to set at work and at home, he said: "It's all related. It's your life. You can't have separate lives. It's all the same. One change can help the other. It's all related."

Self-Assertion Versus Enabling Others to Assert Themselves

A second distinction that falls under the broad heading of self-orientation and other-orientation is having an impact personally versus creating conditions for other people to have an impact. To be self-assertive is to express yourself: make your presence felt, have an impact on the environment, make a difference, achieve, attain mastery, engage in self-expansion, strive to be valued, assert yourself, take the lead, make the rules, set the terms, define the rela-

tionships of which you are a part. To help others to assert themselves is to allow or encourage others to do all of those things, including in relation to you.

Before running across this distinction in the literature on personality, I had developed an understanding of it in the course of
our research-based work with executives. It had struck me, as we
attempted to characterize each individual we worked with, that
many of them were *forces*—forces to be reckoned with, forces in nature—and that their performance problems resulted from being
forceful to a fault. The majority of the executive population tends
to the self-assertive, forceful side, yet a certain proportion leans the
other way, toward enabling others. This distinction was not a new
thought certainly, but one whose particular content and structure
fit the executive-level population that we work with. Just as a par-
simonious theory about an individual manager develops from iterating on that person's data, this theory took shape from iterating
across cases.

Because I first understood the distinction between being self-
assertive and being enabling in relation to the managerial population (Kaplan, 1996), I will describe it here not in general but in
managerial terms. Self-assertive managers make their presence felt;
they let people know clearly what they expect, are not reluctant to
make demands, hold people accountable, step up to the tough decisions (even those that have an adverse effect on people), take
charge, and in general let little or nothing deter them from achieving their objectives, for the organization and for themselves.

When self-assertion is exaggerated, it consists of an excessive
concern with one's own performance and impact. The individual
expends a disproportionate amount of energy on attaining mastery personally. Individual achievement becomes the be-all and
end-all of self-satisfaction. The individual becomes so wrapped up
in distinguishing herself that she has little emotional energy left
over for other people and can be said to lack empathy. This is the
narcissistic personality—one that is much more interested in being
the hero than, as one executive put it, making heroes. Self-assertion
can be taken to the point of domination, outright aggression, and
even abuse of others.

Enabling-oriented managers create the conditions for other
people to put their strength and resources to work. They tap into,

bring out, and place a high value on the capabilities and intensity of other people. In effect, they create the conditions that make it possible for other people to be forceful themselves. They do a great job of involving their people and opening themselves to their influence—in setting strategic direction and in making decisions that affect the unit as a whole.

When enabling is taken to an extreme, managers give their subordinates too much latitude and fail to give direction or hold others accountable. They are overly concerned with what others think, overly responsive to their needs or concerns, overly accommodating. They shy away from conflict and have difficulty confronting people about performance deficits. They do not let their organization know clearly where they stand, strategically or operationally. Overly enabling managers tend to be self-effacing, taking a facilitative or catalytic or behind-the-scenes role to the point where their own direct impact is muted or lost. They are so oriented to others that they subordinate their own sense of self.

Richard, a composite of four people, serves as a case in point. He tilted decidedly toward the enabling side and, as the process of data reduction proceeded, integrated the various elements of his leadership profile around the assertive-enabling duality. His strengths were strategic thinking, knowledge of the marketplace, interpersonal skills, and a generally winning personality. His weaknesses were difficulty with executing, conflict, and delegating. The breakthrough for him came with the realization that he had been overemphasizing one aspect of the forceful-enabling dimension.

Indicative of his historical attitude was his initial reaction to the report. The jumping-off point was the major finding that he had received strong scores on quite a few major managerial dimensions, yet he had underrated himself on most of those dimensions. This discrepancy was telling. Richard immediately recognized his persistent tendency to discount his strengths as an expression of his basic insecurity. And yet when I suggested to him that he would do himself a lot of good if he were to internalize these views of his strengths, he reacted with horror.

Consultant: I suggest that you write down all the strengths as well as the high praise you received. Let in these positives; soak them up through your pores so to speak.

Richard: See, I would have trouble doing that.
Consultant: Let's imagine that you internalized this high praise.
What would happen?
Richard: People would view me as egotistical. I don't like
people like that. Maybe also fear of failure: if I get to
that point, I might fail, from overconfidence.

Affected by his doubts about himself, his hesitance to assert himself acted as a powerful brake on him, as his following comments show:

It's not that I'm not forceful. It's being concerned with how it will be received. It's the acceptance thing. Psychologically, it's back to the fear of rejection. The worst fear is I get up and no one follows.

I can be decisive, but then I say to myself, What if, what if?

People say here in the report that I'm a good guy. Actually, I worry about that. I'm never sure people like me. And this worry inhibits me.

A lot of times I know the decision, but I'm afraid to make it because I don't want to hurt the person's feelings.

I worry too much about whether people are happy versus leading people.

Harmony is very important to me. I don't like fighting at home, and I actually undermine my wife's discipline with our children.

One consequence of this orientation was overwork. Rather than making demands on his subordinates and rather than rejecting unsatisfactory work, he did the work himself. His difficulty with delegation stemmed not, as it often does, from a need to control others, but from a reluctance to assert himself. In general, his scores revealed that he shied away from the tough actions required of managers. His spotty record with implementation arose from an inability to hold his staff accountable for results. People said that he was not truly on top of his job, despite his long hours, in the sense that he lacked personal organization and did not set priorities well.

He was able to break through to a revised understanding of himself, one that put him in a position to grow, with the help of the theory on forceful and enabling leadership. Along with the leadership assessment content, what helped him was the idea, built into polarities as conceptual structures, of polarization. He discovered that he had polarized these two approaches to leadership: "I have thought that people in top positions were sons of bitches." He set the objective of becoming a "better leader," by which he meant a more forceful leader: "I want to go forward versus back into or sidle up to." He also set the objective of "eliminating the aversion to confidence: I've come to believe that confidence is okay." When I suggested that it sounded as if he wanted to sit in the driver's seat, he said, "Yes, and I feel I can drive that car and not be arrogant."

This is a wonderful instance of an increase in clarity. Where previously he had confused confidence and arrogance, he was now able to distinguish the two and free himself to act with greater authority and self-assuredness. This clarification included a cognitive component: he discarded an old assumption or belief. It had also had an emotional component: he overcame his "fear of arrogance" that had kept him from fully recognizing his strengths, solidifying his confidence, and taking strong, decisive action.

Consistent with his difficulty with self-assertion, Richard did not take good care of himself. He felt that when he was home, he owed it to his wife and children to spend all his time with them, a worthy goal if it were not for the fact that he got no time to rest or exercise. His wife actually urged him to take better care of himself. She saw how worn down he got. What kept him from taking time for himself? It would be "selfish." This was another confusion, between meeting one's own legitimate needs and selfishness, a lack of clarity to which people with a strong other-orientation are liable. He was able to make this distinction sufficiently well to allow himself to begin exercising twice a week, getting up early so as not to take away from time with his family. Richard's mistake of confusing taking care of oneself with selfishness is an easy one to make, conceptually speaking. But all human beings need and want things for themselves and are perpetually seeking satisfaction. It is only a question of the routes they choose for getting their needs met. So although it may seem that self-oriented people are more intent on their own needs, other-oriented people are fundamentally no less self-interested.

GETTING AT CHARACTER **221**

Aided by his data and a unifying idea that helped him map the data, Richard was able to locate himself on a psychological and managerial field, see the direction for his further development, and want to move that way. This is a good first step toward self-development.

Uses of Polarities in Assessment

Orientation to self and orientation to others are especially useful as a unifying tool when they are taken together as a polarity. In rolling up the numerous data-based indications about a manager, the self-orientation and other-orientation polarities reveal the extent to which managers emphasize one approach as opposed to the other. Standard practice in management is to assess managerial characteristics piecemeal. By treating them in pairs, especially pairs of characteristics that oppose each other, it is easier to discern patterns. This is especially true when the polarity is broad, basic, and encompassing.

Polarity can prove useful not just in tying together a manager's strengths *or* weaknesses; it can serve as an integrative device that ties together strengths *and* weaknesses. Managers who are heavy on self-orientation are often light on other-orientation, and vice versa. The defining characteristic then becomes lopsidedness on this polarity.

Polarities are unifying ideas that help the manager see not only what is but also what might be. This is a key point. What is revealed is not a static, retrospective analysis, or not only that, but a dynamic prospective opportunity to do better. By organizing data in terms of whether one or the other side is underdone or overdone, one lights up the need and opportunity for a better way. The prescription of what could or should be is contained in the description of what is. What managers take away is an assessment and a direction for development.

The high value in management and life is not on one approach or the other but on versatility, so that individuals are able to take either approach depending on the circumstances. This flexibility does not come easily; human beings have a propensity to identify themselves with one side or the other of opposing ideas. It is almost as if they have trouble holding two ideas in their heads at the same time. Harlan Cleveland (1980) said it well: "The art of executive leadership is above all a taste for paradox, a talent for ambiguity, the capacity to hold contradictory propositions comfortably in a mind that relishes complexity." The ultimate in human development may not be so much a balancing of the opposing self- and other-orientation but an integration of the two into a broad capability.

A larger concept is useful not only for interpreting data but also for informing the collection of data in the first place. We have developed a prototype instrument for measuring forceful and enabling leadership; the results can help integrate all the data on a manager's leadership. The instrument represents only a small subset of the data collected on the individual; the task of ordering the great bulk of open-ended interview data remains. But the results from an instrument like this can help the individual locate himself or herself on the field defined by the polarity. Whether unifying theories are operationalized in the actual data collection, it helps to have them in mind during the process of data reduction. The consultants are in a stronger position to get to the crux if they know what to look for.

Self-Orientation Versus Other-Orientation

In penetrating to the core issue, it can be helpful to understand the individual's adjustment not just as a cross-section but from something of a longitudinal perspective. The ambitious task of laying out the individual's progress through a series of stages to the present point in his or her life is not one we undertake. What we do find productive, for the consultant and for the manager, is to get some idea of where the individual's basic pattern originated—in particular, the relative emphasis on self-orientation versus other-orientation. People tend to be one-sided, relatively speaking, and they tend to get stuck on that pattern. How does this happen?

Two theorists of self- and other-orientation bring a useful historical perspective. Blatt (1995) discussed evolution over a person's lifetime as taking place along these two "fundamental developmental lines." Kegan (1982) proposed a theory of developmental stages operating in spiral fashion, in which the person from birth alternates between an emphasis on one side and an emphasis on the other. He described "a continual moving back and forth between resolving the tension slightly in favor of autonomy or inclusion" (p. 108). At no point in a person's life does the resolution of the tension between an orientation to self and an orientation to other become a matter of either-or. Rather, it is a question of which is primary at a given stage, a matter of which is in the foreground and which in the background at any given time. Problems arise when a person becomes fixated on one of these orientations or processes and fails to swing back after a time to the other one and continue the natural process of unfolding. The individual latches onto that one side as the solution to the problem of how to feel good about himself or herself. Ironically, by depending so heavily on this one solution, the person degrades it.

But individuals who get stuck in a developmental rut are not simply fixated on one of the two opposing poles. A heavy identification with one orientation is not merely the product of having been powerfully attracted to it and therefore gravitating developmentally in that direction, as compelling and in some ways rewarding as that orientation may be. People whose development is seriously arrested actively avoid the opposing pole. As much as they associate themselves with one pole, are wedded to it, they dissociate themselves from the other one, are divorced from it. As Blatt (1995) put it, most developmental problems "can be defined as a distorted and exaggerated emphasis on one of these two developmental lines and the defensive avoidance of the other" (pp. 1012–1013).

We saw this pattern with Zachary. His early experience with relationships was sufficiently aversive that he actively avoided close relationships just as he depended on individual achievement for self-satisfaction. Zach avoided relationships as a defense against being hurt, disappointed, and let down by others. He came to see this, and it sharpened the clarity of his insight into himself in these broad conceptual terms. The next step in his development would be to move from virtually *being* his career to *having* a career, which would free him to invest more in relationships.

Just as the next developmental step for Zachary is to swing in the direction of increasing his investment in relationships, the next step for Richard is to increase his investment in himself. Richard had been stuck in a pattern so thoroughly focused on other people that it was almost as if, as Kegan (1982) would put it, he *was* his relationships. The stage that awaits him is one in which he will *have* relationships, rather than defining his identity primarily in terms of relationships. This is a stage that stresses the person's authority and control over himself and his world (Kegan, 1982). This capacity for self-organization would address Richard's lack of control over his time and lack of organization in his life.

Historically, psychology has viewed independence and individual achievement as the ultimate in human development. Lately, that view has been questioned and has been replaced with one, also taken here, that the relationship side of human nature is no less important to individual functioning and fulfillment (Gilligan, 1982; Kegan, 1982; Blatt, 1995). In fact, as Blatt pointed out, "progress in one developmental line facilitates development in the other." A person evolves through a reciprocal development of these sides of personality. "An increasingly differentiated, integrated, and mature sense of self is contingent on establishing satisfying interpersonal relationships, and conversely the continued development of increasingly mature and satisfying interpersonal relationships is contingent on the development of a more mature self-concept and identity" (p. 1012).

To characterize a particular manager and his or her developmental needs in basic terms like these could easily be superficial and facile were it not for the broad empirical basis of the assessment for this characterization. Because the macroconcept is used to derive simple truths from a large, complex set of data, it is welcomed by the participant as a profound organizing principle rather than dismissed as easy, simplistic typecasting. When existing theory is applied in a given case, we virtually never take it off the shelf and fit it in that form onto the individual. It is usually always altered to fit the person's particular features. Someone who is primarily self-oriented may in certain respects be oriented the opposite way, and the same is true of a largely other-oriented person. The individual's profile on various subcategories is just as significant as the larger category into which he or she falls.

The data and integration of the interpretation are related in a circular fashion. As is true with any other subject, to understand the whole of a person, one must understand the parts, in all of their particularistic glory. And to understand the parts, an individual's various characteristics, it helps greatly to have a grasp on the whole—the person's overall essential character (Hoy, 1978).

The Social Context

The social context has a huge bearing on what data will come to the light, how seriously the individual will take the information, and what use the individual will make of it. The individual's level of trust in the consultants will affect how freely he or she makes data available. The level of support that the individual receives from the consultants will affect how well he or she is able to stand up to the rigors of the feedback process and be equal to the task of encountering disconfirming, disturbing, or painful results. The extent of the network of people, beyond the professionals conducting the assessment, who are involved in the person's effort to change will have a potentially big impact on whether the individual changes and whether the change is sustained. To help an adult make a genuine, lasting change for the better, we need leverage. Information and effective strategies for making use of it is one basic type of leverage in assessment. The social aspect, including who is involved and in what manner and for how long, is another type of leverage. We and the people participating very much need both types.

Conclusions

Although I have concentrated here on psychological assessment done for the sake of the individual's development, the major elements of the approach apply to assessment in general and thus in some respects to assessment for the sake of selection. First, in constructing a picture of the individual upon which consequential judgments can be made, it is obviously important to collect enough information to form a sound basis for those judgments. Second, comes the task of reducing this large and varied set of data to a usable form. Two complementary strategies suggest themselves. First, it is critical to adopt an inductive approach, in which conclusions are inferred from the data through highly systematic, step-by-step analysis. The task is to organize the data into something coherent, so that they hang together. Put another way, we assessors are seeking an understanding of how the individual organizes himself or herself. The ultimate, I feel, is to discover an individual's basic organizing principle or principles. Second, in this process of discovery, it is important to pull down high-level abstractions (for example, archetypelike concepts such as self-orientation and other-orientation) that contribute to the definition of what the individual's basic organizing principle is. However, we must always be sharply attuned to the difference between the lazy, facile pigeon-holing of people into buzzword categories and the careful delineation of an encompassing concept for the specific individual in question.

When the purpose of assessment is the individual's development, then increased clarity on the part of the individual about himself or herself is what we seek to provide. Done successfully, assessment for development leads to genuine change, a change in which participants internalize—actually make a part of themselves—a modified principle, value, belief, or view of themselves. This increased clarity about themselves or about the importance of conducting themselves differently may very well lead to a change in the way they behave. But even if it does not or does not soon after the realization, the realization itself—a "mind-set change," as one manager called it—represents a change. If the new mind-set consists of a principle that the individual embraces but does not immediately practice, that newly embraced principle represents the potential to change in accordance with that principle. Or if the manager goes from being in denial about something she does to recognizing that she does it, even if she does not stop doing it, that realization does some good because she will understand better other people's reactions when she acts that way. In any case, an awareness gained but not immediately acted on amounts to a creative tension that has the potential for later change in behavior. Furthermore, an increase in clarity about oneself is not typically a jump from complete lack of clarity to total clarity. It is a matter of increasing degrees of clarity, gained gradually. It is not often that we suddenly see things clearly; more often, the glass through which we see darkly grows clearer in small degrees.

References

Bakan, D. (1966). *The duality of human existence: Isolation and communion in Western man.* Boston: Beacon Press.

Beck, A. T. (1983). Cognitive therapy of depression: New perspectives. In P. J. Clayton & J. E. Barrett (Eds.), *Treatment of depression: Old controversies and new approaches* (pp. 265–290). New York: Raven Press.

Blatt, S. J. (1995). The destructiveness of perfectionism: Implications for the treatment of depression. *American Psychologist, 50,* 1003–1020.

Bowlby, J. (1988). Developmental psychiatry comes of age. *American Journal of Psychiatry, 145,* 1–10.

Cleveland, H. (1980). Learning the art of leadership: The worldwide crisis in governance demands new approaches. *Twin Cities Magazine.*

Gilligan, C. (1982). *In a different voice: Psychological theory and women's development.* Cambridge, MA: Harvard University Press.

Glaser, B. G., & Strauss, A. L. (1967). *The discovery of grounded theory: Strategies for qualitative research.* London: Weidenfeld and Nicolson.

Holmes, R. (1994). *Shelley: The Pursuit.* London: HarperCollins.

Hoy, D. C. (1978). *The critical circle: Literature, history, and philosophical hermeneutics.* Berkeley: University of California Press.

Kaplan, R. E. (1996). *Forceful leadership and enabling leadership: You can do both.* Greensboro, NC: Center for Creative Leadership.

Kaplan, R. E., & Palus, C. J. (1994). *Enhancing 360° feedback for senior executives: How to maximize the benefits and minimize the risks.* Greensboro, NC: Center for Creative Leadership.

Kegan, R. (1982). *The evolving self: Problem and process in human development.* Cambridge, MA: Harvard University Press.

Lyall, S. (1996, September 23). Forty poems that Eliot wanted to hide, including some on the bawdy side. *New York Times,* p. C11.

McAdams, D. P. (1988). *Power, intimacy, and the life story: Psychological inquiries into identity.* New York: Guilford Press.

Smiley, J. (1991). *A thousand acres.* New York: Fawcett.

Tobias, L. L. (1990). *Psychological consulting to management: A clinician's perspective.* New York: Brunner/Mazel.

Updike, J. (1995). *The afterlife, and other stories.* New York: Knopf.

Wiggins, J. S. (1973). *Personality and predictor: Principles of personality assessment.* Reading, MA: Addison-Wesley.

Wiggins, J. S. (1982). Circumplex models of interpersonal behavior in clinical psychology. In P. C. Kendell & J. N. Butcher (Eds.), *Handbook of research methods in clinical psychology.* New York: Wiley.

CHAPTER 7

A Clinical Approach to Executive Selection

Harry Levinson

Executive selection is complex and difficult, as a number of authors have noted. In a pointed article, Yeager and Brenner (1994) concluded that "the old-fashioned paper and pencil way [of psychological testing] merely gives a generalized label without giving meaningful answers about what is really going on" (p. 6). They complained that contemporary psychological testing for selection is a melange of different tests that tap disparate variables that cannot be integrated; these variables largely describe self-identified behavior but do not explain why the behavior occurs or the causes of whatever behavior is being reported. Essentially, then, reports from psychological tests are fractionated descriptions. Without an underlying integrative theory, psychologists have difficulty tying together the results of different tests. As a result, according to their study of sixty-eight psychologists who reported on their selection work with high-level executives in major corporations, all agreed that the interview, despite its inadequacies as a predictor of behavior, was the one method that was indispensable to the assessment process because the psychologist had to tie the disparate findings into an interpretative summary.

McClelland, Koestner, and Weinberger (1989) compared the interpreted stories of their subjects as predictors of behavior with conclusions formulated from inferences drawn from paper-and-pencil test results. They found that their interpretation of the stories people told about Thematic Apperception Test cards predicted those people's subsequent behavior more accurately than did their responses to the interpretations from inventories.

The problems of selecting executives are compounded by the fact that, to my knowledge, there are no established psychological test norms for predicting the success of high-level executives. At best, peer evaluations and assessment centers predict managerial mobility through several levels. Not many of the thousands of top-level executives in the United States have been nominated by peers or screened by assessment centers.

There is fairly common agreement that certain behavioral traits are fundamental to effective leadership: conscientiousness, energy, intelligence, dominance, self-confidence, sociability, openness to experience, task-relevant knowledge, and emotional stability (Kets de Vries, 1995). Such categories describe behavior but do not explain it.

Although widely used, such measures as the Myers-Briggs type categories and other classifications also largely describe behavior. Despite efforts to relate the variables to each other, these are not readily visible or accepted, nor do they satisfactorily elucidate the origins of various traits, what forces modulate them in what ways under what circumstances, or which, if any, may be integrated by a theory of personality. Nor do they explain how, and to what extent, if any, those traits are learned or given, capable of being developed or encouraged, changeable or resistant to change, age related, reactive, or characterological. The same is true of the Five Factors Model (Digman, 1990) and the Six Personality Types Model (Holland, 1985).

The task of conceptualization may not be so refractory to understanding or integration. Where should one begin? Because "objective" methods for predicting high-level executive success are in such a parlous state, a useful alternative is to fall back on an integrated theory of personality that offers the possibility of describing both the behavioral requirements of a role and the criteria for judging the presence of that behavior in individuals. Such a theory also provides an underlying logic for explaining the origins of the required behavior and also the relationships among its many facets. Those psychologists who are clinically trained may infer less conscious sources of given behaviors. Others may simply summarize them into a consistent, integrated picture of the individual.

A comprehensive personality theory like psychoanalysis, starting with drive theory and ego psychology, is able to do both. From both cognitive psychology and psychoanalysis, we know that feelings precede thinking and thinking precedes behavior. Therefore, a logical theory that enables us to predict behavior should flow from origins in feelings and subsequent mental processes.

A simple way to proceed is to organize the fundamental variables into three categories: thinking, feeling, and behavior (Levinson, 1980). In the first group, thinking, I include the assessment of a candidate's capacity to abstract, conceptualize, and organize and integrate complex data into a coherent frame of reference (Jaques & Cason, 1994). Then I want to assess the person's tolerance for ambiguity: whether and to what degree the candidate can tolerate confusion (under varied circumstances) and still maintain focus. As Andrew S. Grove, CEO of Intel Corporation, has said, competitive changes in the workplace are leading to a less kind, less predictable, less gentle workplace. Managers and executives, he says, need a higher tolerance for disorder and should do their best to drive what is around them to order. "The fundamental idea," he writes, "is that you should run your managerial processes like a well-oiled factory" (Grove, 1995). In this category, too, I include the practicality of one's intelligence under different circumstances and the exercise of judgment in those varied circumstances.

The fundamental feelings, as conceptualized by psychoanalytic drive theory, are derivatives of the drives of sex and aggression. These manifest themselves on the one hand in the need to love and be loved, or the expression of feelings of affection, and on the other in the need to attack or master the environment. Because all human beings start out helpless and ultimately, if they live long enough, become helpless again, the issue of feelings about dependency and its management is also fundamental.

A person who can grow out of her immature ambivalence toward authority figures and develop smooth working relationships with them can also work interdependently with both superiors and subordinates. Thus this person can accept the appropriate dependency of others as well as her own dependency needs. Such a person can take a stand but also invite information, criticism, and cooperation from others. From time to time the person can yield temporarily to the lead of more competent specialized persons without feeling deprived of authority.

A comfortable fusion of aggression and affection and the capacity to accept one's dependency needs manifests itself in a "natural" ability to take charge, when that is role appropriate, with reasonable certainty that one will do so well. That is, the person is able to accept and express his or her own authority and to feel that she belongs in an authoritative situation, one in which power must be exercised appropriate to the role. That stance, coupled with high-level conceptual capacity, enables the person to take a vigorous posture toward the problems and needs of the organization or any of its components that she is to lead. Such a person attacks leadership problems strategically with well-defined targets and plans comprising long-term, step-by-step competitive activity.

When those capacities—abstraction, conceptualization, fusion of affection and aggression, and acceptance of dependency—are found in the context of a high level of aspiration or a distant ego ideal, governed by a power orientation (McClelland, 1975), such a combination orients a person toward attaining gratification from an organization's success rather than from personal aggrandizement. This person is highly motivated toward upward mobility in recognition and appreciation of her competence and talent, not by hunger for applause. In an executive role, such a person sees the organization's achievements as also personal achievements. As Alex Trotman, CEO of the Ford Motor Company, put it, "When the company does things well, that's my ego trip. I don't distinguish between myself and the company" (Taylor, 1995).

Some persons are alexithymic, a label coined by Sifneos (1973); they are unable to experience their own or to sense others' feelings. Leaders, in contrast, must be able to perceive the subtleties of other people's feelings, anticipate them, and take them seriously into account. To be able to do that, leaders must be able to sense their own feelings. Thus they can comfortably involve themselves as participating members of an organization, mixing well with others, seeking information, and maintaining a finger on the pulse of the organization.

A person with these capacities and traits is likely to be able to present herself extremely well. Her colleagues respect her for identifying, verbalizing, and presenting organizational problems, and those in an audience, whose mood she is able to sense, are inspired by her presence and presentation.

In addition to giving rise to mental energy, as reflected in aspects of thinking and mentioned previously, aggression is manifested in a consistently high energy level in behavior. Although always ready to deal with the organization's problems, the person avoids drivenness by careful pacing. She seems to thrive on whatever problems arise, adapting and managing stress well. The fact that this person can do so is also reflected in warm, affectionate humor that eases tensions and makes her welcome company.

Combinations of these factors manifest themselves in what might be described as a super ego–oriented person whose ego ideals give consistent integrated direction to all the facets of her personality. As an executive candidate in her mid-thirties, this person has a sense of the progression of her own life and career, as well as a sense of where the organization should go. (Even a candidate from outside the organization is likely to have investigated the organization before offering himself for scrutiny.) A serious candidate is likely to be actively pursuing well-defined goals consistent with the organization's needs and values.

Such a pursuit implies a certain optimistic perseverance and confidence of finding solutions to obstacles (Seligman, 1991). That is more likely to be the case if a person is well organized and makes good use of time, intuition, and intellect. Because the fundamental issue in all relationships is trust, a person's dependability and possession of a well-established value system that has been tested in various ways in the past lead to the recognition that the person's integrity is beyond reproach. Successful organizational leadership requires people who recognize social responsibility, appreciate the need to assume such responsibility, and relish it as opportunity.

To these criteria, Irving Shapiro (1995), former CEO of E. I. du Pont de Nemours & Co., adds what he regards as the key ingredient: "wisdom." Wisdom provides the capacity to see what followers, however enthusiastic, may not see.

The degree to which these behavioral characteristics are consistent over time and across situations is reflected in the candidate's personal history. That must be carefully investigated, experience by experience, with special attention to the person's reaction to frustration and disappointment. This work enables the assessor to differentiate characterological behavior (the enduring, relatively unchangeable behavioral patterns) from reactive behavior (that occurring in response to varied environmental precipitants or forces).

Behavioral Job Descriptions

With a mode of assessing the character and personality of individuals established, the next logical question is, What for? Some behavioral characteristics are more significant for certain functions than for others. Sometimes groups of behavioral characteristics form a cluster. An aggressive, highly controlling person who would fit one situation in an organization might be inappropriate in another. Therefore, it is more useful to think of behavioral characteristics as a configuration, a pattern or profile.

A good executive, like a diamond, is multifaceted. The larger the number of facets, the more brilliantly the diamond shines. Some facets are larger, some smaller, and not all diamonds are equifaceted. But all facets are part of a whole diamond, which ultimately focuses the light passing through the facets to a single integrated point. Further, few diamonds are without flaws.

The answer to the question What for? is a behavioral job description. Many job descriptions describe only desired or required outcomes, not how those outcomes are to be achieved. More often they describe objectives or targets, less often what activities the person is to perform, with whom, and how. Even headhunters who seek out high-level executives often have only a fuzzy picture of what that person really is supposed to do and with whom. Therefore they often have inadequate understanding of the required fit of the person to the organization, let alone to the specific role.

A job description must be careful to describe all of the significant tasks required in that role. Often there are role senders, who influence a given role even if there is no direct reporting relationship between the person in the role and the role sender. Sometimes role senders have control over resources the person needs: information, material resources, human resources; or they have influence with a person's boss; or they need (or feel they have a right to) that person's cooperation. For a given executive, a role sender may be the organization's controller who has no authority over the executive but can influence his access to funds and financial data. Top management is likely to be involved in relationships not only with members of the board but also with officials in banks or other financial institutions, those in government agencies, and some in powerful political positions or community leadership. The job description should specify the role senders and their expectations, tacit or manifest.

Next, in putting together the job description, it is necessary to consider the mode of thinking needed to accomplish the tasks. One aspect of thinking is the time required for each task (Jaques, 1989). That is, to accomplish each task, how far ahead must a person plan, and what is the time span of the longest task (that is, the time it will take to accomplish it)? The latter defines the time span of the role. For example, the president of a division of a major corporation is likely to have many tasks to accomplish. Some may require a few moments, some a day, some a month, some a year, but it is likely that a person in such a role must be able to think ahead for at least ten years. If a person cannot do that, then he is likely to be overwhelmed by the complexity of the role.

Another issue relates to interaction with the management of affection, aggression, and dependency in the role. Will the job require the person to have frequent, intense contact with others or to take unpopular stands or undertake unpopular actions? What tasks in this role will the person initiate, and to which events must he necessarily respond? Can situations be approached head-on, or must the person modulate his aggression to approach them with greater finesse? What tasks, processes, or problems must be attacked, and how: frontally, as John F. Welch did when he took over the General Electric Company, or more indirectly, as did Reginald Jones, Welch's predecessor?

How does the job require the candidate to manifest trust and credibility, to accept the need for supervision and direction from subordinates, and to accept help from others? Whose trust must the person earn, and how? What will be the inherent returns if the person discharges the requirements of this role well? Will the result be financial rewards? Will the person achieve greater status or recognition? Will the person find greater satisfaction in the results of team effort than in individual achievement? Will the person have to seek pride in the product or service to be offered or in the reputation of the organization? Who or what are the "enemies" to be vanquished?

Formulating a behavioral job description is akin to drawing a picture of the topography of the required job performance in a given organization. This psychological map could show the hazards and dangers of varied interactions, the potential blocks to moving ahead, the psychological shoals, the managerial avenues to be avoided, even the economic mountains to be climbed. Such a map could tell a person what he is likely to have to do, how, with whom, under what circumstances, and with what potential hazards and rewards. Many candidates have appropriate education and experience, but a behavioral job description compels a focus on the one who will work well in *this* company and *this* position. When those who are interviewing a candidate develop a comprehensive picture of the candidate's behavior in the multiple facets of previous roles, then they are in a position to test the fit of that described behavior to the behavior required in the new role.

The critical need here is to have the person describe in explicit detail what he actually did in the various aspects of previous roles. Here are some of the open-ended interview questions (not original with me) that I have found helpful:

1. Tell me what you think I ought to know about you to evaluate how well you are likely to fit the job you are applying for.
2. What do you know about the company you are applying to?
3. What do you know about the specific requirements of the job that you are applying for?
4. What doubts or concerns do you have about either the prospective company or the prospective role?
5. Of all the things you've done, and of all your accomplishments, what has given you the greatest satisfaction and pride?
6. Under what circumstances do you work best in any organization?
7. What things tend to get your goat?
8. How does your spouse or significant other describe you? The people who report to you? Your children? Your closest friend?
9. What important lessons have you learned from your past experiences or mistakes?

10. Describe the best boss you have ever had. The worst?
11. Describe the most difficult crisis you have faced in any one of your roles. How did you resolve it?
12. When you interview people who are to report to you, what are you most interested in learning about? What do you ask? What did you do about problems you discovered? What were the results?
13. What information do you want from me?

Identification

Fundamental to effective leadership is the ability of a person to create identification of her followers with herself. If people cannot identify with the leader, then they will not follow her, and, further, they cannot readily identify with each other. To foster identification, people who are to fulfill leadership roles should be able to create a story of where they are going or where they are planning to take the organization, and why. Ideally, that story will engender enthusiasm, commitment, and dedication on the part of their followers and make clear who or what is the enemy they are to attack. Such a person should be able to foster creativity and commitment by focusing people's attack on appropriate enemies and giving them the freedom and necessary support to master those enemies.

A prospective leader should understand the meaning of the unconscious psychological contract: that change undermines people's preferred mode of handling affection, aggression, and dependency and often interferes with their pursuit of their ego ideals. Therefore all change threatens not merely their conscious expectations but, more important, their deep-seated behavioral preferences. That is the reason people most often experience change as loss. The effective leader, in the words of my colleague Miles Shore, must be the chief mourner of those losses consequent to change. She must openly identify and regret the losses, and then move on to helping the followers find or create new avenues for meeting those needs when previous sources of affectional input and favored foci of attack have been lost.

When the leader helps the followers mourn and thereby detach themselves from their previous sources of gratification, the followers view that as true leadership behavior. That is what a good leader is supposed to do: help them master their regret and move on to new efforts. When they develop such regard for a leader, they identify with that leader and the values reflected in her caring behavior. Not only must a prospective candidate fit the behaviors required in a given role, which may be quite different from those required of the predecessor but she must also know when it is time to leave the role. For some executives who are building organizations, even twenty years in the CEO role may not be too much. Others will have made their most significant contributions in half that time. Many in senior roles feel seven to ten years is long enough. The most important criteria for leaving are boredom, unresolved frustration, repetition, fatigue, and particularly loss of pleasure, especially because of unresolved conflicts. Many executives whose capacity for mastering complexity far exceeds the challenge of their roles must finally leave them in bored desperation. It is important for an interviewer to know what aspects of role performance, as spelled out in the detailed description of tasks, led to the incumbent's frustration. And should a candidate explain the wish to leave a role as due to "personality conflicts," the interviewer should examine in explicit detail the nature of such conflicts.

Avoiding Pathology

The most pervasive problem among people who exercise power over others is that of narcissism in its many forms. All of us need enough narcissism to have self-confidence and to be optimistic about what we can do. However, narcissism can become a conspicuous component of personality. The most obvious form manifests itself when one lavishes one's affection on oneself. There are several prominent variants of this propensity. One simple form is the person who can never get enough attention, recognition, or applause. In a managerial role, such a person may claim others' ideas as his own, give inadequate recognition and credit to others, or fail to support subordinates. In a more pathological vein, such a person may fawn upward and dump downward, gaining the approval of superior while abusing and exploiting subordinates. Such a person has difficulty working on a team, sharing credit, and sensing others' needs and feelings. At higher levels the narcissist may well press inordinately for perquisites, larger bonuses, and sometimes exceptional raises for subordinates. The last is likely when the executive characteristically mobilizes these subordinates against higher management. At highest levels, highly narcissistic people ensconce themselves in opulent offices and with unnecessarily expensive accouterments like large jet airplanes that they rarely use.

A most malignant form of narcissism is the "con man." Such a person has winning ways that result in his being widely liked and too easily trusted, especially by higher management. He often obtains inordinate power in an organization because of his network of friends in powerful places, which enables him to manipulate behind the scenes around channels of accountability. Recognizing his contacts and his popularity, others, even superiors, defer to him. As a subordinate, he is unmanageable and wreaks havoc in an organization. By definition, such a person is contemptuous of others; his gratification lies in outsmarting them.

Another form of narcissism is the psychological core that provides the rationale for attack on others. In organizations, very bright, perfectionist, achievement-oriented people (in McClelland's sense, 1975) frequently are promoted into managerial roles because of their individual competence. The intense demand on and implicit criticism of themselves spills over onto others in the form of abrasive criticism. They are hard on their subordinates and peers just as they are hard on themselves. Because they are so valuable to an organization, higher managements tolerate that behavior for too many years. These people tend to rise in a hierarchy until their behavior becomes too costly in the form of subordinate turnover or customer complaint. A less destructive form of such behavior is that of the disdainful personality, who may not get into vitriolic arguments but who consistently depreciates others' ideas, proposals, and behavior.

Workaholics are likely to combine both forms of narcissism to varying degrees. They not only drive themselves toward impossible ego ideal goals, for example, unconscious fantasied omnipotence, but also tend to demand the same intensity of commitment and level of perfectionist behavior of others that they demand of themselves. When they are particularly competent, they are likely to exude charisma. In their view the whole organization becomes dependent on them—on their proficiency, drive, and imagination. Under such a leader, others are likely to be lesser lights, and to see themselves that way, though perhaps dedicated to the sometimes charismatic leader who often "does it all himself" and does not worry about the limitations of his diminished followers. In his eyes they are all inadequate anyway.

More rarely seen, but often found in tightly controlled organizations like the military, is the alexithymic personality: the "cold fish" who cannot experience his own feelings or sense those of other people. A conspicuous example is a former military officer who is now CEO of a major corporation. When his vice president of human resources suggested a program on stress management, he rejected it, saying that he did not have any stress, he did not know what stress was, and what's more, he did not understand why anybody else should experience stress.

Conspicuous achievement sometimes masks underlying vulnerability. This is especially the case among people who are unconsciously basically passive and dependent and who deny their dependency by high achievement. That achievement appears to others as indicative of great strength and independence. They are likely to lean heavily on their spouses. When the spouses, often frustrated by the executives' overcommitment to work and community service, threaten to leave the marriage or actually do, the executives are vulnerable to psychological collapse (Bird, Martin, & Schuham, 1983).

Other Focuses

Increasingly, contemporary executives will have to work with three kinds of people. First are the achievement-oriented persons who often are outstanding performers. They include a wide range of technical and professional persons, many of whom are on the leading edge of their technical fields. As specialization increases, organizations must have more and more professionals who have spent years learning their specialty and therefore have a very strong identification with their professions. Such people often are difficult to supervise because they are likely to be more self-critical than others, to know a lot more about what they are doing than their managers know about management, and to have a significant body of standards and ethics that govern their performance.

Second, many people in organizations are creative. Members of this creative subgroup may develop new products, new sales and marketing techniques, creative advertising themes, and novel services. They tend not to be conformists and not to live comfortably in bureaucracies. As a result, executives tend to become impatient with them.

The third subgroup of people who must be led carefully consists of those with high potential: the very bright people who are likely to move upward quickly in any organization. With very high ego ideals they demand continuing challenge, and their brilliant competence may frighten their superiors. They are unlikely to wait around for a promotion, yet they must be supported, despite their apparent lack of need for support, and criticized only sensitively.

Those selecting candidates for high-level executive positions must assess each candidate's capacity for sensing the internal strivings of the people in these subgroups and also the candidate's ability to tolerate their sometimes deviant behavior. They require considerable senior management support to assuage their demanding self-criticism, resources to facilitate their achievement, and well-defined boundaries to keep sometimes idiosyncratic behavior within appropriate limits.

The same techniques that enable an assessor to judge a candidate's possibly pathological potential apply also to assessing the candidate's capacity for dealing with professionals, creative people, and high potentials. The fundamental rule is to get the candidate to describe and discuss in considerable detail what he has done in varied situations. It is an old managerial axiom that "the devil lies in the details." Not only are the examples important but even more important are the nuances of detail in which the candidate specifies *exactly* what he said or did in a given situation. Sometimes an assessor may not be able to evaluate all the information, but no one can evaluate information that he or she does not have. An assessor may use various instruments to gather information, but nothing will take the place of an extended interview that probes for detail.

In a global economy, executives, even in relatively small organizations, must manage people who come from diverse cultures and may themselves have to work in such cultures. Given the large number of immigrants in organizations, whether employed in menial roles in the bowels of an organization or in high-achievement professional and scientific positions, an executive's ability to understand and tolerate cultural differences with patience and wisdom will be of growing importance. Some of this capacity is reflected when candidates have taken part of their academic work overseas and have learned several languages, and some is reflected by how they have managed ethnic groups domestically. The management of gender differences, too, will be of growing importance. The African American woman who has become a high-level officer in a financial services firm and the woman who has managed an automobile components factory and whose subordinates are mostly blue-collar men are prominent examples of persons who have mastered cultural diversity.

Some people have a propensity for defeating themselves when they rise to high levels. It is as if they must rise high enough to fall hard or the defeat will have insufficient meaning. Former U.S. Senator Gary Hart is a case in point. Another was a late Hollywood mogul who did not need the money but was convicted of forging checks. Such men usually are the victims of unconscious guilt for having symbolically defeated their fathers by succeeding beyond them. Clues to such behavior lie in the propensity for putting oneself down, for not being able to accept one's achievements without apology, for having made mistakes that are "too stupid to be stupid." "I can't understand why I ever did that," said one otherwise highly successful candidate.

Conclusions

A comprehensive theory of personality (like psychoanalysis) enables psychologists to pursue a highly refined, systematic interview to select executives. Without such a theoretical basis, the interview has not fared well as a predictor of behavior. Yet disparate psychological test data are difficult to integrate into a composite picture of a person, let alone to be an adequate basis for predicting behavior in complex leadership roles. Reasonable prediction from psychological testing requires not only adequate norms for high-level executives but also psychologically detailed behavioral job descriptions. Few exist. Even fewer are based on a theory that relates the required behavior to its underlying psychological dynamics.

The same theory, enriching such a description, also serves to predict more exactly the degree of fit of person to role. In addition, it serves to detect the more subtle aspects of pathology.

References

Bird, H. W., Martin, P. A., & Schuham, A. (1983). The marriage of the "collapsible" man of prominence. *American Journal of Psychiatry*, *140*(3), 290–295.

Digman, J. M. (1990). Personality structure: Emergence of the five-factor model. *Annual Review of Psychology*, *41*, 417–440.

Freud, S. (1957). Instincts and their vicissitudes. In J. Strachey (Ed. & Trans.), *The standard edition of the complete psychological works of Sigmund Freud* (Vol. 14, pp. 67–102). London: Hogarth Press.

Grove, A. S. (1995, September 18). A high-tech CEO updates his views on managerial careers. *Fortune*, p. 229.

Hartman, H. (1958). *Ego psychology and the problem of adaptation.* Madison, CT: International Universities Press.

Holland, J. (1985). *Making vocational choices: A theory of careers* (2nd ed.). Upper Saddle River, NJ: Prentice Hall.

Jaques, E. (1989). *Requisite organization: The CEO's guide to creative structure and leadership.* Arlington, VA: Cason Hall.

Jaques, E., & Cason, K. (1994). *Human capabilities.* Arlington, VA: Cason Hall.

Kets de Vries, M.F.R. (1995). *Life and death in the executive fast lane: Essays on irrational organizations and their leaders.* San Francisco: Jossey-Bass.

Levinson, H. (1980). Criteria for choosing chief executives. *Harvard Business Review*, *58*(4), 113–120.

McClelland, D. C. (1975). *Power: The inner experience.* New York: Irvington.

McClelland, D. C., Koestner, R., & Weinberger, J. (1989). How do self-attributed and implicit motives differ? *Psychological Review*, *96*(4), 690–702.

Seligman, M. E. P. (1991). *Learned helplessness.* New York: Knopf.

Shapiro, I. S. (1995, March 1). How Irving Shapiro hires the right people regularly. *Boardroom Reports*, p. 5.

Sifneos, P. E. (1973). The prevalence of alexithymic characteristics in psychosomatic patients. *Psychotherapy and Psychosomatics*, *22*(6), 255–262.

Taylor, A. (1995, September 18). Ford's really big leap at the future. *Fortune*, p. 134.

Yeager, J., & Brenner, J. (1994). The assessment interview: Metalinguistic strategies in management assessment practices. *Consulting Psychology Journal*, *46*(3), 1061–1087.

CHAPTER 8

Communicating Results for Impact

Pierre Meyer

I have worked for the company for seventeen years, and have never received a performance evaluation. I have no idea what others think of me.

I am really excited about the opportunity to go through a developmental assessment. Then I can compare what you say to what others have told me. I hope we will have a chance to talk about what I can do to improve my performance.

I have no idea why I'm here. I figure you'll tell me. My manager just said to show up, and I couldn't reach anyone in Human Resources.

My team members describe me as positive, enthusiastic, fun, and motivating. My manager says I am too quiet and that senior management does not know if I have potential. I need to know why others see me so differently. Then I can develop a plan for growth and be in a better position for promotion.

The search firm told me I had to see a "shrink" before I could be a finalist for the position. So here I am. Let's go!

Many managers have been through these tests, and a lot of them have said it was useful. I feel fortunate that I am able to participate and that I will get an opportunity to talk about the results.

These statements are typical of the comments I have heard in the years I have done assessments. People who participate in an assessment are curious and cautious. One element that links many of them is the desire for valid, timely, and useful feedback. The external candidate, the experienced manager who is intent on making personal improvement, and the young professional uncertain about career options all want to hear how the results influence decisions made about them. The organization also expects to receive cogent, valuable feedback so that those decisions are effective.

Participants in assessment (this chapter uses the words *assessee* and *participant* interchangeably) and organizational representatives may have different expectations of and reactions to individual psychological assessment. One key element of interest to all is the manner in which results are communicated. They must be judiciously presented, with the understanding that an assessment has no meaning without such feedback. Psychologists must recognize a paradox in the interpretation of the assessment results. On the one hand the information has to be understood easily by persons who are unschooled in measurement methods—generally both the individual assessee and representatives of the organization. On the other hand the interpretation must be consistent with ethical standards and professional practices. The psychologist must consider the communication from these paradoxical perspectives.

The purpose of this chapter is to help psychologists provide substantive and significant information so that the individual receives feedback that affects future behaviors in a positive way and so that the organization is in a better position to make decisions regarding selection, promotion, development, or placement. Psychologists have a duty to both individual and organization.

After individuals have received information about assessment results, they are responsible for directing their own future development. Nevertheless, representatives of the organization can play a significant role in that development. Communicating for impact requires (1) an accurate appraisal of strengths and developmental opportunities, (2) a developmental plan that focuses on specific behavioral goals, (3) continual review and evaluation of progress by the individual, organizational representatives, and the psychologist, and (4) positive reinforcement of any observed changes. A typical developmental assessment process is summarized in Figure 8.1.

The first section of this chapter, on preassessment briefing, gives particular attention to the dual relationship embedded in the process. The second section describes the style and purpose of feedback report, the third section examines the critical elements required for development to occur, and the fourth section describes the activities in an individual feedback session. A fifth section outlines the value and power of holding a second feedback session that includes the individual, the organizational representatives, and the psychologist. I end the chapter with some comments about effective development techniques.

Preassessment Briefing

Effective communication of results begins before the actual assessment. It is important that the individual and the organization understand the purpose of the assessment. The psychologist should describe obligations to each of the parties and give an accurate preview of the assessment activities, discuss the process for evaluating results, and describe how and when feedback will take place.

Purpose

In the remainder of this chapter, it is assumed that the psychologist has a complete picture of the culture, structure, and style of the organization. The psychologist now must be prepared to describe why the organization has requested an assessment and what will occur as a result of it.

The success of the assessment depends on the assessor's having a clear understanding of the knowledge, skills, aptitudes, and other characteristics important for success in the organization. The instruments selected for use in the assessment must show a relationship between the dimensions that are measured and actual work performance. Schmitt and Landy (1993) emphasize that

Figure 8.1. A Typical Developmental Assessment Process.

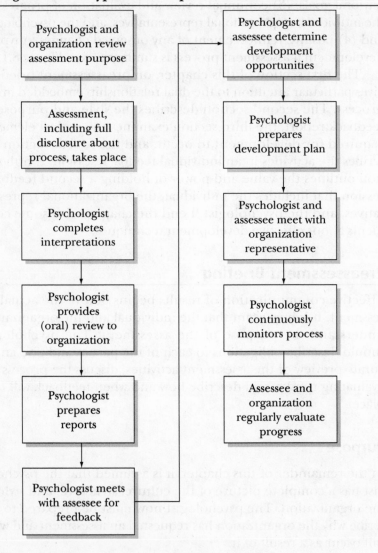

inferences drawn from the selection process must be based on job analyses that "truly reflect critical performance constructs" (p. 289). They note that tests and inventories must directly link to any performance expectations.

In describing the purpose of assessment, psychologists will stress the value of the process and comment on positive reasons for using such an assessment. However, this preview also should recognize, and psychologists should be prepared to discuss, assessment limitations. Guion (1991) ably described some of the limitations that can occur. For example, assessments may evaluate irrelevant characteristics, use poorly designed and inappropriately applied procedures, or be completed by individuals who do not understand good assessment methodology. When assessments are done poorly, the results could be communicated with strong emphasis and yet essentially have no real impact or, worse, have a negative impact.

The assessment purpose should consider ethical standards and best professional practices. Assessees need to be informed about the process and the availability of feedback. Organizations need to understand appropriate uses of assessment information and limitations inherent with any testing program. The assessee might participate in these early discussions.

Psychologists have responsibilities for clear agreement about purpose and use with both the individual and the organization (Cronbach, 1990). Cronbach suggests that instruments selected for the assessment process should include those "whose relevance is easily perceived and that can be explained in lay language" (p. 216), and notes that an organization that wants information about individuals needs to ensure that each instrument and "every question" has genuine relevance to ability to perform the job in question (p. 524). Cronbach's standard is a high one that is tough to implement, but it helps to ensure effective feedback.

A recent report from the Committee on Psychological Tests and Assessment of the American Psychological Association (1996) further guides the prework. The committee's Statement on the Disclosure of Test Data presents a number of major points. First, psychologists are asked to clarify with organizational clients, prior to assessment, the type of data that will be provided to the organization. Second, *informed consent* requires that the assessee be told prior to testing the purposes and intended use of the information, including what information will be released to the organization. Third, once testing has been completed, psychologists are to provide to the assessee explanations about the results. The committee also suggests that there are some organizational uses where such feedback may be limited for legal or security reasons. Fourth, psychologists are reminded that they have responsibility to the assessee as well as to the organization. Fifth, information is to be reported in language appropriate to the persons receiving it and any interpretations are to be carefully explained.

One attempt to balance the responsibilities to individual and organization while also providing informed consent is to give assessees written information about the process. This information can be read, and discussed between psychologists and individuals, prior to commencement of the appraisal. One example of this information is provided in Exhibit 8.1.

Dual Client

The American Psychological Association (APA), the Society for Industrial and Organizational Psychology, state practitioner licensing boards, and other groups have placed much greater emphasis on multiple relationships in recent years. Assessment psychologists are considered to owe an obligation to both the individual participant and the organization requesting that participation. Psychologists are careful to note such joint responsibility and to describe how information will be provided to each. The APA's Standards for Educational and Psychological Testing (American Psychological Association, 1985) clearly define the principles based on the "rights" of participants. Standard 16.1 addresses those rights:

> Informed consent implies that the test takers or representatives are made aware, in language that they can understand, of the reasons for testing, the types of tests to be used, the intended use and the range of material, consequences of the intended use, and what testing information will be released and to whom. When law mandates testing but does not require informed consent, test users should exercise discretion in obtaining informed consent, but test takers should always be given relevant information about a test when it is in their interest to be informed [p. 85].

Standard 16 goes on to indicate that when test scores are an important part of a decision-making process, the individual should receive an interpretation of those scores.

The APA's Ethical Principles of Psychologists and Code of Conduct (American Psychological Association, 1992) describes the expectations for psychologists who represent a number of parties.

Exhibit 8.1. Our Approach to Management Assessment.

This managerial assessment is designed to gain a clear picture of your strengths and style along several dimensions of management effectiveness. These include leadership, problem solving, achievement orientation and initiative, interpersonal style, planning and organizing, and personal adjustment and adaptability. Accurate understanding of this style sets the stage for developmental planning and assistance.

The assessment process is based on a multimethod, multiassessor approach. In general, we ask individuals to participate in three types of evaluation during the day they devote to the assessment.

Paper-and-Pencil Testing

We use a series of psychological and problem-solving tests in the assessment battery. All paper-and-pencil measures are standardized and well validated. Personality and psychological tests are used to understand an individual's traits and characteristics related to interpersonal, occupational, and managerial style and to motivational patterns that are key to job satisfaction. These inventories are completed by the participants and reflect the participants' perceptions of self, compared to people in general and norm groups of successful managers. Ability tests measure approaches used in reasoning and analyzing.

Work-Style Interview

Information about an individual is gained through an interview conducted by the psychologist. The interview is behaviorally based and focuses on past career achievements, background, and the participant's experience, skills, and successes in the various dimensions related to success.

Work Simulations

Work simulations provide a third source of information about an individual. These exercises are set in the context of a fictitious organization. Participants are provided with background information, an organizational history, and information about their role in the organization. From this perspective, they are asked to deal with a wide variety of common problems as if they were a worker in the fictitious organization. By "common problems" we mean those kinds of issues that most persons face on a day-to-day basis. This might include dealing with a dissatisfied customer or resolving a problem with a colleague, for example. The use of work simulations allows us to see individuals' skills "in action."

Based on these methods, the psychologist will compile a comprehensive report about your style and strengths. You will be given a complete debriefing and explanation of the results from each test and exercise used. During this discussion, personal developmental issues will be explored and a plan created so that future growth is most beneficial to you.

They refer to "third party," a phrase synonymous with "dual client." Standard 1.21 states that any psychologist who provides services to an individual, but at the request of a third party, must clarify "to the extent feasible" this multiple relationship. The psychologist is to inform each party about appropriate use of information and any limits to confidentiality. These standards recognize that organizational consulting for such activities as preemployment screening may prevent full discussion of results. However, Standard 2.09 indicates that psychologists should strive to give appropriate explanations when possible.

One of the most important aspects of this dual responsibility relates to the voluntary nature of participation. If results are to be communicated in order to have maximum impact on future behaviors, the individual genuinely should have a choice about participation. It is incumbent on organizational representatives and psychologists to explain fully the reasons for the assessment and to gain cooperation from the individual. Sometimes individuals refuse to participate. I believe it is appropriate for the organization to consider such refusal and, when necessary, drop the individual from consideration. Although individuals have a right to decline participation, they should know that they may lose an opportunity for direct and potent feedback.

The complexity of the dual client relationship leads me to recommend a second written document, this one provided to participants at the beginning of the assessment process so that they give informed consent, based on their understanding of the process and the uses of the assessment instruments. Exhibit 8.2 is an example of such a release of information.

Preview of Activities

When psychologists fully describe the activities in the assessment, participants can ask questions and gain a reasonable level of comfort. Moreover, the psychologist is showing respect for the participant. The kind of information contained in Exhibits 8.1 and 8.2 should be part of the description. Zeidner and Most (1992) remind us that the preview of activities helps to motivate high performance and encourage cooperation. They indicate that psychologists should be sensitive to the participant's physiological needs (room

Exhibit 8.2. Understanding the Release of Information.

To meet our responsibility to you, and to the client organization that requested that you participate in this assessment, we want to inform you about what happens to the results from the assessment.

During your time with us, we will be gathering information about you in order to develop an assessment report. The process typically will include the following:

A work-style interview that will focus on your educational and vocational background, your plans and goals, your strengths and limitations, and other work information

A variety of psychological tests and inventories

In some situations, one or more standardized work simulation exercises

After you complete this work and the psychologist reviews the results, we will be in contact with the organization that requested this assessment. We will tell them about our initial perspectives, based on psychological assessment principles and interpretations. Within approximately two weeks, we will send a written report of our conclusions to the organization.

We are available for a session to provide information to you about the results. We encourage you to participate in this feedback session. For persons already employed by the organization, we generally will make that appointment through the organization. For individuals not already employed by the organization, we will wait for the organization to inform us of their decision and then expect you to contact us for the follow-up session. We prefer that the session be done in person at our offices or at another location; however, we also are willing to provide telephone feedback.

We are certain you will find the process to be a valuable one to you. Please ask any questions that occur to you. We believe strongly that we need to provide as much information to you as possible. We want your work with us to be both valuable for you and helpful to the organization.

Your records are private, and access is limited to our staff, to you, and to those in the client organization who legitimately expect to receive and use the information. No information from the assessment will be released to other individuals or organizations without your written approval and the written approval of the organization. Of course, there is the unlikely requirement that such information would be released upon court order or to conform with state or federal law, rule, or regulation.

It is important to us that you understand this assessment process, the information that will be provided to you and to our client organization, and our responsibility to each. We ask that you indicate that understanding by your signature and the date (below).

Signature: _____

Date: _____

lighting and temperature, for example), emotional needs, and needs for information, such as explanation about the purposes and uses of the assessment. All contribute to establishing positive rapport.

The principles of accurate preview also relate to an understanding of organizations under change. In her 1992 book, Wheatley effectively describes the importance of balance between order and change and also autonomy and control. She writes that "companies organized around core competencies provide a good example of how an organization can obtain internal stability that leads both to well-defined boundaries and to openness over time" (p. 93). Similarly, individuals who participate in assessment need to understand the relationship between organizational expectations (boundaries) and individuals' willingness (openness) to participate. Without both, it is unlikely that results will have any lasting impact on either.

A related issue is a growing question regarding invasion of privacy. More people today are concerned about where their privacy ends and the organization's need for information begins. Psychologists must be open to discussions about this issue. Some parts of the assessment process, especially personality inventories, do ask for information that some people might prefer to keep private. Psychologists can build stronger rapport by acknowledging these concerns and discussing the implications. This rapport again leads to more potential for impact. Cronbach (1990) comments that tests invade privacy when participants do not wish to reveal themselves but that the psychologist is not invading privacy when she or he "is freely admitted and has a genuine need for the information" (p. 522). Other psychologists have noted that information that invades privacy is considered to be less fair even when it is job related (Arvey & Sackett, 1993) or suggest that safeguards are necessary to protect confidentiality and the rights of participants (Jeanneret, 1988). Arvey and Sackett note that the administrative process for testing should demonstrate consistency across candidates, give the opportunity to review scores, inform participants about content and purpose, and describe policies on confidentiality.

Discussion of Results and Feedback

Psychologists should describe what will happen to the results of the assessment and when and to whom feedback will be given. A unique perspective on the importance of this discussion is offered by Smither, Reilly, Millsap, Pearlman, and Stoffey (1993), who suggest that the organization consider itself to be a "vendor of available jobs," with participants viewed as "customers." They note that the degree of understanding that the organization has of participants' preferences, expectations, and needs increases their attraction to the company.

This intriguing notion means that assessment psychologists would devote more time for the explanations they give to assessees/"customers," describing why the assessment process adds value for both the organization and the individual. I do not believe that the psychologist should attempt to persuade the individual to consider a certain job, but there is value in candid and open conversation about the benefits of participation. Through this conversation the customer can become a more willing participant in the process.

Feedback to the Organization

Psychologists want their observations and interpretations to be important to the organization. Their efforts should lead to decisions that make explicit use of the information provided through the assessment. In order for this to occur psychologists must use practical and ethical methods and standards. They then are in a position to communicate results so that they have impact within the organization. Psychologists must know the reason for the assessment and who will receive the report (oral or written or both). Psychologists emphasize that all information is important, help to guide organizational representatives on appropriate use of the results, describe the meaning and limitations of their conclusions, and make recommendations that follow from the data. They also establish guidelines for the future use, storage, and lifetime of the report.

Feedback to Whom?

Psychologists must help to define who inside the organization should have access to the report information. Reports lend an impression that because they are based on "data" or "hard" information, they are more important than other sources of information.

The reports generate curiosity, and numerous individuals who know of their existence may make a case for why they should have access. Nevertheless, access should be limited to those who will make selection, promotion, or placement decisions and those who have a direct coaching relationship in the development of the participant. The psychologist should remind organizational representatives that interviews by nonpsychologists, performance evaluations, leadership surveys, and similar data are legitimate and should have weight similar to that given to the results of the assessment. Guidance in this regard is provided by the APA publication *Responsible Test Use: Case Studies for Assessing Human Behavior* (American Psychological Association, 1993). This publication is based on the deliberations of the Joint Committee on Testing Practices, sponsored by a range of professional organizations. In one of the case reviews the working group that developed the cases notes that test scores should not be the sole source of information used to make decisions and that organizational managers must resist pressure that compromises fair use of an assessment.

Oral Report

Typically, organizations want to receive timely feedback about the results of any assessment. Psychologists can provide such feedback but must understand that this initial review could become the sole basis on which decisions are made. In such cases psychologists should be prepared either to slow that decision process or provide a complete interpretation of results.

This oral report should follow the same format that will be used for written comments and emphasize the same factors and dimensions. The language in this oral description and observations about the participant must be congruent with the written report. That is, organizational representatives expect that oral comments will be similar in tone and value to the final report. If the assessment involves selection or other immediate action, the psychologist probably will be expected to give a recommendation. In my experience these oral comments typically are provided to a human resource representative, no later than two days after the assessment has been completed.

Full Written Report

Psychologists often provide to the organization a written report that fully describes the activities in which the assessee participated, an interpretation of how information fits into an overall perspective, and a balanced review of strengths and developmental opportunities. This written report is made available to the organization under restricted conditions (see comments about Exhibit 8.3 below). Psychologists are alert to the tendency of readers to highlight limited information that they consider to be important. An example is an overemphasis on cognitive aptitude test results, which the reader may think outweigh other legitimate information about personality characteristics, work motivation, and personal adaptability.

In my experience, this overemphasis occurs for at least two reasons. First, aptitude tests result in a specific score that is easy to understand and can be compared against a norm group that the organizational representative understands, for example, middle managers. Second, for many years the psychological literature has emphasized the predictive validity of aptitude tests, often stressing that such scores are the best source of information.

Psychologists work with the organization in making decisions about the report. They emphasize that a judicious and fair review will include all observations, even when multiple interpretations are possible about a single piece of information. Psychologists are aware of, and take action to offset, such misguided reactions to reports. One example of error is provided by Dunn, Mount, Barrick, and Ones (1995), who note, "The attributes that managers attended to were not necessarily the ones they thought they attended to" (p. 507). These authors observe that general mental ability is not correlated with "counterproductive behaviors" (p. 502). It is clear that representatives who attend only to cognitive aptitude measures, rather than to both those measures and personality characteristics, may make poor judgments as they try to apply interpretations and conclusions of psychologists.

A comprehensive written report includes the name of the assessee, the date of the assessment, information about the current work or status of the individual, and identification of the purpose of the evaluation, such as selection, promotion, or development. A typical report might include the following factors or sections:

Leadership style

Problem-solving style

Achievement orientation

Interpersonal style

Administrative style

Personal adjustment

Recommendations

This written report is sent to the organizational representative who contacted the psychologist about the assessment, typically a human resource representative. A reasonable time frame for preparation and delivery of the report is within five to ten days after the assessment has been completed.

Recommendations and Conclusions

The comments that psychologists make in the written report need to add value to the decision-making process of the organization. When psychologists are unwilling to make a recommendation based on the complex interpretations of the data, the organization may minimize or ignore the report. Is there a good fit between the assessee and the organization? Can the assessment participant be successful in the promoted position, or is it likely that she will be unsuccessful? What are the strengths and limitations of this person? Is the assessee better prepared to perform job-based technical functions or general managerial ones? Should the organization consider the assessee for employment? Unless psychologists give definitive statements that answer such questions, results will not have impact. Following is an example of a recommendation:

We consider Ms. Doe to be a good candidate for the position under consideration. She has the skill set and psychological characteristics necessary for success in this role. She has the keen analytical capabilities that are a key ingredient for success, and she will be an active partner in problem-solving situations. She is a team-oriented individual who, with time, can develop positive relationships with a wide range of individuals. She is an extremely well-organized person who appropriately emphasizes administrative operations while also considering strategic consequences. She has a strong drive for success and will continue to take responsibility for her own work, while emphasizing that her associates have accountability for their own performance.

From a developmental perspective, she would benefit from a more dominant and assertive personal leadership style. This approach would be a good addition to her current willingness to provide coaching and developmental suggestions to associates. A combination of a more forceful personal style linked to strong coaching techniques will improve her impact. From an interpersonal perspective, she occasionally needs to be reminded to provide a more empathic and supportive environment for associates. Although she is adept socially, some will view her very strong task orientation as an impediment to relationships.

Guidelines for Future Use

Once the report has been given to the organization, some action will occur. If the report has reached the appropriate individuals and provides specific recommendations, it will be included as a part of the information necessary for personnel decisions. Psychologists help the organization to decide who else may be permitted to review the report. I believe that the report should be restricted to those who are directly involved in decision making or directly engaged in coaching for development. Reports also have a limited time frame for accuracy and impact. Participants do change, and reports written more than three years earlier may not reflect those changes. Jeanneret (1988) notes that organizations need formal assessment policies that include policies on report storage and confidentiality. These policies should protect the rights of the individual. The Principles for the Validation and Use of Personnel Selection Procedures of the Society for Industrial and Organizational Psychology (SIOP) (1987) give recommendations regarding timelines. They note that it is unacceptable practice to retain evaluations in personnel files long after the assessment was completed. They suggest that personnel files be purged when the data have the potential for inaccuracy based on new experience, aging, maturation, or other personal change.

Exhibit 8.3 is an example of a report cover sheet that describes how the report is to be used, stored, and archived. This exhibit succinctly summarizes my concerns about future use.

Critical Elements for Development

A plan for providing feedback should begin with learning theory and the following elements. First, the process follows professional practices and truly adds information the assessee can use to accelerate personal growth. Second, feedback is appropriate and accurate. Third, the participant expresses a genuine willingness to change, and the organization provides coaching and support. Fourth, once change has occurred, there is positive reinforcement. Fifth, the developmental changes generalize to other new behaviors. Finally, others observe the positive changes and understand the value of assessment feedback.

Appropriate and Accurate Feedback

Feedback is a way to help another individual consider the implications and benefits of changed behavior. It depends on information that is important to and understood by the individual. It is a specific description of how behavior can be improved and relates to behavior that the participant can control and modify. Finally, in the communication process, psychologists ask the participant to evaluate and comment on the feedback, in order to ensure that communication is clear. In *Stop Managing, Start Coaching!* Gilley and Boughton (1996) maintain that one requirement for excellent coaching is the provision of accurate feedback: "Improvements can not be made unless your employees understand how well they are doing" (p. 44).

Psychologists have long known that individuals change most quickly when they have a desire for change and focus on developmental feedback and the potential for improvement. They take initiative sooner and cooperate better with those who provide

Exhibit 8.3. Guidelines for Using This Report.

This report is CONFIDENTIAL.

It is based on a systematic, standardized, and objective evaluation that includes interest and personality inventories, aptitude tests, work simulations, and a work-style interview. The process has resulted in the diagnostic assessment and, for some persons, the developmental recommendations that follow.

To be helpful, the report must be read and applied carefully. It is only one source of information. It should be used to clarify and confirm other legitimate observations. The report can enhance the judgment of senior managers and should lead to the individual's active participation in ongoing development. We recommend that the report be part of the framework for directing future development, and sometimes for making decisions about selection and placement.

The report is a profile of results, including strengths and developmental needs observed during the assessment. It is a synthesis of interpretations made by the psychologist. Any developmental suggestions are provided to enhance the strengths and/or to overcome limitations.

The report is to be shared *only* with those who have a demonstrated need to know the results. Generally, it should be delivered by hand and, after review, should be returned to the special file established as a central location for these reports. Copies should *never* be made of this report; access is available when necessary. If other copies were to be made, it would undermine the integrity of the process and improperly overemphasize the value of the report.

There are important responsibilities for those who review this report. First, the participant should have had an opportunity to review the report; in the future, you may wish to provide other opportunities for further review, with the assistance of a human resource representative. Second, the participant should be encouraged to act on the developmental suggestions. Third, after the report has been reviewed in a meeting of the participant and the psychologist, the manager and participant should review the results with the help of a company human resource representative who will assist in implementing appropriate developmental steps. Fourth, all should remember that over time individuals change; the report therefore has limited value after approximately three years. Fifth, the report is to be used only within the company; it may not be shared with others unless there is express approval from the participant, the company, and the psychologist.

support. They also recognize that change requires considerable effort. Assessments rummage deeply into the past experiences and current styles of the participant. Easy changes have already been made. The evaluation process identifies difficult changes, which require time.

Psychologists clearly communicate that fundamental change is difficult and requires the agreement of the participant. Hogan, Hogan, and Roberts (1996) state that "from the data, it appears that when personality changes, it changes gradually" (p. 473).

Coaching and Support

The major elements of effective coaching and support are a plan focused on two or three behaviors, considerable practice, and incremental growth. In all of this the psychologist provides encouragement to the individual. The feedback process permits psychologists to describe how change can take place. Psychologists also engage organizational representatives in that support. Without support and encouragement, it is unlikely that change will persist.

Because the assessment process often identifies long-standing negative behavioral patterns, change does not occur unless someone observes the individual's efforts and provides timely coaching and correction. Effective feedback includes mechanisms to provide such coaching. Senge (1990) notes that few individuals demonstrate the rigor necessary for personal mastery. He says that such competence comes out of the clarification of what really matters to the individual and to the organization. Good coaches assist in that clarification.

Positive Reinforcement and Generalizing of New Behaviors

Nothing else is quite as important as success. Psychologists can continue to exert influence in the organization and on the behavior of the individual. They remind both coaches and participants that pleasant consequences or rewards that follow new behaviors serve to increase or maintain that behavior. When associates of the individual comment that they like the changed behavior, when superiors praise or recognize that change, and when the individual has opportunities to demonstrate new skills and behaviors, those new behaviors continue.

Skill development follows phases, in much the same way that someone learns a new sport. For example, the first-time golfer is very conscious of individual elements of the golf swing, and performance of those elements is awkward. Later, it is the entire swing that feels awkward even though it is performed with less thought to individual elements. It will be some time before the swing is no longer awkward and take even more time for a graceful swing to be habitual and effective. So it is with all other skill development.

Psychologists remind organizational coaches and individuals that change will occur when there is willingness, coaching, and reinforcing but that the change will require time to generalize to other situations. Weiss (1990) states that early performance change requires more thought and is slow and halting, whereas later performance becomes more habitual and smoother. He refers to other theoretical models showing that individuals undergoing change follow a three-step approach. They first make strong use of instructions and focus on tasks. Next, they associate those changes with a wider range of behaviors. Finally, they exhibit the new behavior in an autonomous method, across a range of activities.

Feedback Session

If psychologists are to be successful, their feedback to the organization will influence decision making. The second responsibility of psychologists is to the assessee. Thorough and rigorous assessment of the factors or behaviors under consideration will always point to developmental opportunities. Psychologists must establish a positive relationship with the participant. Test interpretations should be based on appropriate norms and deal with test limitations. Feedback today is a more open process than in the past, and I recommend an unrestricted display of results, including interpretative aids. The assessor and individual should discuss and understand all results. Psychologists should describe access to the report and how it is controlled. There is discussion of identified strengths and developmental opportunities. In some cases there is a written developmental plan.

Establishing a Partnership

Unless psychologists develop rapport with the participant and that person has confidence in the process, any results will have limited impact. I expect that psychologists will give proper attention to building the relationship and that feedback will be pertinent to the individual. In *Frames of Mind,* Gardner (1993) notes that William James, whom he refers to as the "dean of American psychologists and philosophers," was open to the possibilities of individual change and growth and "stressed the importance of relationships with other individuals, as a means of gaining ends, of effecting progress" (p. 238). Herriott (1989) is even more explicit about that expectation. He reports that the selection process is based on a sense of reciprocity and a psychological contract among the psychologist, the organization, and the assessee. He says that participants' expectations and aspirations could be incongruent with those of the organization, and when this happens, participants are likely to stop the employment process and abandon the relationship. He says that "selection is not the gate through which applicants must pass before they can relate to the organization; it is itself part of that relationship" (p. 171). A final comment on partnership comes from the text *Responsible Test Use* (American Psychological Association, 1993), which decries testing without interpretation, and reports that "proper interpretation of results can take place only in a face-to-face meeting between the client and the professional" (p. 132).

Test Interpretation

The next objective is to ensure accurate and useful test interpretation. Psychologists may use one or more cognitive tests and one or more personality inventories, which need to be described to the assessee. Unless the individual has a clear understanding of what has been measured and what the information means, change is unlikely. Psychologists should use appropriate norms, review limitations regarding test procedures, and describe any decisions that are an end product of the process.

Psychologists understand that raw scores have limited meaning, even to other psychologists. Both the organization and the individual expect to receive an interpretation that permits them to compare results to known groups. Norms provide the basis or reference points against which to evaluate raw scores of the individual. These derived scores provide the relevant information the organization and the individual expect. Psychologists can identify appropriate norm groups from the manuals and administrative guides for tests and, where many individuals have been tested, can develop their own norm groups. Zeidner and Most (1992) remind us that before psychologists can draw inferences about an individual, they must understand the characteristics of the norm group, how samples were selected, the size of the sample, and the recency of results. Cronbach (1990) says that raw scores are easily misunderstood; standard scores or some other method of norming is what truly represents differences among individuals. Once again, standards for testing are an important guide. The APA Standards for Educational and Psychological Testing (American Psychological Association, 1985) note that psychologists should base evaluations on evidence of validity for specific interpretations (Standard 9.2), that they must decide whether to use combined gender or separate female-male norms (Standard 9.3), and that normative samples must focus on relevant racial or ethnic differences (Standard 9.5).

A second issue regarding norms occurs when scores have ipsative meaning. Some information is important because the participant's scores can be compared to a relevant norm group; other information is important because one skill or ability can be compared to another skill and ability for that individual. This internal comparison is an ipsative interpretation. Using this approach, psychologists can interpret a single assessee's strengths and developmental opportunities in a more cogent manner. An example can be drawn from the use of cognitive tests. Psychologists can compare an overall standard score against an important norm group. They can also add value by comparing vocabulary development against general verbal development. A second example can be drawn from the use of a personality inventory, where an entire profile can be compared against a normative group. If the profile measures two distinct characteristics, such as leadership dominance and interpersonal empathy, an ipsative interpretation could point to how those differences are evident in managerial behavior. A combination of ipsative and normative interpretation can have the most powerful impact on an individual, because the assessee not only understands the comparison to a specific population such as managers but also knows how his or her individual strengths and limitations are characteristic of behavior.

The interpretative process will also note limitations of tests. This is both an ethical consideration and an important element of communicating for impact. Cognitive tests, personality inventories, and even work simulations are estimates of performance. Psychologists note that scores may change somewhat during different times of test administration. In language easily understood by organizational representatives and assessees, psychologists make important observations about standard error. The APA's ethical principles (American Psychological Association, 1992) are absolute about this in Standard 2.04(b): "Psychologists recognize limits to the certainty with which diagnoses, judgments, or predictions can be made about individuals." Psychologists recognize that some assessment instruments show differences between predictive and face validity and provide information to participants so that they fully understand these differences. For example, Smither and colleagues (Smither, Reilly, Millsap, Pearlman, & Stoffey, 1993) report on the differences between those validities in their use of a variety of selection procedures. The research noted that cognitive tests were perceived to have greater predictive validity than face validity but that the personality inventory was perceived to have greater face validity than predictive validity. Finally, psychologists note that some measures cannot assess technical or skill-based components of the work. Hogan and colleagues (Hogan, Hogan, & Roberts, 1996) write, for example, that personality inventories provide important information about characteristics of the participant but cannot measure technical skills or the ability to learn.

The test interpretation should have some impact on the organization's decisions. Psychologists should discuss the implications of this impact with participants and communicate the differences among selection, promotion, placement, development, and other decisions. The use of assessment methods in selection situations is typically dichotomous because the psychologists must recommend either to accept or reject a candidate. Promotion decisions may also have a dichotomous application but in addition can guide decisions about how candidates could be better prepared for new opportunities. Placement decisions will make maximum use of the current skill set and personality characteristics of the individual under consideration and will identify developmental tasks.

Displaying Results

Effective communication of results can be aided by a variety of interpretative models. Results of work simulations can be scored through use of a rating system, which can be explained to the individual. Remembering the admonitions to provide information that laypersons can understand, psychologists could develop figures, pictures, and other interpretative aids. One example of such an aid is a normal curve or distribution of scores for a particular aptitude test, for a "general population" described by the test publisher. A second perspective could come from a similar comparison to a professional or managerial group, such as production supervisors or bank executive trainees, from norms also provided in the test publisher's manual. These pictures help the assessee to understand how his or her results compare to the results of others who have completed the same test.

Many test publishers provide profiles, narrative reports, and other interpretative aids for personality and interest inventories. Such instruments, when they have been validated for use in these assessments, can be described to assessees.

Discussion and Understanding

Psychologists first describe results from the tests, inventories, work simulations, and other assessment materials. Next, they engage participants in a complete discussion about those results. Participants are encouraged to ask questions and to provide their own self-assessment. Discussion may relate to previous experiences, such as college entrance examinations, career counseling, performance evaluations, or feedback from colleagues. Psychologists should ensure that participants fully understand the specific results and their meaning in terms of selection, promotion, or placement. In this regard, psychologists may once more return to ipsative commentary. An example would be noted in the differences in scores for a test of deductive analysis and a second test of intuitive logic. Psychologists would describe the purpose and meaning of these two tests, and help the assessee to recognize how those differences might be observed in job-related problem solving.

These discussions provide an opportunity for participants to describe elements that may have influenced the results. These influences could be other factors in the limitations of tests. Zeidner and Most (1992) report that there may be contamination based on illness, fatigue, or anxiety; there may have been test conditions such as poor psychometrist-examinee rapport; and there may have been instructional errors or poorly chosen test content. I often hear from mid- and late-career participants that it has been many years since they completed a test similar to the cognitive instruments typically used. They are seeking reassurance that others have been tested in the same manner, and at a similar age or career point.

Cronbach (1990) cautions that psychologists must be acquainted with the logic of all instruments and with possible "misinterpretations that experts on the test have warned against" (p. 20). I add a corollary: that psychologists should be prepared to respond to the possible misinterpretations that assessees initially make of test results. An example of such mistaken interpretation would occur when the participant learns that results for a cognitive ability test are below average when compared to a manager's norm group. The assessee may comment that he or she "never has had difficulty with problem solving" or "others consider [me] to be very creative." Each of these comments requires the psychologist to interpret results further by placing the comments within the assessment context and informing the assessee of the difference between a single aptitude test and general problem solving and the difference between problem solving and creativity.

On the subject of the development of test validation, Schmitt and Landy (1993) note that measures used in assessment are required to undergo "a continual process of hypothesis generation, testing, and challenging" (p. 285). An extension of that process occurs in the interpretation session, when participants should be asked to develop their own hypotheses and to challenge the interpretations presented to them. Psychologists endeavor to demonstrate in these conversations that test results are important to work performance. In describing validation processes for tests, Smither and colleagues (Smither, Reilly, Millsap, Pearlman, & Stoffey, 1993) suggest that it is particularly important for ability tests to be cast in terms of actual work expectations. However, they caution that applicants can misunderstand some of this interpretation. They note that a measure of verbal ability is not the same as the ability to understand or correct business memos. They use as an example of a poor practice an interpretation that is understood by the participant to describe a lack of experience in preparing business memos when in fact the applicant scored low on verbal ability. Finally, professional principles and standards again provide guidance. The SIOP Principles (Society for Industrial and Organizational Psychology, 1987) note that reports of results "should be in terms likely to be interpreted correctly by persons" who receive the report, including candidates (p. 21).

Access to the Report

If the processes used in assessment are to have maximum developmental impact, any written record should be demystified for the participant. I strongly recommend that participants read any such documents. In this way psychologists assure participants that they have access to all information. There may be organizational or consultant restraints on the ultimate disposition of that report (see Exhibit 8.3). Although I do not necessarily believe that participants should get and keep actual copies of the report, I do recommend that the report be available for their reading. Psychologists and organizational representatives give clear statements to participants about future access to the report. The APA's Statement on the Disclosure of Test Data (American Psychological Association, 1996) advises that, wherever possible, psychologists should provide test takers with full explanation of results, while also acknowledging the need for test data security. The statement especially notes that "confidential test materials and data . . . should be safeguarded to avoid disclosure which may harm the individual or undermine the assessments" (p. 647). Although the statement specifically refers only to test results, full use of the standards can be expanded to the report itself.

Identification of Developmental Opportunities

Participants agree to complete assessment processes for a variety of reasons. Sometimes they simply comply with requests from superiors, and other times it is a requirement, which they agree to follow in spite of personal trepidation, as in selection situations. When psychologists want to maximize impact, they focus results on developmental opportunities, providing information to participants that gives them ideas for future performance improvement. This feedback can lead to developmental ideas. Many members of the workforce seldom get effective feedback with guidance for career-enhancing improvement. Effective feedback gives specific focus to the participant and describes ways for self-improvement. Levinson (1992) notes that both praise and criticism must have specificity; otherwise each has limited impact, and the recipient does not learn from it. Development begins with better understanding. Brookfield (1987) says that learning is a process "by which people can be helped to become aware of idiosyncratic tendencies, preferences, biases, habits, blockages, and aptitudes" (p. 83). With Brookfield, I believe that change begins with an understanding of behavior-based developmental needs.

Written Developmental Plan

In-person psychologist-to-participant feedback is the most potent way to ensure change. In addition, written developmental plans, provided to the individual, can add value. Whereas the assessment report itself may be carefully controlled and made available to the participant only in a limited way, the developmental plan should be "owned" by the individual. Written developmental plans must provide a structure for support and refer to specific resources realistically available to the individual. They are limited in focus and reflect that most individuals, at any one moment in a career, can make significant change in only two or three behaviors. They provide behavior-based objectives so that changes can be measured. When possible, they specify time frames.

Typically, a written developmental plan will specify behavior-based goals, describe the action steps necessary for achievement of those goals, include some reference to measuring improvement, note time frames, and describe the involvement of others, particularly superiors and coaches of the assessee. Exhibit 8.4 gives examples of some of these elements.

Power of Three-Way Feedback

When effective feedback is provided to the assessee and a developmental plan focuses on ways to improve, there can be positive impact. A more powerful result occurs when all the partners in the process—the psychologist, the assessee, and representatives of the organization, such as the manager of the assessee and a human resource manager—participate fully at some point during the feedback. I strongly recommend that these organizational representatives be encouraged to participate in one or more of the three-way feedback processes described in this section.

How can psychologists increase the impact of assessment feedback? One approach is to insist that organizational representatives and assessment participants meet to discuss the results of the assessment, the recommendations of the psychologist, and opportunities for development. These sessions are designed to ensure that the three contributors to future growth—the psychologist, the manager of the participant, and the participant—are in agreement about how to proceed. A significant fourth participant can be, when possible, a human resource specialist. A session begins with the psychologist, who describes the process and the materials or tests used in the assessment. In the next step the participant provides a summary of the results, commenting on the strengths and limitations identified during the assessment. This second step gives the psychologist one more opportunity to ensure that the participant fully understood and accepted the feedback. In the third step the psychologist asks for comments from the manager. Finally, all discuss any future steps in the process, giving particular attention to how developmental activities will occur and be measured, evaluated, and rewarded.

A more elaborate process requires additional time and commitment from the organization. In this case the psychologist first meets with the participant alone for a full discussion of results and developmental meaning. Second, the psychologist meets with the manager to discuss the results and to prepare the manager for full

Exhibit 8.4. Sample Comments from a Development Plan.

Developmental Need and Goal. Increased use of a more dynamic and tough-minded leadership style.

Suggestions

You have developed capabilities as a team-oriented leader who gains participation from others. You show appropriate consideration for them and involve them in important decisions. This is a strong base for future development. Our assessment indicates that there are times when you are slow to apply forceful discipline. We believe there will be opportunities in the future for you to be more assertive in your leadership style.

   Our primary recommendation is for placement in a more complex and difficult leadership assignment. We will discuss this recommendation with organizational representatives. We also suggest that you meet with your manager to discuss such a possible position. We believe that this assignment should provide a variety of opportunities to demonstrate your more aggressive style. We hope that this assignment will be made during the next six months.

   We want you to continue to delegate responsibilities to others, but to do so with a strong use of control and discipline. Appropriate delegation ensures that activities are monitored and time frames are enforced. The Training Division of your Human Resource Department offers a two-day program entitled *Making Effective Use of Others Through Delegation and Control.* We believe that it is very important that you attend this program sometime during the next twelve months.

   Once you have completed the seminar, schedule a meeting with your manager. You should describe to this individual what you have learned from the program and one or two specific behaviors that you will begin to emphasize in your work. You should ask your manager to observe your leadership style and to provide feedback to you about your effectiveness. She will be able to describe situations where you missed an opportunity to delegate to others or where your monitoring process was too indirect to be effective. She also will note those situations where you appropriately assigned responsibility and accountability to others and where your monitoring efforts helped your associates to accomplish assignments.

   We recommend that you identify one leader within your organization whom you respect and consider to be highly persuasive and forceful. We suggest that you observe this individual's behavior for the

**Exhibit 8.4. Sample Comments from
a Development Plan** *(continued).*

next three months. During this time, keep a written record about the behaviors you observe and believe make this individual particularly effective. After this period of observation, you should identify a few of those activities that you can begin to practice in your own leadership style. We also recommend that when you begin such practice, you ask a trusted associate to assist in your efforts. Describe to this individual what you are going to attempt to do and ask her or him to give you feedback about your efforts. The person can give reactions to moments when you were more persuasive and can give specific constructive criticism and suggestions about when you could have been more demanding.

This developmental need should be included in your performance goals for next year. You and your superior should identify which of our recommendations are most important and should specify how each of you will evaluate progress. One possibility is for you to complete a 360-degree Leadership Survey at the end of the year. You and I can then meet to discuss the relationship between our assessment and the new results from the survey. If you have been able to make significant changes in your approach, those should be evident from that review.

participation in a third step, the three-way conversation. Fourth, the psychologist holds a follow-up conversation with the assessee to evaluate this participant's understanding of the three-way conversation and the assessee's commitment for action. A fifth possible step is to hold a similar debriefing session with the manager. My own preference is to limit the number of individual conversations because I believe that the candor and mutual support that arise out of three-way discussions are important elements in ensuring understanding by all and confirming their participation in developmental efforts.

A Predictable Problem

If the psychologist has developed rapport with the participant, the two of them are well prepared to discuss the feedback. Further, if the psychologist has provided a normative framework for the participant, that individual fully understands the strengths and developmental opportunities that have emerged from the process. Most often the first two steps of the three-way conversation proceed in an effective manner.

Experience also leads to a prediction about the immediate comments made by the manager once she or he is invited to join the conversation. Almost never do these individuals focus on the positive results or strengths. Many times managers show discomfort about the directness of the feedback and begin to negate, excuse, or minimize developmental limitations. They will comment that the individual only rarely exhibits these ineffective behaviors, knows how to compensate for the predicted behaviors, or that such behaviors are not critical for successful performance. When psychologists are prepared for these types of responses, they can take two actions. First, they can strengthen their relationship with the participant by using the individual feedback session to predict the manager's reaction and to describe how the psychologist will deal with it. Second, they can gently guide the manager into a full discussion about the developmental needs. This might include reminding the manager that the participant already understands the limitations and is committed to change.

Now the feedback is on track again. Psychologists understand why managers react in this manner. In discussing broad organizational reaction to change and renewal, Wheatley (1992) notes that when effective feedback is provided, the organization is "unable to deal with so much magnifying information . . . amplification is very threatening, and there is a need to quell" such feedback (p. 87). She could well be describing managers who are uncomfortable. One reason for this discomfort is based on poor performance evaluation techniques and processes. Goleman (1995) notes that "inept criticism was ahead of mistrust, personality struggles, and disputes over power and pay as a reason for conflict on the job" (p. 152).

Other problems, too, can crop up during three-way feedback sessions. Some assessees may not communicate effectively with managers; in this case, the psychologist can help to facilitate full understanding among all participants. Some managers adhere to their own perspectives about the assessee and do not listen effectively to new or contradictory information. Some managers have not had open and candid conversations with assessees about past performance, and so they are unable to relate assessment information to such past performance. In these situations, and numerous other possibilities, the psychologist should remain focused on assessment data and on how best to help all of the participants to implement effective developmental activities.

Negotiating Support

Now that the predictable problem has been overcome, psychologists move to negotiate among the parties. Because they understand that behavior best changes when there is supportive coaching and reinforcing follow-up, they should ensure that these activities take place. Here, the partnership is expanded to include the manager and human resource representatives. All of them discuss what kinds of activities can be most useful and the degree to which the organization will provide time, opportunities for growth, or any necessary financial resources. Psychologists facilitate these conversations and note when agreements have been reached. They later may provide a written record of these agreements and understandings. In the end, all of the partners leave with a clear understanding about next steps. Settoon, Bennett, and Liden (1996) detail the critical nature of such mutuality within organizations. They state, "The more that relationships or exchanges between supervisors and subordinates are based on mutual trust and loyalty, interpersonal affect, and respect for each other, the better the subordinates' performance" (p. 224). Almost nowhere is such mutuality better exhibited than in these three-way conversations. In their book on coaching, Gilley and Boughton (1996) emphasize the importance of participative communication, where managers shift out of a more authoritative style. They implore managers to "relinquish control and dominance over employees and allow them to participate as equal partners in examining their careers" (p. 131).

A final comment about negotiating support is related to the degree to which the manager understands his or her own strengths and limitations. In the process of discussing growth for the individual, managers will have opportunities to describe their own developmental pattern and growth. Once again, psychologists can encourage these discussions. Kouzes and Posner (1993) describe their observations of a particularly effective executive, who had participated in leadership survey feedback. When he attended sessions at which other individuals described their developmental opportunities, he discussed what he had learned about himself and what he was doing to become a more successful leader. They state, "This action made it easier for others to talk about their own feedback with colleagues and constituents, even about areas in which they had been disappointed or surprised" (p. 188).

Maintaining Efforts

A final responsibility of consulting psychologists is to ensure that the developmental plan is implemented. Here, their partnership with human resource representatives is particularly important. These partners maintain contact with the participant. They are aware of the objectives specified and the time frames established. They make continuing contacts with participants to inquire about progress, generalization of the behaviors to additional work situations, and any further need for support. This information can be shared with managers when necessary in order to ensure that they take continuing responsibility for assistance. Particularly important to this process is that psychologists, human resource specialists, and managers may know of others who could mentor or coach the learning participant. They share this information with the participant and encourage contact; sometimes they initiate the contact to ensure that it takes place. All of these activities lead to more focused and beneficial developmental efforts. Gilley and Boughton (1996) point out that formal training outside the job is effective only when it can be applied on the job. They say, "Performance improvement can't occur until employees apply what they learn," which then leads to improved organizational competitiveness (p. 53). In their research on transfer of training, Tracey, Tannenbaum, and Kavanagh (1995) make a similar point about innovative and competitive organizations. They say that such organizations encourage application of new behaviors, emphasizing that "a continuous-learning culture can influence specific behaviors associated with a particular training program" (p. 249).

Goleman (1995) describes why helpful criticism is part of the emotional support a manager provides to associates. He says that such criticism is "a question of feedback, really, of people getting the information essential to keep their efforts on track" (p. 150). Brookfield (1987) deals with developing critical thinkers, a specific application of development that can be broadened to other applications. He notes that role models help individuals to define changes and practice new behaviors. Such modeling has clarity, consistency, openness, illustrative communication, and specificity. He ends this discussion by noting that very effective modelers (and I would add managers) "are seen as accessible . . . do not threaten or intimidate potential imitators by presenting visions of themselves as people whose abilities are far beyond the reach of mere mortals . . . and are open to inquiries concerning their activities" (pp. 85–88). All of these comments apply to maintaining the developmental efforts of participants in order to ensure that assessment results have impact.

Developmental Techniques

Psychologists understand that different individuals can be guided in different ways toward developmental growth. A final element of communicating with impact relates to those differences. Individual learning style varies in significant ways. Generalization of new behaviors occurs best when activities are focused around actual job performance. People can learn quickly and effectively because of new organizational assignments or through community or professional activities. Some can make good use of suggested readings, and others learn best by attendance at formal seminars or training programs. Some prefer lecture-style seminars, whereas others learn more in experiential settings.

Individual Learning Style and Successive Approximation

Psychologists are keenly aware that individuals differ in their preferences for learning. Information derived from the assessment materials and techniques helps psychologists in understanding those differences. The developmental plan prepared in cooperation by psychologists, organizational representatives, and participants makes suggestions consistent with individual learning style. Whereas some enjoy reading and are quickly able to apply written ideas from authors, others are hands-on learners who best show improvement through practical application. Some want to participate, and can usefully do so, in professional organizations. Others are most effective in showing improvement when they can work one-on-one with a mentor or coach.

The next step in the process is for psychologists to recall the importance of successive approximation. No individual moves quickly to acquire the complex skill set that typifies most behavioral improvement. Each participant will have a different timetable for growth, but in all cases individuals take small steps that demonstrate incremental improvement. Developmental plans should be designed to be consistent with the notion of stepwise improvement and individual time frames.

From a psychological perspective the early work of Piaget (Piaget & Inhelder, 1969) on intellectual development in children is applicable. Piaget explained that learning is a combination of organizing new behaviors and adapting those behaviors. He clearly saw that behaviors become more complex with growth and time. He reported that assimilation occurs when current structures are used to understand the world and accommodation occurs when those structures change in response to external pressure. In his description of learning organizations, Senge (1990) makes a similar observation that also provides more direction for the developmental process. He worries that individuals become "locked into" ways of dealing with external forces and therefore are less open to change. He writes, "As we get older, our rate of discovery slows down; we see fewer and fewer new links between our actions and external forces" (p. 170).

Brookfield (1987) notes that it is important to understand how those in a developmental process create and maintain motivation for learning experiences. He reminds us that it is important to understand how people integrate new ideas and explore new opportunities. He asks, "Do they use trial-and-error methods, problem-solving, or careful planning of short-, intermediate-, and long-term goals?" and, "In what ways do people feel most comfortable entering the new and potentially frightening" developmental experiences (p. 83)? In terms of both individual style and successive efforts, the work of Schneider and Hough (1995) is important.

They summarize earlier research noting that low-ability and low-anxiety individuals are similar to high-ability and high-anxiety individuals in that they benefit most from highly structured learning situations. Those with the opposite patterns of low ability and high anxiety or high ability and low anxiety benefit more from developmental experiences that are low in structure.

On-the-Job Activities, New Assignments, and Community or Professional Activities

Developmental growth occurs when individuals have an opportunity to participate in work-based activities. New behaviors are learned from practical experience when individuals have specific objectives to meet in their assignments. This approach works best when there are specific things that an individual must do in order to improve personal performance. These activities may relate to personal organizing and time management, influencing others through dynamic presentations, or moving away from a directing style of leadership to one that is more open to the participation of others. The efforts might include specific use of project planning systems or software, better active listening techniques, or written records of how to use a new analytical process.

Sometimes new skills are best acquired and practiced in non-work situations—for example, coaching skills, public presentation, and elective leadership (which is different from leadership based on position power). Individuals can be encouraged to volunteer in a community-based organization, participate in a business service group, or become active in a professional organization. Skill development might occur because of coaching in Little League baseball, learning how to gain support from volunteers, or giving impromptu presentations or comments, as suddenly assigned by a club president. Individuals also get to observe others who are more competent at a certain skill. They can ask for their ideas and guidance and practice these new skills in a relatively safe nonwork environment.

Sometimes the acquisition of new behaviors requires major changes in assignment. These developmental needs focus around key behaviors that cannot be learned in a current role. It is only through temporary or permanent transfer to a very different job that the participant can experience growth. For example, a manager fully embedded in daily operational activities may not have an opportunity for growth in strategic thinking. If this person is given a temporary assignment to a strategic planning task force, growth can occur. Someone who needs to learn team-based leadership will find it hard to do when given supervisory responsibility for a group of inexperienced employees who both want and need to be told how to function. King and Kitchener (1994) give specific recommendations for how faculty members can develop reflective judgment in students, and some of their ideas are directly applicable to work situations. They note that "people are not passive recipients of experience, and development is inexorably tied to active processing" (p. 248). Learning environments that require active development of new behaviors will be more effective in changing past behavior.

Reading and Formal Training Programs

If psychologists and organizational representatives want to maximize developmental impact, they will be prepared to recommend books, articles, magazines, and other reading references. Individuals who demonstrate strong academic orientation typically enjoy such reading. In this reading they will find two or three specific techniques to apply in their own developmental efforts. Sometimes this reading is a good way for them to develop a broader vocabulary or learn about a broader range of content. Books are available on virtually every imaginable developmental topic. For example, they can help individuals understand the importance of systems and processes, introduce participants to conflict management techniques and models, advise managers on team-building skills, and give individuals a stronger base of financial and technical expertise. Magazines can be specific to an organizational function or more general. Some people are interested in basic research, which might be reported in a professional journal, whereas others are fascinated by the leadership style of individuals as covered in a general distribution business magazine.

Individuals also learn through participation in workshops, seminars, and other training programs. Sometimes those programs are organizationally sponsored. Many companies have "universities" that emphasize continual learning and improvement. Specific courses can help some participants not only to develop personal skills but also to deepen their understanding of the company culture. Many colleges and universities offer seminars ranging from ten-week courses to one-day continuing education seminars. Psychologists and human resource representatives should know what is available in the immediate area and may know which seminar leaders or instructors are best matched to which participants.

It is incumbent on assessment psychologists to understand a range of developmental techniques and opportunities. Psychologists know which job-based behaviors need changing and what special assignments will increase the speed of change. They are aware of the potency of community and professional organizational participation. They must read broadly, track important information and articles, and be prepared to call attention to this information so that individuals are guided through appropriate avenues for improvement.

Conclusions

In his extensive review of personnel assessment, Guion (1991) challenges psychologists about better use of assessment. He notes, "most personnel decisions are more job oriented than person oriented" (p. 387). He adds that there are some situations where an applicant is not an appropriate fit for a placement but that such an individual can be "immensely valuable to the organization," and he asks for greater efforts on the part of psychologists to find and use that value. He agrees that persons can be better prepared for certain jobs if they receive potent feedback and developmental assistance.

Senge (1990) adds an organizational perspective to Guion's job- and person-perspective. He writes that personal mastery is a process requiring lifelong discipline. He notes that individuals committed to such mastery are aware of their areas of incompetence and their opportunities for growth. He says, "People with a high level of personal mastery live in a continual learning mode. They never 'arrive'" (p. 142).

Those two observations nicely conclude this chapter. There is no purpose for individual assessment that cannot be communicated in results with individual and organizational impact. Individuals must understand the process and assessment tools used, must receive complete and open feedback that describes their strengths and limitations, and should be guided toward effective developmental efforts. Organizations must receive feedback that aids in selection, promotion, and placement decisions; organizational representatives need to provide the developmental emphasis and recognition required for significant change; and all should be informed about the professional principles and standards that guide assessment. When all of this occurs, there will be a clearer definition of what individual assessment means and a more significant application of growth-producing impact.

References

American Psychological Association. (1985). *Standards for educational and psychological testing.* Washington, DC: Author.

American Psychological Association. (1992). Ethical principles of psychologists and code of conduct. *American Psychologist, 47,* 1597–1611.

American Psychological Association. (1993). *Responsible test use: Case studies for assessing human behavior.* Washington, DC: Author.

American Psychological Association. Committee on Psychological Tests and Assessment. (1996). Statement on the disclosure of test data. *American Psychologist, 51,* 644–648.

Arvey, R. D., & Sackett, P. R. (1993). Fairness in selection: Current developments and perspectives. In N. Schmitt, W. C. Borman, & Associates, *Personnel selection in organizations.* San Francisco: Jossey-Bass.

Brookfield, S. D. (1987). *Developing critical thinkers: Challenging adults to explore alternative ways of thinking and acting.* San Francisco: Jossey-Bass.

Cronbach, L. J. (1990). *Essentials of psychological testing* (5th ed.). New York: HarperCollins.

Dunn, W. S., Mount, M. K., Barrick, M. R., & Ones, D. S. (1995). Relative importance of personality and general mental ability in managers' judgments of applicant qualifications. *Journal of Applied Psychology, 80,* 500–509.

Gardner, H. (1993). *Frames of mind: The theory of multiple intelligences* (2nd ed.). New York: Basic Books.

Gilley, J. W., & Boughton, N. W. (1996). *Stop managing, start coaching!* Burr Ridge, IL: Irwin.

Goleman, D. (1995). *Emotional intelligence.* New York: Bantam Books.

Guion, R. M. (1991). Personnel assessment, selection, and placement. In M. D. Dunnette & L. M. Hough (Eds.), *Handbook of industrial and organizational psychology* (2nd ed., Vol. 2). Palo Alto, CA: Consulting Psychologists Press.

Herriott, P. (1989). Selection as a social process. In M. Smith & I. Robertson (Eds.), *Advances in selection and assessment.* New York: Wiley.

Hogan, R., Hogan, J., & Roberts, B. W. (1996). Personality measurement and employment decisions: Questions and answers. *American Psychologist, 51,* 469–477.

Jeanneret, P. R. (1988). *Are psychological assessments legal and ethical in the selection and hiring process?* Paper presented at the National Assessment Conference, Minneapolis.

King, P. M., & Kitchener, K. S. (1994). *Developing reflective judgment: Understanding and promoting intellectual growth and critical thinking in adolescents and adults.* San Francisco: JosseyBass.

Kouzes, J. M., & Posner, B. Z. (1993). *Credibility: How leaders gain and lose it: Why people demand it.* San Francisco: Jossey-Bass.

Levinson, H. (1992). Feedback to subordinates. In *Levinson letter: Addendum.* Waltham, MA: Levinson Institute.

Meyer, P., & Davis, S. (1992). *The California Psychological Inventory applications guide.* Palo Alto, CA: Consulting Psychologists Press.

Piaget, J., & Inhelder, B. (1969). *The psychology of the child.* New York: Basic Books.

Schmitt, N., & Landy, F. (1993). The concept of validity. In N. Schmitt, W. C. Borman, & Associates, *Personnel selection in organizations.* San Francisco: Jossey-Bass.

Schneider, R. J., & Hough, L. M. (1995). Personality and industrial/ organizational psychology. In C. I. Cooper & I. T. Robertson (Eds.), *International review of industrial and organizational psychology* (Vol. 10). New York: Wiley.

Senge, P. M. (1990). *The fifth discipline.* New York: Doubleday.

Settoon, R. P., Bennett, N., & Liden, R. C. (1996). Social exchange in organizations: Perceived organizational support, leader-member exchange, and employee reciprocity. *Journal of Applied Psychology, 81,* 219–227.

Smither, J. W., Reilly, R. R., Millsap, R. E., Pearlman, K., & Stoffey, R. W. (1993). Applicant reactions to selection procedures. *Personnel Psychology, 46,* 41–76.

Society for Industrial and Organizational Psychology. (1987). *Principles for the validation and use of personnel selection procedures* (3rd ed.). Arlington Heights, IL: Author.

Tracey, J. B., Tannenbaum, S. I., & Kavanagh, M. J. (1995). Applying trained skills on the job: The importance of the work environment. *Journal of Applied Psychology, 80,* 239–252.

Weiss, H. M. (1990). Learning theory and industrial and organizational psychology. In M. D. Dunnette & L. M. Hough (Eds.), *Handbook of industrial and organizational psychology* (2nd ed., Vol. 1). Palo Alto, CA: Consulting Psychologists Press.

Wheatley, M. J. (1992). *Leadership and the new science.* San Francisco: Berrett-Koehler.

Zeidner, M., & Most, R. (1992). *Psychological testing: An inside view.* Palo Alto, CA: Consulting Psychologists Press.

Strategies

CHAPTER 9

Assessing and Changing Managers for New Organizational Roles

Larry Fogli
Kristina Whitney

Many organizations are facing the challenges of assessing and developing managers for new roles. Traditional command-and-control methods are ineffective in today's environment, and new behaviors, skills, and styles are needed to inspire, motivate, and facilitate employees. Most current individual assessment practices were developed under dramatically different conditions from those facing U.S. organizations today. This chapter examines the viability of current practices today and suggests changes and additions to them.

To set the stage for *why* assessors need to take another look at their assessment practices, we describe the new role of the manager and discuss how to use assessment results to help managers change styles and behaviors for new roles. We also offer thoughts on the future of assessment and of managerial roles.

Our focus is on *managers* rather than *leaders*. Leaders develop a vision for the future and create direction through vision and inspiration; managers ensure that the organization's vision, mission, and strategy are executed. Although many managers are being asked to provide leadership today (McFarland, Senn, & Childress, 1994), we treat the two as distinct.

Our perspective is that the design of individual assessments for new and evolving managerial roles should be driven by competencies linked to organizational mission, vision, values, and strategy and be explicitly future oriented. Throughout the chapter we provide examples from our work in the retail supermarket, apparel, and banking industries to illustrate our points.

The New Role of Managers

Over the past decade, there has been a shift from control to commitment in the workplace (Lawler, 1986), along with a shift in the role of the manager. In terms of management style, there has been a move away from being autocratic, militaristic, boss dominated, and command-and-control oriented and toward being empowering and participative. The role of the manager has shifted from taskmaster, micromanager, enforcer, and dictator to coach, helper, facilitator, team builder, and problem solver.

Traditional management roles emphasized control and supervision, work allocation, evaluation and reward, decision making and integration and interfacing. In contrast, the new role emphasizes guiding, mentoring, nurturing, educating and developing employees, removing obstacles from their paths, providing resources, resolving performance problems, ensuring optimal utilization and deployment of talent, and building teams. Old role managers focused primarily on results; new role managers must focus on process as well as results.

Although it emerged earlier, this new role became more widely acknowledged after it was described by Champy and Hammer (1994) in *Reengineering the Corporation:*

> Traditional bosses supervise, monitor, control, and check work as it moves from one task performer to the next. . . . Traditional bosses have little to do in a reengineered environment. Managers have to switch from supervisory roles to acting as facilitators, as enablers, and as people whose jobs are the development of people and their skills so that those people will be able to perform value-adding processes themselves. . . . Managers in a reengineered company need strong interpersonal skills and have to take pride in the accomplishment of others. Such a manager is a mentor, who is there to provide resources, to answer questions, and to look out for the

long-term career development of the individual. This is a different role from the one most managers have traditionally played [p. 77].

Many authors have documented and elaborated on this shift. For example, in *Twenty-First Century Leadership* (McFarland, Senn, & Childress, 1994), the authors describe a paradigm shift in management, from

> being a boss, controlling people, centralizing authority, micromanaging and goal-setting, directing with rules and regulations, establishing "position power" and hierarchy, demanding compliance, focusing on numbers and tasks, confronting and combating, stressing independence, encouraging "old boy" networks, changing by necessity and crisis, being internally competitive, and having a narrow focus ("me and my organization")

to

> being a coach and facilitator, empowering people, distributing leadership, aligning with broad vision and strategy, guiding with winning shared values and a healthy culture, building "relationship power" and networked teams, gaining commitment, focusing on quality, service and the customer, collaborating and unifying, fostering interdependence, respecting, honoring, and leveraging diversity, continuously learning and innovating, being globally competitive, and having a broader focus ("my community, my society, my world") [p. 345].

The new role of managers differs from the old role in four important ways. First, there has been a shift in ownership and accountability from the manager to the person doing the work. Second, the relationship between manager and employee has shifted from parent-child to adult-adult, based on the idea that if you treat employees like high performers they are more likely to act like high performers. Third, there has been a shift in the interaction between managers and employees, from a "tell" approach to an "ask" approach. Fourth and finally, as more managers have to manage without direct authority, there has been a shift from achieving goals through control to achieving goals through influence.

For the past five years, we have worked with organizations to help incorporate the new role into management cultures. For example, we have worked with supermarket retailers to establish a new style of management to support superior customer service strategies. Although we have worked with managers at all levels, in this case we targeted the store manager job because of its relationship to front-line service employees. Some of these stores were able to execute their customer service strategies and deliver superior service on a consistent basis, but others were having difficulty. On closer examination, it became clear that the superior service stores were being managed differently from the other stores. We examined the specific practices of the managers of these stores and conducted focus groups with employees to find out what their managers did that was so effective. We talked with employees to find out how they wanted to be managed to facilitate their superior service delivery. The results of this research were remarkably similar to the new role descriptions (see Table 9.1).

The new role has four components.

- Being a *helper* involves providing direction, knowledge, resources, advice, and support to employees.
- Being a *facilitator* involves simplifying and expediting organizational issues so that the employee can perform more effectively.
- Being a *problem solver* involves working with employees to identify obstacles, brainstorm solutions, and develop implementation plans for problems related to scheduling, supply, out-of-stock items, performance issues, and so forth.

Table 9.1. Old Role Versus New Role Management.

Old Role	New Role
Enforcer	Helper
Dictator	Facilitator
List maker	Problem solver
Micromanager	Team builder

- Being a *team builder* involves building a cooperative spirit and showing employees that they can achieve more by working together than by competing with and sabotaging each other.

Research with these companies has shown that managers who successfully adopted the new role had better unit financial results than those who did not. Although more research is needed, one possible explanation for this is that the way managers treat employees has an impact on how employees treat customers, the way employees treat customers has an impact on customer satisfaction, and customer satisfaction has an impact on sales and profits.

Conditions Creating the Need for New Role Managers

Changing economic conditions have produced downward pressure on managers to change their management style. Over the past decade, U.S. organizations have faced unprecedented competitive pressures due to increasing globalization, rapid advances in technology, the shift to an information economy, and the accelerating pace of change. In response, organizations have begun to pursue new strategies that require them to recognize their employees as a strategic resource and to find ways to tap employees' full potential. In particular, reengineering and process-centered work have raised expectations for high performance, placed more responsibility on employees, reduced the need for traditional supervision, and created a need to motivate and enable employees to do the job themselves. At the same time, spans of control have increased from 7–10:1 to 25–40:1, making it impossible to micromanage. Thus managers have received downward pressure to adopt a more facilitative and supportive style of management.

In the banking industry, for example, competition, deregulation, financial innovation, and technology have eroded many of the comparative advantages of banks. Emerging technology and newer distribution channels such as the Internet and telephone banking have made traditional branch networks less important for delivering financial services. To limit the decline in revenues from brick-and-mortar branches, there has been a shift away from traditional transaction processing toward a sales orientation and culture. As a result the role of the branch manager has shifted to that of sales manager. Many branch employees are having difficulty making the transition from the tradition and formality of old-style retail banking to the new-style retail sales culture. The new branch manager needs to motivate, encourage, and facilitate branch staff to operate as sales associates, a task that requires a different set of skills from the past.

The supermarket industry has always been fiercely competitive. However, new threats have emerged from several different directions (among them, warehouse operators, specialty retailers, and supercenters), and it is anticipated that 20 to 33 percent of supermarkets will disappear by the year 2000 (Saporito, 1995). At the same time, consumers are spending less money on groceries (Pollok, 1995). The primary response of supermarkets has been to adopt superior customer service as their key differentiating strategy, because superior service delivery leads to increased store profitability and growth through the creation of customer loyalty.

Many supermarket chains have a notoriously old role management culture. Many store managers learned a command-and-control style of management from previous old role managers and have been using that style successfully for many years. Old role store managers are commonly seen ordering, directing, list making, and focusing on the negative, to the exclusion of the positive. Employees respond to this management style with poor customer service. Thus many store managers are being asked to change the way they manage their store employees.

The same shift is seen in the apparel industry, which is feeling increased competition due to globalization, technology, changing demographics, and shifting consumer buying patterns. Competition from low-wage countries has forced many U.S. clothing factories to close their doors. Along with an increase in catalogue shopping, new delivery channels such as the Internet and television home shopping networks have provided increased competition. Consumers are demanding more value for their money and are less interested in shopping overall compared to the 1980s. Finally, changing demographics have had an impact on sales; for example, baby boomers spend more on home goods than on clothing (Dunne, Lusch, & Gable, 1995).

Service and sales has always been a key strategy for the apparel industry. Now many organizations are focusing on new ways to satisfy customers: reengineering the store around the customer, initiating customer loyalty programs, and offering special services such as personal shopping, fashion shows, special size promotions, customer information kiosks, and newsletters. And apparel organizations too are examining and implementing new roles for their managers.

At the same time, changing demographics and the values of the new workforce have shifted the expectations of employees, providing upward pressure for managers to abandon their command-and-control methods. For example, many organizations are focusing on superior service delivery to increase sales and gain competitive advantage. This strategy requires that frontline employees be managed in a positive way. How a manager treats an employee affects the service that the employee delivers to the customer. Many employees today are not motivated by authority alone.

Challenges

Organizations that attempt to develop new role managers are likely to face tremendous resistance. New role management requires unlearning old behaviors that brought success in the past. Managers must learn how to trust employees and keep out of the way, and must content themselves with achieving through others. Some managers do not believe in the new role; others do not want to change. Some lack the confidence to change or the skills needed for the new role. And finally, managers have been put through a lot over the past several years and may not be motivated to change.

Many managers who survived the reengineerings, downsizings, and delayerings report feelings of *survivor guilt* and burnout. They have had to trim jobs, cut back staff, and demote subordinates. As a result of ever-increasing time pressures, their workdays have been long and hard. And with measurement as the new "religion" of company leaders, they always have someone looking over their shoulder for financial and numerical results (Mintzberg, 1996).

The middle manager is in perhaps the most difficult position, getting squeezed from all angles (Schellhardt, 1997). Middle managers report being unable to please all of their constituencies—customers, employees, peers, and bosses—which leads to high levels of stress. The results of a recent survey showed that 40 percent of managers would quit their jobs tomorrow if they could afford it financially (Morris, 1996).

These are not the kind of conditions that foster change, particularly to a new management role that is more difficult than the old one. Managers are no longer protected by hierarchy and position power, they are supposed to be human and admit their flaws, and they must have even more self-control than before, because they can no longer vent their frustration at employees at will.

Future of the New Role

In addition to assessing and developing managers on the skills and competencies needed for the new role that is already in place, there is also a need to help them prepare for the future. Although no one can predict exactly what the future role of managers will entail, certain skills will help them make the transition effectively.

New role skills such as coaching, recognizing, and empowering employees will be important in the shift from the culture of empowerment to the next management paradigm. As information and knowledge continue to increase in importance, communication skills will be needed to share and disseminate them. To the extent that teams are used in organizations, managers will need team-building and team leadership skills. Finally, in organizations that adopt sales and service strategies, managers will need sales, sales management, customer service, and customer service management skills.

The context in which managers operate suggests that possessing skills and abilities such as these is already insufficient for success. Instead, skills and abilities are minimum entry requirements; personal qualities differentiate the best from the average performer. We believe that qualities such as resilience, stress tolerance, and adaptability will be increasingly important in the future as managers face increasing pressures and constant change. High levels of motivation will lead them to persist when conditions are difficult. And personality fit with job requirements and company culture may reduce stress in the long run. As Levinson (1996) notes: "Whether we are naturally levelheaded, spontaneously enthusiastic, artlessly charming, or born to persevere, we take our behaviors with us into everything we do. If what you do is at the core of who you are, your stress level will go down" (p. 163).

"Self-awareness" has been described by the *Harvard Business Review* as its "candidate for No. 1 managerial aptitude of the next decade" ("Faultlines a Manager Must Walk," 1996). Tolerance will help managers work with people from different cultural backgrounds within and across national boundaries. And values such as "integrity, honesty, trust, 'can-do' spirit, personal accountability, respect for all people, and openness to change" have been described as self-empowering and may give managers a competitive edge (McFarland, Senn, & Childress, 1994, p. 344).

White, Hodgson, and Crainer (1996) describe five skills that are required of managers and leaders in this era of change and uncertainty

- Difficult learning: learning from difficult situations or mistakes
- Maximizing energy: channeling energy into activities with added value
- Simplicity: inspiring others by simplifying the complex
- Multiple focus: focusing on multiple agendas simultaneously while creating corporate clarity
- Inner sense: possessing and using tacit knowledge about managing oneself, others, and tasks

Given that change and uncertainty are unlikely to diminish in coming years, these skills should continue to be important. In designing individual assessments for new and evolving organizational roles, it will be important to consider future job and role requirements such as these in addition to current requirements.

Identifying New Role Competencies: Future-Oriented Job Analysis and Competency Modeling

The analysis of current and future job requirements is critical to the design of individual assessment programs for new and changing organizational roles. Traditional job analysis methods, however, do not provide all of the information required in these circumstances. Future-oriented job analysis is needed to determine assessment techniques and processes and also to evaluate which competencies should be assessed.

The analysis of current and future job requirements has been a major part of our work to design and conduct assessment and developmental systems for new and changing organizational roles. A common scenario requires the consultant to determine what the future jobs should be and who should fill them and also how to change the skills or styles of the current workforce to fit the needs of the "transformed" organization.

A retail banking client seeking to shift from an operations and credit culture to a retail sales and service culture in order to remain competitive and the supermarket retailers implementing superior customer service strategies to differentiate themselves from their competitors wanted and needed useful information about the current jobs and also about how the future jobs needed to be performed to implement the strategies to meet the new mission and vision. In all of the situations, jobs were key components of these strategies.

Objectives of Job Analysis and Competency Modeling for New Role Managers

Many observers have begun to question the utility of traditional job analysis techniques in the face of the rapid changes facing jobs and organizations today. They argue that job analysis is not needed for the design of individual assessments for new or changing organizational roles, nor do they believe that competency modeling should replace job analysis in this situation. Nevertheless, we have found that some form of job analysis is needed to provide a basis for content validation and to obtain information for the design of simulations and work samples. Traditional job analysis techniques, however, are not future oriented enough, and other techniques need to be added to determine the following components:

- The company direction (vision, mission, values, and strategy)
- The role of managers in achieving strategic objectives
- The competencies required to achieve strategic objectives

- The activities and responsibilities of future job(s)
- The managers already performing new role requirements

In addition, we obtain initial judgments regarding which critical competencies can be assessed, what the most appropriate way is to assess them (assessment techniques and processes), and which competencies should be acquired through hiring and which should be developed on the job.

Identifying competencies that differentiate high from average performers has been more useful than developing the traditionally exhaustive laundry lists of knowledge, skills, abilities, and personal qualities (KSAPs) that traditional techniques tend to produce. However, we have had to get to a more detailed level in order to develop simulations, write test questions, and choose personality questionnaires. We have done this by determining the specific behaviors that define each competency and occasionally by using competencies as an organizing framework for the more specific KSAPs.

Shortcomings of Traditional Job Analysis

Traditional job analysis approaches fall short when it comes to meeting these objectives in the context of changing jobs and roles. The following areas seem most in need of change when assessing for new and changing organizational roles:

1. The job analysis must be both *descriptive* of existing job requirements and *prescriptive* of future job requirements.
2. The job analysis must include a stronger focus on the organization's *vision, mission, and strategies* and the role that managers will play in helping to achieve the new vision.
3. The job analysis must broaden its focus beyond a single job to include *work processes* that cut across jobs and *how the job fits into the structure of the organization.*
4. The job analysis must focus more strongly on *personal qualities, attitudes, values, motivational factors,* and other "soft" skills.
5. Although some existing job analysis tools can provide useful information about emerging jobs and roles, the *way in which the tools are used* must change.

Descriptive and Prescriptive

Job analysis must be descriptive of existing job requirements and prescriptive of future job requirements. Traditional job analysis approaches define the job as it currently exists in terms of the specific activities performed and the KSAPs needed to do those activities. However, as organizations go through downsizings, delayerings, right-sizings, layoffs, restructurings, and, the latest trend, growth, the definitions of jobs must be dynamic. Thus current jobs can be used as a starting point to lay out all of the activities being performed in an organization and the competencies associated with them. That information can be compared to the future scenario of the organization to make reorganization, restructuring, and placement decisions and to identify future training and developmental needs.

An additional implication for assessment design is that the assessment dimensions, techniques, and processes must be determined at the same time that the job is being defined. The results of the assessment can then be used to inform the definition and future direction of the job.

In one situation, we worked with a fashion retailer that was redesigning its stores around the customer. We first analyzed current store and field jobs in relation to current structure, work processes, vision, mission, and strategy. We used the resulting information to test the viability of various future scenarios, including different jobs, structures, store layouts, and work processes. Once a final scenario was selected, information such as the amount of time spent on current tasks, coordination requirements across different job functions, and the competencies needed to perform these tasks was used to design the new jobs and structure at a moderately detailed level. Assessment and developmental systems were then designed around the future job descriptions.

In being prescriptive, the resulting descriptions of future jobs should still include the activities to be performed *and* competencies needed to perform them. However, these descriptions have to be less specific than traditional ones due to the fact that the future jobs are only conceptualizations. Once the new structures and jobs are implemented, many changes and modifications are typically made.

Stronger and Broader Focus

Job analysis must include a stronger focus on the organization's vision, mission, and strategies and the role that managers will play in helping to achieve the new vision. In addition, it must broaden its focus beyond a single job to include work processes that cut across jobs and how the job fits into the structure of the organization.

Traditional job analysis tends to look at jobs in isolation. In order to develop a viable description of future jobs, job analysis must also consider the job in relation to current and future vision, mission, and strategy; jobs and structure; work processes; and competencies.

In our work with the fashion retailer, current jobs were examined in relation to all of these factors. In addition, we retained a reengineering firm to reengineer key processes such as merchandising and displaying, communications, and personnel planning. We incorporated information from the current and redesigned process maps to analyze jobs in relation to other jobs and work processes. This information provided a broader perspective than we would have had if we had examined each job in isolation.

Soft Skills Focus

Job analysis of new or emerging managerial roles must focus more strongly on personal qualities, attitudes, values, motivational factors, and other soft skills. Traditional job analyses focused on tasks, activities, knowledge areas, skills, and abilities, and only to a lesser extent on personal qualities and softer skills. The softer areas are more likely to differentiate successful from unsuccessful managers in emerging environments and thus should be a greater focus of job analysis.

In the banking organization that was shifting to a sales and service culture, we found that personal qualities of flexibility, resilience, energy, self-confidence, interpersonal insight, and achievement orientation were better predictors of which managers could adapt to the new managerial role than were traditional business skills and knowledge.

New Uses for Old Tools

Some existing job analysis tools can provide useful information about emerging jobs and roles, but the way in which they are used must change (May, 1996). Rigid, structured approaches work when jobs are rigidly defined and static. A more eclectic approach is needed that combines multiple techniques, draws on different sources of expertise (senior management, marketing department, customers, and subordinates), focuses on the present as well as the future, and is descriptive as well as prescriptive. The process is messier than traditional job analysis: less precise, more iterative, and more dynamic. The consultant must be able to use an experience-based framework and understanding of company strategy to make judgments based on incomplete and changing information.

To gather information on current and future jobs in the fashion retailer example, we used nontraditional sources of information, such as customer interviews, market research data, competitor studies, literature reviews about the changes occurring in the fashion industry, reengineering process maps, and interviews with reengineering design team members. As part of the job analysis questionnaire, we asked job incumbents to rate the importance of various tangible and intangible customer service dimensions to customers and their perception of the store's performance on those dimensions. By constructing a matrix of customer importance to store importance, we were able to test the viability of proposed process redesign changes and thus the likelihood that various new job designs would be implemented.

Key Questions for Job Analysis

One way we have determined to modify existing tools is to frame the job analysis in terms of the questions that we need answered and then choose techniques and tools to help us answer those questions. Following is a list of questions that we have found useful to ask:

- What are the vision, mission, and strategy of the organization?
- What is the role of managers in achieving the new vision, mission, and strategy?
- What automation and process changes are planned (for example, new computer systems and processes for purchasing, pricing, delivery, scheduling, and inventory control)? How are they expected to affect future job requirements?

- What is the transition process for getting to the vision of the job as it fits the organizational vision and mission?
- What are the immediate job requirements for filling the jobs at the outset of strategy implementation? How do they differ from the long-term job requirements?
- What are the critical differences in job duties and responsibilities anticipated for the future?
- What decisions do managers make today and what decisions are they likely to make in the future?
- What are the most critical differences in competency and KSAP requirements anticipated for the current versus the future job?
- What are the key competencies that underlie many of the jobs in the new culture for implementation of vision, mission, and strategy?
- What are the major barriers, obstacles, and solutions to superior job performance in the job today?
- What job design changes would facilitate superior performance?
- What are the best practices of current managers?
- What do managers like and dislike currently about the job and organization?
- What is the impact of these factors on job performance?

Following are some traditional questions that remain useful for analyzing new and evolving organizational roles:

- What parts of the current job are most important?
- What do managers spend the most time doing?
- What are the most challenging parts of the job?
- What are the most important KSAPs needed to perform the job well?
- Which ones differentiate the best performers from average performers?

New Role Job Activities and Competencies

We have used future-oriented job analysis techniques to analyze the changing requirements of managerial jobs in several different industries. For example, we used these techniques to analyze the job of store manager for a major retailer during the 1980s and again in the mid–1990s. We found that the job changed in terms of activities and the competencies required for success (see Figure 9.1).

Store managers today spend less time on the task side of the job (for example, store operations and expense control) and more time on the people side (for example, spending time with employees and customers). In fact, the most effective managers—those with the best financial, service, and leadership scores—have redesigned their jobs so that they can spend almost all of their time with employees and customers.

This new set of job activities requires different competencies than in the past. The following list contains a summary and integration of new role management competencies, based on work with several management jobs in different industries.

New Role Management Competencies

1. Communicating effectively
   Verbal communication and presentation
   Listening
   Informing
   Persuading
2. Interpersonal skills
   Sensitivity
   Directness, openness
   Approachability
   Relationship building
   Influencing
   Networking
3. Leadership
   Motivating and inspiring
   Fostering a shared vision
   Coaching and mentoring
   Building and leveraging teams
4. Problem solving, cognitive skills
   Analytical thinking
   Decision making
   Continuous learning
   Thinking outside the box

**Figure 9.1. Time Spent on Major Job Activities,
1980s versus 1990s.**

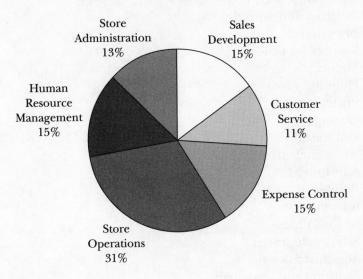

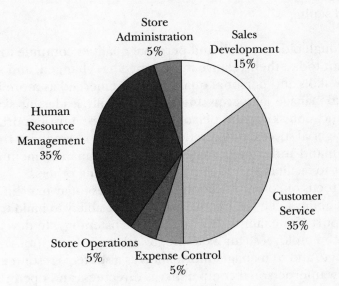

5. Drive for results
   Initiative
   Resourcefulness
   Ownership, accountability
6. Integrity and attitude
   Integrity
   Respect for others
   Maturity
   Humility, modesty
   Pride
   Courage
   Optimism
   Willingness to take risks
7. Adjustment
   Resiliency
   Adaptability
   Self-awareness
   Self-development
8. Administrative skills
   Planning and organizing
   Delegating
   Goal setting

Although old role skills and personal qualities continue to be important today, their relative importance has changed, and several new skills and personal qualities have emerged as more important to managerial success. Interpersonal skills, leadership skills, communication skills, and personal qualities are most important for managerial success today, reflecting the shift in emphasis from the command-and-control structure and micromanagement approaches to facilitating, coaching, and developing others.

The focus of communication competencies today has shifted from the ability to be clear and effective to the ability to build trust and support (for example, through active listening), to develop and coach employees (for example, by asking key questions), to sell change, and to manage information as a strategic resource.

A new interpersonal competency is directness and openness. Effective managers today are more direct and open than was the norm in the past. They are able to create an environment in which people feel comfortable expressing ideas and opinions. They accept criticism openly and nondefensively. This style fits well with the changing values of the workforce and empowerment strategies.

Managers must be very comfortable with people. Back-office managers are not available, accessible, or approachable enough to perform the new role. Many managers who were effective operators or financial whizzes in the past are finding themselves struggling as they shift to being a coach and facilitator.

In addition, relationship building and networking have increased in importance, reflecting the wider net within which managers now operate, for example, of suppliers, consultants, distributors, and others.

Leadership competencies are more differentiated than in the past and include a greater emphasis on teams. With teams now an integral part of the organizational landscape, managers must be able to create a sense of team unity as they also help each individual team member understand his or her contribution to the overall effort.

Traditional problem-solving skills remain important, particularly as the workplace becomes more complex and changes more frequently. There is a greater need for managers to think strategically, learn new skills, learn from failure, and use common sense to determine how to handle different situations. Effective managers have always relied on common sense or intuition to make decisions, but consulting psychologists did not have assessment tools to measure these qualities. However, newer thinking views intuition as the immediate perception of nonlinear patterns learned through experience. This definition helps us understand how managers use pattern recognition to match features of current situations to the vast database of experiences they carry with them to identify solutions and make decisions.

Personal qualities appear to be key differentiators of highly successful and less successful managers today. Higher levels of commitment and motivation are required. Managers with the strongest drive, the greatest resourcefulness, and the strongest sense of ownership have a key advantage over the rest.

Integrity and attitude factors play a key role. Certainly they have always been cited as important components of management; they take on added importance in situations involving reorganizations, downsizings, and delayerings. Managers are often faced with conflicting loyalties and sensitive information in these situations. Egomaniacs are no longer tolerated; managers must have humility and must respect the needs of others. They must have the courage to take on tough issues such as terminating perpetual underperformers; otherwise, the other employees, overworked, are resentful. Managers must communicate optimism and a positive attitude to motivate their employees during times of change and uncertainty.

Finally, to be able to adjust to the changing and complex workplace, managers must continually learn and develop to accommodate the changes in their jobs; this involves openness and self-awareness. They also must be adaptable and resilient in dealing with constant change.

As the list of competencies shows, managers today and in the future must possess a higher-level, more complex skill set with a stronger focus on people skills than managers in the past. A question we often hear from client organizations is, "But will we ever find anyone with this profile?"

Assessment Techniques and Methods for New and Evolving Organizational Roles

Designing and conducting individual assessments for new management roles presents several challenges to the consultant or psychologist:

- Designing assessment systems that are inclusive of the current and evolving job and personal requirements
- Developing assessment systems that go beyond traditional knowledge, skill, and ability approaches
- Integrating multiple sources of data and information about a manager to make judgments about the person's fit with the organization's current and future needs and strategy
- Ensuring the validity of the individual assessment process

Many of these challenges can be overcome by adapting existing assessment methods and techniques. We have used different sources of information to assess managers for new and evolving roles, including tests, interviews, simulations, upward evaluations and 360-degree feedback ratings, employee surveys, performance appraisals, and financial results. These techniques can be grouped into four categories of competency measurement: experiences, attributes, abilities, and skills.

Traditional competency areas, such as management skills and cognitive abilities, are often only minimum requirements for new and evolving managerial roles. Personal characteristics like self-awareness, adaptability, energy level, motivation, interests, values, and expectations have become more critical in predicting whether an individual will meet the challenges of new managerial roles. The breadth and depth of past experiences, relevant achievements, and accomplishments have become more important as managers are repeatedly moved from one assignment to another. Our challenge is to measure these new role job requirements reliably, some of which may not be measurable. For example, a manager who possesses the KSAPs for the new role may not make the personal sacrifices of extended work hours, travel, relocation, and career over family choices for job success.

In conducting assessments of current employees for future jobs, we have used a process of integrating multiple sources of data and information about an individual. Because individual assessment consists of multiple assessment methods, the evaluation of and conclusions about any individual are derived from the consistency of results across these multiple methods. The process of individual assessment should comply with assessment center guidelines ("Guidelines and Ethical Considerations," 1989) that lead to accurate assessment and predictions of job performance. For example:

1. Assessment should be based on clearly defined dimensions of managerial behavior.
2. Multiple assessment techniques must be used.
3. A variety of job-sampling techniques should be used.
4. The assessors should know what it takes to succeed. They should be thoroughly familiar with the job and organization.
5. The assessors should be thoroughly trained in assessment procedures.
6. Behavioral data should be observed, recorded, and communicated among the assessor team.

7. Group discussion processes should be used to integrate observations, rate dimensions, and make predictions.
8. The assessment process should be separated into stages that delay the formation of general impressions, evaluations, overall ratings, or final predictions.
9. Assessees should be evaluated against a clearly understood norm, not against each other.

Validation of assessment techniques for new role jobs is based on content validation and validity generalization. Techniques must be content oriented to measure task and related competency requirements and must have evidence of previous validity in predicting job performance for similar jobs, that is, must be transportable. Future-oriented job analysis information is essential for validation to determine new role competencies; valid measures of those competencies can then be part of the assessment process. Assessments should include both proven predictors of managers and leaders across situations and history, such as intelligence and personality factors, as well as new role competencies that differentiate successful performers from average performers. In this section we review existing assessment methods and techniques in the light of these challenges.

Experiences

Future behavior is predicted from past relevant behavior. Accordingly, the performance of managers in future roles can be predicted from their past performance. Assessment data and information about a person's past experiences, achievements, accomplishments, and job performance are therefore essential to predicting how the person will perform in new role jobs. Four techniques to assess past relevant experiences—the accomplishment record, biographical data, structured interviewing, and performance assessment—provide useful information in assessing managers for new roles.

Accomplishment Record

Hough (1984) developed the accomplishment record as the "let my record speak for itself" technique for professionals who often resist traditional testing, among them attorneys. Past, recent, and long-standing achievements that relate to job requirements are valid predictors. McDaniel, Schmidt, and Hunter (1988) report validity ($r = .45$) for the behavioral consistency accomplishment record. An applicant fills out a structured resumé or supplemental application form (SAF) that is evaluated for relevance to the requirements of the new role job. Behavioral consistency is measured by how responses are related to a current and evolving job.

When one of our retail clients was undergoing a major reorganization, we helped identify and develop competencies for new role management and leadership positions in the redesigned organization. Applicants were provided with definitions of these competencies and were required to describe their accomplishments and achievements by answering a set of questions. Following is an example for one of the competencies, Relationship Building:

> *Relationship Building.* Builds and maintains relationships and networks with people who are, or might someday be, useful resources in achieving work-related goals. Develops and nurtures customer relationships. Understands others and is able to get their cooperation without regard to reporting relationships.
> 1. What was the problem or objective?
> 2. What did you actually do and when (approximate dates to the nearest year)?
> 3. What was the outcome or result?
> 4. What is the estimated percentage of this achievement directly attributable to you?
> 5. Who would verify your achievements?

Biographical Data

Biographical data are well documented as a valid predictor of management, executive, and leadership success. Gatewood and Feild (1994) reported studies showing biodata validities (for example, $r = .33$) for managerial performance. Among the variety of job criteria that are predicted by biodata relevant to new role management sales and service leadership positions are job choice, vocational preference, turnover, overall performance, communication skill, coping with stress, customer service, leadership, learning rate, management skill, problem solving, promotability, sales skill, sales performance, teamwork, trustworthiness, and work ethic.

The types of biodata items that have proven useful in assessing applicants for new roles cover areas such as

- Prior work and job experiences
- Work interests
- Preferred work characteristics
- Preferred job characteristics
- Work style
- Interest in leisure activities
- School experiences
- . Self-concept
- Directness, openness
- Affiliativeness
- Learning ability
- Achievement motivation
- Resourcefulness
- Ownership, accountability
- Humility, modesty
- Optimism
- Self-awareness
- Self-development
- Adaptability

Structured Interviewing

Structured interviews integrate the latest in interviewing technology to provide reliable and valid information for selection and promotion decisions. The process involves multiple interviewing steps and multiple interviewers. Job analysis provides the foundation for each step. Interviewer training is required to implement systematic information gathering and reliable applicant ratings. This approach has been used successfully for new role jobs. A typical process to assess new role competencies (for example, relationship building, team building, developing others, adaptability, resourcefulness, influencing) follows:

1. Describe new role job requirements.
2. Ask minimum job qualifications (salary, travel, licensure, credentials, relocation, hours and days of work).

3. Ask follow-up questions on the accomplishment record (SAF). This includes probing for missing factual information about the cited accomplishment, as well as more description of how the new role competency was demonstrated.
4. Ask other behavioral description questions (Janz, Hellervik, & Gilmore, 1986). Standardized questions are prepared to gather more information about new role competencies.
5. Ask situational judgment questions (Latham, Saari, Pursell, & Campion, 1980) about what the applicant would do given situations that can happen in the new role job.
6. Ask questions that measure the applicant's interest and motivation for the new role job.

Behavioral description questions focus the interview on past behavior rather than opinions and views about oneself. These questions keep the interview on track, focusing on important job-relevant behaviors.

We have developed an inventory of behavioral description and past experience questions to assess new role competencies. Following are a few examples for relationship building:

- Sketch out two or three key strengths you have in dealing with people. Can you illustrate the first strength with a recent example? When did this example take place? What possible negative outcomes were avoided by the way you handled this incident? How often has this type of situation arisen? What happened the next time this came up? (Repeat same probes for other strengths.)
- Can you tell me about a time when you effectively used your people skills to solve a customer problem? When did this take place? What did the customer say? What did you say in response? How did the customer react? Was the customer satisfied?
- Maintaining a network of personal contacts helps a manager keep on top of developments. Describe some of your most useful personal contacts. Tell me about a time when a personal contact helped you solve a problem or avoid a major blunder. How did you develop that contact in the first place? What did

you do to obtain the useful information from your contact? When was the next time this contact was useful? What was the situation at that time? How often in the past six months have personal contacts been useful in this way?

- Given the usefulness of contacts, building new contacts pays off. Focusing on the past six months, describe an example of the way you build your contacts. When did this example take place? Has this particular contact paid off yet? How? How often have you used this type of approach to building contacts during the past year?

Performance Assessment

Evaluation of current job performance for new job competencies is an important part of individual assessment. Multirater evaluations and feedback provide measures of competencies as well as feedback for employee development. Ratings by self, manager, coworkers, employees, and customers on performance, behaviors, skills, traits, and attitudes provide useful information for assessment. Examples of such ratings are

> Listens to what others are saying
> Treats others with courtesy, consideration, and respect
> Behaves consistently regardless of his or her mood
> Likes being around people
> High personal integrity

The typical system collects feedback by questionnaire. Feedback is provided graphically with norm comparisons and written comments and also narrative recommendations for development. When one of our retail clients decided to improve customer service as a competitive strategy, a multirater feedback system was implemented for all executives and managers. Some of the competencies and items follow:

- Communication
  Communicates clearly and concisely
  Listens to what others are saying

- Feedback and recognition
  Gives feedback on progress toward store and department goals
  Provides timely, specific performance feedback to employees
- Leadership and empowerment
  Creates a feeling of energy and excitement in the store
  Inspires others to achieve outstanding results
- Team building
  Makes everyone feel like an important part of the store team
  Encourages and facilitates cooperation and teamwork among employees
- Interpersonal skills
  Establishes and maintains good working relationships with others
  Treats others with courtesy, consideration, and respect
- Adaptability and stress tolerance
  Behaves consistently regardless of his or her mood
  Remains calm under stressful or difficult situations
- Delegation
  Delegates the right amount of work
  Provides clear instructions when assigning work
- Managing for superior customer service
  Manages the store to ensure that the entrance and outside area are well maintained (for example, parking lot is well lit, clean, and free of clutter; store entrance is well kept)
  Manages the store to ensure that the shelves are well stocked

Attributes: Personality and Style Inventories

Organizational fit and emotional IQ are critical to success for a new role manager. Personality, leadership, and management style inventories provide useful new role manager profiles.

Personality Inventories

The resurgence of personality measures as valid predictors of job and career success has been documented by several authors (Barrick & Mount, 1991; Costa & McCrae, 1995; Murphy, 1996). Some of this evidence shows that personality predicts management performance. Costa and McCrae (1995) cite evidence showing that conscientiousness, emotional stability, and extroversion predict managerial success. We have found validities for management and leadership performance using scales on the California Psychological Inventory (CPI) (*California Psychological Inventory,* 1995) and the Occupational Personality Questionnaire (OPQ) (Saville & Holdsworth, 1996).

California Psychological Inventory. The CPI measures aspects of both new and old role orientations. Several scales assess interpersonal style and manner of dealing with others (dominance, capacity for status, sociability, social presence, self-acceptance, independence, and empathy) and provide an impression of how a manager approaches others and of qualities such as self-confidence, poise, and initiative. Scales pertaining to the internalization and endorsement of normative conventions (responsibility, socialization, self-control, good impression, communality, well-being, and tolerance) illustrate how a manager views social norms and how conduct is affected by these considerations. Scales pertaining to cognitive and intellectual functioning (achievement through conformance, achievement through independence, and intellectual efficiency) show how a new role manager behaves with respect to achievement in either structured or open situations. CPI has seven Special Purpose Scales, including those for leadership, work orientation, managerial potential, and amicability directly related to occupational issues. Using these scales, CORE Corporation has developed composite CPI scores for retail management positions, with validities ranging from .20 to .31 for managerial performance.

We have found certain CPI scales to be most important for new role managers. The new role manager should be at or above the sixtieth percentile on sociability, social presence, self-acceptance, responsibility, sense of well-being, tolerance, intellectual efficiency, psychological mindedness, and flexibility. He or she should be between the fiftieth and sixtieth percentile on independence, capacity for status, socialization, self-control, good impression, commonality, achievement through conformance, and achievement through independence. And we look for new role managers who score at or above the sixtieth percentile on leadership, work orientation, managerial potential, and amicability.

Occupational Personality Questionnaire. The OPQ (Saville & Holdsworth, 1996) is used to describe personality for a number of organizational purposes, including managerial selection, training and development, and team building. Relationships with people, thinking style, and feelings and emotions are the three general personality factors measured in specific attributes, as described below:

- Relationships with people
  Persuasive: enjoys selling, changes opinions of others, convincing with arguments, negotiates
  Controlling: takes charge, directs, manages, organizes, supervises others
  Independent: has strong views on things, difficult to manage, speaks up, argues, dislikes structure
  Outgoing: fun loving, humorous, sociable, vibrant, talkative, jovial
  Affiliative: has many friends, enjoys being in groups, likes companionship, shares things with friends
  Socially confident: puts people at ease, knows what to say, good with words
  Modest: reserved about achievements, avoids talking about self, accepts others, not status conscious
  Democratic: encourages others to contribute, consults, listens and refers to others
  Caring: considerate to others, helps those in need, sympathetic, tolerant
- Thinking style
  Practical: down to earth, likes repairing and fixing things, enjoys using hands
  Data rational: likes to work with data, operates on facts, enjoys assessing and measuring
  Artistic: appreciates culture, sensitive to visual arts and music
  Behavioral: analyzes thoughts and behavior, psychologically minded, likes to understand people
  Traditional: preserves well-proven methods, prefers the orthodox, disciplined, conventional
  Change oriented: enjoys doing new things, seeks variety, prefers novelty to routine, accepts changes

Conceptual: theoretical, intellectually curious, enjoys the complex and abstract

Innovative: generates ideas, shows ingenuity, thinks up solutions

Forward planning: prepares well in advance, enjoys target setting, forecasts trends, plans projects

Detail conscious: methodical, keeps things neat and tidy, precise, accurate

Conscientious: sticks to deadlines, completes jobs, perseveres with routine, likes fixed schedules

- Feelings and emotions

Relaxed: calm, relaxed, cool under pressure, free from anxiety, can switch off from work

Worrying: worries when things go wrong, keyed up before important events, anxious to do well

Tough minded: difficult to hurt or upset, can brush off insults, unaffected by unfair remarks

Emotional control: restrained in showing emotions, keeps feelings to self, avoids outbursts

Optimistic: cheerful, happy, keeps spirits up despite setbacks

Critical: likes probing the facts, sees the disadvantages, challenges assumptions

Active: has energy, moves quickly, keeps busy, doesn't sit still

Competitive: plays to win, determined to beat others, poor loser

Achieving: ambitious, sets sights high, career centered, results oriented

Decisive: quick at conclusions, weighs things up rapidly, may be hasty, takes risks

The OPQ provides useful new role style scales for teams and leadership styles. Tables 9.2 and 9.3 contain examples of outputs from the OPQ for a manager assessed for a new role managerial job.

Our case studies of new role managers show they score higher than old role managers on the following OPQ characteristics: outgoing, affiliative, socially confident, modest, democratic, caring, behavioral, change oriented, forward planning, relaxed, tough minded, optimistic, active, competitive, achieving, and decisive.

Table 9.2. OPQ Team Styles Profile.

Style	Description (Case Example)
Coordinator	Sets the team goals and defines roles
	Coordinates team efforts and leads by eliciting respect
Shaper	The task leader who brings competitive drive to the team
	Makes things happen but may be thought abrasive
Innovator/plant	Imaginative, intelligent, and the team's source of original ideas
	Concerned with fundamentals
Monitor-evaluator	Offers measured, dispassionate critical analysis
	Keeps team from pursuing misguided objectives
Resource investigator	Salesperson, diplomat, resource seeker
	Good improviser with many external contact
	May be easily diverted from task at hand
Completer	Worries about problems; personally checks details
	Intolerant of the casual and careless; sees project through
Team worker	Promotes team harmony; good listener who builds on the ideas of others
	Likable and unassertive
Implementer	Turns decisions and strategies into manageable tasks
	Brings logical, methodical pursuit of objectives to the team

Table 9.3. OPQ Leadership Styles Profile.

Style	Description (Case Example)
Directive leader	Maintains responsibility for planning and control Issues instructions in line with own perception of priorities
Delegative leader	Minimal personal involvement Believes in delegation of task and responsibility
Participative leader	Favors consensus decision making Prepared to take time over decisions Ensures involvement of all relevant individuals
Consultative leader	Pays genuine attention to opinions and feelings of subordinates, but maintains a clear sense of task objectives and makes the final decisions
Negotiative leader	Makes deals with subordinates Influences others by identifying their needs and using these as a basis for negotiation
Adaptability	A measure of the individual's capacity to adopt different styles of behavior in different sets of circumstances

New role managers also score higher on coordinator, shaper, resource investigator, team worker, and implementer team styles and have higher scores on participative, consultative, and adaptable leadership styles.

Management Styles

In addition to psychological traits, new role managers need to possess effective behavioral styles in the workplace. We have measured style constructs such as customer service, sales style, interpersonal, conflict, empowerment, learning, stress resiliency, and power orientation to assess managers for important job competency requirements. Some of the tests and inventories that assess these styles are ServiceFirst (CORE Corporation, 1990), Firo-B (*Firo-B,* 1989), Thomas-Kilmann Conflict Mode Instrument (Thomas & Kilmann, 1974), Empowerment Inventory (Thomas & Tymon, 1993), Stress Resiliency Profile (Thomas & Tymon, 1992), Power Base Inventory (Thomas & Thomas, 1991), and the Strong Interest Inventory (*Strong Interest Inventory,* 1994). Besides providing assessment information, these types of tests provide useful coaching and personal insight feedback for the person.

Abilities

It is widely accepted that cognitive abilities are valid predictors of job success (Murphy, 1996). Hunter (1986) has shown that cognitive abilities predict managerial job performance ($r = .51$). We have used both standardized tests, such as the Watson-Glaser Critical Thinking Appraisal (Psychological Corporation, 1980), and specific tests, such as the Retail Management Situational Judgment Test (Fogli, 1991), to measure learning and problem-solving abilities and skills. Situational tests that measure tacit knowledge (Wagner & Sternberg, 1985) or experiential learning have added unique variance to the prediction of management success in retailing (Fogli, 1991). There are twelve work-related situations in the Tacit Knowledge Inventory (Psychological Corporation, n.d.) for which the respondent must rate the quality of alternative plans of action related to the situations. These items are designed to measure *practical intelligence.* Scores are provided on scales indicating a person's knowledge in terms of managing one's self, managing others, and managing tasks. The Tacit Knowledge Inventory correlates ($r = .30$) with retail management job performance.

The Retail Management Situational Test (Fogli, 1991) contains thirty-three work-specific situations for which the respondent must rate the quality of alternative solution strategies pertaining to the work situation. It has a format similar to that of the Tacit Knowledge Inventory and measures similar knowledge and abilities, specifically knowledge of retail management and decision making in work-oriented situations. The Retail Management Situational Test correlates ($r = .46$) with retail management job performance.

Our approach to cognitive ability assessment is to use one general and one specific test. For example, if critical thinking and financial calculations are needed, we could use the Watson-Glaser test and a specifically designed financial calculations test. The approach is to assess for both the general and specific types of thinking essential to future job success.

Skills

The competencies and skills to perform specific new role job activities can be measured by simulation exercises. Interpersonal, leadership, communication, problem-solving, organizational, and job-specific skills and competences can be assessed by performance tests.

Gatewood and Feild (1994) report meta-analytic coefficients for performance tests and job simulations of $r = .53$ with managerial job potential and $r = .36$ with managerial job performance. New performance tests and simulations have been designed to measure old role and new role skills and competencies. For example, branch managers of banks of the future need to be able to sell directly to clients, develop and manage a sales team, and manage the branch as a franchise. Following are examples of simulations designed for a new branch manager role.

New role branch management plan. The participant is asked to develop a plan to take over a branch from an old role manager and improve service, sales, and profitability. The participant is assessed on the extent to which he or she uses new role techniques (for example, helping, facilitating, problem solving, team building) to improve branch performance.

Coaching employee performance simulation. The participant plays the role of a new branch manager who has replaced an old role manager. One of the tellers has had difficulty adapting to the new sales focus of the branch because of the old role tactics used by the previous manager. The participant is asked to coach this teller to improve his or her performance. As part of a coaching discussion, the participant is asked to role play a sales interaction with the teller and give feedback on how it was handled.

Sales simulation. The participant plays the role of a new branch manager who reschedules a customer appointment that had been canceled previously by his or her old role predecessor. The appointment is with a doctor who had responded to a mailer two months ago indicating an interest in more information about business checking, business credit, personal checking, personal credit, investments, and certificates of deposit. The participant meets with the doctor to assess his needs, establish a relationship, and sell financial products and services.

Existing assessment techniques are useful in conducting assessments for new role management jobs. For traditional competencies that are still needed in new role jobs, techniques can be used as is. Newer competencies can be measured by adapting traditional assessment techniques, for example, by changing the content of performance simulations or using newer techniques such as multirater feedback. The overall process of designing and validating individual assessments for new role jobs, however, remains much the same as it has been. We have found individual assessment techniques to be quite transportable to new role jobs when the job analysis provides prescriptive information about future job requirements.

Developing Managers to Meet New and Emerging Organizational Role Requirements

Perhaps the most important use of assessment results is in developing new role managers. Because there is and will continue to be a shortage of qualified labor, organizations cannot replace all current managers with new managers who possess new role competencies. First, even if an organization decided to replace its managers, it would likely have a difficult time finding enough managers who have new role skills. Second, current managers have a wealth of knowledge of and experience with the organization that would be difficult to replace. Thus organizations must work with the resources they have, coaching and developing current managers to be able to manage in a manner consistent with the new role.

In this section we describe some of our experiences and lessons learned in developing new role managers. There is a vast literature describing the different strategies and tools available to develop managers (Peterson & Hicks, 1996), and we will not cover this material here. However, we will describe an approach that we have found to be effective in situations specifically focused on developing new role managers. At its core it includes efforts to develop managers through feedback and coaching, but these efforts are subsumed within broader efforts to change the management culture of the organization.

Unique Issues in Developing New Role Managers

Several unique issues relate to the ability to develop new role managers: issues about people, about coaches, and about the conditions for change. First, the new role is difficult to perform for some individuals. Because it is based on personality and style factors, it is not just what a manager does that makes him or her effective but also how he or she does it. New role managers are rewarded not just for their results but how they achieve them. In other words, process is more important today than in the past, and process depends on the manager's personality, interpersonal skills, and communication skills. Becoming a new role manager is more difficult than learning how to read operational reports. As Roger Enrico, vice chairman of PepsiCo, put it, "Human interactions are a lot tougher to manage than numbers and P&Ls" (Sherman, 1995a, p. 91).

Some people cannot change and may not be coachable. Many managers and executives developed their skills and style in a different culture and environment. It is difficult to give up what has worked so well for them in the past. Many have not had the proper role models, and others disagree with the whole concept of the new role. Attitude, self-insight, and the ability to accept responsibility for one's behavior all contribute to determining whether a manager can change. Managers may or may not want to change, and they may or may not possess the skills needed to do so. And deeply entrenched or frequent negative behaviors are very difficult for anyone to change, even if they want to do so.

The second set of issues concerns the coach. Not everyone has what it takes to be an effective coach. Old role managers who need coaching are often angry that they need to change, confused about how to change, and demotivated in their jobs as a result. Some resent that the world has changed and they have not. Others feel that they have been successful in the past so why change now? These individuals need understanding, acceptance, and focus from their coach. The coach must be able to show trust and understanding to help the manager accept the need to change, focus on specifics, and take action to change.

Many organizations are turning to their own managers to become coaches to others who are having difficulty adapting to the new role. The role of internal coach is different from that of traditional manager. Traditional managers tend to be competitive; quick to think, act, judge, and speak; and short on time—all qualities that are not conducive to the coaching relationship (Waldroop & Butler, 1996). The coach must take on the role of teacher or helpful colleague, not competitor or judge. The coach must be patient and have a long-term rather than short-term focus, have the time to develop the relationship through regular meetings, and be able to step out of his or her regular job and just listen and focus in order to help move the individual from understanding to action.

Internal coaches must also have credibility with the individuals they are coaching and must be able to perform the new role themselves. Some of the best internal coaches we have seen are district sales managers who have changed from the old role to the new role themselves. This gives them tremendous credibility with the individuals they coach and sends the message that it is possible to change.

In addition to providing an effective coach, there are other important conditions for change: communicating clear expectations regarding the new role, providing feedback (such as multirater or upward evaluation results, test data, and observations) to the manager to increase his or her awareness, and holding the manager accountable for change.

Creating a New Role Culture

We have used coaching as one component of a broader effort to change the management culture of selected organizations. Exhibit 9.1 summarizes the approach we have used

Typically, we first work with the organization to identify the management practices and style it needs to achieve its strategic objectives. Top management then communicates the new job

Exhibit 9.1. Steps to Create a New Role Culture.

1. New role is determined based on company mission, vision, values, and strategy.
2. New role expectations communicated formally and through upward evaluation.
3. Managers participate in upward evaluation process (new role competencies and behaviors).
4. Managers receive upward and other feedback.
5. Managers develop new role behaviors through workshops, action planning, and individual coaching.
6. Managers communicate feedback and action plans to staff.
7. Managers receive ongoing feedback through upward evaluation and continue to develop new role behaviors.
8. Human resource systems are aligned with new role and with new role competencies (such as assessment, hiring, promotion, training, compensation, and reward systems) to provide consistency and accountability.

expectations and requirements to managers, usually through an upward evaluation or multirater feedback process. These tools are useful both in communicating role expectations and in providing feedback to managers on their performance. A critical element here is to show how the new role relates to the company's direction and strategy. Specifically, management needs to communicate the link between the competencies and personal qualities measured by the upward evaluation and their role in helping the company achieve its strategic objectives.

Once the new expectations have been communicated, managers must receive feedback on their management style. This feedback is a key component in helping them change old role behaviors and developing new role behaviors. In developing new role managers, it is not always possible to work one-on-one with each manager using an approach tailored to that person's level of skills and commitment. In most situations where an organization is trying to create a broad-based shift in management style, we have had to work with large numbers of managers simultaneously. The most viable solution has been to do some work at the group level and to work one-on-one with individuals who are having difficulty creating change. In these situations we have designed new role workshops as a first step in helping managers use upward evaluation feedback to change their behaviors.

The objectives of these workshops are typically for managers to understand their new job requirements in specific terms; relate the new job requirements to the organization's mission, vision, and strategy; understand their employees' perspective about how they should implement the new job requirements; prepare to implement new role skills and techniques for superior performance; develop a realistic action plan to implement new job requirements; and prepare to communicate their upward evaluation results and action plan to their staff.

We have found that on-the-job, tangible, developmental activities have been the most effective way to change managers' behavior, accompanied by coaching. Thus a key part of the workshop is to work with participants to identify developmental assignments that will help them develop new role skills and create a change in perceptions of their style.

A key component of our work is to build in internal supports and accountability structures. One example has been to set up internal coaching teams within the work unit, as well as an internal coach-mentor, typically the manager's boss. The internal coaching team is a group of employees chosen by the manager to provide understanding and support, monitor performance, provide ongoing feedback, and help the manager take action. Often the manager is encouraged to include someone who has *not* been a supporter. The relationship between the manager and this person is often improved by involving him or her in the manager's development. The group commits to pointing out when the manager strays from the action plan as well as reinforcing positive behaviors.

It is helpful to train the manager's supervisor as an internal coach-mentor, with specific and tangible roles and activities for internal "boss" coaches. If the manager is to change, the coach-mentor needs to understand the critical behaviors and what has worked to change managers in other situations. All coach-mentors need to learn specific coaching activities and skills.

When the manager is not successfully implementing the new role or the internal coach is not strong enough, we have provided external coaching to the manager. Typically, these managers have had difficulty understanding or accepting their upward evaluation results. Therefore, if needed, we start the process by going back to the results and working with the manager to increase understanding, acceptance, and commitment to action. A key strategy here is to help the manager simplify the feedback and prioritize areas for change. Some managers we have worked with come to us with pages and pages of analysis and long lists of behaviors they think they need to change. They do not know where to begin. We help them review their results, look for consistencies across ratings and comments, and draw key conclusions about the major areas that need to change. We also help them interpret the results with respect to the situation (for example, we ask, "What was going on at the time you were evaluated?").

Most managers we work with are committed to changing and just need help with their action plan and learning new skills and behaviors. Some, however, cannot get beyond their resistance. In these cases, we discuss the feedback and new role requirements in relation to their career goals and help them make a determination whether they want to change. Sometimes they decide that the new role is not for them and leave the organization or move to another position in it.

Once the manager has a better understanding of the feedback and is committed to action, he or she revises the action plan and begins working on the plan activities. After a certain period of time we spend time with the manager in his or her work environment. With the manager's permission we gather feedback from employees on how the manager is doing and how the action plan is going. For example, with store managers, we spend about four hours in the store, do a store walk with the manager, and attend key meetings. We unobtrusively support the manager, observe his or her progress, and gather more feedback from employees. We then provide feedback based on our own observations and interviews with employees. We present the feedback in terms of themes and do not overload the manager with too much information. Our objective is to continue to increase insight, acceptance, and commitment and to help the manager adjust his or her action plan to include activities that will have the most impact. The coaching process continues until the manager changes in behavior, as measured by informal interviews with employees and upward evaluations.

Success Factors

Many managers can and have changed to the new role. We have noticed certain similarities among managers who have been successful. Almost all have focused on specific activities (such as having more personal conversations with employees)and also on how they have done the activity (for example, being genuine or taking appropriate time).

Implementation of a new role for managers is difficult to initiate and challenging to sustain. At a minimum, it needs to be linked clearly to organizational vision, mission, and strategy; managers need to see how it will help them achieve their goals; they need support to develop new role behaviors; they need ongoing feedback and accountability structures; and all organizational systems need to be aligned to reinforce that new role.

Conclusions

In this chapter we have shared some of what we have learned about assessing and changing managers for new organizational roles. We summarize our learnings by providing answers to three questions.

1. *How do you determine what to assess and develop in new role managers?* Job analysis traditionally has been the foundation for identifying the requirements for assessment and development. Because of rapid change, several authors (for example, Morgan & Smith, 1996) have questioned the concept of "job." In regard to managers, the more important question is not the job but what managers and leaders will be expected to do in the future. Organizations will always need leaders and managers. Future-oriented job analysis and competency modeling are requirements for identifying what to assess and develop in managers of the future. Our approach includes organizational analysis. Jobs change in a prescriptive manner as organizational strategies get implemented. Organizational strategies are ways to achieve organizational mission, vision, and values. We have learned to go beyond the job and the present. Job analysis for new role managers is an eclectic process. Our results in three service industries show convergence in the competencies that differentiate new role from old role managers.

2. *How do you design assessments for new role managers?* Many current techniques for assessment are appropriate for assessing new

role managers. In the past ten years meta-analytic studies have shown evidence of the validity generalization of techniques for predicting managerial job performance: performance simulations, cognitive ability testing, personality testing, biographical data, and structured interviews. Assessors do not need to reinvent the wheel in techniques; rather they must become more creative and flexible in implementation. Our individual assessments have included techniques that provide the participant with more self-awareness about interests, values, motivation, preferences, perception of others, and other areas. The design of assessment for new role managers must be creative and expansive in order to include simulations for future job requirements; personality indicators for interpersonal job and organizational requirements; and tests and interviews that assess for and integrate the candidate's motivation, interests, values, expectations, career orientation, and other needs critical for traveling the challenging path to success in managing today and the future. The psychologist and consultant must be capable of using a variety of existing techniques and be willing to do so, making necessary modifications as appropriate to measure new role managerial requirements and making sound judgments about people for managerial selection and developmental decisions.

Assessments must be comprehensive and inclusive of broad organizational requirements and not just job requirements. Psychologists or consultants who conduct these assessments require multidisciplinary skills and knowledge (for example, business and industry knowledge) if they are to have credibility with senior management. They need to understand organizational vision, mission, and strategies and be able to translate them to the managerial job and personal requirements.

3. *What are the challenges for organizations in selecting and developing new role managers?* Our parting comment relates to what we believe to be an irony in the requirements for the new role manager. The new managerial role is difficult and challenging from every perspective: time on the job; pressures to show results; the need to please boss, customers, and other employees; and the knowledge, skills, abilities, and personal requirements for success. Where do we find people with all these qualifications to do this job? There are a limited number of extraordinary individuals who can meet these demands. From our experience, the best approach

is to assess and develop current managers for the new role. Perhaps organizations need to become more realistic about what they can expect from managers to meet the increased demands of organizational changes and strategies. We cannot reengineer man and woman into Superman and Superwoman.

References

Barrick, M. R., & Mount, M. K. (1991). The big five personality dimensions and job performance: A meta-analysis. *Personnel Psychology, 44,* 1–27.

California Psychological Inventory. (1995). Palo Alto, CA: Consulting Psychologists Press.

Champy, J., & Hammer, M. (1994). *Reengineering the corporation.* New York: Harper Business.

CORE Corporation (1986). *Performance skills for effective store management.* Washington, DC: Food Marketing Institute.

CORE Corporation (1990). *ServiceFirst.* Pleasant Hill, CA: CORE Corporation.

Costa, P. T., & McCrae, R. R. (1995). Domains and facets: Hierarchical personality assessment using the revised NEO personality inventory. *Journal of Personality Assessment, 64,* 21–50.

Dunne, P. M., Lusch, R., & Gable, M. (1995). *Retailing* (2nd ed.). Cincinnati: South-Western.

Faultlines a manager must walk on the way to the 21st century. (1996). *Management Update, 1,* 1–3.

Firo-B. (1989). Palo Alto, CA: Consulting Psychologists Press.

Fogli, L. (1991). *Retail Management Situational Test.* Pleasant Hill, CA: CORE Corporation.

Gatewood, R. D., & Feild, H. S. (1994). *Human resource selection.* Orlando: Harcourt Brace.

Guidelines and ethical considerations for assessment center operations. (1989, Winter). *Public Personnel Management, 18(4),* 457–470.

Hough, L. M. (1984). Development and evaluation of the "accomplishment record" method of selecting and promoting professionals. *Journal of Applied Psychology, 69,* 135–146.

Hunter, J. E. (1986). Cognitive ability, cognitive aptitudes, job knowledge, and job performance. *Journal of Vocational Behavior, 29,* 340–362.

Janz, T., Hellervik, L., & Gilmore, D. C. (1986). *Behavior description interviewing.* Needham Heights, MA: Allyn & Bacon.

Latham, G. P., Saari, L. M., Pursell, E. D., & Campion, M. A. (1980). The situational interview. *Journal of Applied Psychology, 65,* 422–427.

Lawler, E. E., III. (1986). *High-involvement management: Participative strategies for improving organizational performance.* San Francisco: Jossey-Bass.

Levinson, H. (1996, July–August). When executives burn out. *Harvard Business Review,* pp. 153–163.

May, K. E. (1996). Work in the 21st century: Implications for job analysis. *Industrial-organizational psychologist, 33*(4), 98–100.

McDaniel, M. A., Schmidt, F. L., & Hunter, J. E. (1988). A meta-analysis of the validity of methods for rating training and experience in personnel selection. *Personnel Psychology, 41,* 283–314.

McFarland, L. J., Senn, L. E., & Childress, J. R. (1994). *21st century leadership: Dialogues with 100 top leaders.* New York: Leadership Press.

Mintzberg, H. (1996, July–August). Musings on management: Ten ideas designed to rile everyone who cares about management. *Harvard Business Review,* pp. 61–67.

Morgan, R. B., & Smith, J. E. (1996). *Staffing the new workplace: Selecting and promoting for quality improvement.* Milwaukee, WI: ASQC Quality Press.

Morris, J. (1996, August 31). Many would flee jobs if suddenly wealthy. *Contra Costa Times,* pp. 1C–4C.

Murphy, K. R. (1996). *Individual differences and behavior in organizations.* San Francisco: Jossey-Bass.

Peterson, D. B., & Hicks, M. (1996). *Development first: Strategies for self-development.* Minneapolis: Personnel Decisions International.

Pollok, J. (1995). Supermarkets: Caught in the crossfire. *Chain Store Age* (Section 2: State of the industry: Reengineering for revenue), pp. 17A–21A.

Psychological Corporation. (n.d.). *Tacit Knowledge Inventory.* Orlando: Harcourt Brace.

Psychological Corporation. (1980). *Watson-Glaser critical thinking appraisal.* Orlando: Harcourt Brace.

Saporito, B. (1995, May 15). What's for dinner? *Fortune,* pp. 50–64.

Saville & Holdsworth. (1996). *Occupational Personality Questionnaire.* Boston: Saville & Holdsworth.

Schellhardt, T. D. (1997, April 4). Want to be a manager? Many people say no, calling job miserable. *Wall Street Journal,* pp. A1, A4.

Sherman, S. (1995a, November 27). How tomorrow's leaders are learning their stuff. *Fortune,* pp. 90–102.

Sherman, S. (1995b, December 11). Wanted: Company change agents. *Fortune,* pp. 197–198.

Strong Interest Inventory. (1994). Palo Alto, CA: Consulting Psychologists Press.

Thomas, K. W., & Kilmann, R. H. (1974). *Thomas-Kilmann Conflict Mode Instrument.* Tuxedo, NY: XICOM.

Thomas, K. W., & Thomas, G. F. (1991). *Power Base Inventory.* Tuxedo, NY: XICOM.

Thomas, K. W., & Tymon, Jr., W. G. (1992). *Stress Resiliency Profile.* Tuxedo, NY: XICOM.

Thomas, K. W., & Tymon, Jr., W. G. (1993). *Empowerment Inventory.* Tuxedo, NY: XICOM.

Wagner, R. K., & Sternberg, R. J. (1985). Practical intelligence in real-world pursuits: The role of tacit knowledge. *Journal of Personality and Social Psychology, 49,* 436–458.

Waldroop, J., & Butler, T. (1996). The executive as coach. *Harvard Business Review, 74,* 111–117.

White, R. P., Hodgson, P., & Crainer, S. (1996). *The future of leadership: Riding the corporate rapids into the twenty-first century.* London: Pitman.

CHAPTER 10

Assessment Across Cultures

John R. Fulkerson

At its conceptual core, the assessment of the knowledge, abilities, traits, and competencies required to predict success in a given endeavor is relatively simple. Once an outcome or criterion has been identified, a potentially predictive variable is identified, measured, and then correlated with the criterion or outcome. The relationship found between predictor and criterion, if sufficiently robust, is then used to select, place, diagnose, or plan an intervention so that positive outcomes are maximized. This conceptual core remains relatively simple as long as the assessment process is carried out within the boundaries of understanding associated with a single national or ethnic culture. Assessment across multiple or different cultures, however, can be quite complicated due to the influence of cultural differences that contribute to potential variability in often unexpected ways.

For the sake of simplicity, this chapter will focus on some of the sources of cultural variability that have an impact on cross-cultural assessment, and will use the selection of managers and executives who lead and work in multinational organizations as the discussion platform. The discussion will also assume that the cross-cultural assessment is being done primarily from a U.S. reference point, even though the general principles discussed apply to any assessment where the cultures of the assessor and assessee differ. The latter half of the chapter will explain more about how to deal with the practical problems caused by cultural variability.

The majority of today's cross-cultural assessment work may be described as a focus on the validation of a particular test instrument or measurement in a specific culture where there is also a common language. While this single-validation, one-country approach may be scientifically appropriate, it is not broad enough to be practical when assessment is required simultaneously across many cultures. In today's economy it is not uncommon for a global company to have products or businesses in a hundred or more countries and to have executives or managers who are representative of all of these countries. The United Nations claims a membership of 185 countries, and depending on the geopolitical situation at the given moment in time, there may be as many as 200 or more countries recognized as sovereign nations. Each of these nations has a potentially unique and specific culture. The very practical problem that a multinational commercial organization faces is that it must assess and select individuals for leadership positions in all countries where it has a business interest.

Business Considerations and Cross-Cultural Assessment

A host of statistical tools and uniform guidelines are available to ensure that both scientific and legal protocols are observed during assessment in the United States. Indeed, assessment has developed into a refined art that is perhaps as much the purview of attorneys as it is of psychologists. U.S. assessment, for purposes of selection and subsequent employment, is steeped in questions of fairness to racial or gender groups. In today's global economy, where business is conducted in more than 200 sovereign nations and only a relative few of these nations have industrial and organizational (I/O) psychologists, uniform selection guidelines, or laws pertaining to assessment, the quest for the silver or ultimate selection bullet turns from simply complex to enormously complicated.

The search for generalizable, cross-cultural assessment tools and truths is difficult at best and constantly uncovers exceptions to interpretation that can be explained only by understanding some of the unique aspects of the cultures in which the assessment is done.

It is here, in the international arena, that psychological science and art are challenged to deliver some degree of practicality to an ongoing assessment process that is primarily managed and driven by global executives charged with producing business results. This global executive asks simple business questions: Can I turn over a multimillion dollar investment to an individual who is quite different from me in terms of language, culture, background, and nationality, and what assurances are there that I will get an appropriate return on my investment? And further, What assurances are there that the business results delivered will be in tune with the accepted business practices and the standards for conduct established by my company and my government?

Any discussion of cross-cultural assessment must start with an understanding of the assessment customer or the line manager who must select and develop executives to run a business in an emerging or exotic location like Russia, China, or India. In a very real sense, this last sentence speaks to the heart of the cross-cultural assessment challenge. This assessment challenge centers on the necessity of finding ways to predict outcomes in a context and in situations that are likely to be very different from that of a typical U.S. business. To refer to certain countries as *exotic*, for example, has meaning only to someone not familiar with those particular countries. It is unlikely that a Russian, a Chinese, or an Indian would characterize his or her home country as exotic. He or she would be far more likely to describe that country as familiar. Simply stated, the cross-cultural assessment challenge is the attempt to measure or understand behaviors and mind-sets that may be the product of fundamental and basic differences in human philosophy or values. In other words the challenge of cross-cultural assessment is to determine the most practical way to measure the unique aspects of a particular culture and translate that meaning into data that can be used to facilitate selection or assessment decision making. The business decision maker faces a formidable challenge and must select individuals whose standards of behavior may be unfamiliar and then entrust substantial amounts of capital to that individual. The primary objective of cross-cultural assessment is, then, to reduce the uncertainty of selection and improve the odds of business and personal success.

Examples of Cross-Cultural Misunderstanding

A few examples will help to make the cross-cultural assessment challenge clearer. Consider a Japanese executive who visits the United States and participates in a leadership training seminar. This executive is viewed as quiet but does engage in the free-flowing discussions that are a normal part of a U.S. learning experience. The executive explains that he is uncomfortable in the U.S. classroom environment because he feels compelled to participate actively in the discussions. When questioned about his "nonparticipation," he points out that in Japan, a senior executive would do more observing than participating and would be more likely to offer summaries only after his subordinates had recommended a course of action. He further notes that his English is not fluent and that he feels awkward speaking to the seminar group. The net result of observing the Japanese executive's behavior, however, is that his U.S. boss wonders about the Japanese executive's leadership skills because he sees very little evidence of leadership in an American sense.

Eventually the story has a positive outcome because the U.S. boss makes a point of observing the Japanese executive's leadership behavior as it plays out in Japan, in the Japanese language, and in a Japanese sales meeting. The behavior observed in this sales meeting is seen as highly energized, verbal, assertive, and powerful. Not only is the executive producing business results, but he has a highly motivated and effective organization. If he were assessed in a traditional U.S. manner with paper-and-pencil instruments and a traditional interview by a nonculturally sophisticated U.S. executive, he might be seen as lacking leadership in the Western sense. The point is that the behavior observed and measured in the U.S. classroom does not measure behavior that can be observed or measured in a sales meeting conducted in Japanese and in the Japanese culture. Without an understanding of cultural differences, our judgment of this executive's capability could be off the mark. Our descriptions of the observed classroom behaviors might be accurate, but our interpretations of those behaviors and how those behaviors play out in real situations are quite another matter.

Another example of the cross-cultural assessment challenge concerns a Russian who was learning about Western notions of leadership and struggling to find a conceptual framework within which to understand and apply the concepts of empowerment and pay for performance. For the Russian executive the notions of letting workers decide on the best course of action and of paying for individual gains in productivity were exotic and foreign. It was not until he made the connection between leadership as an *ideology* and communism as an ideology that he was able to begin to understand how to communicate and adopt management practices that are matter-of-factly accepted in the United States but still somewhat exotic and new in Russia. For example, describing leadership as an ideology might strike an assessor as unusual, but to the Russian, that description has significant meaning. In a Western sense, ideology may seem an almost negative term, but to this particular Russian, it connoted a whole system of meaning around how things get done in a large organization. The Russian executive could easily understand the notion of producing results but could not fully grasp the "how" of producing results in a Western sense. Conceptualizing leadership as an ideology allowed the Russian to find some personally familiar ground from which to develop a new mind-set and a potentially expanded set of leadership behaviors.

From an assessment perspective, if the Russian executive were interviewed and asked to explain how he leads and what empowerment is, the interviewer might hear words like ideology and communism and draw some rather erroneous conclusions. Only by understanding the Russian culture could the interviewer fully appreciate the conditions leading to and driving the mind-set and behaviors that the interviewer is seeking to assess.

To frame our cross-cultural assessment problem in terms that are literally grounded in semantics and meaning, consider an individual who is color-blind. About 5 percent of males are red-green color-blind and experience red and green colors in ways that cannot be fully communicated to a non-color-blind person. To a color-blind person, green on a traffic light is seen as the color on the bottom (at least in the United States) and perhaps as having more intensity or white to it than red. The usual question asked of a color-blind person is, "Well, what color do you see?" In one sense the question is meaningless. The color-blind person may verbally describe the color on the bottom of the traffic light as green but will not experience that color in the same way as the non-color-blind person and, further, will not be able to share that color experience. The color-blind person has simply learned to label as green what the non-color-blind person describes as green, but his actual experience of green is quite different. The behaviors of the color-blind and non-color-blind persons will be the same at a busy intersection (we hope), but their personal experience will be quite different.

Assessing across cultures is much like the color-blind, color-sighted example. I hear what you say, but I do not know what you mean or what the underlying assumptions are. So it is with cross-cultural assessment. Without understanding the impact of culture, I may not have a common ground for understanding and may make erroneous assumptions about assessment results.

Finding Meaning Across Cultures

The cross-cultural assessment problem may be approached in terms of attempting to predict a set of desired outcomes or behaviors from the perspective of a color-blind person attempting to share his experience of color with a color-sighted person. The assessment problem is made a little less complex if we assume that a shared, common, and positive business outcome is the sole selection criterion. That business criterion, at least from a global executive's perspective, can be communicated in terms of numbers. Numbers are a lot easier to communicate than behaviors. It is when we attempt to measure and frame a construct or set of behaviors around a Western concept, like the notion of optimism, that the assessment problem becomes much more difficult.

Optimism, at a basic personal or value level, suggests that a locus of control exists within an individual. Behaviorally, optimism might mean an executive would take the actions needed to improve or make a bad business situation better without waiting for instruction from a superior. However, taking positive action without approval could lead to big problems for an executive living and working in a totalitarian state. In such a situation, optimism could mean simply having the guile to survive and maintain employment—read that as, "Don't get fired or into trouble." Further read that as, "Wait for instructions." The point is that the behaviors attached to the word optimism can be culturally quite different. Optimism may also take on very different meanings philosophically. If I am a Hindu and believe in the circle of life and reincarnation, then optimism may be focused on achieving nirvana rather than fixing today's business problem. I may fix the problem in question, but as a Hindu, I do not relate or characterize my behavior as optimistic.

The cross-cultural assessment problem demands that we be clear about what the desired behaviors are and then that we discover the conditions under which those behaviors manifest themselves. We must also understand what the behaviors are called locally and the appropriate measures for those specific behaviors in that specific culture. Before we go further, we should consider a model that will help us understand the range of complexities that exist when assessing across cultures.

Limits of U.S. Assessment Technology

As sophisticated as U.S. assessment technology is, that technology may have a built-in blind spot when applied to non-U.S. cultures. One source of potential bias is the possibility that different interpretations may be applied to management language (for example, words like *empowerment*). It is also relatively easy to offend someone who is unfamiliar with U.S. assessment processes. A non-U.S. assessee may not understand why any assessment beyond an employment interview or check on previous work history is needed. Assessment questions phrased in U.S. terms may also seem to some nationalities as too personal or prying. In Europe, for example, an essay is often the preferred university exam method and allows students to justify and fully explain their answers. When we contrast this free-flowing European response mode with the U.S. preferences for multiple-choice questions, it becomes clear that another opportunity for misunderstanding and misinterpretation is possible. A non-U.S. student may do well on essay exams but poorly on multiple-choice exams. And finally, consider a U.S. assessee being evaluated with U.S. assessment technology for characteristics needed for successful work in a non-U.S. culture. If *flexibility*, for example, is seen as important for working in a non-U.S. culture, but flexibility has a different meaning or ideology associated with it in that culture, then there is another opportunity for misinterpretation. Semantically, flexibility can mean "getting along," or it can mean "changing when confronted with obstacles."

Any assessment technology applied across cultures must be based on an understanding and translation of the key differentiating characteristics between the two cultures in question. The U.S. assessment practitioner must recognize what he or she does not know and assume from the start that some bias is highly probable.

A Model for Understanding Assessment Across Cultures

The number of potential variables that must be considered when assessing across cultures far exceeds those found in a one-country assessment, dealing with one language, one set of cultural norms, and fundamentally a background of shared experiences that can be readily understood by an assessor. The model for describing assessment across cultures is complex because culture acts as a geometric multiplier of the potential combinations of behaviors and their antecedents. Simply stated, culture creates complexity.

The conceptual model for assessing across cultures that I developed has six key components (see Figure 10.1) that must be taken into account if an accurate and valid prediction of an assessment outcome is expected:

1. The specific dimensions of an individual's culture
2. The individual characteristics of the person being assessed as they are influenced by culture
3. The specific behaviors being assessed
4. The measures employed to assess the individual
5. The way a particular culture bends or distorts our ability to understand a culture that is different from our own (the cultural lens or filter)
6. The outcome or criterion

Each of these components needs to be explored to understand cross-cultural assessment complexities. At the close of this chapter, we will explore some of the ways assessment across cultures can be

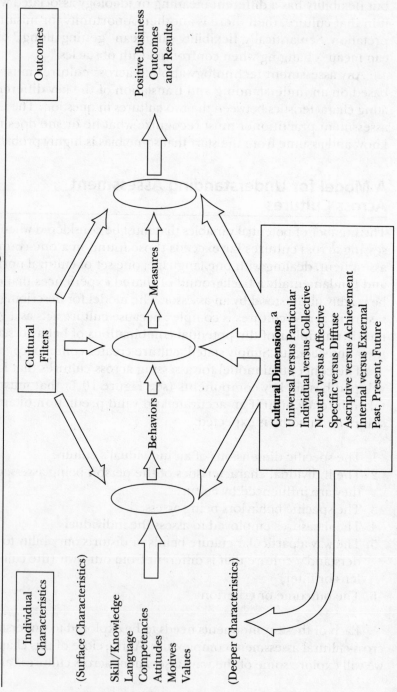

Figure 10.1. Conceptual Model for Assessing Across Cultures.

Individual Characteristics

(Surface Characteristics)

Skill/Knowledge
Language
Competencies
Attitudes
Motives
Values

(Deeper Characteristics)

Behaviors

Cultural Filters

Measures

Outcomes

Positive Business Outcomes and Results

Cultural Dimensions [a]
Universal versus Particular
Individual versus Collective
Neutral versus Affective
Specific versus Diffuse
Ascriptive versus Achievement
Internal versus External
Past, Present, Future

[a]The cultural dimensions are from Trompenaars (1994).

improved and made more practical, and I will present a picture of the future of assessing across cultures. For now, we will focus on some of the problems and complexities.

Descriptive Dimensions of Culture

Fons Trompenaars (1994) and Geert Hofstede (1991) have done a great deal of research to frame some of the critical dimensions that help describe how cultures differ. Although this work is not directly related to assessment methodology, it does provide an important starting point for looking for differences in meaning that can affect the outcome of an assessment. The specific dimensions specified in the cross-cultural assessment model described here are the result of Trompenaars's work. Understanding these dimensions helps explain how cultures may differ and how cultural differences may affect assessment outcomes. This chapter will not attempt to offer a treatise on cultural differences, but without a rudimentary grounding in the key differences between cultures, we cannot fully appreciate the cross-cultural assessment problem.

Trompenaars (1994) and Hofstede (1991) have sorted out major dimensions along which different cultures may be described, measured, and compared. We will assume the dimensions are sufficiently accurate and descriptive for our purposes. The examples provided here are somewhat general; moreover, even within a specific culture, there is a normal distribution of behavior around a given cultural dimension. As each of Trompenaars's dimensions is described, consider the implications for assessment and how assessment accuracy can be improved or confounded depending on the level of understanding or misunderstanding attached to each of his dimensions.

Universal Versus Particularist Cultures

In a universalist culture, rules are seen as applying to everyone. A red light always means stop. Everyone pays taxes. The law is the law. Even if there are exceptions to the rules, there may be rules that explain the exceptions. In a particularist culture, there may be rules, but the rights of an individual friend are more important than the rights of the larger community.

If individuals from a universalist and a particularist culture are asked if they would help a friend avoid responsibility for causing a traffic accident, the responses are likely to be quite different. The universalist would be more likely to say the friend is responsible and must accept the consequences of his actions. The particularist would be more likely to say she would do almost anything to help her friend avoid getting into trouble. In an assessment context, and when asked if performance is more important than friends or family ties, the universalist would be more likely to say yes, whereas the particularist would be more likely to say, "It depends on the circumstances." Regardless of the assessment instrument, responses around how things get done in a group setting may be quite different given a particular cultural background. Not understanding where the assessee is coming from can lead to erroneous assessment conclusions.

Universalists tend to reside more in Western countries, whereas particularists reside more in Asian countries. Trompenaars identifies South Koreans and Russians as more particularist and Canadians and Americans as more universalist. The implications for assessment are immediate and obvious. If I am attempting to assess a Russian's ability to lead an organization, I may see behaviors that are focused on building informal, personal relationships, whereas an American might be more concerned with establishing a business vision that will be communicated more uniformly to everyone in the organization. In order to assess the Russian properly, I, as an American, must understand the context under which the Russian establishes mental rules and process, and I am likely to get rules and process that are quite different from the American context.

Individualist Versus Collectivist Cultures

In an individualist culture the individual is assumed to be the repository of responsibility and action. In a collectivist culture the group or team collectiveness is more important than individual action. If I am assessing an individualist, the person may tell me what he or she has done at an individual level with a lot of emphasis on "I." If I am assessing a collectivist, I may soon wonder if the person has ever done anything as an individual. The collectivist, the ultimate team player, is much more likely to use "we." It is possible for a collectivist almost never to speak in "I" terms and yet be enormously effective in getting a group to act in a prescribed manner in a collectivist culture. By the same token, if I assign a collectivist to lead a team in an individualist country, I should not be surprised if problems occur.

Trompenaars describes Canada and the United States as individualist cultures, whereas Nepal, Japan, Greece, and Egypt are less so.

Neutral Versus Affective Cultures

In a neutral culture, self-control is prized, and individuals are reluctant to show emotion. In an affective culture, spontaneous actions and feelings are more highly valued. In the United Kingdom and Japan, there is likely to be very little emotion shown in the workplace, whereas in Italy or France, there is likely to be a great deal of spirited interaction. If I, as an American, am assessing someone from the United Kingdom, I may see the person as aloof and cool. If I, as an American, am assessing someone from Argentina, I may see the person as passionate and spirited. I could be wrong on both counts. Because so much of interview assessment depends on the "feel" of the interview and particularly the first few minutes, I must guard against rushing to judgment.

Assessors must be careful to dig deeply into not just the specific behaviors being observed but also the context and background that give rise to those behaviors. The same is true in an assessment center where visible behavior is so important. When assessing across cultures, starting off with the wrong, or perhaps any, assumption can lead to an inappropriate conclusion. Face validity can be very misleading in this situation. The principle holds true for a paper-and-pencil assessment as well. If asked if I agree with the statement, "Do you believe it is important for a leader to have personal charisma?" my answer is potentially fully confounded by cultural differences.

Specific Versus Diffuse Cultures

In a specific culture, relationships are usually based on a specific need or action attached to that particular purpose only. In other words, an individual may be viewed as more like a functionary than a person. A manager, for example, is dealt with as a manager, and very little of that person's interaction with others will be on personal level. In a diffuse culture, relationships deal more with the entire person and almost all aspects of his or her life. The boundaries between personal and private are very soft, if they exist at all.

Trompenaars lists Sweden and Switzerland as examples of specific cultures and China, Indonesia, and Thailand as examples of more diffuse cultures. In cross-cultural assessment terms, specifics will get to the point very quickly and stick to the agenda. Diffuses may wander around from topic to topic and appear very much off agenda to an American or a specific. This wandering is very exasperating to specifics. Specifics, in contrast, are likely to be seen as cold and unfeeling by the diffuse community.

Ascriptive Versus Achievement Cultures

In an ascriptive culture, social status depends on family, wealth, or background. In an achievement culture, status is earned more through hard work and personal achievement. Austria and Nigeria are seen as more ascriptive than Denmark and Iceland by Trompenaars. An ascriptive, for example, might be offended by even being asked to submit to an assessment. Questions regarding personal achievement asked of an ascriptive might be seen as offensive or prying. Achievements, on the other hand, are more likely to welcome an opportunity to demonstrate and prove their abilities.

Internal Control Versus External Control Cultures

In an internal control culture, power comes from within the individual, and conflict is natural, aggression is accepted, and humans control the environment, not vice versa. In an external control culture, there is a view that nature is a mighty force, and harmony with that force is more important than attempting to change or control it. Externals may be seen by internals as too willing to compromise and too flexible. Internals believe they are responsible for their fate, whereas externals may be more willing to accept what has happened as inevitable. In a divided Germany, East Germans would be classified as more external and West Germans as more internal.

Past, Present, and Future Cultures

This dimension deals with the use and perception of time. Past-focused cultures (such as Russia and Belgium) may be more concerned with tradition and protocol. Present-focused cultures (such as Venezuela and Spain) are more worried about the here and now. Future cultures (such as the United States and Italy) talk a great deal about the prospects for the future and future aspirations. Although these temporal views are generalities and always in flux, the point is that certain assessment measures or observations can be influenced by an individual's perceptions about whether things should be traditionally managed or constantly changed to meet new circumstances and conditions.

The point of this cross-cultural excursion is that an understanding of context is essential if cross-cultural assessment is to be both accurate and useful. How we view the world is shaped by our experience of our own unique cultures that have embedded in them a rich and often specific context of meaning. To assess that meaning and the resultant behaviors requires a broad understanding of potential sources of behaviors and values.

Individual Characteristics and Competencies

The second major source of complexity in the conceptual model for cross-cultural assessment deals with individual characteristics as they are manifested in a particular culture. If we assume there is a cross-cultural impact on individual characteristics and behaviors, then the number of possible combinations or permutations that may have an effect on assessment outcomes becomes staggering. If every one of the two hundred or more countries in the world has some unique characteristics of culture that may affect behavior, it would be easy to assume that cross-cultural assessment is impossible due to the potential variability.

The key point is that all behavior is influenced by the cultural dimensions I have described. Behavior is also influenced by inner states or experiences that are the result of those same culturally determined values. It must be recognized that these values are often so integrated into an individual's makeup that the individual may not be able to explain how these personal values affect behavior. If I value hard work and effort, I will work hard and put forth effort, but I may not be able to explain how I came to hold this value. As another example, a sense of urgency may be an integral part of a future-oriented, individualist culture but much less important in a past-oriented, collective culture. My understanding of those behaviors will certainly differ depending on my cultural background. Further, an assessor's ability to assess those behaviors accurately and predict outcomes will also depend on an ability to understand something about those cultural differences. It will be much more difficult to assess a value (such as hard work) than it will be to assess ability to perform mathematical calculations. In other words, surface characteristics and behaviors are easier to assess than deeper characteristics or behaviors, and yet it is those deeper behaviors that the assessor must understand in order to predict the broad range of outcomes typical of executive assessment. In cross-cultural assessment, deeper characteristics will have more generalizability and perhaps predictability, but they are inherently difficult to assess accurately.

Each of the individual characteristics mentioned in the cross-cultural assessment model—skill/knowledge, language, competencies, attitudes, motives, and values—presents some unique problems for the assessor, and each ultimately may require a specific assessment methodology. Culture differences add complexity and may be a source of frustration for the assessor who demands a great deal of scientific accuracy.

The cross-cultural assessor must first determine whether a construct can be understood broadly, if not universally, and then if that construct can be measured parsimoniously. If these first two conditions are met, it must next be determined whether the construct is practical (that is, predictive of behaviors and actions that make a business successful). The achievement motive, as defined by McClelland (1989), for example, may be broadly understood, but may be difficult to measure and translate into useful, predictive terms outside the U.S. culture. Most successful cross-cultural assessments focus on more objective, quantifiable behaviors. Again, accuracy in performing mathematical calculations will be more easily assessed than achievement motivation. Although limited in its generalizability, accuracy of performing mathematical calculations could be very practical and predictive. Achievement motivation, a highly generalizable concept, may be much more difficult to measure and make practical for predictive purposes.

The assessment of general intelligence as an individual characteristic and as defined by paper-and-pencil tests is seen as predictive of general success. However, all of the biases of test methodology and cultural differences make even general intelligence suspect as a universal cross-cultural predictor. There are very few tools available that do not have some racial or cultural bias associated with them. Even so-called culture-free instruments like the Raven Progressive Matrices are not totally culturally free. It could also be argued that in a collective culture, individual problem solving is not as highly valued as group problem solving. This could mean that a collectivist might not be as motivated as an individualist when confronted with a Raven matrix test and consequently might not score as well as an individualist.

It is likely that competencies may turn out to be the most useful descriptors of individual behavior for cross-cultural assessment purposes. This is true particularly when the competencies are defined in terms readily understood within the framework of a global business organization. Competencies that are empirically developed actually become part of an organization's fabric. Once defined and behaviorally described and shared, a given competency takes on a meaning that is understood and internalized by an entire organization.

PepsiCo, as an example, uses a number of competencies that seem to hold up as both descriptive of desirable executive behaviors and also predictive of success in the PepsiCo culture. More important, the competencies are being applied across many different cultures. This effort has produced competencies that are useful in describing and communicating corporate values as well as being an aid to assessment and selection. Over time the competencies may come to be well understood, almost paradoxically, in multicultural terms but also similarly understood across the organization. These competencies were developed by looking at the behaviors most often associated with outstanding versus not-so-outstanding executives. These competencies and their abbreviated definitions may be grouped into the following buckets:

Business Leadership: "Setting the Business Agenda"

- Customer driven: discovers and meets the needs of customers
- Drive for results: stays focused on outcomes and works efficiently and effectively to produce results; willing to work hard to get things done

- Initiative: takes sustained action when confronted with new situations or circumstances without waiting to be told what to do; anticipates and acts on future possibilities
- Thinking out of the box: creates new and unique solutions to overcome problems and reconceptualizes process or actions
- Analytical thinking: able to see the relationships between complex sets of data and lay out appropriate courses of action
- Intellectual curiosity: always looking for new ideas and insights into how things work

Organizational Leadership: "Taking Others with You"

- People and organizational savvy: understands and diagnoses reasons for individual or organizational behavior and establishes an agenda to address issues.
- Organizational impact: able to influence an organization to move toward a desired goal
- Alignment and team leadership: views self as a leader and is able to motivate others to get behind and support initiatives by clearly communicating a compelling vision
- Empowerment: comfortable with making others powerful and capable; allows others to take the actions required to achieve objectives
- Developing others: enjoys fostering the development of others and helps them build their skills

Personal Leadership: "Doing It the Right Way"

- Self-confidence: having the confidence to attack difficult issues and confront tough situations
- Objectivity (sometimes labeled executive maturity): knows and understands personal abilities and limitations; makes decisions and takes actions based on objective data
- Respect for others: believes people are fundamentally good and strives to treat people fairly and support their actions
- Openness (sometimes labeled integrity): deals with issues and individuals in a candid manner; welcomes directness, openness, and honesty
- Leverages diversity: understands and respects the customs and norms of other countries and cultures

- Relationship building: builds strong and effective relationships between groups and individuals
- Flexibility: works to find ways to cope with unexpected situations and issues

A great deal has been written elsewhere about the usefulness of competencies for assessment, but the point is that competencies are rooted primarily in behavior and thus may be very useful for cross-cultural assessment. The list of competencies is provided as an example of how behavioral descriptors may be used across cultures to begin the development or codification of behaviors that may be predictive of executive success. Competencies, at least in the cross-cultural sense, transcend nationality more readily than traits. Certainly, there will always be some cross-cultural influence on any behavioral descriptor, but the bias represented here is that a competency can be framed and translated into understandable terms more easily than constructs like emotional stability or assertiveness. Competencies may also be framed in business outcome terms and thus are more easily understood by the assessment end user. Producing a positive business outcome is easier to define in behavioral terms than a wide range of mental states.

Competencies may become self-fulfilling prophesies as they are integrated into and become part of the culture of an organization. Drive for results means, for example, a willingness to work hard and stay focused on a positive outcome. These drive for results behaviors in a sense become codified as well as descriptive of an organization's culture. The implication is that a consistent use of competencies may ultimately help to decomplexify cross-cultural assessment. In a multinational, global context, an organization's culture transcends many boundaries and binds individual members of the culture together for a common outcome: the success of the enterprise. If such a global culture is relatively strong, the rules for behavior can become sufficiently generalizable to be translated into and out of different cultural contexts. For example, an Indian can demonstrate drive for results just as easily as an American or a Mexican. How each of these nationalities specifically demonstrates drive for results may differ slightly, but the respective behaviors can all be labeled as drive for results. Over time, drive for results begins to assume a common behavioral meaning and becomes much more useful for assessment purposes.

By achieving greater clarity around the competencies that make an enterprise successful, assessment can at least focus on named, defined, and observable behaviors that have a potential common meaning outside one particular culture. This is not to suggest that competencies are the only way to approach cross-cultural assessment, but they seem to offer significant potential for being both understood and measurable.

Behavioral Differences

The example of the Japanese executive helps to illustrate the interaction of dimensions of culture, individual characteristics, cultural filters, measures, and behavior. All of these elements can serve to confuse the assessor about what is actually being observed or inferred. Simply stated, change the setting (cultural filter), and the understanding attached to a given behavior may change. Behavior is also potentially changed by our measurement technique. In physics, this is known as Heisenberg's uncertainty principle. In a behavioral sense, this principle posits that the actual or true behavior can only be inferred, never truly known. Our very act of measuring may change the observed behavior. Measuring the Japanese executive in a U.S. classroom made him quieter and more reserved than he might be in his native culture. If behavior has potentially different meanings, the assessment judgment or outcome prediction can be off target unless we measure it reliably and under the same relative conditions. The point is that behaviors may have different meanings depending on the context, and the cross-cultural assessor must at least be grounded in the particular culture or context in question.

Potential Predictors and Measures

Although many assessment psychologists would likely disagree vigorously, the number of measurement opportunities or techniques for assessing executive behavior is somewhat finite. For our purposes, there are three main categories: background or historical data, behavioral observations, and self-report data. (Examples of these categories and examples of measures for each may be seen in Figure 10.2.) Background data are often easier to verify and potentially quantifiable. Behavioral observations, as they apply to

Figure 10.2. Potential Predictors and Measures.

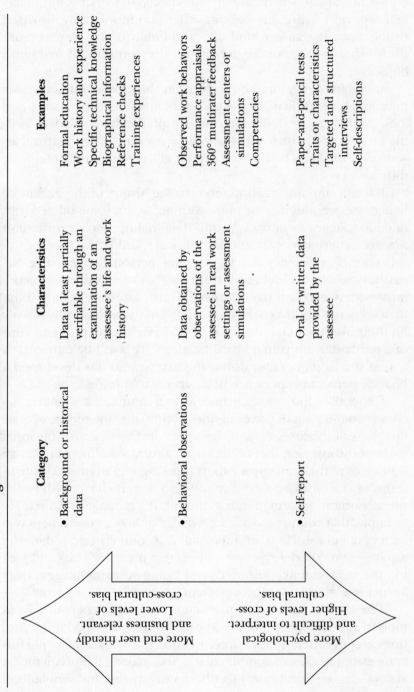

Category	Characteristics	Examples
• Background or historical data	Data at least partially verifiable through an examination of an assessee's life and work history	Formal education Work history and experience Specific technical knowledge Biographical information Reference checks Training experiences
• Behavioral observations	Data obtained by observations of the assessee in real work settings or assessment simulations	Observed work behaviors Performance appraisals 360° multirater feedback Assessment centers or simulations Competencies
• Self-report	Oral or written data provided by the assessee	Paper-and-pencil tests Traits or characteristics Targeted and structured interviews Self-descriptions

More end user friendly and business relevant. Lower levels of cross-cultural bias.

More psychological and difficult to interpret. Higher levels of cross-cultural bias.

cross-cultural assessment, are directly related to work performance. Self-report measures are seen as softer and more easily distorted by the assessee. Background data and behavior are seen as more useful than self-report data because they potentially are more objective.

In all three measurement categories the cross-cultural assessor must weigh the difficulty and expense of attaining the measure and look carefully at the desired outcome or prediction needed. In looking at a list of measures that would be useful in cross-cultural assessment, the list is relatively short but at the same time potentially difficult to use.

Background information refers to the history of the individual being assessed and may be more verifiable than some other forms of data. Categories of background data include such information as work experience, education, technical training, specific technical expertise, reference checks, and even personal appearance. Regardless of what is included, this category of information is the most widely used source of cross-cultural assessment data. Line managers rely almost exclusively on it. They invariably rely heavily on their own personal "expert system" to weigh the pros and cons of a particular individual's qualifications. This will be particularly true if the line manager doing the assessment has developed a body of personal experience in a particular culture.

Generally a line manager interviews a candidate and makes decisions on the basis of two categories of thinking: the technical qualifications of the assessee and then the competencies (or personal style) of the assessee. Part of the cross-cultural assessment challenge is to capture the manager's expert thinking and then add value in terms of reliability and validity and also the efficiency with which the assessment information is gathered. If a manager believes, for example, that country-specific knowledge of how a government regulatory agency works is an important selection criterion, then the assessment methodology must address that manager's bias and seek to validate and make knowledge of how government regulatory agencies work part of the assessment process.

The second category of predictors and measures comes from more direct behavioral observations. Sources of data falling into this category include assessment centers, work samples, performance appraisals, and competencies. Also making the predictor list are 360-degree (multirater) feedback instruments and simulations.

Managers have a positive bias for this category of information and will refer to its utilization as looking for "evidence" to validate a hypothesis about behavior.

The third type of measure includes self-reports and paper-and-pencil instruments. Without country-specific validations, these measures are likely to be a major source of error in cross-cultural assessment. A bias in cross-cultural assessment is that "behavior is better" as a predictor. This, in turn, suggests that detailed, in-depth behavioral or targeted interviews are seen as more appropriate than paper-and-pencil assessment. In general terms, and without country-specific validation, cross-cultural assessment may best be done with behaviors at this stage of methodology and process development.

Geisinger (1994) and Riordan and Vandenberg (1994) have provided a thorough analysis and description of some of the critical issues related to potential cross-cultural predictors and measures. Geisinger lays out an approach for adapting a test measure to a new target population. It is important to understand whether test scores, for example, have the same meaning across cultures or whether there is total score or item bias occurring as a result of translation. Riordan and Vandenberg have studied the issue of whether a translated questionnaire measures the same construct intended in the original version.

Trompenaars (1994) and Hofstede (1991) raise the same issue but are more focused on differences in conceptual meaning than on test scores. The cross-cultural assessor must use caution when dealing with conceptual generalities. The notion of meaning for any concept (such as leadership or empowerment) may play out quite differently across cultures. This is just as true in test or assessment construction as it is in organizational development. I have had numerous experiences with attempting to install U.S. leadership concepts into non-U.S. environments. The key learning is that the behavior may travel well, but the language may not. An assessor must be certain that constructs, meaning, and behavior are interpretable across cultural borders.

Cultural Filters

Although I have described the cultural dimensions that help differentiate between cultures, I have not explored how these dimensions add to the complexity of assessment. Each time a behavior is observed or manifested, it does so only in the context and within the background of cultural difference. This means that there is always a chance of misunderstanding or misinterpretation if there is less than a full understanding of that particular cultural influence. In that sense, culture acts like a color filter; if we do not know the color of the filter, we are likely to make an error in judgment about the type of behavior coming through. Stated another way, culture can act as a lens that bends the behavior coming through.

Cultural filters work at every intersection of the cross-cultural assessment model and demand that we keep open at least the possibility of cultural distortion if we are to avoid surprises. If an individual is believed to have a competency, like drive for results, the cultural filter can change the behavior in a way that makes it difficult to observe or interpret. The example of the reserved Japanese executive in the U.S. classroom who becomes much more active and animated in the Japanese business meeting is an excellent illustration of the point. This executive was assertive, but our U.S. cultural lens and assessment circumstance distorted and mislabeled what was meant by assertiveness and where assertiveness could be seen.

It should also be noted that assessor bias can have an impact on the cultural filters. If an assessor does not have a thorough understanding of a particular culture, then the assessor literally does not know what he or she does not know. The potential for assessor bias based on almost subconscious beliefs about a particular culture is also a potential source of error in interpretation. In all cases of cross-cultural assessment the assessor must, at a minimum, ask if there is a possibility of misinterpretation due to not fully understanding cultural differences. Knowing and exploring how cultural filters affect behavior is essential to successful cross-cultural assessment.

The Outcome

The final and perhaps most important component of the cross-cultural assessment model deals with outcomes or, in psychometric terms, criteria. Outcomes, if properly defined, offer at least the beginning of a solution or way out of the complexity of assessment across cultures. In business assessment the most important outcome is related to helping predict the growth and health of a business. A business must be profitable to succeed.

It has been long suspected that the refinement of criteria has not received the same attention as the development of predictors and psychometric instruments. In a cross-cultural setting, it is imperative that criteria be rigorously defined. Even if we are not certain whether a particular outcome is exactly the correct one, we must have a point of view regarding the most appropriate criteria as a starting point. Defining criteria requires an expert system that is understood by the individual business decision maker and the assessment expert. For example, to assess the potential success of an individual tapped to open a new business venture in the Czech Republic, there must be great clarity of judgment around what is required to get the business running. Business decision makers also must think in future terms—in this case, what will be demanded of an assessee beyond the start-up.

Business decision makers often employ a hierarchy of selection criteria (see Table 10.1). This hierarchy is somewhat different from one that might be posited by a psychometrically oriented practitioner. At one end of the hierarchy are the criteria related to language, country experience, industry experience, and the ability of the executive and family to live "in country." In the middle of the hierarchy are observations around competencies and leadership characteristics. At the other end of the hierarchy are the judgments about whether the assessee can produce the desired business results. A business decision maker will weigh all of these criteria before reaching a conclusion.

That ultimate assessment decision will certainly use assessment data, but the majority of the data used will be based on the internal, expert system of knowledge and experience residing in the decision maker. Assessment data, from the psychological community, must focus on providing as clear a picture of the assessee's behavioral tendencies as possible. The cross-cultural assessment must add value by also assessing relationships between the personal data and the desired business outcomes. This means that a good cross-cultural assessor must have some grounding in and understanding of business outcomes. The decision maker's thought process is not grounded in psychometric science. It is grounded in a practical

**Table 10.1. Decision Maker Thought
Processes: A Hierarchy.**

	Comments
Easier or more obvious Language expertise Country experience Family adaptability to living "in country" Industry and functional experience Critical skills	Decision maker and assessor share expertise and selection decision making.
Competence Leadership skills Motives Drive Analytical skills Intellectual flexibility	Assessor can add value by explaining how competencies affect assignment success. Business decision makers may have strong biases.
Business outcomes: more difficult Strategic skills Understanding/knowledge of the business Business savvy Market or country knowledge Technical knowledge, skills	Assessor generally has a lower level of business knowledge. The business decision maker's expertise must be captured and understood.

weighing of all of the potential variables that can lead to an overall successful outcome. Table 10.1 emphasizes the point that as a decision maker reaches a conclusion, many factors must be considered. The cross-cultural assessor must at least be aware of and reflect an awareness of the subcriteria employed by the business decision maker.

A Decision-Making Model for Cross-Cultural Assessment

It may seem illogical to suggest that a simplified model for cross-cultural assessment is a starting point for dealing with the complexity outlined in this chapter. If it is not yet practical to validate tools and instruments from across the globe for every single nationality, then a simple starting point is required. A decision-making model is shown in Figure 10.3. The model starts with a decision maker's mind-set and typical questions that may be raised during an assessment and requires that the assessor have a clear sense of the desired or satisfactory business outcome in order to reach an appropriate conclusion.

Keeping the business end point firmly in mind allows the assessor to stay anchored to the consumer of the assessment service. Without meeting those decision maker needs, cross-cultural assessment will not have initial credibility. If we are looking for ways to make this assessment work, we need a thinking or expert system sequence to help us. The decision-making model, in contrast to the conceptual model, says, "Let's step back from the complexity and make some judgments about what we really need to know to make the best assessment decision that is also in the best interests of our business."

Most leadership research shows similar, if not totally consistent, themes or behaviors associated with leaders. Competencies (read that as "behaviors") have been found to have some consistency of understanding across a number of cultures. Drive for results is understood cross-culturally to mean behavior that is proactive and pushing for results and change. Although that behavior may look different in Japan and Kenya than in the Untied States, the observers of that behavior, even if culturally color-blind, may use the same phrase: drive for results. They will then be able to understand that behavior in both local and global terms and describe what the Japanese or Kenyan manager will do to produce a positive outcome. Behaviors, because they can be described and seen, offer the beginnings of a descriptive system that will allow the assessor and manager to discuss in intelligent terms what is important to a particular satisfactory outcome. The thought process leading to an assessment decision starts with a mental factor analysis of the satisfactory outcomes required and then the behaviors believed to predict most effectively.

The third component of the model for decision making is to look for the most practical tools and measures available at the moment. If the most practical tool is an interview, then how does the assessor make certain it is appropriately robust to get at the key

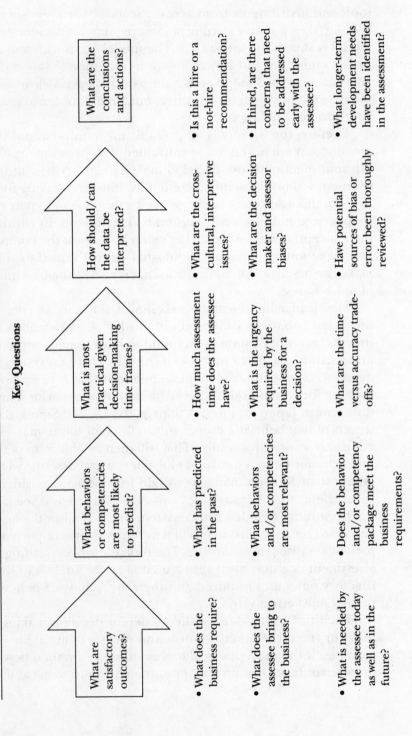

Figure 10.3. A Decision-Making Model for Cross-Cultural Assessment.

Key Questions

What are satisfactory outcomes?

- What does the business require?
- What does the assessee bring to the business?
- What is needed by the assessee today as well as in the future?

What behaviors or competencies are most likely to predict?

- What has predicted in the past?
- What behaviors and/or competencies are most relevant?
- Does the behavior and/or competency package meet the business requirements?

What is most practical given decision-making time frames?

- How much assessment time does the assessee have?
- What is the urgency required by the business for a decision?
- What are the time versus accuracy trade-offs?

How should/can the data be interpreted?

- What are the cross-cultural, interpretive issues?
- What are the decision maker and assessor biases?
- Have potential sources of bias or error been thoroughly reviewed?

What are the conclusions and actions?

- Is this a hire or a not-hire recommendation?
- If hired, are there concerns that need to be addressed early with the assessee?
- What longer-term development needs have been identified in the assessment?

assessment questions? Practical considerations related to the time available for the assessment (such as telephone interview versus assessment center) will dictate the methodology of the moment. In the real world of global business, speed of assessment and decision making is critical. This may be why the standard interview (usually not more than an hour), combined with reference and experience checks, remains the decision maker's most popular assessment method.

The fourth step in decision making is to look at all of the possible sources of confounding suggested by the cross-cultural model and take those points into consideration. This chapter has reviewed some of the points that must be considered as sources of confounding. Suffice it to say here that this process step is often clinical and requires a thorough grounding and understanding of the particular culture being assessed.

The final component of the simplified decision-making model is the application of judgment based on an expert system of business and cultural understanding. In the absence of large statistical samples, there is no substitute for judgment grounded in an understanding of culture and business context. This is another way of saying that a statistical model for cross-cultural assessment is ideal but not yet practical for broad-gauge, multinational assessment.

Eventually our statistical models will become sufficiently grounded to permit more scientific rigor. For now, clinical judgment and an almost anthropological understanding of decision makers and their expert decision-making systems are required. Currently the best expert systems for cross-cultural assessment reside with the decision makers who are making assessment judgments on a daily basis. If we lived in an ideal world, we would interview every decision maker regarding his or her specific business and country knowledge and collect a body of facts, hunches, and insights. That collection of information would provide a solid foundation for further refining our cross-cultural assessment "tricks" and insights. To be good psychologists, we may also need to be good cultural anthropologists.

In summary, our thinking model for cross-cultural assessment starts with positive business outcomes as criteria and a belief that there are some competencies or behaviors that may help predict that outcome. We then seek to determine if those competencies somehow differentiate between groups of successful versus less successful leaders. This type of research was the source of the PepsiCo competencies. Once that competency foundation is complete, with all of its inherent flaws, we have a starting point to guide our assessment and judgments. The PepsiCo competencies were developed and refined with a broad cross-cultural sample but are also specific to PepsiCo. Behavioral evaluation and the correlation of that behavior with business outcomes are at the heart of cross-cultural assessment. A key partner in the cross-cultural assessment endeavor must be the line manager who also makes the final decision about whether an individual will be placed in a particular job.

Lessons and Learnings

Cross-cultural assessment is very much in an evolutionary state. Much has been learned, but much remains to be understood. Nevertheless there are a number of general conclusions from the practitioner's point of view that can serve as a guide to our future efforts.

Cross-Cultural Assessment Is Complex

The model outlined in this chapter seeks to make the practitioner at least humble about the scientific accuracy of cross-cultural assessment. The potential sources of variance are considerable, and unless practitioners have at least some knowledge of those sources of variance, many errors are likely to creep into practical assessment conclusions. A simple, uniform, statistical guidelines approach, although satisfying scientifically, may not be appropriate at this stage of cross-cultural assessment process development.

Cross-Cultural Assessment Is Not Impossible

The assessment of executives for global assignments is occurring constantly. However, it is being done by business experts, not assessment experts. These assessors are using criteria gained from business experience and knowledge. Part of the psychological challenge is to understand better the cues and behaviors the expert decision makers see as most predictive. The behavioral/competency

model outlined in this chapter offers a viable alternative for cor-
relating the behaviors and the measures of those behaviors with
successful outcomes. In that sense, a grounding in business fun-
damentals is essential for the cross-cultural assessor.

The Focus Is on Outcomes

To avoid the trap of being locked into an overly complex model of
assessment, our initial thinking about assessment should focus on
outcomes. The simpler and more general the outcome, the better.
Where possible, the outcome should be focused on business success criteria. This strategy serves the purposes of forcing administrative simplicity and keeping the business decision maker focused
on what counts in his or her terms. An outcome focus will also
drive a more thoughtful and targeted dialogue on what behaviors
are present in a candidate and whether those behaviors are useful
predictors of real behaviors in real business situations.

Judgment Is Needed

Sound and reasoned judgment must be an integral part of the
cross-cultural assessment process. Because statistical validity may
be limited, it is important to start with some hypothesis about the
behaviors in question and test conclusions with the cross-cultural
model. The large range of possible interactions requires the assessor to start with a reasoned and personal factor analysis as to
what is most important to the outcome of a particular assessment.
This kind of thinking starts with the question about what will satisfy the requirements of the decision maker and also be scientifically sound.

Thought and Thoroughness Are Important

A great deal of focus on the tools and methodology of measurement may not add significantly to the accuracy or predictive nature of the cross-cultural assessment. For example, a carefully
crafted and detailed interview may be just as useful as a paper-and-
pencil test. A targeted selection interview that drives deep into the
exact nature of actions taken by the assessee and the conditions

under which those behaviors were demonstrated can be quite powerful. This is particularly true if the evaluation of that assessment interview is done by an expert skilled in business, psychology, and cultural differences. The one variable that is critical to a satisfactory assessment outcome is time. No interview or measure should be rushed. A three- or four-hour selection interview can do a great deal to validate and correlate a person's background and experience with the job requirements in question.

Patience, Patience, Patience

Patience is required to build a sufficiently broad understanding of the personal factor analysis or expert system required to get good cross-cultural data. Each additional assessment of a different nationality will build a database and a storehouse of hypotheses about the extent to which certain cultures manifest certain behaviors. Until that knowledge base has sufficient data, the broad understanding required to predict business outcomes should not be expected to be particularly robust.

Expect the Unexpected

When certain behaviors are probed, outcomes may vary widely. Welcome these unexpected behaviors as an opportunity to learn something new. Finding something unexpected may not mean that the model is wrong but simply that it is not sufficiently robust. To that end the models presented here are viewed as hypotheses and starting points, not as solutions to cross-cultural assessment issues.

Consider Expert Systems

Use the line manager as an expert system, and start with a grounding in what the line manager or decision maker is attempting to accomplish. Look for the cues used by the decision maker, and develop a thorough understanding of where those cues came from and whether they are actually related to the critical outcomes.

Behavior Comes First

Finally, most work to date suggests that behavior, or observed behavior, is a best bet for a successful cross-cultural assessment. Cross-cultural assessments should focus primarily on specific examples of work product or actions leading to a result if the grounding to business outcomes is to remain solid.

Conclusions: The Future of Cross-Cultural Assessment

The future of cross-cultural assessment is exciting and challenging. In one sense, we have just landed on Mars and must learn how to interact with cultures and languages that are quite different from ours. Our U.S. traditional one-country model of assessment and uniform guidelines may not be broad enough to capture the richness of cross-cultural assessment. We will have to learn how to deal more effectively with interactions and multiple levels of complexity. A much broader way of thinking about behavior may be required for psychological science to advance the cause of cross-cultural assessment fully. To that end the references cited at the end of this chapter are not about assessment methodology. Instead, they will serve to broaden readers' understanding of the context within which cross-cultural assessment takes place. The practitioner is encouraged to think outside normal assessment paradigms. To do that, a foundation of cross-cultural understanding is helpful. If we think primarily about methodology and process, we may not be sufficiently open and innovative to find the new tools and techniques needed for cross-cultural assessment. Once we leave the relative safety of one language and venture into the fullness of cross-cultural assessment, a breadth of business and cultural understanding is also needed. The intent of this chapter has been to challenge traditional assessment assumptions and stimulate us all to think in different terms. As we become members of a global village, our thinking and methodologies must continue to evolve if we want to continue to provide scientific rigor as well as practical assistance. Cross-cultural assessment offers a real opportunity to learn how to do both.

References

Barham, K., & Oates, D. (1991). *The international manager.* London: Business Books.

Copeland, L., & Griggs, L. (1985). *Going international.* New York: Random House.

Evans, P., Doz, Y., & Laurent, A. (Eds.). (1989). *Human resource management in international firms*. Houndmills: Macmillan.

Fulkerson, J., & Schuler, R. S. (1992). Managing worldwide diversity at Pepsi-Cola International. In S. E. Jackson (Ed.), *Diversity in the workplace: Human resource initiative*. New York: Guilford Press.

Geisinger, K. F. (1994). Special section: Cross-cultural issues. *Psychological Assessment, 6*(4), 304–312.

Hampton-Turner, C., & Trompenaars, F. (1991). *The seven cultures of capitalism*. New York: Doubleday.

Hofstede, G. (1991). *Cultures and organizations*. London: McGraw-Hill.

McClelland, D. C. (1989). *Human motivation*. Cambridge, England: Cambridge University Press.

Mitrani, A., Dalziel, M., & Fitt, D. (Eds.). (1992). *Competency based human resource management*. London: Kegan Paul.

Morrison, T., Conaway, W. A., & Borden, G. A. (1992). *Kiss, bow, or shake hands*. Holbrook, MA: Bob Adams.

Rhinesmith, S. H. (1993). *A manager's guide to globalization*. Burr Ridge, IL: Business One Irwin, 1993.

Riordan, C. M., & Vandenberg, R. J. (1994). A central question in cross-cultural research: Do employees of different cultures interpret work-related measures in an equivalent manner? *Journal of Management, 20*(3), 643–671.

Schuler, R. S., Fulkerson J. R., & Dowling, P. J. (1991). Strategic performance measurement and management in multinational corporations. *Human Resource Management, 30*(3), 365–392.

Spencer, L. M., & Spencer, S. M. (1993). *Competence at work*. New York: Wiley.

Trompenaars, F. (1994). *Riding the waves of culture*. Burr Ridge, IL: Irwin.

CHAPTER 11

Assessment as Organizational Strategy

Sandra L. Davis

Sometimes assessment fails. Practitioners and organizations invest time, money, and expertise in creating outstanding assessment processes that fail because they do not last. An example of such a failure occurred several years ago with a major retailer. Two management development assessment centers for store managers and buyers were created. Initially, there seemed to be an impact. Participants reported significant learning, the client praised the real-life feeling of the simulations, and all involved celebrated the apparent success of the assessment process. But within a few months it became clear that the organization had only given lip service to management development, no one was ever held accountable for using the results, and within twelve months the materials and the participant reports gathered dust on the shelf.

Consider another kind of failure. Sometimes assessment does not live up to its potential. Assessment impact (however it is defined) is becoming increasingly important. Organizations demand greater measurability and results from their proposed or existing assessment approaches. Each placement or hiring decision becomes increasingly significant as organizations trim their employee populations, companies face greater competitive pressures, and new worldwide organizational structures evolve. Practitioners may believe that they can respond to the demands for measurable results by designing the most reliable, valid, and state-of-the-art methodology. They assume methodology alone should guarantee impact and results. It does not.

This chapter aims to prevent such failures and to capitalize on assessment as a means to further the goals of the organization. It zeroes in on assessment from two directions by addressing how to approach assessment strategically and how to use assessment as a means to drive strategy. In either case the central issue is designing assessment for a lasting impact.

The model in Figure 11.1 serves as a framework for designing assessment in a way that creates lasting results. Such long-term effects are possible only when all of the stages in the figure are considered. If context is ignored, the process will have no roots. If design is shortchanged, it will have no substance. If implementation is neglected, it will have no longevity.

In the subsequent sections of this chapter, each of the three stages in Figure 11.1 is considered separately. This is not meant to imply that context variables surface only in the beginning or that implementation can be thought about only after design has ended. On the contrary the stages are more interrelated than they appear on paper. Nevertheless, because they do follow a rough sequence, this chapter will do the same. In addition, ideas and challenges for using assessment in more creative ways are embedded in the discussion about each stage.

Stage One: Assessment Context

Assessment does not occur in a vacuum. Just as a human resource system needs to align with an existing culture and future demands, so does assessment. By considering the following factors, or variables, the practitioner builds a strong strategic foundation for assessment.

Context lends a backdrop and provides opportunities for making assessment a value-added program. The variables examined here range in an approximate fashion from those that simply have to be taken into account to those that offer possibilities for driving strategy. History, culture, workforce needs, and organizational problems give substance to later choices of design and implementation. But business strategies, core human resource (HR) strategies, and change initiatives are about the future. They drive choices

Figure 11.1. A Strategic View of Individual Assessment.

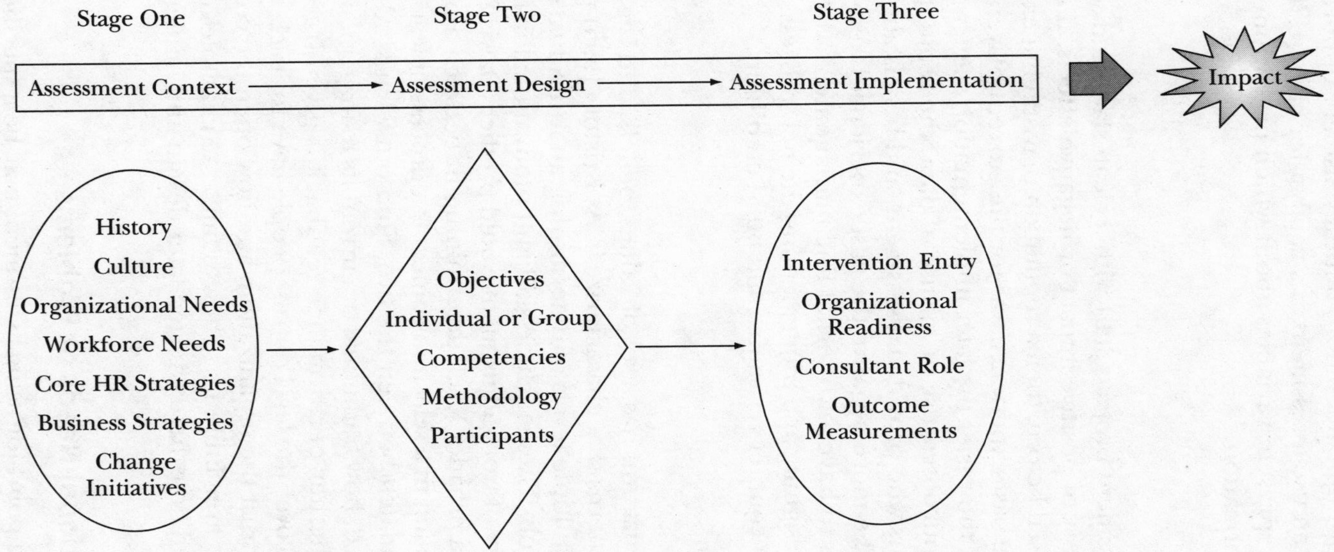

Stage One   Stage Two   Stage Three

Assessment Context → Assessment Design → Assessment Implementation

History
Culture
Organizational Needs
Workforce Needs
Core HR Strategies
Business Strategies
Change Initiatives

Objectives
Individual or Group
Competencies
Methodology
Participants

Intervention Entry
Organizational Readiness
Consultant Role
Outcome
Measurements

Impact

of design or implementation, but they also are opportunities for which we can use assessment as a catalyst for change. The following ideas represent variables about which practitioners need to gather information.

History

Some assessment projects start with a clean slate, and some begin with a history of positive impact or negative effects. If assessment has been used before, then a reputation may still linger. The more positive the past experience was for the current players in the organization, the easier the later implementation stage will be. Consider past purposes, use or misuse of data, the reputation of the practitioners who provided assessment, and beliefs about its overall value. The more negative the past experiences were, the more critical it is to have an internal line management work team involved in designing and implementing the new process. That team can help to counter resistance and build credibility.

Culture

Each organization has a set of values, beliefs, and ingrained behavioral patterns that characterize it. As Kristof (1996) points out, there are multiple levels of determining an individual's fit with a particular job. These include skill and motivational match, much as the theory of work adjustment would predict (Dawis & Lofquist, 1984). On a broader level, determining fit between a person and an organization in a selection context is a process of learning about the values match between the two. Find out what kind of leadership is valued, how traditional or current its management practices are, and whether performance feedback is given freely and accepted. Discover the level of trust people have for each other, how much they trust the organization, and how open the communication systems are. Table 11.1 shows some case examples of cultural variables and how these affected later design and implementation decisions.

Organizational Needs or Problems

The starting point for using assessment may be a specific problem or need. If the turnover rate for newly hired customer service

Table 11.1. Cultural Factors Addressed in Design and Implementation.

Cultural Factor	How Design Addressed the Factor	How Implementation Addressed the Factor
Lack of effective performance feedback	Involved potential assessees in designing the competencies.	Trained managers on how to use assessment data and give additional feedback to participants.
Team-based culture and values	Involved several work teams in the design; used group exercises; created several team behavior competencies.	Had intact work teams participate in assessment process together.
Aggressive, fast-paced culture	Selection assessments included motivational tests and a simulation where speed was important.	Used behavioral checklists to integrate data faster; assessment process completed in three days.
Lack of trust	Involved trusted, informal leaders in design as champions.	Participation was voluntary; manager received oral summary.

representatives is high or too many managers fail within a year of promotion, there may be an obvious selection problem to solve through the use of systematic selection assessment. The need or the problem generates a measurable business result that assessment must produce.

Consider the case of the customer service function in a large credit card company. Turnover rates were running at 40 percent, well above national averages for such functions. Turnover is expensive. The cost of hiring new staff, training them, and integrating them into the work group is significant. The company estimated the cost of hiring and training to be at least $20,000 per employee. Moreover, the cost of dissatisfied customers and increasing complaints affected the strategy of gaining market advantage by having superior customer service. This was the assessment context. The assessment had to be created with this goal in mind: reduce turnover and customer complaint rates.

Workforce Needs and Attitudes

Individuals or work teams have needs that affect the assessment process. Attitude survey researchers know, for example, that people often feel they want more feedback than they are getting. This desire for feedback paves the way for the acceptance of assessment as a valuable experience. Typically, many individuals feel apprehension at the thought of assessment (who will see the data?), some are excited by the opportunity, and others adopt a wait-and-see attitude. If assessment has been used before in the organization and most people perceive it as a painful process that was misused, then the organization needs to explore what benefits would make assessment worthwhile to potential assessees.

Most people are interested in feedback; some want confirmation, some want to use the data for career planning, and others want to know how to improve their skills or their chances for advancement or broader roles. Those interests and desires give practitioners a chance to create assessment processes that are a form of reward or recognition. Taking the perspective of the participant interested in personal growth allows a design to be quite broad ranging.

A primary use of assessment centers and an individual assessment process is as a catalyst to development. The design assumes that feedback and developmental suggestions have an impact on personal growth. Anecdotal and testimonial evidence abounds testifying to the efficacy of this approach, but the empirical evidence to support the power of developmental centers is scarce. Jones and Whitmore (1995) concluded after comparing a subgroup of assessees with a control group of equally performing nonassessees that there were no differences in career advancement. Frankly, it is doubtful that significant development occurs for a given group just because individuals have had feedback.

The Jones and Whitmore data suggest the need to be more creative about ways to link developmental goals with job performance objectives. If we begin with an HR strategy that promotes continual learning, we ought to be asking, How can assessment be used to show measurable results?

When developmental assessments are coupled with coaching activities focused on individual behavioral change, there is at least anecdotal evidence that change occurs. Committing resources to developmental assessment follow-up activities extends the original investment of time and resources.

Core HR Strategies

Most assessment processes are sponsored by HR or by HR and a key line manager. HR strategies often encompass an analysis of the organization's long-term talent and competency needs. Other strategies seek to address a deficit, for example, by outlining a specific initiative for developing stronger leaders and managers. The design should incorporate these elements, and later efforts to measure assessment impact should tie back to these.

We also need to understand the role that HR currently plays in the organization. HR roles have ranged from those that are purely administrative, to those that police organizational functions, to those that partner with line management. Although HR is moving toward partnering with line management and succeeding in some settings, one needs to know what is happening now and where the function is heading. Assessment implemented in the right way can help to reinforce or further the role and strategies of the HR function.

A recent case illustrates a process that provided HR with a means of strengthening its role as partner to line management in developing leadership talent. In designing a selection process for an insurance company, the external psychologist established a feedback loop that included a discussion between the psychologist who conducted the hiring assessment, the hiring manager, and the HR generalist. In the past, feedback had been given only to the HR generalist, who "told" the hiring manager about bottom-line assessment results. Through the change, HR relinquished some control and gained the ability to collaborate with the line manager about the hiring decision itself and subsequent possibilities for how best to work with the new employee. Had the consultant not asked about long-term HR goals, she might have accepted the status quo of providing assessment feedback only to the HR staff.

Another organizational need that can be addressed through a systematic assessment process is evaluation of an organization's HR capabilities. The goal is to have an accurate and complete audit of skills, motives, and potential in an entire class of employees (such as managers or technical employees). The data are useful on both an individual and an aggregate basis. If, for example, assessments show that team leaders in a team-based manufacturing environment have a limited or deficient skill set in facilitation or conflict management, group training programs or individualized coaching might be implemented. The best place to begin such an audit is with a definition of the most needed skills, given the organization's strategy and mode of operation. The strategic value is obvious, and certain skill sets can then be targeted in specific hiring or promotion decisions.

Core Business Strategies

Although debate exists about whether different skill sets are needed for different strategies, understanding an organization's core success factors leads to powerful assessment designs. Knowing the organization's strategic plan sets the stage for the design process. Consider using the Treacy and Wiersema (1995) model that delineates three primary strategies an organization may adopt: customer intimacy, technological innovation, or operational excellence. The chosen strategy affects competency design in particular and makes certain leadership factors more critical than others. In general, interpersonal skills tie to customer intimacy, creativity or wide-ranging thinking to technological innovation, and implementation skills to operational excellence.

A medical products company has adopted a technological innovation strategy that includes dramatic annual investment in research and development (R&D). The management of the R&D function is central to keeping the best technical talent, so assessment plays a key role in the selection of R&D managers. Knowing the organization's strategy led to competencies that include leadership of the creative technical professional, the ability to stimulate innovative thought, and a willingness to take risks.

A Silicon Valley high-tech company's strategy was to be on the cutting edge of technology and be the first to come to the market with a new product. It therefore needed the best new talent from superior technology colleges. Those new players entered a campus in which it was not uncommon for individuals to put in eighty–hour weeks, working around the clock at critical stages of product development and even sleeping on site. New employees had no time to come up to speed, nor were they given much training. They were immediately made part of a design team. The company's challenge was to select the best talent and make few, if any, selection errors. The company was most concerned about immediate effectiveness and placed relatively little importance on individuals' remaining for the long term.

The psychologist designed a selection process that was itself intensive, including performance demands, short time frames, teamwork, and situations requiring the ability to give and take criticism. That same process was not transferable to other organizations with different strategies. It would have offended a training and development–focused company whose strategy was to support and train key professionals so they would stay and contribute for the long term.

Strategically paying attention to the leadership talent needed in the future is critical for an organization's survival. Collins and Porras (1994) contend that developing leadership talent from within is one of the factors that predict organizational longevity and exceptional performance. Assessment ought to be used more often than it is to stimulate effective succession planning. Several forward-thinking organizations have worked to define the critical leadership competencies needed for the organization of the future. Then they moved into using assessment as an integral part of identifying and developing leadership talent.

Current Change Efforts

This area poses tremendous opportunities for assessment to drive, not just respond to, new strategic initiatives. Broad organizational change efforts currently seem geared toward developing stronger teams, flatter organizations, or learning environments. Why are assessment practitioners not taking the lead to provide momentum and energy for this initiative?

A prime example of using assessment to drive a change process occurred in a regional banking organization that was moving from a traditional service and operational structure to a sales-driven environment. The HR staff proposed the use of assessment centers to send a message about the future and the new structure of jobs. As the change process was rolled out in each bank, the new job roles and competencies were described, and individuals were asked to participate in an assessment after indicating which roles interested them. The simulation exercises were designed around future job tasks, and the feedback incorporated the new competencies. Following the centers and the feedback process, some participants indicated that the experience of a realistic job preview convinced them that this change would not fit them, and they chose to leave. Others found the changes exciting, and the assessment experience increased their level of comfort in the new organization.

Stage Two: Strategic Assessment Design

This section covers design variables with an eye to their strategic ties and implications. It is not intended to serve as a primer of everything to do in designing assessments but rather suggests strategic considerations for practitioners as they make design choices.

The variables chosen for inclusion here begin with those that are broadest in scope and thus have the most impact on the subsequent design. Assessment purpose is touched on from a strategic perspective. Similarly, the inclusion of competencies is meant to promote creative thinking about them. The list of variables then becomes more detailed and specific, to cover choices of which people to assess and the use of 360-degree instrumentation.

Assessment Objectives

The first step in assessment design is to clarify assessment objectives. There is a distinction between assessment purpose at a strategic level and assessment objectives at the tactical level. The previous section, in addressing such broad factors as business strategy and change efforts, gave a context for assessment activities. In this section the concern is to translate those strategic opportunities into specific objectives. Table 11.2 contains some examples of translating strategic purpose into tactical objectives.

Most important, the practitioner needs to write a clear statement of what assessment is designed to accomplish. Assessment designs, like performance appraisal systems, can fail because they try to meet too many needs with a single intervention. That means limiting the number of objectives and being clear about which are primary.

Although individual assessment has been used historically for a variety of reasons, including selection, development, career planning, coaching, and personal growth, the most common combination in the past has been selection paired with development. Regardless of which objective is primary, clarifying it will guide several other choices about assessment, including who will have access to the data, the kinds of questions that are posed in an interview, and the choice of testing methodologies. Table 11.3 shows some common assessment objectives and the implications each has for other design or implementation actions.

Design of Competencies: What Should We Assess?

Addressing the question of what should be assessed lies at the heart of assessment design. No assessment methodology can be chosen until the competency question is answered. If a potential client were to ask, "How do you do assessment?" the answer ought to be, "It depends. What do you need to measure?"

Competencies summarize behaviorally the critical knowledge, skills, abilities, and other characteristics needed in the target job

Table 11.2. Translating from Strategy to Tactical Objectives.

Strategic Purpose	Tactical Assessment Goals
To position the organization to be technologically innovative	To select the best technical leaders
	To provide data about the organization's technical leadership so management talent can be developed
To develop international operational stability	To select executives for expatriate assignments
	To understand better who succeeds and who fails in such assignments
	To provide data that will guide the placement process
To ensure continual learning and skill growth	To help individual assessees take ownership for his or her growth and development
	To provide assessees with feedback and resources to plan their development
To build the organization's leadership talent pool	To identify future leaders from a pool of nominated candidates
	To provide accurate feedback and information on the organization's leadership talent
	To provide feedback to participants for development
To change from operational excellence to being sales driven	To communicate about the organization's new competencies
	To provide a realistic job preview
	To give managers a blueprint for individual and collective training needs
To support the development of a team-based organization	To help individuals communicate with each other about their needs, motivations, and skills
	To provide intact work teams with data for team assessment and development

Table 11.3. Assessment Purpose and Design Implications.

	Selection	Personal Growth	Succession Planning	Support of Organizational Change
Who is the client?	Organization	Participant	HR and the organization	Organization and participant
How important is job analysis?	Critical	Not necessary	Less important than creating leadership competencies	Important; but if the target job does not exist, create a model
What are the competencies?	Specified for position	Generic or specified by person	Strategic competencies for the organization	Competencies for the future using trends
Who has access to the data?	Decision makers	Participant	Participant, line management, and HR	Participant, line management, and HR
How important is content validity?	Important	Not important	Important in matching task complexity	Important
What is the focus of the participant interview?	Behavior-based questions tied to success predictors	Career pathing, personal goals, self-assessment	Motivational factors, behavior-based probes tied to competencies	Behavior-based questions tied to competencies

or job level. Most practitioners understand the process of creating competencies from interviews, observation, critical incident techniques, or other methods. In many cases the competency set already exists when an individual assessment practitioner is brought in to the system.

Understanding how to write a competency definition and behavioral anchors is not enough. The competency set or measurement targets need to be as broad as possible. Many competency models (with the exception of Spencer, McClelland, & Spencer, 1994) fail to specify motivation as part of the model; however, traditional work adjustment theory does consider motivation (Dawis & Lofquist, 1984). In making selection or placement decisions, we need to take more than skills and competencies into account. Turnover remains high if those selected have the skills to do the job but are not motivated to remain.

The turnover of the customer service unit of a large credit card company was running at 42 percent. The company had a well-designed and validated set of skill-based competencies, and those who were selected based on those competencies proved to have the ability to learn and carry out the job functions. So why was turnover still so high? What was missing was an understanding of the motivational match between the individual and the job. Once the structure of the job was understood and current incumbents with strong performance and longevity were assessed, it became clear that patience with detail and lack of overriding career ambition led to job satisfaction and longevity. By assessing motivational fit, turnover was reduced to 19 percent.

The bottom line is that the practitioner needs to consider motivational variables when competencies are developed. If motivational fit appears to be an important factor, then assessment design will include motivational interviews, interest inventories, or motivational instruments.

We also need to look beyond traditional leadership and management competencies toward what research across companies tells us. If, as McCall (1991) contends, a critical variable in successful executive performance is the ability to learn from experience, then our assessments need to incorporate it. In this instance, McCall points out three aspects of the ability to learn from experience: (1) openness to experience (if one has little curiosity or sense of adventure, there will not be many experiences from which to learn), (2) openness to feedback (includes seeking feedback and trying to determine what the lessons of experience are), and (3) ability to use what was learned and apply it to the next situation.

Incorporating organizational values or competencies such as ability to learn from experience has an enormous impact on the selection of assessment methodologies. The more creative the competency set is, the more the practitioner needs to look beyond traditional methodologies for data.

Choices of Methodology: How Should We Assess?

When methodologies are chosen based solely on the capacity of the methodology to measure the desired competencies, values, or motivational variables, they can miss the mark. If strategic purpose is not considered, measurement may be psychologically sophisticated and accurate but not put into practice.

Notice, for example, how many companies have become captivated with the use of 360-degree feedback as a tool for learning and personal growth. In response, we have experienced a proliferation of 360-degree instrumentation, and many clients now expect this feedback to be an integral part of developmental assessments. However, some organizations have implemented multirater processes with no understanding of when the practice adds value. When performance rewards have nothing to do with the impact of one's leadership style on others, then the majority of assessees will discard the data.

Peer ratings and information about the interaction between leaders and followers provide a far richer picture of leadership style than objective measures, simulations, and tests alone. As Hogan, Curphy, and Hogan (1994) noted in a far-reaching article about the measurement of leadership effectiveness, a "leader's credibility or trustworthiness may be the single most important factor in subordinates' judgments of his or her effectiveness." Therefore, there are many circumstances in which learning about one's credibility can be a central aspect of assessment.

Adding a 360-degree instrument is especially helpful when the organization is clearly committed to increasing the quality of leadership as seen through the eyes of those who are being led. Adding such an instrument is also especially valuable in the context of an assessment conducted for coaching purposes and when the individual is curious about his or her impact on others. Yet using a 360-degree instrument for a coaching assessment in an organization that has never been exposed to such practices is questionable unless the participant can sell it to others so they answer candidly.

One advantage of multirater feedback instruments is the ability of people other than psychologists to use and interpret them. Some assessment methodologies are more psychologist dependent than others. That can be highly appropriate in a selection assessment where the primary focus is evaluative. But if a strategic goal of the organization involves individuals' directing their own learning and developmental processes, then we need to choose or design assessment methods that are easily interpreted or accessible to people other than psychologists. For example, when an organization is encouraging individual responsibility for learning, the practitioner ought to be finding creative ways for the assessee to take an active role in the feedback process. The practitioner would be working at cross-purposes to the organization if the feedback process required only passive listening by the participant.

A case that illustrates moving away from being psychologist dependent and toward participants' taking a more active role in feedback occurred in a large retail organization. As part of the developmental assessment center, the participants evaluated themselves. They viewed videotapes of their own role plays and other interactions. They used guides and checklists for observing and rating their own interaction skills. In subsequent meetings, they compared their self-assessments with similar ratings done by assessors and by their peers.

Individual or Team Focus

If selection assessment is to help predict whether an individual will be an effective addition to a work team (responsible for producing a group result, such as a new product design or a technical innovation), then it is imperative that we are not so myopic as to think only about assessing the individual. Those who historically have conducted individual assessments have based much of their work on the understanding and measurement of individual differences. In selection they ask whether an individual fits well with the job in question.

Now assume that the individual is to become a member of an intact work team. By helping to predict which candidate will best fit with the work team in question, we are attempting to increase homogeneity. And striving for greater homogeneity may be exactly the wrong tactic. As Schneider (1996) and other organizational development theorists have pointed out, contributing to the heterogeneity of the group, not its homogeneity, may be more important for its effectiveness.

There are several ways in which the assessment design could have a powerful group focus. One would be to conduct team assessments to provide feedback to the entire team about the effectiveness of its communication, decision making, and work management processes. Another would be to use team assessment exercises with various combinations of individual members to determine the most effective team assignments (something athletic coaches and conductors of small musical ensembles have been doing for years). Another would be to assess an intact team to determine what team member roles or expertise are missing (see team member roles in Belbin, 1981) so an appropriate new team member could be identified. Another possibility would be to use team assessments to assess how well the group interacts and provides data to other teams in an interdependent environment.

Organizational or Job Function Fit

The world of jobs and work appears to be shifting dramatically. Rather than assuming an individual will join an entry-level career track and progress up or across, organizations are hiring individuals with broad skill sets or high levels of adaptability. Hiring the employee of the future may mean enrolling an individual in a flexible workforce that shifts with changing projects and tasks. Thus we need to consider what selection assessment has to say about the degree of fit between the individual and multiple job functions, not just the fit with a single, specific job function. At a minimum, we may need to assess an individual's competencies against clusters of tasks. The implications for assessment design or selection of methodologies are apparent. Many researchers have noted the tendency of assessment center variance to be exercise specific rather than competency specific. That fact can be an advantage as we seek to evaluate performance within a set of discrete tasks.

Another component of organizational fit is cultural match or values match. Indeed, many hiring managers have confidence in their ability to assess an applicant's skills and knowledge but find the assessment of fit more elusive. The model Kristof (1996) proposed provides insights about what assessment might target. She argues that in selection, person-organization fit at the broadest level is needed. If fit at that level includes the organization's culture and values, then those factors must show up in the competency model. In fact, values and culture variables do not always emerge as significant in job analysis. That happens because cultural variables do not tend to be the factors that distinguish superior performers from good performers.

The company culture of one medical products company is heavily weighted toward humanistic values and an international perspective. The competency model includes the usual leadership and interpersonal competencies but also one competency that deals with international understanding and one that reflects commitment to helping people. The competencies have behavioral anchors and are measured in both selection and developmental assessments.

In a small specialty manufacturing company, assessment of fundamental leadership and management competencies was not enough to predict ultimate position success or failure. Thus management involved employees in defining the company's fundamental cultural values. One value was being organization focused rather than self-focused, and another was flexibility (because the products involve significant customization). Those values are now incorporated in the company's competency model and included in selection assessments. That simple addition has increased the success rate of new employees. In fact, after cultural fit was included in the assessment of external candidates for management positions, all newly hired employees have been rated as good fits with the culture of the organization.

Choice of Participants

One of the more specific design questions is, Who should be assessed? Rather than considering this as a tactical question, we need to bring the focus back to strategy once again.

Anyone who has conducted individual assessments in an organizational setting has heard the question, "Why me?" Decisions about inclusion or exclusion of certain individual employees need to rest on a solid rationale. For example, if one of the broader purposes is to communicate about organizational change, then more rather than fewer participants will be involved. A broader group of employees should be included as well when the culture is highly inclusive.

Consider too the issue of whether assessment is a voluntary activity. If the organization's culture is moving toward empowerment, then it would be contradictory to require developmental assessments of all individuals in a certain job category (say, managers). Potential assessees should be given as much information as possible so they can determine whether to participate. The practitioner may need to educate the executive sponsor about the realities of assessment ethics so that potential assessees can say no to assessment if they do not want to participate. The only time that assessment should be mandatory is when it functions as part of a standardized selection or promotion decision-making process.

Stage Three: Strategic Assessment Implementation

This final section deals with organizational development considerations in implementing assessment. Achieving a successful assessment intervention requires attention to three primary elements, each posing opportunities or stumbling blocks for the practitioner: assessing the readiness of the organization to embrace an assessment strategy, beginning the intervention in the best way possible (point of entry), and defining the role of the external or internal consultant.

Assessing Organizational Readiness

Organizational readiness level drives other intervention variables. Exhibit 11.1 contains a questionnaire for assessing organizational readiness. Use it as a rough guide for determining whether the organization has a low, medium, or high level of readiness for implementing assessment processes. Simply answer the questions and

Exhibit 11.1. Assessing Organizational Readiness.

Answer the questions and total the points.

1. What kind of experience do the assessment process sponsors have with assessment?

Never used it before	Used it in only a limited way	Have used it recently for some years	Have used it extensively
1	2	3	4

2. How informed are the assessment process sponsors about the appropriate use and limit of assessment data?

Know very little	Have some general background	Are very well informed
1	2	3

3. Describe the communication systems in the organization across levels.

People tell each other little; many secrets	People sometimes communicate freely	There is an open flow of information across levels
1	2	3

4. How well is performance feedback handled?

People complain that they are rarely given any feedback	Feedback is given only at performance appraisal time	People are used to getting considerable feedback (performance appraisal, 360-degree data, for example)
1	2	3

5. How open is the executive in charge to participating in assessment?

Thinks assessment is for others	May participate to a limited degree	Has participated in assessment or is interested in feedback
1	2	3

6. To what degree does assessment coincide with significant organizational changes that threaten job stability?

Nothing highly unusual underway that might affect job security	Systems are changing but employees have some small concerns about security	A fundamental shift in how work is performed or significant downsizing is occurring; employees fear losing their jobs
6	4	2

Scoring: add points from all six questions to determine readiness, as shown in the following table.

Low Readiness (12 or Fewer Points)	Medium Readiness (13–17 Points)	High Readiness (18–22 Points)
Many barriers are likely to impede acceptance and accuracy of assessment.	Barriers to assessment are not large, but current circumstances suggest reluctance.	Assessment seems to be a known process, and people tend to be open to feedback.

add up the point values to determine approximate readiness level. Then refer to Table 11.4 to see case examples of how design or implementation actions can take readiness into account.

An example of a low-readiness situation occurred in the customer service unit of a Fortune 100 company. Participants had no prior experience with assessment, the organization was in the midst of a reengineering effort, and even the human resource staff had limited previous exposure to the use of assessment information. Therefore the line executive in charge of the area participated in the assessment first. She shared her assessment experience and even her report with potential participants and explained how the data would be used in selection decision making. Her openness eased some of their anxieties, but they were still openly skeptical and questioned the consultants and their leaders intensely at each stage in the assessment process. The organization held meetings to communicate about the process and gave participants personalized attention prior to and following the assessment.

The opposite dynamic occurred in a retail organization that had been using assessment for more than fifteen years to determine promotability and developmental needs. Instead of needing such extensive communication, participants seemed disinterested. Had a meeting been called to explain the assessment process, few would have shown up. A brief introductory letter filled the bill.

Another aspect of readiness exists in the individual apart from the organization. Individuals may have emotional barriers to being assessed. The practitioner should be aware of how potential participants feel about assessment. The overly anxious or the highly disinterested are not the best candidates for assessment. For different reasons, their data may not truly reflect their normal work selves. The practitioner can help to calm the overly anxious individual, and the line manager or executive sponsor can help to set the tone for motivated participation.

Determining a Good Point of Intervention Entry

Assessment is intervention. The more visible, broad-reaching, and central the individual assessment process is, the more carefully the process needs to be introduced, announced, or marketed. Because there are often barriers to assessment or to the use of assessment results, the practitioner needs to determine how to get started.

Table 11.4. Organizational Readiness and Assessment Implementation.

Readiness Level		Suggested Action Needed		
	Role of Line Sponsor	Orientation of Participants	Education of Line Management and HR	Dissemination of Results
Low (<13)	Participate in assessment first.	Consider holding a pilot program.	Psychologist holds briefing session about assessment, its uses and abuses.	If development only, consider report as belonging to the individual.
Medium (13–17)	Participate in the assessment process in some way.	Hold a Q&A meeting with participants, psychologists and sponsors.	Present information and reminders about assessment and its use.	Ensure all know where copies of reports go and how they will be used.
High (18–22)	Communicate about the goals of the assessment.	Provide written information about the assessment process.	Compare and review details of logistics and confidentiality with HR contacts.	Explain report process in preliminary letter.

Perhaps assessment should not be the first intervention activity. Consider the following case. The CEO of a large health care organization decided he and his executive team should participate in individual developmental evaluations. He had several reasons for using assessment. He wanted other employees to see that the executives were serious about improving their management skills (a recent employee attitude survey had proved there was considerable dissatisfaction with the management skills of the executive team). The CEO wanted to know more about the talent depth of those he had reporting to him, and he was anxious to provide the team with more knowledge about itself.

The consultant began interviewing members of the executive team to understand their level of readiness for this effort. Discovering that their readiness level was low and their distrust of each other was high, the consultant and the CEO decided to start with a team-building process. Assessment was introduced after the group members developed a sense of trust with each other, with their CEO, and with the consultant who ultimately conducted the assessments.

In another instance the director of a multilocation psychology clinic asked to participate in an individual coaching assessment so he could better work with his board and address board members' concerns about his leadership. The practitioner discovered, however, that the board had demanded an assessment because employees had complained about the director to the board. Therefore, the practitioner began with staff and board interviews to determine the dynamics of the situation and to find out others' expectations for leadership in this setting. Eventually an assessment was conducted, but only after all agreed on the primary components of effective leadership in that clinic.

These cases illustrate how critical it is to determine client needs. In every circumstance the practitioner needs to determine whether the client request for assessment is actually the best solution given the situation. Requests for assessment services are no different from requests for a specific kind of therapy. Both are for a predetermined solution; practitioners need to make sure the solution implemented meets the needs of the client.

Defining the Role of the Consultant

If we make assumptions about the clients' expectations of us as consultants, we may be in for a rude awakening. Many practitioners intend to operate in partnership with their clients, yet not all organizations welcome such efforts. In addition, some individual executives have quite explicit demands. For example, a practitioner might expect to discuss a selection assessment recommendation with a client, only to discover that he or she expects the consultant to "leave the bottom line and intelligence test score data on my voice mail."

Some line managers believe they are purchasing a commodity; that is, they believe that assessment is the same no matter how it is carried out. If they operate with a commodity mind-set, they emphasize cost and expect that assessment will just "give them the answer." If they truly have a partnership in mind, they expect to be part of planning the intervention and actively using the results. It is our job to help educate potential clients about our roles and about what assessment can and cannot do (see Chapter Four on assessment ethics).

To illustrate these dynamics, Schein's model (1988) about the role of consultant is useful. Schein contrasts three models: purchase of expert information, doctor-patient (diagnostician), and process consultation. Assessment, because of its evaluative aspects and the fact that certain tests can be interpreted only by licensed psychologists, pushes us professionally toward being experts and diagnosticians. When we assess fit of the job and the person or of the person and the organization, we operate as experts. In fact, some managers would like to have something or someone else make the difficult choice about hiring or placement.

Though some would like to keep psychologists in the role of expert, if practitioners want to operate as process consultants, they have the power to make that happen. First, educate the client about the use of assessment data prior to conducting the assessment. Second, discuss possible outcomes and the steps needed to make the most use of the dollars and time being spent. Third, be willing to walk away from an assessment contract if the client expects assessment to be a substitute for judgment and decision making. Fourth, demonstrate your understanding of the strategic business opportunities and show how partnering can help the organization capitalize on them. Fifth, plan the intervention to extend beyond the assessment and its immediate outcome. This could include developmental planning and later measurement of results, using assessment data in team building, measuring the ongoing effectiveness of individuals hired using assessment, and fine-tuning the process to measure all competencies important to job success.

Outcome Measurements

The final step in the intervention process is measurement. Deciding what ought to be measured should be easy if stage one has been done well. In fact, consider defining tangible results or outcomes that assessment will help to produce as part of stage one actions. At a minimum, if assessment is being conducted for selection, keep track of effectiveness and monitor assessment accuracy over time.

Take a second look at the business and HR strategies of the organization for ideas about what is important and for the kind of impact that might be measured. Always look for creative ways of measuring impact. As practitioners, we know to measure validity, reliability, retention, and job performance. But we should also be looking at performance improvement, increases in employee satisfaction, lowered costs of the hiring process, ease in attracting high-quality candidates to the organization, behavioral change, individual case data, increased quality in the organization's leadership talent pool, and even bottom-line business goal achievement.

Conclusions: Ideas and Opportunities

Sometimes assessment exceeds even our highest expectations. This chapter began with a disappointing story of failure. It is only right that it ends with an exciting picture of success. In each stage of developing assessment as strategy, we have opportunities to be creative and deliver significant results. Here are a few of those opportunities.

In stage one we can use our knowledge of the organization and the context in which assessment occurs to advance the organization's goals. Here are a few options:

- Use competency modeling to communicate about the new organization of the future.
- Choose an element of the company's goals and show how assessment could be used to advance these.

- Develop behavioral measures of culture and values fit.
- Study positions and tasks of the future and use them as the basis for assessment.
- Use assessment to show system knowledge or skill gaps.
- Help to define what is truly meant by effective leadership or effective teamwork.
- Consider what assessment can do to improve internal communication systems.

Stage two provides an opportunity to think about assessment in another way. We have only scratched the surface in rethinking our own assessment methodologies. Here are ways in which the design can begin to mirror our changing organizational and communication systems:

- Assess teams, not individuals.
- Customize the assessment to find the skills a team does not have.
- Use methodologies that can be interpreted by participants and trained laypeople.
- Incorporate multirater data into the process.
- Use multimedia venues.
- Involve participants in the design of the assessment process.
- Make sure the design process matches the culture and style of the organization.
- Design simple measures of charting progress on developmental goals.

Preventing failures is also a key objective of stage three, but this step in particular provides strategic opportunities. If assessment is recognized as the organizational development activity or intervention strategy that it is, we will be far more active in this stage than we historically have been. We need to shift from the mind-set of practitioner as expert and diagnostician to practitioner as process consultant. What do we believe a specific client organization needs to do to leverage assessment? We need to tell our clients what is needed. We have to take an active role in determining assessment timing. And we must be willing to dissuade clients from using assessment when it has a slim chance of advancing strategy or producing tangible results. We have the power to have significant strategic impact through assessment.

References

Belbin, M. (1981). *Team roles at work.* San Francisco: Pfeiffer.

Collins, J. C., & Porras, J. I. (1994). *Built to last: Successful habits of visionary companies.* New York: Harper Business.

Dawis, R. V., & Lofquist, L. H. (1984). *A psychological theory of work adjustment.* Minneapolis: University of Minnesota Press.

Hogan, R., Curphy, G. J., & Hogan, J. (1994). What we know about leadership. *American Psychologist, 49*(6), 493–504.

Jones, R. G., & Whitmore, M. D. (1995). Evaluating developmental assessment centers as interventions. *Personnel Psychology, 48*(2), 377–388.

Kristof, A. L. (1996). Person-organization fit: An integrative review of its conceptualizations, measurement, and implications. *Personnel Psychology, 49*(1), 1–49.

McCall, M. W. (1991). *Identifying leadership potential in future international executives: Developing a concept.* Los Angeles: University of Southern California School of Business Administration.

Schein, E. H. (1988). *Process consultation, Vol. 1: Lessons for managers and consultants.* Reading, MA: Addison-Wesley.

Schneider, B. (1996). When individual differences aren't. In K. Murphy (Ed.), *Individual differences and behavior in organizations* (pp. 548–571). San Francisco: Jossey-Bass.

Spencer, L. M., McClelland, D. C., & Spencer, S. M. (1994). *Competency assessment methods: History and state of the art.* Boston: Hay McBer Research Press.

Treacy, M., & Wiersema, F. (1995). *The discipline of market leaders.* Reading, MA: Addison-Wesley.

CHAPTER 12

Shaping Organizational Leadership
The Ripple Effect of Assessment
Rob Silzer

> *The CEO succession here is still a long way off,*
> *but I think about it every day.*
> JACK WELCH, 1993

Identifying, developing, and utilizing leadership talent is often a top priority for CEOs, particularly those who are genuinely committed to improving the long-term viability and competitiveness of the organization. Their efforts are complicated by the realization that the leadership skills required for future organizational success are different from the skills that produced past success. Business environments now demand strategically driven leadership that can manage constant organizational change. Sometimes managers can learn new leadership behaviors in order to adapt to changing business needs. Frequently, however, organizations must resort to using selection decisions to identify new leadership. Both developmental and selection approaches rely on accurately evaluating an individual's leadership skills, and individual assessment is widely used for this purpose.

Leadership change and succession issues can be seen in the corporate sagas at Apple Computer and AT&T. Each organization has gone through a very public discussion of how the next leadership needs to be different from past leadership. Neither of these organizations has had very smooth leadership transitions, which has been reflected in their inconsistent financial performances. Although leadership succession is a complex challenge with many variables, it rests on determining the future leadership needs of the organization and finding the leadership talent to meet these needs. In addressing their challenges, many organizations are assessing all candidates for executive positions. One well-known financial services corporation requires that all internal and external candidates for the one thousand officer positions complete an individual psychological assessment.

Simultaneously, human resource (HR) interventions including psychological assessments are expected to demonstrate their effectiveness in achieving business strategies. Some past human resource practices that have benefited individuals have diminished in use because their value to the organization has not been apparent. For example, assessment centers, so widely used in the 1970s, were less frequently used in the 1980s and 1990s. No doubt, there are several contributing factors to this decline. However, in some organizations, the indirect, and sometimes unseen, developmental benefit to the individual was not seen as clearly benefiting the organization. What primarily survived in the assessment center field were initiatives directly focused on screening or selecting individuals for key positions and having direct and obvious benefits to the organization.

Although there are a number of ways in which individual psychological assessment can have broad impact in shaping organizational leadership, this chapter focuses on four specific initiatives: leadership selection, leadership team development, leadership planning, and strategic leadership change. Each of these efforts addresses the changing leadership needs in an organization.

Organizational Applications

Individual psychological assessment has become widely used in organizations for selecting and developing individuals; however, the broader benefits to the organization are often overlooked. There are at least four applications of leadership assessment that can have a transforming influence in an organization.

Leadership Selection

It has become common practice in many American corporations to use individual psychological assessment to help select executive leaders. Key management positions become open for a variety of reasons but are less likely to be due to retirement and more likely to be due to organizational restructuring and change than they were twenty years ago. Silzer, Hollenbeck, and DeVries (DeVries, 1993; Hollenbeck, 1994; Silzer, 1991; Silzer & Hollenbeck, 1992) have discussed many of the critical issues related to managerial assessment and selection.

In some organizations where significant strategic change is occurring, all key management positions may be refilled with new leaders. One example is an American corporation that decided to replace all five business unit presidents within a year because of weak financial performance and a need to redirect the organization. Although this is a striking example, it is becoming more common for organizations to replace key managers when organizational performance is not up to expectations. The executive leadership selection process often starts with discussions and interviews with senior managers on the following issues:

- What external business trends will have an impact on our business strategies and our leadership needs?
- What implications do the current and future business strategies have for leadership performance?
- What are the specific roles and priorities for the organizational leadership?
- What are the leadership's responsibilities and decision-making authority?
- What specific performance objectives or results are expected?
- What leadership skills and competencies will be needed?
- What organizational experience, expert knowledge, or technical skills are needed?
- What are the expectations of the CEO, board of directors, or immediate manager?
- What resources will be available to the leadership to accomplish objectives and results (for example, human resources, financial resources, information systems, physical facilities)?

- What time period is reasonable for the leadership to have demonstrated an impact on the organization?
- What supports or hurdles are there from the culture and other managers?
- What strengths or performance issues were related to the last incumbent's effectiveness, and what changes from the last incumbent are expected?

Frequently this process involves having discussions with numerous senior managers and sometimes key direct reports to the target leadership position. The outcome of these interviews is a written leadership profile that summarizes and documents the following issues:

- External business trends
- Business strategies
- Leadership roles, responsibilities, and priorities
- Performance objectives, expected results, and time windows
- Decision-making latitude
- Available organizational resources
- Required leadership competencies
- Preferred organizational experience, expertise, and technical skills
- Organizational, cultural, and peer issues

Typically the leadership profile is circulated and a consensus reached among the hiring managers. This profile is then used to design the search, assessment, and selection process.

Often this requires the assessment psychologist to interact with executive recruiters who are assigned to finding external candidates. This situation presents some ethical concerns because the psychologist needs to maintain independence and objectivity in reviewing candidates and not be compromised by any relationship with the executive recruiters. This may be an issue particularly with executive recruiters whose fees are contingent on successfully placing their candidate in the organization.

If there are strong internal candidates, they are identified and often assessed simultaneously with external candidates, so all are treated equally. The selection decision process often winds up being sequential, however, due to candidate availability, indecisive hiring managers, early candidates who are poor matches for the position, political corporate environments, and early strong candidates who reject the opportunity.

Once the position is filled, it is useful and ethically important that the successful candidate have an opportunity to understand the assessment results. Rejected candidates should be given feedback on their assessment process, but the depth of feedback may vary, with internal and successful candidates getting more complete feedback. It is also useful to identify several key strengths and developmental areas and to suggest possible developmental action steps. Some organizations even create developmental plans for both the successful candidate and rejected internal candidates, operating on the principle that everyone has room to develop. Creating a developmental plan for the successful candidate is relatively easy; implementing that plan is more difficult.

The newly selected leader, particularly if an external candidate, has a lot of areas to learn quickly regarding the company, the culture, expectations, and peer managers but is often expected to produce results quickly. This learning process can be very consuming and allows little time for the individual to focus on developmental needs. Implementation of a developmental plan is most likely to occur when the person's immediate manager puts a priority on developmental progress.

After the manager has been in the position six to twelve months, it is often useful for the assessment psychologist to have follow-up conversations with that manager, the immediate manager, and the senior human resource officer in order to determine whether the placement was successful and whether the initial psychological assessment was accurate in predicting the individual's performance. This information is valuable to the assessment psychologist for reviewing the assessment and prediction process.

Leadership Team Development

Many organizations have created management teams and looked for ways to improve their effectiveness and increase their collaboration (Goodman & Associates, 1986; Guzzo, Salas, & Associates, 1995; Hackman, 1990; Mohrman, Cohen, & Mohrman, 1995). A good deal of attention has been paid to the process of selecting and developing teams over the last decade (Cannon-Bowers, Tannenbaum, Salas, & Volpe, 1995; Klimoski & Jones, 1995), and numerous models and approaches have been proposed (Guzzo, Salas, & Associates, 1995).

Often a senior manager, unsatisfied with the effectiveness of individual team members and their ability to work together, will search for ways to improve team performance and collaboration. The manager or team leader may consider issues related to work design, organizational structure, the decision-making process, or individual or team skills and abilities.

The leader may decide to initiate a team development process (historically referred to as team building), which can take many forms depending on the issues, the team, and the team facilitator or consultant. Frequently the real issues are not readily apparent, and if the leader jumps to conclusions, she may deal with only superficial problems. A broad team development process that is structured appropriately can address a wide range of underlying problems.

One common approach to leadership team development is to assess the leadership and team skills of the team members and the team as a group. Psychological assessment can collect data at both the individual and the team levels. The individual and team assessment results are then summarized and provided to the group. The results can serve as a foundation for introducing change and developing individual and team skills.

Leadership Planning

Many organizations spend a good deal of time focusing on leadership succession planning efforts. At the most fundamental level, this approach historically has been geared entirely toward replacement planning, that is, having a list of individuals who are potential successors for specific positions in the organization. Replacement planning is driven by expected turnover and frequently has a short-term focus of one or two years.

A more contemporary planning approach involves broader talent pool management and identifies talent needs and internal individuals who can meet those needs in the future. Although this process may include replacement planning, it also creates long-term and comprehensive developmental plans for certain individuals, specifying skill development steps and career experiences necessary to prepare them for leadership roles. Similarly, it often leads to broad organizational initiatives that build the internal talent pool to ensure that a sufficient number of strong candidates are ready when the organization needs them (Silzer & Graddick, 1996; Silzer, Slider, & Knight, 1994).

In the most progressive corporations, leadership planning is driven by business strategies. The leadership that is needed to accomplish the business strategies is specified, and the organization is inventoried to determine whether the leadership talent is available internally to implement those strategies. This approach, which leads to creating strategic organizational leadership plans, is a benchmark for state-of-the-art leadership planning.

All of these efforts typically require an assessment process, frequently individual psychological assessment, to analyze the current leadership talent pool in the organization (Silzer & Graddick, 1996).

Strategic Leadership Change

Many organizations have recently made significant changes in their strategic direction. In some cases the strategic change happens quickly and does not allow for long-term planning of a talent pool. The ability to redirect the organization fairly quickly (within a few years) becomes critical. This is a special application of leadership planning that often draws on individual psychological assessment to identify available leadership talent in the organization.

Strategic Leadership Change Model

When organizations face any of these leadership issues, they find that there are four common steps for making leadership changes in the organization. In fact, many leadership issues can be addressed with a four-step leadership change model:

- Determine business strategy.
- Identify leadership needs.

- Assess leadership talent.
- Develop and implement leadership plans.

These four steps help an organization ensure that the leadership talent is ready when needed to accomplish the business strategies.

Determine Business Strategy

An important starting point for any leadership change model is to identify the business strategies in the organization. Typically, these strategies are linked to financial resources and goals and often have implications for organizational structure, product development, marketing, manufacturing, and other functions. A wide range of business environment key variables can have an impact on business strategy (Hamel & Prahalad, 1994; Porter, 1980, 1985).

HR professionals are discovering the implications of business strategies for their work in organizations (Beer, 1997; Ulrich, 1997). They need to align their work efforts, systems, structure, and staff around these strategies. In the future, HR managers will have a role in shaping and setting business strategies (Hewitt, 1997; Ulrich, Losey, & Lake, 1997).

Consequently, the first step in the strategic leadership change model is to understand the business environment and the business strategies as the foundation for leadership change in the organization (see Figure 12.1).

Figure 12.1. Step One of the Strategic Leadership Change Model: Determine Business Strategy.

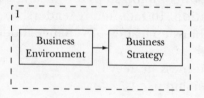

Identify Leadership Needs

A critical step in implementing a leadership initiative is translating business strategies into leadership strategies. Only a few organizations have been successful in making this connection (Heskett & Schlesinger, 1997).

What is an organization's leadership strategy? Historically, it has been unwritten, informal, and often unstated. In the past the talent strategy for many organizations was to hire exceptional individuals out of college or graduate school, put them in a management training program, let them burrow into the organization, and hope they find a career path to the top. In some organizations this talent is identified and more carefully managed as management trainees, high-potential individuals, or early identification individuals.

Typically, the careers of most people in an organization take unpredictable twists and turns. Some career moves are based on the individual's interests and skills, others on business needs or marketplace changes. In many organizations, it is informally known that the way to the top is through a particular functional area, such as marketing, operations, merchandising, or finance. Some organizations formalize this career path, but most do not. For example, a widely known marketing-driven consumer products organization has only five hundred people in the marketing function compared to fifty thousand in the manufacturing, packaging, and distribution of the product. However, it is common knowledge that successful candidates for business unit head positions have almost always either been marketing managers or people who have spent an extended period of time in the marketing function. Clearly, marketing know-how and skills are seen as necessary to be a successful business unit head.

The talent strategy in this organization clearly emphasized marketing expertise, even though it eliminated 99 percent of the population from consideration as a business unit head. This rule, never written down, was nevertheless widely known and accepted; to have significant influence in the organization, one needed to be on the leading edge of consumer marketing. In this case the business strategy of being a leading consumer-driven company dictated a specific leadership talent strategy.

In identifying their leadership strategy, organizations need to determine the specific leadership skills necessary for accomplishing each business strategy (Gerstein & Reisman, 1983). An organization with a customer-driven consumer product or service strategy may need talent that is service oriented in areas of customer service management, consumer products, and marketing. An organization strategically focused on marketing products and services to overseas markets may look for talent with international expertise, specifically in the targeted markets. This strategy has been difficult for U.S. corporations to implement. Over the past twenty years, many U.S. corporations have included global expansion as a key business strategy. But they have discovered that it is far more complicated and time-consuming than they initially expected, primarily because they were not very insightful or experienced in understanding the unique talent needs necessary to fulfill that strategy.

A leadership strategy is a general framework for the organization's approach to resourcing leadership talent and addresses the following issues:

- What will be the impact of the business strategies on organizational structure, the nature of the work, decision-making processes, and other areas, and how will this affect the management and leadership approach?
- What type of leadership will be needed to implement each business strategy?
- What leadership competencies and experience will be needed?
- What will be the primary sources of talent for filling leadership needs?

The leadership strategy is translated into specifications or needs (see Figure 12.2), which are predictions of the nature and the number of specific leadership positions and of the skills, expertise, and experience needed by the organization in the immediate and short-term future (typically one to five years). Leadership needs are often documented as:

- The specific leadership roles needed in three to five years to accommodate anticipated changes

Figure 12.2. Step Two of the Strategic Leadership Change Model: Identify Leadership Needs.

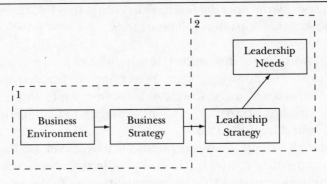

- The number of leaders needed
- The specific leadership competencies needed in each position
- The anticipated turnover expected in key positions
- The impact of future start-ups, acquisitions, and mergers on leadership needs
- Other special leadership talent needs such as technical expertise or cultural experience

Moving from talent strategy to specific leadership needs can be difficult because it requires envisioning the future and anticipating, with some guesswork, what the specific needs will be in concrete terms. This step requires visionary thinking. Some organizations do nothing more than extrapolate from historical records to future needs, but this is rarely effective in anticipating market or company changes and promulgates a backward-looking view that tends to be conservative and reactive. It does nothing to anticipate future change. It is most often found in stable businesses and markets and in organizations led by concrete, nonvisionary thinkers.

An effective way of specifying leadership needs is to have a series of discussions with senior managers, particularly those who set the business strategy, with the following goals:

1. To understand the business strategies.
2. To outline anticipated growth and change in the organization.

3. To identify the leadership implications of strategies and anticipated changes.
4. To specify the specific leadership competencies, experience, and key positions that will be needed.

Following these discussions, it is helpful to arrive at a consensus in order to allow for specific projections of leadership needs. Typically, however, projections can be wrong. An example of connecting business strategies to talent strategies to leadership needs can be found in Table 12.1.

Since the 1980s, many corporations have developed a leadership competency model or success profile that defines the skills and abilities required for the organization to fill its leadership needs. Most organizations develop a leadership profile that appears to be tailored to the organization. Nevertheless, after reviewing numerous leadership profiles, it is apparent that there is much commonality.

There seems to be a pool of sixty to eighty leadership competencies that typically appear in corporate leadership profiles. Each corporation often selects a subset of this pool for its own "unique" success profile. An organization trying to enter new markets, for example, may choose a subset of leadership competencies different from that selected by an organization focusing on its current markets. Although the mix of competencies varies among corporations, it often includes very similar competency factors. These common factors are listed in Table 12.2 along with competencies that often show up in leadership success profiles.

Some organizations have their own competency labels and language specific to their cultures. For example, business integrity may show up in various success profiles as business ethics, business values, showing honesty, acting professionally, following through on commitments, following legal and organizational policies, or something similar. Typically, leadership success profiles have eight to twenty competencies. Organizations with fewer competencies tend to give each competency more focused attention and generally have more success in identifying or developing people with those skills. Organizations that have a longer set of competencies (some profiles contain twenty-five or more) often have more difficulty taking action and fulfilling their leadership needs, because the larger number results in less focus and more confusion.

Table 12.1. Converting Business Strategies to Leadership Needs.

Business Strategy	Leadership Strategy	Leadership Needs
Pursue global markets.	Gain global and cross-cultural management experience.	Identify five country managers with both the leadership experience in specific cultures and the skills to launch a start-up organization.
Acquire specialty companies in our market that are not performing up to their financial potential.	Build a leadership team that can analyze, acquire, and turn around business acquisitions.	Identify ten candidates with corporate financial skills and turnaround leadership skills.
Increase our share of our primary market to be the market leader in revenue and innovation.	Create world-class functions in consumer marketing, sales, product development, and operations.	Identify enough candidates to fill five new executive positions in each of these functions who have the skills to transform the function into a market leader.
Seek a merger with a direct competitor that is a strategic fit.	Build a leadership team that can successfully accomplish a large-scale merger.	Identify a corporate merger team with ten executives experienced in organizational and cultural change.

Table 12.2. Common Leadership Factors and Related Competencies.

Common Factors	Related Competencies
Thinking skills	Analyzing information Solving problems Making high-quality decisions Leveraging financial information Thinking innovatively Using seasoned judgment Taking calculated risks Dealing with ambiguity Developing strategy
Work management skills	Planning and organizing work Being resourceful Managing projects Executing and implementing Involving others Achieving results
Interpersonal and communication skills	Building networks Relating to others Showing sensitivity and respect for others Communicating with others Delivering presentations Listening to others Keeping others informed Managing conflict Valuing diversity Collaborating with others
Leadership skills	Recruiting and staffing Motivating and inspiring others Coaching and developing others Providing direction and vision Building and using teams Influencing and negotiating Empowering others
Motivation skills	Adapting to change Showing drive and taking action Maintaining high standards Showing initiative Taking responsibility Providing feedback

**Table 12.2. Common Leadership Factors
and Competencies** (*continued*).

Common Factors	Related Competencies
Personal characteristics	Demonstrating integrity and trust Modeling cultural values Learning continually Acting professionally
Organizational skills	Focusing on customers Committing to quality Driving change Pursuing continuous improvement Managing a large scope
Technical skills	Demonstrating functional expertise Knowing the business Demonstrating industry knowledge Showing business acumen

Typically, leadership needs also include a competency profile that captures the key skills and abilities required for future leaders. This profile is often useful as a complement to the more concrete numbers of positions and candidates that are needed for the leadership change process.

Assess Leadership Talent

Once the leadership needs have been specified and a leadership success profile has been identified, an inventory of leadership talent in the organization can be pursued (see Figure 12.3). This inventory is often an assessment process that identifies and evaluates internal candidates against the leadership needs.

Three key questions need to be addressed in conducting a leadership inventory in the organization:

1. Who should be included in the talent inventory?
2. What skills, abilities, and experiences should be evaluated?
3. What assessment tools and process should be used?

Figure 12.3. Step Three of the Strategic Leadership Change Model: Assess Leadership Talent.

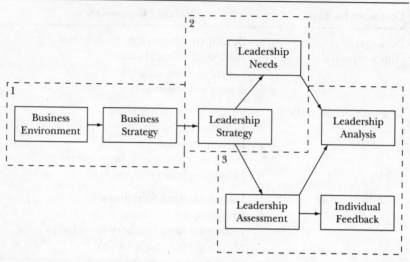

Organizations approach the first question in various ways. Some organizations, particularly those with small exempt populations, include all exempt personnel in the inventory each year. This exercise creates an annual database of information on all exempt personnel. Eventually decisions are made to determine whether individuals should be promoted into specific positions. This decision is often made when the position becomes open. This approach tends to be more primitive than replacement planning and is mostly found in small organizations (see Figure 12.4).

Other organizations use a screening or nomination process to identify a more select group of individuals to be considered for the talent pool. In these organizations leadership talent pools are created by focusing on high-potential, early identification, management trainee, or special talent individuals. Each of these groups may have unique screening processes. In some cases the talent pool may be very small, such as for candidates for the CEO position. In other cases, the talent pool may be quite large, such as all exempt individuals in the organization who have potential for moving one organizational level higher.

Figure 12.4. Leadership Inventory Approaches.

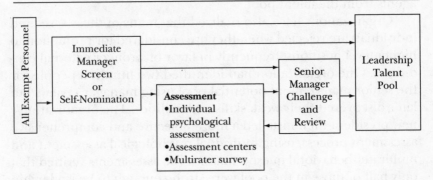

The purpose of the screening process is usually clear: for example, to identify replacement candidates for a particular job position, candidates for a particular talent pool (high potential, early identification, management trainee, and the like), or candidates for a particular team, task force, or corporate initiative. Immediate managers are asked to screen and identify candidates who have certain skills and abilities, certain areas of expertise, or certain career experiences that qualify them for career opportunities. Sometimes the hurdle is set fairly high. In large, hierarchical organizations, candidates often need to have the potential to move at least two organizational levels higher to be included in the high-potential talent pool. Often the screen is focused on the individual's past work experience and expertise. The immediate manager may also broadly screen on leadership skills.

The screening process is often seen as ineffective because it can produce ineffective candidates. Many immediate managers have difficulty separating past or current job performance from the potential to handle larger future responsibilities effectively. Screening can also be contaminated with a number of other purposes. The immediate manager may inflate an individual's potential to encourage her to stay with the organization. Frequently individuals who do not always agree with their immediate manager may not be included in the talent pool. This can produce talent pools of norm-following individuals who fit well into an organizational hierarchy and are selected because they are loyal to and supportive of their immediate manager. It also often eliminates many change agents from the talent pool.

Organizations have also realized that many of these screened individuals are rejected when they are considered for promotion to higher-level positions, frequently in favor of stronger external candidates. One organization had identified two hundred people for the senior management potential pool using manager reviews but later discovered their weak skills and abilities. The organization's new president then installed a more objective and comprehensive assessment process, using individual psychological assessment and multirater behavioral questionnaires. The assessments verified that only half of those in the pool were strong enough to be leadership candidates.

Other organizations have introduced sophisticated assessment tools, not only to provide a more objective and accurate evaluation but also to assess skills needed for the future. Immediate managers may not understand or recognize future-oriented skills, much less evaluate these skills in others.

Sometimes individuals have the opportunity to self-nominate themselves for consideration and thus express their career interests and ambitions. Self-nominations are typically followed by an immediate manager screen. Occasionally, the individual is allowed to self-nominate directly into the assessment process. In this way organizations use personal motivation as a screen.

In more sophisticated organizations, screened (or self-nominated) individuals are reviewed and challenged by senior managers. In these reviews, individuals are more thoroughly discussed and vetted. They are removed from the talent pool if managers have sufficient doubt about their candidacy. Any significant talent pool reductions at this stage, of course, raise questions about the adequacy of the screening process. Candidates are then sent through an assessment process to document their leadership skills. Sometimes all those who pass the immediate manager screen are assessed. In one organization, individuals can self-nominate themselves to participate in an assessment, and the assessment results are shared with the organization only voluntarily by the individual.

Assessment Approaches

The assessment process is usually designed to capture the skills, abilities, and career experiences outlined in the leadership needs profile. This means identifying assessment tools that can evaluate not only leadership skills and abilities but also specialized skills such as financial analysis, business planning, or strategy development and situation-driven skills such as the ability to handle business start-ups, business turnarounds, presentations to the investment community, or media press conferences.

In addition, corporations capture a career history of each individual that includes past job positions and responsibilities in different functional areas and also specific organizational experiences such as a business start-up, turnaround, or expansion. Other experiences may also be noted, such as working for a difficult and demanding manager or managing a tough financial situation. In some organizations, experience working for specific managers may be considered important.

The assessment process is designed to capture a wide range of information and follows one of three paths.

An Individual Psychological Assessment. This process is widely used particularly for leadership selection and leadership team development objectives. The process often includes these components:

- A background history questionnaire
- A career and competency focused interview
- Cognitive tests
- Personality and interest inventories
- Leadership simulations
- A multirater feedback instrument

During the process, either on the background form or in the interview, the individual's past positions and responsibilities, organizational experiences, and specific technical skills and abilities are explored. The assessment process often uncovers unusual experiences or expertise that might be leveraged by the organization in the future.

An Assessment Center. This process usually covers two or three days of simulations, testing, and interviews. Often a multirater feedback instrument is also included. In some ways this is similar to an individual psychological assessment except that greater time is devoted to simulations and groups of individuals experience the assessment at the same time. Simulations allow for direct observation of how an individual handles organizational situations, rather than just asking for self-report descriptions. Typically, assessment centers are used only in organizations that can justify the expense and the time associated with them by assessing large numbers of individuals. One large organization that has long used assessment centers schedules several executive-level assessment centers and ten to twelve upper-management-level assessment centers each year. There is some evidence that assessment centers once developed and implemented can have drifting validity if they are not carefully administered and monitored (Schmitt, Schneider, & Cohen, 1990). This means keeping the staff well trained and the assessment center process standardized.

A Multirater Assessment Process. A written questionnaire or an interview can be used to collect ratings and input from a range of individuals who regularly interact with a candidate at work. Written multirater feedback instruments are standardized behaviorally based questionnaires that are frequently customized specifically for an organization and that have become widely used (Tornow, 1993). The results can be useful to highlight a consensus by the respondents on an individual's effective and ineffective behaviors and to identify very specific behavioral development needs. This tool, widely used to evaluate individuals, can also can be used to identify the strengths and developmental needs of a group or talent pool.

Another approach, one pursued by fewer organizations, is a leadership assessment based on telephone or in-person interviews with ten to fifteen people who have working relationships with the individual candidate. The interviews are one to two hours long and follow a structured list of questions in an effort to identify the individual's skills. This technique can be particularly effective at collecting rich behavioral examples and anecdotes. It is less effective as a standardized data collection process, because the unique views and observations of each person interviewed limit the opportunity to standardize the responses in order to summarize the data easily across interviewees. Although this process produces data that are harder to integrate into an overall profile of the candidate because of the diverse views, it does provide a deeper understanding of some unique issues or talents associated with a candidate. The interview process is also more expensive and time-consuming than a written survey. Assessment psychologists will find it difficult to conduct more than a few of the interview processes simultaneously, not only because of the time demands but also because of the difficulty in keeping the collected data clearly separated and not commingling information across candidates.

Individual Feedback

The assessment process should include a feedback session with each individual, communicating the results of the assessment. This session helps the individual to understand his strengths and developmental needs in comparison to the leadership success profile and to develop an individual development plan. This actively involves the individual in the assessment results without requiring that the organization inform the individual whether he is in a specific talent pool. Consequently, an organization can maintain confidentiality over the composition of the talent pools.

Leadership Analysis

The process of analyzing the leadership assessment data and matching it to the leadership needs of the organization usually occurs on several different levels: individual, team, departmental, or functional level or unit or organizational level.

Individual Candidate Level. The first step is usually to look at the assessment results of each individual to determine if the profile of strengths and developmental needs qualifies her to be included in a particular pool. Usually, organizations list criteria necessary to qualify for certain talent pools. Progressive companies emphasize future-oriented rather than past-oriented competencies. For example, the skills of managing and driving change may be more important to future organizational success, whereas being loyal and following orders may be less important in the future. Some talent pools require specific career experiences or functional knowledge to qualify. For example, individuals in a start-up talent pool may be required to have at least some past start-up experience. A rapidly growing retail corporation that is regularly opening new stores may want to identify district manager candidates who have had past experience opening new stores. In order to qualify for a finance high-potential pool, an individual may be required to have specific accounting or auditing experience.

Individuals who are considered for talent pools typically need to qualify in several areas: requisite skills and abilities, work experience, and an interest in career advancement. Some highly talented individuals may be included in several talent pools, such as a functionally specific talent pool, a position-specific talent pool (for start-up managers or candidates for plant manager positions, for example), or a broad leadership potential pool.

Team, Departmental, or Functional Level. The next level of analysis occurs at a functional, department, or team level. A particular department in an organization such as accounting may want to determine how many people have potential for being accounting managers and how that compares to accounting manager needs expected over the next three to five years. A start-up team that is developing and marketing a new product line and is facing fast growth may want to determine whether the organization has the talent necessary to manage and sustain that growth. A marketing-driven organization may want to know if there is sufficient marketing talent in the organization to continue an aggressive consumer marketing campaign. In these situations the numbers of individuals in each talent pool are compared against the anticipated needs.

This level of analysis may also take into consideration the career stages of those in the talent pool to determine if there is an appropriate number of individuals at various career levels to provide a constant flow of candidates for the target positions. Does the manufacturing talent pool have sufficient numbers of individuals at different career stages to be a constant source of strong candidates for plant manager positions? Will there be enough candidates ready in the next two, five, and eight years? In some organizations this means having a new hire, early identification, or management trainee talent pool in which individuals hired following college or graduate school are assessed and followed for several years at the beginning of their careers.

Business Unit or Organizational Level. The broadest level of analysis usually is conducted at the business unit or corporate level and compares the organization's leadership needs (executives, senior managers, and general managers) to the leadership potential pool. This analysis usually requires summarizing across departmental and functional areas to cull out and identify those who have the greatest potential for advancement into senior leadership positions.

These analyses are usually completed annually or biannually and document

- The actual skill levels and competencies of each individual in the pool
- The group strengths and developmental needs of each talent pool
- The promotion readiness and availability of the candidates in the pool
- The specific developmental needs or work experience needs of the candidates

Develop and Implement Leadership Plans

The final step is to review the results of the leadership analysis, then develop and implement plans for leveraging the talent that exists and building the talent that is missing. This step can have a major impact on the organization's future performance.

Organizational Reviews

Once the leadership analysis has been completed, organizations typically hold a series of organizational review meetings to discuss the analysis and make decisions about the adequacy of the available talent. The review meetings may focus on particular functional areas or business units but ultimately look at the broad organization-wide analysis (see Figure 12.5).

The review discussions often focus on three levels: individuals, departments and functions, and business units and the overall corporation. The discussion of individuals may focus on the following questions:

1. *Should the individual be in the talent pool?* The review of the individual's assessment profile should decide whether the individual sufficiently meets the criteria for inclusion. The review group may also identify missing skills or work experience.

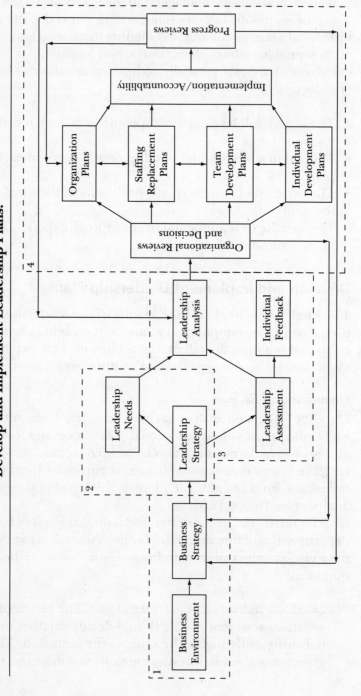

Figure 12.5. Step Four of the Strategic Leadership Change Model: Develop and Implement Leadership Plans.

2. *What career opportunities should this individual be considered for given the skill profile?* Some candidates have unusual skills, talents, or work experiences that may make them more qualified for some career moves.

3. *What competency or work experience deficits need to be addressed in the future?* Frequently, a candidate overall is qualified to be included in a talent pool but may be missing some experiences or skills. The review group often identifies these areas and in the planning discussion specifies career moves or developmental plans that can overcome these deficits.

In rising to the function- or department-level discussion, the organizational review may concentrate on the following issues:

- Are there sufficient individuals in the candidate pools to meet our functional and department leadership needs?
- Is the talent available at different organizational and career levels to sustain a constant flow of talent?
- Are there any unique issues associated with the talent pool? For example, given the perceived shortage of strong information technology (IT) managers that currently exists in the United States, the organization might anticipate an unusually high turnover in this talent pool and more aggressively recruit IT talent from outside the organization.

The final part of the review, usually at the business unit and the corporate level, may consider the following issues:

- Is there sufficient internal leadership talent to lead the organization over the next five to ten years?
- Does the leadership talent have the necessary skills and expertise to change the organization, meet changing business needs, and accomplish business strategies?
- Does the talent pool contain a sufficient number of broadly based, diverse general managers who could readily step into a variety of leadership roles?

Leadership Plans
Many organizations then make plans for individual development, team development, staff replacement, and organizational devel-

opment to address talent shortages, to capitalize on existing talent, or to anticipate future strategic shifts.

Individual Development Plans. Following the leadership analysis, organizations may put plans in place for building the needed leadership skills internally. In the case of leadership selection this may mean working with the hired or promoted candidate to shore up skill areas that need development. It might also mean creating and implementing developmental plans for other internal candidates rejected for the position in order to strengthen their candidacy in the future.

Similarly, developmental plans are often created for individuals who are part of a leadership team or are included in a leadership talent pool. These plans not only address specific skills but also frequently recommend career moves to provide individuals with specific organizational experiences that will prepare them for other responsibilities.

Team Development Plans. Team development initiatives include both individual development plans and plans for developing the entire team. This may involve identifying group skill strengths or deficits and determining how well the team profile matches the team's business objectives and goals. Team development plans may focus not only on specific skills and abilities for the team but also on changes in how the team operates and functions (for example, in its decision-making and communications processes).

Staffing Replacement Plans. Organizations commonly try to determine whether they have sufficient internal talent not only to fill current positions for the next several years but also to staff positions emerging in the near future. This means identifying a slate of candidates and developing their skills and abilities for a target position. If the target position has numerous incumbents, such as plant managers, then the organization may take a broader staffing initiative, perhaps building stronger ties with universities and colleges that produce effective plant management trainees so that more high-potential candidates can be hired directly out of school for entry-level positions that will lead to plant management. More careful tracking of internal candidates in the plant management career track might also be initiated.

Organizational Plans. In many situations, broad organizational plans are needed. In the case of a shortage of plant manager candidates, plans might include putting in place a plant manager development program with job rotations, plant manager assistant positions, or management trainee programs, or even an external hiring initiative to bring in seasoned plant managers. All of these tools are available to an organization that wants strong internal replacements for key positions.

At times the organization may anticipate a significant change in the leadership skills needed in the future. A skill shortfall is more likely in the management ranks—for example, when an organization is shifting from a technical orientation to a consumer-driven orientation, it is likely that the organization needs to develop a customer-driven mentality, marketing expertise, and consumer leadership skills. Sometimes individuals who have had little visibility in the past emerge with skills uniquely suited for the future organizational direction.

Organizational plans can include a broad range of recruiting, staffing, and internal development initiatives. An organization might decide to focus on developing a single competency to ensure corporate viability. This focus might include broad training and developmental efforts or even the acquisition of another organization that has the needed talent. This occurs in the investment community, where different organizations have developed an expertise in mergers and acquisitions or in bonds or currency exchange. In order to move an organization quickly into one of these areas of expertise, it is not uncommon for investment firms to merge with or acquire another firm in order to obtain the expertise. Wall Street firms frequently adopt a strategy of buying intact groups that have developed the competency as opposed to starting from scratch and building the talent inside. Some organizations now have annual leadership initiatives in which they focus on one or two leadership skills each year, leveraging the organization's resources to build the talent pool.

Implementation, Accountability, and Progress Reviews

Once the plans have been determined, the next step, rarely taken by most organizations, is to hold individuals and teams accountable for the implementation of the plans. Only a few organizations do this well. By assigning accountability to specific senior managers and holding progress reviews, the organization can monitor plans and evaluate their success. Periodically, organizations also need to review the entire leadership change process to identify what seems to be working well and what needs to be changed to overcome ongoing obstacles. By reviewing progress against plans, organizations provide a feedback loop for modifying plans and sometimes modifying business strategies.

Impact on Business Strategy

Progressive companies are now understanding the relationship of internal human resources to strategies. Once an organization has taken a close look at its internal leadership talent, it may consider refining, or in some cases redirecting, its strategies based on that available talent.

One design engineering company, which had a staff of five thousand employees and was known worldwide for technical expertise in designing nuclear power plants, faced a major organizational challenge when the nuclear power plant industry collapsed in the 1980s. Few, if any, nuclear power plants were being designed or built because of safety concerns. The challenge was to take a close look at organizational capabilities and internal human resources to determine how best to redirect the organization. After a careful review and analysis of all exempt staff, the decision was to pursue business opportunities that focused on building technical and manufacturing facilities for corporations. Particularly targeted were industries with complex technical requirements for their facilities, such as the chemical, oil, and pharmaceutical industries. This organization focused on internal talent and technical expertise as a foundation for setting new business strategies.

Leadership talent issues may also affect business strategies when an organization has extended difficulty filling the leadership needs required by the current strategies. An example is a large textile manufacturing organization that provided greige goods to consumer product apparel companies. Their clients converted the greige goods into products sold directly to the consumers. However, because of changes in the industry, the organization started seeing the value of providing branded greige goods that could be sold at a premium and also opportunities for producing consumer products itself that it could sell directly to end use consumers. These changes required marketing and consumer product talent.

Once the top managers realized that no one in the organization had these skills, they developed plans for identifying and recruiting the necessary talent from the outside. After two years of trying to identify the necessary talent for their business strategies, the organization realized that it was going to have difficulty finding and attracting the type of consumer product expertise needed for its narrow market niche. As a result, the managers decided to focus on providing branded greige goods that could be marketed to their corporate clients at a premium, rather than trying to sell products directly to consumers. In this case the organization pursued certain business strategies that could not be fulfilled because of a lack of talent and expertise. As a consequence, it had to modify its strategies to reflect available talent.

Critical Steps

Although there are numerous steps in the strategic leadership change process, four are critical:

1. Once the business strategies have been specified, it is important to convert those strategies into an organizational leadership strategy.
2. The exact leadership skills and expertise that are needed should be specified.
3. A cornerstone of the process is to complete a valid and reliable assessment or inventory of available leadership talent.
4. Leadership plans need to be specific and accountability for the plans needs to be assigned to ensure organizational progress and leadership change.

These are the key leverage points that often differentiate successful efforts from less successful ones.

Critical Assessment Issues

A cornerstone of effectively implementing a leadership change process is accurately evaluating the leadership talent. Increasingly, organizations are using psychological assessment for that purpose, particularly as they begin to realize that different types of leaders are needed for different business situations. The process of using psychological assessment to evaluate key individuals in leadership positions takes a variety of forms. Often leadership assessments occur as part of a larger organizational initiative that may include the assessment of individuals, an entire senior management team, all high-potential individuals, or all managers in a particular function.

Key Issues

When completing leadership assessments, psychologists need to consider some key issues.

Assessment Purpose

Managers are often concerned about why they need to go through an assessment process. They question the benefit to the organization and to themselves. Organizations need to be effective at clearly communicating the benefits to both. The individual manager needs to understand why it is in the organization's interest to collect assessment data on individuals. The organizational purpose may be to develop the management team, plan for leadership succession, or implement an organizational strategy.

The primary benefit to the individual is individual development. Although there seems to be a lot of homage to individual leadership development in organizations, it frequently gets lost in the list of other priorities and demands on managers. Although developmental priorities might get identified and developmental suggestions generated, an actionable developmental plan for the individual does not always result. Even when the plan is drafted and agreed on by the individual manager, progress against the plan is usually intermittent, and the plan is often forgotten in a few months. Most leaders and managers have experienced various developmental programs in their careers and are often not enthusiastic about going through an assessment process. Therefore the organizational purpose needs to be clearly stated and convincing in order to get managers' involvement and commitment.

Confidentiality

Most leaders during their career have been gaining experience, building their reputation, and learning additional skills. Consequently, they may be concerned that a psychological assessment process may uncover unflattering characteristics or that skill deficits may be misinterpreted or overshadow their reputations. They generally dislike activities they cannot control or influence or whose outcomes they cannot accurately predict. Assessors may be seen as potential threats who may inappropriately share assessment information, particularly if an assessor has a strong relationship with senior managers.

Consequently, many organizations and assessors provide a written statement outlining the limits of confidentiality so that managers clearly understand what data will or will not be shared in the organization. This is a critical step in gaining their commitment.

Commitment

An organization's ability to use psychological assessment effectively is based partly on the trust level in the organization. Individuals will be concerned that assessment data may outweigh their performance records. It is not uncommon, for example, for some senior managers to misuse or misinterpret an individual's scores on cognitive tests; these managers may allow the scores to overinfluence their perspective and opinion about the individual.

Many managers may base their commitment to the process on their trust in how the organization will use the assessment data. If there has been a history of trust and openness in the organization and a CEO or president who has forged strong relationships with the other managers, then there may be a greater willingness to participate in the process. In these organizations, the managers will have more confidence that the assessment data will be used in an objective and professional manner. This is not always the case, however. Managers' suspicions are often based on

- A lack of trust in the company culture
- A highly political culture
- A distant CEO, president, or immediate manager
- A history of subjective and questionable judgment in human resource decisions
- A highly competitive peer group
- A poor internal communications system
- An environment of uncertainty or ambiguity

- Pressure on managers to improve organizational performance significantly

Frequently the executive who is driving the assessment initiative, often the CEO or president, will clearly communicate to the participants the organizational benefits and why participation is important, and at the same time issue a directive in which the CEO or president either clearly expects that everyone will participate or even mandates participation. In some organizations, participation is stated as optional; nevertheless the CEO or president states a preference that everyone will participate. In this case, individual managers may have a hard time resisting the informal pressure. Usually, though, once the CEO or president is committed and clearly communicates the purpose and benefits, other managers and leaders usually make a commitment to the process.

Logistics

Because of the busy schedules of most managers and the complexity of the assessment process, the logistics of actually conducting the assessment can present some challenges. Because leadership assessments frequently take at least one day, and sometimes several days, planning must be done well in advance in order to reserve contiguous time on the individual's calendar. Having a group of managers assessed in the same time period only increases the scheduling challenge. Because most managers carefully schedule and control their own calendar, the assessment schedule is usually negotiated with each individual or administrative assistant separately. Not infrequently, managers insist on breaking the assessment process up into pieces, which might require two or three half-day sessions.

Providing Results and Feedback

It is particularly important to distinguish what assessment results are shared with the manager and what are shared with the organization. For many assessment initiatives, only group data are reported back to the organization. This may be a condition requested by the managers to gain their participation. Typically, individual data are reported to the organization for succession planning and leadership selection efforts.

In team development efforts, individual data may be presented to the whole team but not connected to individual names. Therefore the group can see the distribution of individual scores without knowing the scores of any particular individual. Often group members will decide to be free and open with their scores and will actually share their individual data.

Individual managers may be concerned that the organization will receive a report or summary that the individual has not seen. At higher organizational levels the individual almost always gets a copy of whatever is provided to the organization. Even in succession planning activities the individual gets a clear understanding of the assessment results, though perhaps not his status in the succession plan.

Use of Information

Once the assessment has been completed, the individual will watch to see if the data are used in a way consistent with the original purpose. The most typical problem is that the organization emphasizes a developmental purpose, but senior managers use the assessment results in selection decisions. This not only violates the ground rules underlying the original commitment but also exacerbates the concerns of the managers about misuse of the information. This problem can be solved by putting the original purpose in writing and distributing it so that it is widely read at the beginning of the process. In this way, individual managers can hold the organization accountable to the original purpose.

Who sees the information is also of some concern. Generally the individual's manager reads the assessment report, which is shared with the organization and typically an HR representative. In some cases the report is shared with the CEO and senior managers. In succession planning activities a senior HR staff member may have responsibility for summarizing the data across individuals, with results shared only on a need-to-know basis. Who has access to the data is an important decision for the integrity and trustworthiness of the process.

Storage

Related to the question of who uses the information is the question of how the assessment data and results are stored. Some organizations prefer to have individual assessment data maintained by an external assessor. If an internal assessor is used, then the assessment data should be stored to strictly limit access. Preferably the data should be in an assessor's office under lock and key and not released to anyone who is not professionally qualified to review psychological data.

In most cases the assessment reports are securely stored somewhere in the organization—typically in restricted HR files that are not part of general personnel files, with access on a need-to-know basis. In at least one organization the reports are not distributed at all; senior managers can read the report in a special reading room but may not take a copy with them. This organization also will read the report to certain managers over the telephone. In most organizations, however, a copy of the report may be sent to select managers if there is a clear purpose. Access by the immediate manager varies depending on the purpose and on the level of the individual going through the assessment. At senior levels, it is more likely that the immediate manager would get a copy of the report. At lower levels, it is less likely.

Organizations need to have a written policy on handling and storing the assessment data and need to follow that policy carefully in order to maintain the trust of the individual participants and the integrity of the system.

Organizational Applications

Following are four cases of actual organizations where the leadership change model has been applied relying on individual psychological assessment. (Identifying information has been changed to protect the identity of the organizations. In some examples, two organizations have been blended into one case.) These four examples show how psychological assessment can be used to produce significant impact in an organization.

Case One: Leadership Selection

This $3 billion chemical manufacturing company has grown significantly over the past twenty years, developing a market niche by producing high-quality specialty products. The tremendous growth occurred under the leadership of a single person, the CEO. This individual thoroughly knew the product manufacturing process, was a dominant personality in the organization, and made all the decisions herself. Because of some minor health problems and being at an age approaching retirement, the CEO decided that she needed to find her replacement. She had tried to do this several years earlier on her own, but with no success. The heir apparent, hired from a European partner, lasted no more than a few months. The president tended to dwell on that candidate's faults, which indeed were numerous. However, there was some question of whether the CEO was really ready to let go of the corporate reins.

This was a significant leadership selection step for the organization. The CEO did not want to fail a second time. She decided to identify a replacement again and hired an external consulting psychologist to design and assist with the selection process. The process began with numerous discussions with the CEO and other managers on business strategy and the specific leadership skills that would be needed to implement that strategy over the next ten years. The strategies focused on branded products and expansion overseas. A very specific list of leadership skills, abilities, and experiences was identified. The list grew long, primarily because the incumbent insisted that her replacement have not only all of her product manufacturing skills and leadership abilities but additional skills in consumer marketing, reengineering, and computer-assisted manufacturing, as well as international experience in order to take the organization to a new performance level. This created a significant challenge because it seemed that such candidates would be impossible to find. Further discussions then separated competencies and experiences into primary and secondary categories.

The specific leadership assessment process was designed to evaluate those skills and abilities and included a lengthy background interview, a multirater feedback instrument (for internal candidates), and two leadership simulations (problem analysis and role play exercises), as well as cognitive, personality, and interest inventories. The assessment process took a full day with the assessment psychologist. Five internal candidates and three external candidates were identified. The president had clear opinions about all the candidates, but she kept them to herself while the assessments were being conducted. The assessment process hinged not only on accurately evaluating each candidate against the needed leadership profile but also on providing a thorough and credible process that the CEO could believe in. After all, the CEO was willing to let the psychological assessment process have a major influence on who would run the corporation in the future. It was also important that the selection process have credibility with the investment community.

After all the assessments were completed and assessment reports were written, a presentation to the CEO and board members compared all candidates, weighing the strengths, deficiencies, and developmental needs of each. They identified a single candidate who seemed to stand above the rest. This person happened to be an internal candidate who had a history of significant conflict with the president, having been fired and later rehired. After much discussion the CEO decided that she was prepared to appoint the individual as chief operating officer immediately and then as president within two years. The candidate had significant manufacturing experience but was not as knowledgeable in this area as the CEO. However, the candidate did have consumer marketing and international experience.

After the CEO's decision, feedback was provided to all candidates, and individual development plans were developed for all internal candidates, including the successful candidate. A plan of action was laid out for the successful candidate that not only emphasized developing certain skills, among them being how to build a stronger relationship with the CEO, but also a timetable for adding additional responsibilities.

Five years later, the transition process is working well. The consulting psychologist continued to work with both the CEO and the president to build their relationship, transfer authority to the president, and help both learn their new leadership roles The former CEO, now chairman, is ready to retire officially, and the appointed president is not only thriving but expanding the organization. Over the five years, several senior managers in the organization have been replaced. Many had been with the organization a long time, and their job responsibilities had grown past their ability to accomplish them. They had survived primarily because a dominant CEO had made all the key decisions and had given them little latitude or authority. The new CEO has the vision and insight to bring in stronger talent.

The individual psychological assessment process was the key factor in providing for CEO succession and providing the leadership talent needed to accomplish business growth strategies. The corporation has been growing 10 to 15 percent annually for the last five years. The impact of this leadership selection process was not only to identify an effective CEO replacement but to influence the relationship with the board chairman and carve out a new role for the chairman. The objective and comprehensive assessment process was the foundation of this leadership intervention.

Case Two: Leadership Team Development

A relatively young organization in the insurance industry was spun off from a well-known New York financial institution, having developed a unique quantitative approach to personal insurance. The organization was started by four bright entrepreneurs who first sold the idea to the financial institution, then joined the organization, built the business unit, and spun the unit off as a separate corporation. The strategy was so successful that the organization has grown rapidly over the last six years to be a highly successful and highly profitable organization of eighty-two hundred employees. The company leaders have introduced some innovative ideas, particularly computer-based marketing, into their market and have captured significant market share.

The four leaders decided to staff the organization with very bright talent straight out of college. Therefore most of the current managers and executives in this organization are under thirty years old, with no prior management experience and little prior working experience. The challenge was to develop the leadership talent in this organization quickly enough to keep up with the rapid growth. Most of these young managers and executives thought they knew everything there was to know about managing an organization; they thought their school success and the company's success proved their individual leadership skills.

Clearly the business strategy in this organization was connected to its talent strategy, which focused on specific technical skills and abilities needed for the computer-based marketing strategy. However, the stated talent needs were quite narrowly focused and did not include many other competencies necessary for effective organizational leadership.

The leadership team development approach began by looking at business strategies, particularly growth expectations, and determining the range of talent that would be needed to achieve those objectives. This led to a broad discussion of leadership needs.

All twenty senior executives were encouraged to participate in a team development process that included not only a focus on team dynamics and effectiveness but also individual psychological assessment of leadership skills. The process led to lengthy team discussions about the skills, abilities, experiences, and decision-making processes that would be needed to help the team meet its aggressive objectives. A comprehensive leadership profile was outlined that captured the competencies needed to build the organization and sustain growth in the future. Fifteen senior executives participated in the process; the other five decided that the process was either irrelevant to their work or too time-consuming. Each of the fifteen leaders participated in individual psychological assessments.

Following the assessments, written assessment reports, and in-person feedback sessions, the participants held a series of meetings in which they discussed group assessment results, identified team strengths and developmental needs, and created team development plans. The plans addressed not only the team's leadership needs competencies, but also steps for improving the effectiveness of team communications and decision making. In addition, each team member drafted individual development plans. Twelve individuals agreed to participate in a one-year executive coaching process. Periodic team meetings focused on the team's ability to implement those plans.

At the two-year mark, progress on those plans is mixed. Some members have made outstanding progress on their individual plans, and others only a little progress. After several organizational restructurings, several members have left the organization; other members, particularly those who seem to take their development seriously, have moved into more significant positions. Efforts at improving communications among the team and changing the decision-making process were seen as successful according to a follow-up team survey.

The individual psychological assessments served as the cornerstone of the individual development, team development, and coaching initiatives. The impact of the assessment intervention was to help a new organization recognize the full range of leadership skills needed to build and effectively manage a business organization. The assessment data gave individuals objective feedback on their leadership skills and potential. Some capitalized on that opportunity, whereas others, confident in their existing technical skills, never fully appreciated the importance of leadership skills and as a consequence have not progressed in developing their skills or advancing their careers.

Case Three: Leadership Planning

This technically driven computer manufacturing organization had a long-standing dominant position in its market, primarily because of the difficulty competitors had in gaining competitive technical expertise. The organization produced leading-edge computer specialty products for business. In the past five years, however, it had become evident that a few domestic and international computer corporations had emerged as strong direct technical competitors in the business market. The competitors were also known for strong direct marketing and customer service skills and were well established in computer products for nonbusiness consumers.

This organization historically provided quality products and service at a premium price and had a long track record of significant and steadily increasing earnings. The emerging competitors were providing competitive technical products to business at lower prices and using their marketing skills to erode the organization's revenue base. Although the organization remains the largest player in its market, its executives realized that its business strategy needed to focus on both the business and consumer markets. Because the new technologies being introduced were widely shared, the organization no longer had a significant technology advantage and needed to become more customer-marketing driven.

In this situation the business market environment required a change in business strategies. The organization estimated that it would have approximately five years to identify and build the talent pool needed to implement the strategies and meet this new competitive threat. The first year was focused on thoroughly analyzing market opportunities, developing the appropriate business strategies, and building a leadership talent strategy. These strategies were carefully developed given the huge financial cost of significantly changing the organization.

Interviews were held with twenty senior officers to help articulate the appropriate talent strategy and leadership needs, based on the newly identified business strategies. The interviews were particularly helpful in translating business strategies to talent strategies.

In addition, two other initiatives were undertaken. The first was to develop an internal leadership needs survey that was sent to 450 internal managers and executives, asking them to clarify the important issues existing in the organization related to identifying, developing, and using leadership talent; to state their opinions of currently used leadership assessment services and assessment tools that should be useful in the future; and to rate the importance of sixty leadership competencies for effective future performance in the organization. The other major initiative was to conduct a benchmark study of leadership practices in twenty-one major U.S. corporations known for leading HR development practices. This study was conducted in conjunction with another major corporation and involved one-day visits to each of the corporations participating in the study. Together with this study of corporate practices, a literature review was conducted on each of the topical areas in the corporate practices study: HR development, succession planning, executive development, training and development, career planning and development, and leadership assessment.

The outcome of these initiatives was a leadership success profile that defined the leadership skills, expertise, and organizational experiences that future leaders would need. This leadership profile served as a foundation for defining future leadership needs. Additionally, the different types and numbers of leaders were determined. The emphasis in the leadership profile was on innovation, customer service, marketing, motivating and developing subordinates, and taking calculated risks. The profile was widely discussed and supported by most executives. It was clear, however, that changing a hierarchical, technically oriented organization into a quick-moving, customer-driven marketing organization would take some time. Many of the senior officers had built careers based on their technical abilities and had little insight into what it would take to be customer driven.

The next step was to build a leadership planning process that would identify, develop, and use the leadership talent that was needed. This meant conducting a wide-scale inventory of existing leadership talent in the organization. An immediate manager screening process surveyed all exempt employees to identify candidates for early identification, management potential, and executive potential talent pools.

A series of organizational review meetings followed at functional and business unit levels to review all the candidates for the three talent pools and to brainstorm individual development plans for those who were included. The next step was several corporate-wide review meetings in which senior officers presented their candidate pools for discussion. In addition, 25 percent of the individuals were recommended for a full individual leadership assessment. The intent by the organization was to put approximately 25 percent of the talent pool through leadership assessment in each of the next four years in order to evaluate the complete talent pools fully and objectively. In the first year, 25 percent of the individuals with the highest management and executive potential were selected for assessment. It was also decided that all candidates for the early identification talent pool would be assessed in the first year. The results of the assessments were reported back to the senior officers so that formal individual development and career plans could be determined.

As it turned out, the first year of this process was in fact a trial year. Managers and officers in the organization were trying to grasp the expected organizational changes based on the changed business strategies. Although some effort was made to redefine the leadership talent pool, many of those who were nominated tended to match the old executive skill requirements, not the new leadership success profile. As a consequence, when the candidate nominations were presented at the corporate-wide meetings, it became apparent that many of the candidates did not qualify for the newly redefined talent pools. In fact, the senior officers significantly reduced the candidates in each pool and kept only those candidates matching the new leadership profile.

Plans were put in place not only to assess and develop individuals in the talent pools but to move key individuals so that they could gain specific organizational experiences to prepare them as replacement candidates for key positions. Organizational initiatives were taken to introduce managers to the concept of an innovative, customer-driven organization and to train them to help create that organization. Staffing plans were put in place to recruit external managers and executives with needed leadership skills. Commitments were made among executives to exchange candidates and implement certain developmental strategies. The senior officers also committed to an eighteen-month cycle of quarterly meetings to monitor the progress of the leadership planning process and hold each other accountable for achieving certain goals.

This process has been in place for five years, and the organization has made dramatic improvements in its manager and executive staffing decisions. It is also making significant inroads into the consumer product market while stopping the erosion of its business market.

The impact of individual assessment and the leadership planning process on the organization cannot be underestimated. It has influenced the design and implementation of a broad range of HR and business initiatives, including modifications to organizational structure, compensation systems, executive selection decisions, and numerous leadership training and developmental interventions. The full impact on the organization will be seen in the next few years.

Case Four: Strategic Leadership Change

Approximately fifteen years ago, this organization, a $10 billion consumer products company, entered a new, larger market offering a new line of consumer food products in an attempt to challenge the dominant competitor in that market. For the first ten years, it pursued the dominant leader using aggressive marketing and pop culture icons to appeal to younger consumers and create generational differences in product preference. The organization, clearly marketing driven, became widely recognized for innovative approaches and creative thinking. A good deal of the financial and human resources were devoted to the marketing effort, and the strongest talent was identified and leveraged in the marketing function.

The organization gave creative, bright individuals an opportunity to have significant marketing visibility and responsibility early in their career, but it also put them under a great deal of pressure. The turnover rate in the marketing department tended to be high, with an emphasis on recruiting individuals with creative talent early in their careers, putting them in major management positions, and installing an up-or-out culture in which those who were not getting promoted every six to twelve months were seen as not being the strongest players. Many soon left for highly visible and more stable positions in other organizations.

The organization made such significant advances in increased market share that the market became almost evenly split with the primary competitor. This changed the business strategy from a high-growth, aggressive marketing approach to a head-to-head competition between two formidable competitors, neither of which was likely to capture a dominant market position again. The business strategy switched from gaining market share domestically to maintaining market share domestically while growing globally. The focus shifted from being a high-growth start-up organization to being a well-managed corporation that could be a major competitor in the mature market. After numerous discussions, it became evident that the talent strategy needed to shift from emphasizing only marketing talent to finding strong leaders in all functional areas. Clearly the leadership needs had shifted to broader management and leadership skills. The organization decided to identify internal candidates with leadership potential, particularly individuals with skills in motivating, influencing, and developing others; building interpersonal relationships; and managing work through others.

Individual psychological assessments were completed on the top one hundred managers to identify the depth of leadership potential in the organization. The assessment process included two management simulations (a problem analysis in-basket exercise and a problem subordinate role play), cognitive tests, personality and interest inventories, and a career background and competency interview. These assessments were typically done with groups of four or eight individuals in order to cost effectively involve assessors, psychometrists, and participants.

Analysis of the assessment data revealed that only 25 percent of the individuals currently had potential to be effective leaders. Although a majority were seen as being bright, personally motivated, and creative, they also were independent and self-focused, and had little interest in or skills for managing and motivating others.

Organizational discussions and reviews of the information resulted in decisions to modify existing HR systems in order to shift the focus toward identifying and rewarding leadership talent as opposed to only marketing talent. The organization put together a five-year organizational plan designed to change the recruiting, selection, promotion, performance appraisal, and compensation systems with the objective of becoming a well-managed corporation. Although the organization wanted to maintain its marketing expertise, it wanted to put an equal emphasis on similarly rewarding leadership talent. Organizational and replacement plans were put in place for identifying and promoting individuals with leadership potential. The marketing team participated in leadership development and training. The organization also put in place a review process that annually surveyed the talent in the organization.

This is an example of an organization that consciously identified how a change in the business environment directly affected its business strategies and leadership strategy. The impact of psychological assessment in this organization was significant. The leadership change process was driven first by business environment changes and then by the assessment process that not only uncovered the widespread shortages of leadership potential but also identified the specific developmental needs of the talent pool.

The organization's ability to meet the business challenge was dependent on identifying the skills that were needed, the leadership talent that existed internally, and the plans necessary to build the talent pool.

Ripple Effect on the Organization

Leadership assessment, of course, can have a significant impact on the individual being assessed. For all four organizational applications, the assessment process allowed individuals to:

- Understand their skills, abilities, and developmental needs
- Construct an action plan that encourages them to leverage their strengths and to build their skills in areas that need development
- Identify gaps in their experience or knowledge that may need to be addressed to advance their career
- Understand how well matched they are with current and future career opportunities

These benefits should not be underestimated, particularly in leadership selection, where the selected individual not only faces new challenges and learning opportunities but has increased influence over changing and modifying the entire organization.

Frequently organizations overlook the impact of psychological assessment on the organization; it often ripples through HR systems, leadership strategies, and even business strategies. In all four cases, individual psychological assessment has had a range of potential influences on the organization.

Impact of the Individual on the Organization

Assessment results and feedback can give individuals insight into their own talents and their influence on others. The results and feedback help individuals see how they can leverage their skills to gain influence and effect change in the organization. By capitalizing on existing skills while also learning new ones, individuals can identify situations and positions that are well matched to their skills profile.

An example is the manager who is uncomfortable and ineffective when speaking to large groups but feels confident and is more effective when speaking to small groups or individuals. Besides working on her public speaking skills, this person can look for opportunities to influence others through small groups such as informal get-togethers, employee lunches, or one-on-one meetings. By knowing their strengths and capitalizing on them, individuals can increase their effectiveness and their impact.

Impact on Team Collaboration and Productivity

Individuals who go through a psychological assessment process simultaneously with their peers or direct reports get the double benefit of understanding not only their own assessment results but also how their skills and abilities match the skills and abilities of others on the leadership team. Individuals thereby see their unique contributions to the team and ways to be more collaborative with other team members.

Assessment also allows team members to have a better understanding of team strengths and developmental needs, so they can leverage their talents and consciously take steps to address team shortcomings. Team members gain insight into how the team profile may affect the team's ability to deliver on business goals.

An example is the case of a team of detail-oriented, structured, and norm-following individuals that is asked to reengineer a work process. Frequently this group focuses on tried-and-true, narrow approaches and has difficulty coming up with truly innovative approaches. This team may be handicapped by not having the conceptual thinking skills to see significantly different possibilities. The members are more likely to make small and minor changes in the process than to challenge their own assumptions and consider more significant changes. The group's assessment profile can help members understand the group problems or limitations and the skills that are missing on the team. By addressing team deficits and developmental needs, the team can improve its effectiveness and its productivity.

Impact on the Organizational Culture

Organizations have often been identified as marketing driven, technology driven, or finance driven. Often a single functional area gains a reputation in the organization not only for being highly effective but also for being the major driver in achieving business goals and strategies.

Similarly, organizations may consciously or unconsciously emphasize certain competencies over others through their recruiting, selection, and promotion systems. In the past, certain corporations, such as IBM, PepsiCo, and American Express, had well-known and distinct profiles of specific skills needed to succeed in each organization. One company profile might hire individuals who are highly aggressive, bright, very motivated, and competitive, while another might select individuals who are thoughtful, analytical, comprehensive, and cautious. Although these organizational profiles exist, they typically are not well articulated. Often organizations drift into habits that encourage the proliferation of certain types of individuals, and are not fully aware of the extent to which a skewed distribution of skills may exist in the organization.

In both of these situations, where the leadership profile is either well known and encouraged or unknown, it can be useful to an organization to use leadership assessment to determine its actual distribution of skills. Where the profile is well known and seemingly monolithic, the organization needs to know whether other types of leaders exist in the organization. Leadership diversity is often critical if the organization must adapt to a variety of business situations.

This raises the question of whether an organization should create a specific leadership success profile and insist that all managers and executives match it. It may skew the decisions and the performance of the organization if all the managers have the same strengths and presumably the same biases, deficiencies, and blind spots. Most organizations need a balance of strengths, particularly in different functions. Only in select single-minded groups is it helpful to have homogeneity. For example, small start-up organizations often benefit from having a similar group of entrepreneurial leaders. In most organizations, however, the leadership profile should be able to accommodate some range of leadership diversity.

Leadership assessment can play an even greater role in organizations where a specific leadership profile is not well defined and or promoted. In these organizations, there usually is poor information about the skills and abilities of the talent pool. Leadership assessments and a thorough leadership analysis can clarify what talent exists and point to the steps that can improve the leadership talent pool. By determining a leadership profile, the process can also help define the organizational culture.

Impact on Business Strategy

In some organizations the leadership assessment and analysis process has led to revised business strategies. Some organizations have changed their strategic plans and time lines because of the realization that they have insufficient talent to accomplish certain strategies. For example, some organizations, realizing that there is a significant shortage of leadership in information technology, have decided to outsource the function instead of trying to compete for the talent in the market.

The idea widely held in the 1970s and early 1980s that a strong leadership executive team could effectively and profitably run any type of business has been replaced by a view that organizations ought to identify their organizational competencies or areas of effectiveness and focus on them, or as a few well-known authors (Peters & Waterman, 1984) have stated, they need to "stick to their knitting." In essence, this is a realization that certain types of leaders with certain skills, work experiences, and expertise are best matched to specific business situations (Gerstein & Reisman, 1983).

Although it has been clear that the effective manager in a consumer products company may be different from the effective manager in a heavy industrial manufacturing organization, it also is emerging that the type of leadership skills needed for a start-up organization may be very different from those needed for other business environments such as turnaround or high-growth situations. Organizations are now starting to differentiate strategically driven leadership needs.

In general, organizations need to match the leadership talent to the business situation. This matching process requires organizations to specify the business situation and do a thorough job of assessing the leadership talent pool. Some refer to this as a strategic selection (Gerstein & Reisman, 1983). As organizations become more sophisticated in their HR practices, they are moving toward a strategic matching of leadership talent to business needs and in some cases changing their business strategies to capitalize on their existing leadership talent.

Conclusions

This chapter has addressed the use of psychological assessment as a cornerstone for strategic leadership change in an organization. The strategic leadership change process typically has four key steps:

1. Determine business strategies.
2. Identify leadership needs.

3. Assess leadership talent.
4. Develop and implement leadership plans.

Most organizations specify their business strategies but have difficulty translating those strategies into a leadership talent strategy and specific leadership needs. This connection tends to be a weak link. Once specific leadership needs are identified, organizations often have difficulty objectively and reliably assessing leadership talent against those needs.

Once organizational plans and action steps are in place, it is important to assign accountability and have periodic progress reviews. This step of accountability and progress reviews currently defines the leading-edge organizations in the area of strategic leadership planning. Very few organizations have taken this step. Those that have are seeing clear benefits.

Strategic leadership decisions can have a critical impact on the effectiveness of an organization and the ability to achieve business strategies. Since the late 1980s, organizations have begun to understand the significant impact that leadership resources can have on the success of an organization. As a consequence, the HR function has gained increasing influence and is more likely now to be seen as a strategically important function in the organization. In the future, organizations will become as sophisticated about managing their leadership resources as they are about managing their financial resources, using those resources to influence the strategic direction of the corporation.

References

Beer, M. (1997). The transformation of the human resource function: Resolving the tension between a traditional administrative and a new strategic role. In D. Ulrich, M. R. Losey, & G. Lake (Eds.), *Tomorrow's HR management* (pp. 84–95). New York: Wiley.

Cannon-Bowers, J. A., Tannenbaum, S. I., Salas, E., & Volpe, C. E. (1995). Defining competencies and establishing team training requirements. In R. A. Guzzo, E. Salas, & Associates, *Team effectiveness and decision making in organizations* (pp. 333–380). San Francisco: Jossey-Bass.

DeVries, D. L. (1993). *Executive selection: A look at what we know and what we need to know* (Rep. No. 321.) Greensboro, NC: Center for Creative Leadership.

Gerstein, M., & Reisman, H. (1983, Winter). Strategic selection: Matching executives to business condition. *Sloan Management Review,* pp. 33–49.

Goodman, P. S., & Associates (1986). *Designing effective work groups.* San Francisco: Jossey-Bass.

Guzzo, R. A., Salas, E., & Associates. (1995). *Team effectiveness and decision making in organizations.* San Francisco: Jossey-Bass.

Hackman, J. R. (Ed.). (1990). *Groups that work (and those that don't): Creating conditions for effective teamwork.* San Francisco: Jossey-Bass.

Hamel, G., & Prahalad, C. K. (1994). *Competing for the future.* Boston: Harvard Business School Press.

Heskett, J. L., & Schlesinger, L. A. (1997). Leading the high capability organization: Challenge for the twenty first century. In D. Ulrich, M. R. Losey, & G. Lake (Eds.), *Tomorrow's HR management* (pp. 25–38). New York: Wiley.

Hewitt, G. (1997). Corporate strategy and human resources: New mind sets for new games. In D. Ulrich, M. R. Losey, & G. Lake (Eds.), *Tomorrow's HR management* (pp. 39–47). New York: Wiley.

Hollenbeck, G. (1994). *CEO selection: A street smart review* (Rep. No. 164). Greensboro, NC: Center for Creative Leadership.

Klimoski, R., & Jones, R. G. (1995). Staffing for effective group decision-making: Key issues in matching people and teams. In R. A. Guzzo, E. Salas, & Associates, *Team effectiveness and decision-making in organizations* (pp. 291–332). San Francisco: Jossey-Bass.

Mohrman, S. A., Cohen, S. G., & Mohrman, A. M., Jr. (1995). *Designing team-based organizations: New forms for knowledge work.* San Francisco: Jossey-Bass.

Peters, T., & Waterman, R. H., Jr. (1984). *In search of excellence.* New York: Random House.

Porter, M. E. (1980). *Competitive strategy: Techniques for analyzing industries and competition.* New York: Free Press.

Porter, M. E. (1985). *Competitive advantage: Creating and sustaining superior performance.* New York: Free Press.

Schmitt, N., Schneider, J. R., & Cohen, S. (1990). Factors affecting validity of a regionally administered assessment center. *Personnel Psychology, 43,* 1–12.

Silzer, R. F. (1991, June). *Executive assessment.* Workshop presented at the Metropolitan Washington, DC, Personnel Testing Council, Washington, DC.

Silzer, R. F., & Graddick, M. (1996, April). *Corporate leadership planning: Identifying, developing, and utilizing leaders to accomplish corporate strategies.* Workshop presented at the annual conference of the Society of Industrial and Organizational Psychology, San Diego.

Silzer, R. F., & Hollenbeck, G. P. (1992, April). *Executive assessment.* Workshop presented at the annual conference of the Society of Industrial and Organizational Psychology, Montreal.

Silzer, R. F., Slider, R. L., & Knight, M. (1994, June). *Human resource development: A study of corporate practices.* Atlanta, GA: BellSouth and Anheuser-Busch.

Tornow, W. W. (1993). Introduction to special issue on 360-degree feedback. *Human Resource Management, 32,* 211–220.

Ulrich, D. (1997). *Human resource champions.* Boston: Harvard Business School Press.

Ulrich, D., Losey, M. R., & Lake, G. (Eds.). (1997). *Tomorrow's HR management.* New York: Wiley.

PART 4

Perspectives

CHAPTER 13

Anticipating the Future
Assessment Strategies for Tomorrow

Rob Silzer
Richard Jeanneret

The only way to predict the future is to have
the power to shape the future.
ERIC HOFFER, 1954, P. 78

Individual assessment is not only about predicting the future but also about shaping it through selection recommendations, organizational interventions, and behavioral change programs. Although assessors are not the only decision makers involved in selecting individuals, they can have significant influence over many human resource decisions. This power to influence the future needs to be used ethically, wisely, and professionally. We recognize the value of individual assessment but also want to provide some cautions against its misuse.

This chapter focuses on our views of the future. We provide an integrating framework, possible new directions, and some professional guidelines that will continue to be important for assessment practice.

Individual Assessment Framework

There are a number of different assessment approaches, different in terms not only of procedures but also of theoretical frameworks.

445

Nevertheless we think that there is enough common ground for proposing a general framework for individual assessment (see Figure 13.1).

For experienced assessors, many of these steps will seem obvious, although some might argue with the order of the steps. Kaplan (Chapter Six), for example, approaches interpreting and integrating data simultaneously with reaching conclusions and communicating results. Levinson (Chapter Seven) might take the position that the process of reaching conclusions is influenced by understanding the organizational context. However, what a number of assessors do not sufficiently pursue are the steps of facilitating the impact of assessment in the organization and following up on assessment outcomes. We outline each of the assessment steps and consider several key issues and some future directions for each step.

Understanding Organizational Context

Key Issues

Most assessors initiate the individual assessment process by receiving a request for an assessment from a client. This historical approach often places the assessor in a reactive and order-taking role. We believe, however, that the assessor has a responsibility for knowing the organizational context before considering the request. Assessor psychologists need to be partners with their clients in recognizing organizational issues and responding with alternative solutions that will influence the assessment process and outcomes. Davis (Chapter Eleven) has provided an insightful discussion of the organizational variables that need to be considered before making the decision to conduct individual assessments. Both Davis and Silzer (Chapter Twelve) emphasize the need for assessors to understand the business strategies of an organization. We believe that the assessor has an obligation to know the organizational context before a discussion about assessment is even initiated. Some of the key contextual issues to consider include

- Business strategies
- Organizational structure
- Executive roles and responsibilities

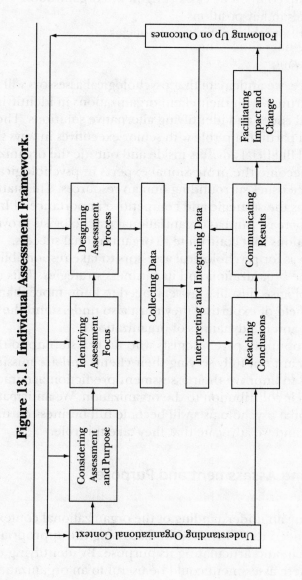

Figure 13.1. Individual Assessment Framework.

- Organizational capabilities
- Organizational priorities
- Cultural and political environment
- Leadership competencies existing in the organization
- Individuals in key positions
- Human resource initiatives and policies

Future Directions

In the future, we anticipate that psychological assessors will be integrated partners with their client organizations in identifying organizational issues and identifying alternative solutions. They will move into a partnership role with senior executives in ways similar to legal and financial advisers inside and outside the organization. They will become the professional experts in psychological and performance issues surrounding human resources. This status will be earned as the strategic and competitive importance of human resources increases and as organizational psychologists provide effective solutions that contribute to organizational success.

The key is for psychological assessors to take responsibility for knowing the organization and its business strategies. This means that psychologists, just like lawyers, need to know more than their particular field of expertise; they must also understand the world of business and the dynamics of organizations.

In our opinion, psychologists who do not step up to this responsibility are not fully serving their clients and are missing opportunities to improve their assessment prediction accuracy and increase their contribution to the organization. We anticipate that organizational psychologists will become full business partners in the future, and we advocate that they take this role.

Considering Assessment and Purpose

Key Issues

After gaining an understanding of the organizational context, psychologists need to be involved in discussing the appropriateness of assessment and articulating its purpose. By identifying opportunities where assessment could be useful to an organization and discouraging situations where it might be misused or inappropriate, psychologists can help organizations learn how to use individual assessment effectively. Again, this requires the psychologist to be a partner and an early participant in the discussion about the role of assessment in the organization.

Assessment has been used for a variety of purposes. There are certain critical points at which individual psychological assessment can make a significant contribution to organizational and individual effectiveness. These critical points, often described as organizational needs or assessment purposes, include the following:

- Evaluating external candidates for selection into important positions
- Evaluating current employees for promotion opportunities
- Gaining an in-depth understanding of an individual to develop that person's skills and abilities
- Helping an individual understand his or her skills and interests in order to plan his or her career
- Diagnosing an individual's current performance issues
- Helping the organization make decisions about the fit between the person and the job when significant changes occur in job performance requirements and expectations
- Surveying for critical competencies in the redeployment of human resources
- Planning leadership change and succession in an organization
- Analyzing the leadership competencies of a broad organization
- Collecting team assessment data in developing team effectiveness, decision making, and communications
- Helping individuals plan for retirement and lifestyle changes.
- Conducting an inventory of leadership and management talent in order to implement or modify business strategies
- Evaluating compatibility or bench strength during mergers or acquisitions

Any of the above purposes may be the reason for assessment, but in fact many assessments have multiple purposes. Obviously the purposes should be stated and communicated to all parties involved in the assessment process.

Organizational psychologists may also need to consider alternatives to individual assessment, especially when there is very little trust within the organization or when the potential participant is hostile to the assessment process. The alternatives might include assessment centers, multirater feedback surveys, or a series of interviews; each needs to be understood for its benefits and drawbacks.

Future Directions

The psychological assessor who functions as a business partner needs to work with organizational clients to assist them to understand the value and determine the appropriateness of assessment for the business situation. Individual assessment will be used for a broad range of organizational needs and purposes in the future. In particular, the use of individual assessment for personal development and behavioral change will become even more widespread. Assessors will also become personal coaches to assessment participants in an effort to leverage assessment data to support behavioral change.

We believe that some psychological assessors will emerge as major players in helping an organization to understand the strategic importance of its human resource competencies. This means not only having an active role in leveraging psychological assessment for leadership planning, organizational restructuring, and executive team development, but also advising the organization on the implications of human resource competencies for business strategies and organizational effectiveness.

Not only will the range of purposes broaden, but the influence of psychologists in determining when to use individual assessment and how to leverage the assessment data for organizational benefits will continue to grow. Many organizational psychologists will become key advisers to CEOs and presidents, as some already are.

Identifying Assessment Focus

Key Issues

Once individual assessment has been selected as a course of action, the key issues surrounding the assessment need to be identified. If the purpose of the assessment focuses on selecting or matching individuals to particular job or career opportunities, then a preassessment analysis seeks to identify the requirements, success factors, or performance expectations associated with those job or career opportunities. If the assessment is for the purpose of developing personal skills and changing behavior, then the skills, abilities, or competencies to be evaluated need to be specified. Assessment issues that need to be explored include the following:

- Job requirements and performance expectations
- Key competencies that are required
- Unique expertise or experiences that are needed
- Organizational environment or culture
- Reporting relationships
- Organizational change initiatives
- Historical context of the position, job performance, and job incumbents
- Organizational values
- Cross-cultural issues

Assessment is no different from any other tool or system used for human resource decision making in the need to consider job-relevant information. It does not matter whether this information is labeled as job requirements, skills and abilities, or competencies. What is important, however, is that the information be documented so that it can have an important role in designing the assessment and in interpreting, predicting, and communicating results. The link to job information also provides the job-relatedness connection mandated by both statutory guidelines and professional principles. It is valuable to remember that jobs are changing rapidly and that job information should be focused on tomorrow's demands as much as today's requirements.

The focus of an assessment may involve one or more measurement constructs:

- Integrated personality: attempts to understand the assessee in a holistic way
- Aptitudes or cognitive abilities: those most frequently measured are verbal, numerical, and abstract reasoning
- Traits: dispositions to behave in certain ways
- Skills: abilities learned from experiences
- Behavioral responses: descriptions or actual samples of behavior

Each of these constructs can be matched to the competencies that are being evaluated. For example, thinking competencies are often evaluated by focusing on cognitive aptitudes and behavioral responses, whereas interpersonal skills may shift the focus to traits and behavioral responses. Some competencies may involve all the measurement constructs.

Psychologists need to have an understanding of what they are assessing prior to the assessment (surprisingly, some do not and discover this only after the assessment). Assessors need to have an understanding of the assessment focus ahead of time but also need to be open to discovering unexpected data during the assessment. There needs to be a balance. An exclusive emphasis on one approach or the other will likely lead to more limited results.

Future Directions

We anticipate that in the future assessors will better understand these assessment issues and their direct impact on the assessment process. In addition, we anticipate that case studies will be used to help assessors understand the interrelationship of competencies, measurement constructs, and performance outcomes. We anticipate as well that organizations and assessment psychologists will develop a greater openness to and a research framework for studying and reporting on these relationships. We need to know far more than we do about the situational variables and psychological constructs that influence the effectiveness of individual assessment.

Designing the Assessment Process

Key Issues

Frisch (Chapter Five) has noted many of the issues to consider when designing an assessment. The assessment process should be planned to collect the information needed to evaluate the competencies that are the focus of the assessment. Many assessors and consulting organizations tend to use a single standard assessment process for all purposes and all business situations. This often misses the opportunity to tailor the process to specific business situations and needs. A one-design-fits-all approach may compromise assessment validity.

A variety of assessment tools can be included in the process. Assessments that only use a single assessment tool such as an assessment interview or a battery of cognitive tests significantly limit the validity of the assessment. We still periodically encounter clinical psychologists who rely exclusively on an assessment interview for data collection or industrial psychologists who rely exclusively on a battery of cognitive tests. In fact, one psychologist, with little attention to test administration issues, not only collected data solely through cognitive tests but faxed these timed tests to participants to take and had the participants fax back their completed answer sheets. We strongly believe that this violates basic assessment principles and calls into question business and psychological testing ethics.

Assessment tools can fall into several categories: tests and inventories, interviews, simulations, multirater surveys, and other types of questionnaires. The psychometric properties differ among them. Generally the reliabilities (test-retest, parallel form, or internal consistency) of most objective assessment instruments are high (Jeanneret & Silzer, 1990; Silzer & Jeanneret, 1987). Alternatively, the reliability of information obtained with projective techniques is usually below .60 (Jeanneret & Silzer, 1990; Lanyon & Goodstein, 1982). For behavioral measures such as work simulations, a wide range of reliability data is reported, but the overall conclusion is that most are satisfactory (Jeanneret & Silzer, 1990; Silzer & Jeanneret, 1987). Assessor interview reliability research is not prevalent, and indications are that reliabilities may be marginal (Arvey & Campion, 1982). Unfortunately there is no clear trend for assessors to convert to the more reliable structured interview approach (Chapter Three).

One technique often overlooked or rarely used is behavioral observation of how an individual in a natural work environment makes decisions and addresses issues. Such observation can be a rich source of information, although it is a somewhat unstandardized data collection approach that can be intrusive and costly and is not feasible to use with external selection candidates.

Assessment tools fall into three categories: psychometric, observational, and interview based.

Psychometric approaches rely on standardized tests or inventories as vehicles for data collection. These tools usually are accompanied by information on test reliability, validity, and norms. However, a number of psychological instruments used for selection assessment in organizations were not designed for that specific purpose. Unfortunately, assessors may frequently rely on tests that have little face validity and do not relate to job performance behavior. The Thematic Apperception Test is an example.

Observational tools such as work simulations provide opportunities to observe and evaluate the individual's behavior directly in worklike situations. Examples include group discussions and some types of role plays. The key issues are to choose tools and design a process that uniquely fits the specific organizational needs, addresses the assessment purpose, and evaluates the relevant competencies.

Interview-based tools such as the assessment interview typically involve the assessor listening to the individual's responses and hypothesizing about characteristics of the individual with little systematic analysis. Although it is possible to develop and implement structured and scored interviews, we believe most interviews rely on the psychologist's intuitive judgment about the assessee's response. Some assessors are prone to use only the interview method because of their views regarding the inadequacies of psychometric tests. The interview is also expedient in that it combines data collection and data analysis. We advocate that assessors test their interview-based hypotheses against other predictors and criteria obtained as part of the assessment process.

Future Directions

The range of assessment tools has been broadening over the decade with an emphasis on behavioral data and standardized tools. A good deal of attention recently has been devoted to multirater feedback instruments and also personality inventories. We anticipate that each of these will be validated for specific assessment purposes and competencies, although we do not believe that either one, used exclusively, can provide a comprehensive assessment.

We think the future direction of assessment design will have two major themes. The first will be to continue to develop, validate, and standardize assessment tools. This means not only redoubling efforts to validate existing tools but developing new ones too. We anticipate that tomorrow's tools will include cognitive ability tests that operationalize new theories of intellectual functioning (Gardner, 1993), new personality inventories that are more directly applicable to work behavior, and behavioral interview methods that are more competency driven and are evaluated in a less intuitive manner. We also anticipate more widespread use of work simulations as part of individual assessment. In addition, a number of other assessment data collection efforts that are now often only a tangential part of the assessment process need to be standardized and validated: biographical data, resumé information, work experience questionnaires, and on-the-job observations.

A second major thrust will be the broader use of computers and information technology in the assessment process. Currently research efforts are investigating the administration and scoring of tests and inventories by computers. This effort will continue and may become standard practice. It will also be extended to simulations and exercises and to multirater questionnaires. The one exception might be the assessment interview. Although interviews could feasibly be accomplished over computer networks, the technology might limit the assessor's ability to have an intuitive understanding of the individual through face-to-face interaction. However, even in this area, as computer screens accommodate live video images, assessment interviews might be conducted over the Internet. It would be interesting to determine the comparability of Internet assessment interviews with face-to-face interviews. In addition, computers will be more involved in integrating assessment data and in aiding assessors to reach assessment conclusions and predictions.

These two themes will be coming together so that individual assessment not only will be accomplished using more reliable and more valid instruments and tools but also will be conducted over computer networks. This is the future of assessment design.

Collecting Data

Key Issues

The process of collecting data is fairly straightforward and has received attention in the preceding chapters. The basic data collection process follows some fairly clear principles of standardized administration. We advocate using written administrative procedures and certainly having well-trained psychometrists and assessors.

The most challenging aspect of this step is for assessors to be well trained not only in the exercises, tools, and competencies but also in the ability to create and test hypotheses about the individual during the interview. This may mean following up during the assessment interview on certain intuitive ideas about the individual in order to verify them or to identify alternative explanations.

This raises the issue of whether interviewers should know the results of other collected assessment data prior to conducting an initial assessment interview. There are differences of opinion here. One position advocates that the cognitive tests and personality inventories provide strong clues of areas to probe and hypotheses to test in the assessment interview. The other view is that the data collection tools should be independent sources and not contaminated by each other. By using test data to guide the assessment interview, the assessor will find it difficult not to look for and find confirming information. Although this second perspective may lower the possibility of validating the test data during the interview, it also raises the standard by insisting on getting confirming but uncontaminated data from two independent sources. In the long run this will strengthen the assessment process by using a higher standard for reaching conclusions.

Future Directions

The direction of data collection will move toward computers and electronic administration. Although we believe that this is feasible for many assessment tools, it may take a while for the technology to become sufficiently sophisticated for interviews and interpersonal simulations.

Interpreting and Integrating Data

Key Issues

Once assessment data are collected, they must undergo interpretation by the psychologist. The interpretation process includes understanding the meaning of test scores or individual responses, integrating the information from the various data sources, and organizing the information in a manner that will lead to useful predictions.

This is a key step in reaching sound, valid conclusions. Assessors need to consider the reliability and validity of various data sources; understand what inventories, tests, and tools are actually measuring; and objectively weigh and integrate the data. There are many ways in which judgment error can enter into the process. This may be particularly true for assessors who have been conducting assessments for a long time and have fallen into habits of judgment and integration without ever validating or objectively reviewing them. Every assessor needs to be aware not only of potential errors made in particular situations but also of the fallacies of human judgment in general (Einhorn & Hogarth, 1978, 1981).

Individual assessment in some situations involves several assessors and offers an opportunity to provide multiple independent perspectives. Assessors should periodically have other assessors review and integrate the same assessment data in an assessment case and derive independent conclusions for comparison as a double check on the assessment process. Reviewing case studies and holding case discussions among trained assessors is a valuable way of improving the assessment integration process.

Where comparative judgments are necessary, psychologists will be evaluating the assessment data on more than one individual. For example, the results for two or more individuals may be compared in order to determine who is the strongest candidate for a particular position. Unfortunately, there is virtually no research that addresses the psychometric quality of these comparative judgments.

Kaplan (Chapter Six) has shown that integrating and interpreting data can be an iterative process involving the participant in reaching conclusions and communicating results. This can be particularly true for personal development assessments but is less feasible for selection assessments. Certainly there has been considerable discussion among clinical psychologists about interpreting and integrating data, particularly in the debate over clinical versus mechanical data collection and data integration approaches (Dawes, Faust, & Meehl, 1989; Meehl, 1954; Wiggins, 1973).

The practice of psychological assessment could benefit from a strong research base that has evaluated the psychometric characteristics of all of its components. Psychologists now must rely on whatever is known about the psychometrics of various assessment techniques, with the expectation that these qualities carry forward to the individual assessment process. For the most part, this is the point at which psychological research knowledge stops. Consequently, there is minimal research knowledge about the capabilities of assessors to make reliable and valid interpretations of assessment data or predictions about an individual's behavior and performance. Clearly there are numerous research opportunities to expand this knowledge, although the research design issues are especially difficult because of small sample sizes and unique assessment cases.

Future Directions

There have been several attempts since the late 1980s to integrate assessment data mechanically, and there is some support for this, particularly when standardized, reliable, and valid psychometric instruments have been used (Dawes et al., 1989; Silzer, 1984). However, efforts so far to use mechanical integration for complex competencies and jobs have not yet been successful.

For years, the advantage has been given to statistical or mechanical integration methods based on the analyses of Meehl (1954) and Sawyer (1966). However, individual assessment psychologists have traditionally avoided this approach. Even those who rely on some statistical combination of test data still use clinical judgment to modify the interpretations and reach their final conclusions. It seems reasonable that assessor judgment will always be required.

We advocate that the next step is a more formal combined mechanical and clinical integration process. There is evidence that reaching predictions based on a mechanical data integration process and then providing that prediction to the assessor to consider in making a final clinical judgment integration seems to have some merit (Silzer, 1984). We encourage assessors to look for ways to introduce mechanical integration processes but still provide a role for the assessor. Assessors should be able to modify the mechanical prediction, taking into account the reliability and validity of various instruments, as well as their own assessment knowledge and judgment on how the different pieces of data fit together.

Reaching Conclusions

Key Issues

Reaching conclusions is a complex challenge of considering not only the integrated assessment results but also the organizational context. It produces predictions of performance effectiveness or future behavior. Sometimes the process of communicating results to the individual or to the organization may also influence or facilitate reaching sound conclusions (Kaplan, Chapter Six). Few assessors really understand the range of issues or the dynamics involved, much less how organizational variables should be integrated in reaching sound predictions.

Future Directions

As assessment psychologists become partners with their business clients and are more involved in organizational issues, they gain sophistication in understanding the impact of organizational variables on accurate predictions. Earlier chapters explored the range of organizational, situational, and individual variables and their impact on reaching accurate conclusions. We anticipate that these relationships will begin to unfold with some clarity as assessors better understand organizational dynamics. However, the speed of organizational change in some ways has complicated the ability to research these issues adequately. One future direction is to document the important interrelationships and to provide case studies that demonstrate them.

Communicating Results

Key Issues

Meyer (Chapter Eight) has explored a broad range of issues related to communicating assessment results to individuals and organizations. He also has documented the professional and ethical issues described in Chapter Four. Certainly assessors need not only to be aware of their professional and ethical responsibilities but also to work toward understanding how the communication process affects both the individual and the organization.

Future Directions

It is likely that the communication process will become more electronically based. Assessment reports may be transmitted with some security code to the organization and in some instances to the individual participant. Telephone communication will also be used more widely to provide feedback and further discussion of the assessment conclusions to the participant. Eventually video computer monitors may be used for interactive feedback sessions, just as video conferencing is currently used for group interactions.

Second, assessment results will be communicated increasingly in ways that are useful to both the organization and the individual. Results will become more behavioral and less psychometric, concentrating more on clear and understandable behavioral issues and even specifying the work environments, immediate managers, job challenges, and business situations that will be effective or ineffective matches for the individual.

Although assessments for developmental purposes are becoming more prevalent, there still is widespread use of assessments for selection and promotion decision making. However, even in selection circumstances, there is a need for feedback to the individual of the assessment results. Every individual assessment should provide some form of feedback to the participant. We believe this should be and will become standard practice.

Facilitating Impact and Change

Key Issues

There is a widespread movement toward using individual assessment as a foundation for individual development and behavioral change. This outcome will become even more prominent in the future as many organizations insist on leveraging the data for specific individual development benefits.

In addition, the connection between individual assessment and organizational change will become evident as assessor psychologists delve more deeply into organizational issues. More frequently, assessment is being initiated for organizational change and impact (Chapters Eleven and Twelve), but it will also be seen as an influence on future organizational direction.

Future Directions

In the future we will become more knowledgeable and sophisticated about effective or ineffective behavioral change efforts following certain assessment results and in certain business situations. We may find that a particular developmental strategy or technique for building interpersonal communication skills is effective in certain organizational settings and not in others. The ability to change individual performance behavior becomes an important field itself.

Increasingly we see the involvement of assessment in broad-scale organizational change. Silzer (Chapter Twelve), in particular, has outlined how assessment can play a fundamental role in executive selection, leadership team development, leadership succession planning, and strategic leadership change. The question will be whether assessment psychologists dealing with individual cases and psychological data can learn how to leverage assessment data for broader organizational uses.

Not only should assessments be designed in a manner consistent with an organization's business strategy; they also should be recognized as part of an effort to create organizational change. The change occurs because the assessment process has helped to identify, select, or develop people who can help achieve the business strategy. This gives increased importance to assessment in the development of individuals and organizations.

Following Up on Outcomes

Key Issues

Clearly this step is the one that is rarely taken but critically needed. For many years, the clinical research literature has demonstrated the importance of validating assessment predictions. Anyone trained in empirical research methods understands this as a fundamental premise of the work. However, it is rarely addressed by assessor psychologists. Part of the problem has been that assessors have not had access to follow-up criterion measures of performance (and have not insisted on this access) in trying to validate assessment predictions. In addition, the techniques used to measure behavioral job performance accurately have measurement problems themselves. We urge assessors, particularly those doing large numbers of assessments for single organizations, to design validation projects and follow up on them to strengthen their understanding of the relationship between assessment results and job performance.

Future Directions

We believe that the future is likely to provide increased opportunities for psychologists to do informal as well as empirical research follow-up on their behavioral predictions. Assessors using assessment for large organizational initiatives should try to collect both predictor assessment and performance criterion outcome data in order to document the organizational benefits.

Similarly we anticipate that standardized multirater behavioral questionnaires may become more reliable and valid performance criteria measures. We challenge assessors to create and test more sophisticated performance measures. Certainly the work of Borman and Motowidlo (1994) has helped us understand job performance in a more complex way. We are hopeful that their research, along with other initiatives in measuring job performance, will lead to more sophisticated criterion measures. Designing these more sophisticated measures is critical to conducting better follow-up on assessment outcomes.

Broad Issues

The individual assessment framework provides an opportunity to focus on particular stages in the assessment process and discuss key issues. Additionally, there are a number of overarching issues in the assessment process that are not focused on any particular step but are nevertheless important to highlight.

Assessment Theory

Key Issues

In order for assessment to continue to evolve as a science and to be supported by research, there is a strong need for assessors to begin with and be influenced by relevant theories. The value of theory is evident when it is realized that the purpose of assessment is to predict behavioral components of job-relevant performance. Although it is possible to rely on the theoretical perspectives of those who developed assessment instruments, the more valuable theories are those that help assessors make accurate predictions about performance and behavior. Hogan and Hogan (Chapter Two) make a strong argument for bypassing the traditional trait theory and even the Big Five theory of personality. They believe that psychological assessment should be organized around socioanalytic theory. From this perspective, the assessment focus should be on measuring and predicting factors associated with individual differences in power and status, individual differences in respect and admiration, and how accurately the individual is able to understand social reality.

Although it is not our intent to endorse any specific theoretical position, clearly some theoretical perspective is essential if individual psychological assessment is to continue to evolve from art to science. Furthermore, we believe that a theoretical basis should influence an assessor's thinking whether or not the purpose of assessment is focused on selection or development. More important, when individual development is the dominant purpose, it may be especially important for the assessor to be aware of how well the assessment strategy fits the theoretical model of choice and whether the model can be useful in guiding a coaching strategy that might evolve as part of the assessment process.

Assessment is a complex process, and it will grow more complex in the future as assessors consider organizational influences and impact. We believe that assessors need to be familiar with theories behind psychological measurement and behavioral prediction but also need to be well rounded as psychologists. They need to understand learning theory, social psychology, and group psychology as well as the individual differences literature. Assessors also need to understand organizational behavior theory, particularly business strategies as they relate to human resource needs and organizational change. Without understanding business issues in organizations, psychologists are limiting their ability to make accurate predictions in the organization and diminishing the relevance of their assessments to the organization. As interest in assessment spreads and assessment providers face increasing competition, assessors will find that they will have no choice but to understand organizational context and how it influences assessment.

Future Directions

We concur with the importance of theory in advancing assessors' understanding of individual assessment in organizations, and we believe that assessors in the future will need to understand the broad range of variables that influence and are influenced by individual assessment. We also believe assessment psychologists need to be trained broadly in psychological theory as it applies to business organizations. Consequently we challenge academic graduate programs in industrial-organizational and counseling psychology to teach the importance of theory in predicting behavior and behavioral change. We also want to encourage cross-disciplinary efforts to integrate different theoretical approaches. How does social learning theory, for example, integrate with individual differences in predicting the behavior of an individual? We also see advantages to assessors gaining some understanding of organizational behavior theory.

Research

Key Issues

Although the practice of individual assessment dates back more than twenty-two hundred years, the research that has taken place is sparse and often lacks rigor. Assessment psychologists are guided for the most part by research studies that examine instruments not designed for measuring job performance or business issues.

The measurement properties important to individual psychological assessment are the same as those that are relevant to any other selection or evaluation program. The standard psychometric parameters of reliability (internal and test-retest) and validity (content, criterion-related construct, and generalized) apply, as does a concern for the adequacy of test norms. Additionally, it is appropriate to consider the fairness of assessment procedures and reasonable to determine the utility (cost-effectiveness) of an assessment. However, the psychometrics are confounded from a measurement perspective because of the very nature of the individual assessment process. Figure 13.2 outlines opportunities to evaluate the psychometric properties of individual assessment data, although virtually all the research focuses on just a single issue in any given study.

Ryan and Sackett (Chapter Three) have pointed out the dearth of research focused on individual assessment. Most of the available research has examined particular assessment tools or has been borrowed from assessment center research. Because of the increasing importance and use of individual assessment, it is critical that assessment psychologists conduct sound research in this field.

It is also critical that universities and colleges, particularly psychology departments with industrial and organizational psychology graduate programs, encourage and support research on

Figure 13.2. Opportunities to Evaluate the Psychometric Properties of Assessment Data.

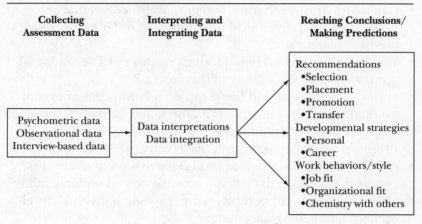

Collecting Assessment Data	Interpreting and Integrating Data	Reaching Conclusions/ Making Predictions

individual assessment. In many schools, such as the University of Minnesota, there has been a cross-disciplinary effort between the counseling and industrial-organizational psychology programs. Unfortunately, individual assessment is almost never taught in graduate industrial and organizational psychology programs, and although it is part of clinical and counseling psychology programs, it typically focuses on diagnosing psychopathology or helping individuals with personal or vocational issues. Rarely do these fields combine their efforts to concentrate on individual assessment in organizations.

Assessor psychologists have escaped the necessity of documenting the usefulness and validity of their efforts. There is a long list of research issues that need to be addressed, including the following:

- What assessment tools are more valid and effective in evaluating particular competencies?
- Are certain assessment tools and procedures more effective than others for certain assessment purposes?
- How effective are new assessment tools such as multirater feedback instruments and new personality inventories in predicting on-the-job behavior?

- What are the critical components and likely judgment errors in the data integration process?
- Can we identify mechanical integration processes that are more effective than clinical integration in order to increase prediction accuracy?
- What else should we know about the impact of assessment administration on the validity of the process?
- How can we understand the complex relationships of organizational variables, situational variables, and individual assessment results in order to reach sound conclusions and decisions regarding selection, placement, and development?
- Are there more effective or less effective ways of communicating results to others to facilitate acceptance and understanding?
- How can assessment best be used to provide individual development and behavioral change?
- How can assessment results be leveraged for broad organizational impact and change?
- How do different assessment tools compare in predicting behavioral performance on the job?
- What situational or business constraints contribute to accurate and valid assessment results?
- What assessor skills are important to conducting valid assessments?
- How should assessor skills be trained?

Future Directions

We want to encourage additional research on individual assessment. As individual assessment gains organizational visibility and more widespread use, organizations may insist on clearer documentation of the benefits and the validity of individual assessment. We anticipate that research may occur in large organizations that are currently using individual assessment extensively or in external consulting firms that conduct a large number of individual assessments and can leverage their assessment database.

Clinical versus Behavioral Approach

Key Issues

Assessors also disagree on whether to use a clinical person approach or a behavioral competency approach to individual assessment (Silzer & Hollenbeck, 1992). The most effective individual assessment process probably is a mix of both approaches. It is important to predict specific on-the-job behavior in an organization, using performance competencies and behavioral assessment tools that can contribute to accurate prediction. However, the individual being assessed needs to be considered as a whole person. Assessors need to understand the interaction of beliefs, values, and behavior in order to understand the individual in a more holistic way. This is particularly true when predicting behavior in a fast-changing, complex organization. This increases assessors' ability to predict accurately the individual's fit in a number of different positions, business situations, and organizational contexts. Assessors need to understand the individual not only at a behavioral level (the way the person motivates direct reports, for example) but also at a broader level (the way the person will function in a start-up situation with inexperienced direct reports and a demanding, micromanaging immediate manager, for example). Is the individual flexible and adaptable to changing organizational demands?

Many assessors have approached assessment in a narrow sense, focusing solely on the individual's scores on various assessment tools. More sophisticated practitioners have focused on integrating that assessment data into specific predictions about behaviors in certain competency areas. However, assessors also need to understand the larger organizational context and situational variables and to consider the whole person before making final predictions.

Future Directions

We anticipate that as assessor psychologists become organizational psychologists, they will learn the interactions of organizational variables with assessment results. We can only hope that this bridge will be crossed by individuals who approach issues in an analytical way and pursue research efforts to document what they are learning.

Diversity

Key Issues

Many organizations are learning how to use individual assessment in a broad range of cultural settings both internal and external to the organization. Clearly in the United States, many challenges are occurring inside corporations as they hire employees with more diversity in their backgrounds. Many organizations, such as NCR and PepsiCo, have already struggled with how to use individual assessment in other countries and globally. Fulkerson (Chapter Ten) identifies a number of the key hurdles in making this bridge.

With the increase in workforce diversity and business globalization, there is an equivalent and growing demand for assessors to understand ethnic, cultural, nationality, and other diversity influences and how they affect the assessment process. Also, psychologists need to consider disabilities and the accommodations that can be made in the assessment process. It is likely that most assessors operate from stereotypes based on past experience. Most of the norms used in assessment interpretations probably lack sufficient diversity to be fully representative of the relevant employee groups. The need for such information will continue to grow, and assessors are rapidly falling behind.

Individuals now participating in assessment are also likely to differ from past participants in other important ways, such as education, experience, and socioeconomic background. The influences of these variables on assessment measures and interpretations are rarely known and are likely to be overlooked by assessment psychologists.

Future Directions

We anticipate that individual assessment in other countries will become more widespread, particularly as U.S. corporations introduce their human resource assessment systems globally. Many assessments now completed on a global basis outside the United States for U.S. corporations are conducted by psychologists native to that country. We anticipate that assessment psychologists will form global networks and learn from each other what tools and techniques are effective in different cultures. This process is only beginning, though some corporations have already faced it; many more corporations will be struggling with this challenge in the next ten years. We anticipate that assessment psychologists around the world will find common interests in sharing knowledge and forming global alliances.

Organizational Influences

Key Issues

Davis and Silzer (Chapters Eleven and Twelve) have noted organizational influences on individual assessment. These influences can permeate the assessment process, even influencing the selection of assessment tools. A deeper understanding of the organization's influences on assessment and a connection of assessment to business needs and strategies should be pursued.

The client organization has a major influence on the entire assessment process. This influence is actually two-way. The organization initiates the influence by deciding to use an individual assessment process for some specific purpose. When a relationship is established, the organization communicates its values and culture, goals, and expectations to the psychologist. It is also useful for the assessor psychologist to gain an understanding of organizational strategies that exist or are evolving that will characterize how the organization will operate in the future. These strategies may be embedded in the core business plan or in other efforts directed toward change. Additional insight may be found in the culture itself, especially in the level of trust that exists, or in the workforce needs and attitudes. Finally, the human resource strategies and the role played by human resource professionals can influence assessment activities. The psychologist must be sure that these contextual variables are in alignment with the outputs that will be delivered as assessment results and predictions. In other words, it is imperative that the psychologist realize that most individual assessments are not just one-on-one events but occur within a defined organizational context that will have significant influence on both the process and the outcome.

Future Directions

We anticipate that as assessors become more involved in broad organizational initiatives that use assessment, they will begin to understand and articulate the organizational influences on each step in the assessment process.

Professional Roles and Responsibilities

Key Issues

The roles of psychologists and managers have changed over the previous ten years. Fogli and Whitney (Chapter Nine) have outlined some of the new organizational roles for managers. Assessors are also taking on new organizational roles as they become partners with the organization.

The professional responsibility of assessors is a critical consideration in the acceptance, design, and delivery of individual assessment services. These responsibilities frequently require psychologists to make ethical choices or decisions that are in conformance with current statutes and professional principles. One strategy for maintaining these responsibilities is to have well-defined policies and practices that address the parameters associated with professional conduct when assessing others. A complement to this strategy is to have well-defined roles for both the assessor psychologist and the clients who are responsible for assessment information and outcomes.

Certainly Jeanneret (Chapter Four) has identified a range of ethical and professional issues that need to be considered in assessment practice. Unfortunately, there are few written guidelines in this area. Some of the approaches that assessors have used have been not only been clearly unethical but in violation of general practice principles outlined by the American Psychological Association. An example are the ads for mail-in assessments that are found in some newspapers. Not only are these often blind ads but they promise validity and accuracy that are never documented.

Future Directions

Once an assessor-client relationship has been initiated, specific written policies and procedures should outline the responsibilities of both the organization and the psychologist. Critical to these responsibilities is the recognition by both parties that there is a two-way client relationship. There must be equity in that relationship without either side having an advantage. At the same time, every effort must be exerted to protect the individual's rights, dignity, and confidentiality.

Assessment psychologists can remain ethically fit by having a full appreciation of relevant professional values and principles. Assessors must understand their duties and obligations as set forth by professional associations and licensing and certification boards. Although there is ample information available to understand these professional responsibilities, we are not certain that every psychologist who provides assessment services is aware of them. Frequently it is not a case of intentionally violating a code of responsibility, a professional standard, or an ethical principle, but rather a lack of information about the proper course of action. If we are correct, then the psychological profession needs to provide more information to assessors to guide them in their practices.

We believe that ethical and professional practice will be more clearly defined in the future. In fact, as part of an effort to facilitate this, we are proposing some guidelines for professional practice.

Guidelines for Professional Practice

The general guidelines that follow are intended for assessors who are conducting individual psychological assessments within an organizational setting. These guidelines are derived in part from the work of Sundberg (1977) and in part from the preceding chapters. The guidelines are relatively broad and are intended to fit many, but perhaps not all, assessment situations.

Clarify the Assessment Purpose

Once an assessor has begun to establish a relationship with a client organization, an early initiative should be to clarify the purpose of the assessment, how the information will be used, what decisions will be made, and in what form the assessment results will be most useful to both the client and participants. This frequently requires an educational process for those requesting the assessment services. In many instances, it also may be useful to help the organization write explicit assessment policies and procedures.

Understand the Organizational Context

Assessment information is typically used to make decisions about individuals who are performing their jobs within a particular organization. This organization has a variety of characteristics that will exert considerable influence on the assessment process and decisions based on the assessment outcomes. It is important to obtain as much information as possible about the organizational context to use in the design and delivery of assessment services.

Obtain Relevant Job Information

The more information there is regarding relevant job performance criteria, the more effective the assessor can be. The assessment psychologist needs to take the time required to learn about the characteristics or competencies that will make a significant difference in job performance. In turn, assessment interpretations and predictions should be focused on these relevant performance competencies.

Standardize the Assessment Process

In most instances, standardization of the assessment process within an organization is likely to benefit all participants. This is especially true if multiple assessors are involved in serving an organization and there are several recipients of the assessment results. Standardization should include not only the assessment procedures and instruments but also the feedback and reporting (oral and written) mechanisms. The expected value should be a level of consistency that will help control for unknown biases or sources of error that might contaminate assessment outcomes. Whenever possible, the input of other assessors to the interpretation and prediction processes should be considered.

Rely on Objective Measures

Generally, instruments that have undergone reasonable psychometric development (scored personality tests, in-baskets, role plays) have the greatest value in making assessment predictions. These objective qualities also should help minimize cultural or social biases that might affect the assessor's interpretations and predictions. Use of objectively scored instruments permits the assessor to develop and use appropriate norms that can guide interpretations and predictions.

Rely on Relevant Assessment Data

The assessment program that relies on collecting as many data as possible may not be more effective than one that focuses on obtaining specific relevant information from fewer sources. This usually requires the assessor to begin with a sound understanding of the job requirements and competencies that lead to successful performance. The intent should be to measure the critical characteristics, rather than "shotgun" every participant with the assessor's favorite assessment protocol.

Make Conservative Interpretations and Predictions

Assessors should stay within the bounds of the information available to them. Tendencies to go beyond the assessment results, sometimes tempting to the assessor and potentially more satisfying to the client, are risky. In response to inquiries that are outside the parameters of the assessment information, assessors should explain that the data are not sufficient to answer that question or should clearly qualify their answers.

Be Aware of Potential Biases

The diversity of individuals who will undergo assessment is destined to increase. With diversity comes the potential for biases on the part of the assessment process, either because of the instrumentation, the interpretations, or the assessors' biases, which influence their predictions and recommendations. Awareness and understanding are the best protection for unwanted bias. Self-evaluation can bring about awareness.

Evaluate Your Effectiveness

Assessors need to learn about the accuracy of their predictions. This opportunity is available during every individual feedback session with the individual. If there are areas of disagreement, the assessor should not assume the individual is being defensive or is not self-aware. Rather, a full exploration of the individual's own evaluation should be made so the psychologist can determine the best possible interpretation for the behavior being discussed. Further, for situations where hiring or promotion decisions have been based in part on assessment outcomes, the accuracy of the predictions and subsequent successes and failures should be reviewed. Assessors then need to evaluate their procedures, interpretations, and predictions in the light of the knowledge obtained about performance and organizational fit. Additionally, assessors should continually look for opportunities to learn about the effectiveness of their assessment practices and seek ways to improve them.

Communicate Results Clearly

The value of the assessment rests on the psychologist's ability to communicate clearly and accurately the information needed by the decision maker. In most assessments, the decision maker is a representative of the organization who is not conversant in psychological terminology. In all instances the other important person to receive information is the individual. This information can be used for self-development whether or not that was the specific assessment purpose. Consequently, the psychologist must use a communication style and language that ensures that assessment information will be correctly understood and that follow-up decisions will be consistent with the assessment results.

A Final Word

We have provided an array of perspectives and opinions on individual assessment in organizations. We have consciously avoided producing a book that is a how-to assessment manual. Our goal was to stimulate and challenge thinking on broad issues related to individual assessment. We hope we have accomplished our goal.

When we consider all the information and issues associated with the assessment of individuals for some organizational purpose, it is clear that the practice relies more on art than science. Although scientific endeavors may expand the basic knowledge about assessment and strengthen the capabilities of psychologists to be more effective as assessors, it is still very likely that individual assessment will continue to remain an art into the foreseeable future.

Psychological assessment is having a significant influence on the lives and careers of a large number of individuals in American organizations, and it has been used for a wide range of purposes in a variety of organizational settings. However, assessment practice has not been well defined or researched. Little effort has been made to provide ethical and professional guidelines for assessment or to understand how individual assessment can be effective in an organizational context. Despite all of these limitations, it has become a widely used human resource tool for addressing individual and organizational decisions and issues. We believe that the time is right for organizations and assessors to document ways in which assessment can be an effective and valid tool for contributing to organizational and individual success.

We challenge practitioners in particular to take their professional and ethical responsibilities seriously. We also challenge academics to initiate research programs in collaboration with practitioners and organizations to understand more fully if and why assessment is effective.

A few years ago, while working in a major U.S. corporation, one of us (Rob Silzer) had the opportunity to design and implement individual assessment for a number of different organizational and business needs. This organization had been involved in leveraging assessment, particularly assessment centers, for twenty years. Assessment had become an integral part of the organization's human resource practices. The motto of the internal leadership development group responsible for managing assessment was: "Assessment Is My Life." Although you could argue that this may be overstating the importance and centrality of assessment to the human resource function and organizational effectiveness, you would not be able to convince many executives inside this organization that the systematic and objective use of assessment in the organization did not play an important role in contributing to the success of the organization. This organization over the past twenty-five years has consistently been financially successful and, despite facing major competitive threats in recent years, continues to use assessment and continues to post record earnings. If psychologist assessors could establish some clear link between the use of individual assessment in an organization and organizational performance, then they would have an immensely powerful psychological tool for building successful organizations. We believe there is a link. We challenge assessment practitioners and academics to document it.

References

Arvey, R. D., & Campion, J. E. (1982). The employment interview: A summary and review of recent research. *Personnel Psychology, 35,* 281–322.

Borman, W. C., & Motowidlo, S. J. (1993). Expanding the criterion domain to include elements of contextual performance. In N. Schmitt, W. C. Borman, & Associates, *Personnel selection in organizations.* San Francisco: Jossey-Bass.

Dawes, R. M., Faust, D., & Meehl, P. E. (1989). Clinical versus actuarial judgment. *Science, 243,* 1668–1674.

Einhorn, H. J., & Hogarth, R. M. (1978). Confidence in judgment: Persistence of the illusion of validity. *Psychological Review, 85*(S), 395–416.

Einhorn, H. J., & Hogarth, R. M. (1981). Behavioral decision theory: Processes of judgment and choice. *Annual Review in Psychology, 32,* 53–88.

Gardner, H. (1993). *Multiple intelligences: The theory in practice.* New York: Basic Books.

Hoffer, E. (1954). *The passionate state of mind.* Boston: Harvard Press.

Jeanneret, P. R., & Silzer, R. F. (1990). *Assessment of personality for selection and development.* Society for Industrial and Organizational Psychology Workshop presented at the thirty-eighth convention of the American Psychological Association, Boston.

Lanyon, R. I., & Goodstein, L. D. (1982). *Personality assessment* (2nd ed.). New York: Wiley.

Meehl, P. (1954). *Clinical versus statistical prediction.* Minneapolis: University of Minnesota Press.

Prien, E. P. (1962). Assessments of higher-level personnel: III. Rating criteria: A comparative analysis of supervisor ratings and incumbent self-ratings of job performance. *Personnel Psychology, 15,* 187–195.

Sawyer, J. (1966). Measurement and prediction, clinical and statistical. *Psychological Bulletin, 66,* 178–200.

Silzer, R. F. (1984). *Clinical and statistical prediction in a management assessment center.* Unpublished doctoral dissertation, University of Minnesota.

Silzer, R. F., & Hollenbeck, G. P. (1992, April). *Executive assessment.* Workshop presented at the annual conference of the Society of Industrial and Organizational Psychology, Montreal.

Silzer, R. F., & Jeanneret, P. R. (1987). *Psychological assessment: Getting at job-related skills and abilities.* Society for Industrial and Organizational Psychology Workshop presented at the thirty-fifth convention of the American Psychological Association, New York.

Sundberg, N. D. (1977). *Assessment of persons.* Upper Saddle River, NJ: Prentice Hall.

Wiggins, J. S. (1973). *Personality and prediction: Principles of personality assessment.* Reading, MA: Addison-Wesley.

Name Index

Subject Index

A

Accommodation, in design process, 139

Accomplishment record, for managers, 306–307

Accountability, and implementation, 417–418

Adjective Checklist, 191

Adjustment, for managers, 302, 304

Adverse impact, research on, 76–77

Age Discrimination in Employment Act of 1967, 100

Alexithymic personality, 231, 239

American Educational Research Association, 102–103, 128

American Psychiatric Association, 32, 50

American Psychological Association (APA): and assessment, 7; and design, 141, 176; and ethical issues, 94–98, 102–103, 105–107, 111–114, 128–129, 470; and feedback, 247–248, 250, 254, 262–264, 267, 280; and research, 55

Americans with Disabilities Act (ADA) of 1990, 100, 139, 151, 156

Ascendance-Submission Test, 8

Assertion, by self or others, 216–221

Assessment centers: decline of, 392; exercises and simulations by, 153–155; and lawsuits, 101; for leadership talent, 409–410

Assessments: character, 178–227; components of, 150–161; credibility for, 185–195; cross-cultural, 330–362; follow-up steps for, 169–171; issues of, in leadership change, 419–424, 432–434; for leadership talent, 408–411; polarities used in, 221–222; policy statements on, 115–117, 121, 142, 173, 248–249; previews of, 245–253; reporting outcomes of, 163–169; ripple effect of, 434–438; schedules for, 163–164; standardized process for, 472; structuring, 161–164; techniques for, 304–319. *See also* Developmental assessment; Individual psychological assessment; Selection assessment

Assessors: consistency for, 75; as consultants, 93–94, 138, 386–388; dual clients of, 90, 140–141, 247–250; ethical and practice issues for, 104–114, 119; evaluating, 474; functions of, 12–22; responsibilities of, 88–131, 470–471, 475; training of, 123–125

Autonomy, in character assessment, 214–216

B

Behavior: cultural dimensions of, 343–344, 348, 360–361; in executive selection, 231–232, 233–236; feedback for generalizing, 260–261, 277–278; of managers, 309–310

Behavioral approach: in future, 466–467; and procedures, 40–41

Bias: awareness of, 473; in self-presentation, 13–15; of tests, 76–77

487